Natural Resources
and the
Macroeconomy

Centre for Economic Policy Research

The Centre for Economic Policy Research was established in 1983 as a private educational charity to promote independent analysis and public discussion of open economies and the relations among them. It is pluralist and non-partisan, bringing economic research to bear on the analysis of medium- and long-run policy questions. Institutional (core) finance for the Centre has been provided through major grants from the Economic and Social Research Council, the Leverhulme Trust, the Esmée Fairbairn Trust and the Bank of England: these organizations do not necessarily endorse the views expressed in the Centre's publications. The research work disseminated by the Centre may include views on policy, but the Board of Governors of the Centre does not give prior review to such publications, and the Centre itself takes no institutional policy positions. The opinions expressed in this volume are those of the authors and not those of the Centre for Economic Policy Research.

Natural Resources and the Macroeconomy

Edited by

J. PETER NEARY

and

SWEDER VAN WIJNBERGEN

The MIT Press
Cambridge, Massachusetts

First MIT Press edition, 1986

First published 1986

Basil Blackwell Ltd
108 Cowley Road, Oxford OX4 1JF, UK

Library of Congress Cataloging-in-Publication Data
Main entry under title:

Natural resources and the macroeconomy.

   "Proceedings of the conference 'Natural Resources and the
Macroeconomy,' organized by the Centre for Economic
Policy Research, London, on June 10–11, 1985"—Pref.
   Includes bibliographies and index.
   1. Nonrenewable natural resources—Economic
aspects—Congress aspects—Congresses. I. Neary, J.
Peter. II. Wijnbergen, Sweder van, 1951–   III.
Centre for Economic Policy Research (Great Britain)
HC59.N3194   1986   333.7   85–23767
ISBN 0–262–14041–1

Typeset by Photographics, Honiton, Devon
Printed and bound in Great Britain by Billing and Sons Ltd,
Worcester

Contents

Tables

Figures

Preface

This volume contains the proceedings of the conference 'Natural Resources and the Macroeconomy', organized by the Centre for Economic Policy Research and held in London on 10–11 June, 1985.

Financial support for the conference was provided by the Ford Foundation, to whom we express our gratitude. We wish in particular to thank Tom Bayard of the Foundation's staff for his interest in the project. We would also like to thank the CEPR's permanent staff for their constant encouragement and support, especially Richard Portes, who first suggested holding a conference on this topic; Monica Allen, who ensured the smooth running of the conference; Stephen Yeo, who oversaw the preparation of the conference volume; and Wendy Thompson, who supervised the conference's financial arrangements. Thanks are also due to Tim Callan of Nuffield College, Oxford who acted as rapporteur for the conference and to John Black of the University of Exeter, whose painstaking work as Production Editor was essential to the book's swift publication.

Finally, our major debt is to the authors and conference participants whose enthusiastic cooperation and adherence to deadlines ensured that the volume provides an accurate reflection of the profession's current thinking on the paradoxes of prosperity.

Contributors

Editors

J. Peter Neary   *University College, Dublin and CEPR*
Sweder van Wijnbergen   *World Bank and CEPR*

Authors

Iulie Aslaksen   *Central Bureau of Statistics, Oslo*
Olav Bjerkholt   *Central Bureau of Statistics, Oslo*
Shahid A. Chaudhry   *World Bank*
Sebastian Edwards   *UCLA and World Bank*
Peter Forsyth   *The Australian National University*
Alan H. Gelb   *World Bank*
Jeroen J. M. Kremers   *Nuffield College, Oxford*
Ricardo Martin   *World Bank*
Lance Taylor   *MIT*
Peter G. Warr   *The Australian National University*
Kadir R. Yurukoglu   *World Bank*

Discussants

William H. Branson   *Princeton University and CEPR*
W. Max Corden   *The Australian National University*
Partha Dasgupta   *University of Cambridge and CEPR*
John Flemming   *Bank of England*
Jean M. G. Frijns   *Central Plan Bureau, The Netherlands*
Patrick Honohan   *Department of the Taoiseach, Dublin*
Ronald W. Jones   *University of Rochester*
John Kay   *Institute for Fiscal Studies*

David M. G. Newbery *University of Cambridge and CEPR*
M. Hashem Pesaran *University of Cambridge*
Douglas D. Purvis *Queen's University, Kingston*
Alasdair Smith *Sussex University and CEPR*

Other participants

Michael Beenstock *City University Business School and CEPR*
John Black *University of Exeter*
Christopher Bliss *Nuffield College, Oxford and CEPR*
Tim Callan *Nuffield College, Oxford*
Ravi Kanbur *Essex University and CEPR*
Juan Carlos Moreno-Brid *University of Cambridge*
David Pearce *University College, London and CEPR*
Richard Portes *CEPR and Birkbeck College*
Frances Ruane *Trinity College, Dublin*
Anthony J. Venables *Sussex University and CEPR*

Introduction

J. PETER NEARY and SWEDER VAN WIJNBERGEN

A striking feature of the world economy in the 1970s and 1980s has been the frequency and magnitude of the shocks to many economies as a result of changes in the price or availability of natural resources. Resource-poor countries have suffered of course, but, paradoxically, resource-rich countries have not been immune. Resource-based booms have frequently been blamed for a tendency towards 'deindustrialization', while the macroeconomic performance of many countries with large resource sectors has been less than satisfactory. The problems associated with resource booms have even been given a name – the 'Dutch Disease' – which prompted *The Economist* to comment that 'to refer to a vast, valuable energy resource as the source of a disease is surely rather ungrateful'.

Academic researchers have not been slow to subject these problems to scrutiny, and a sizeable literature has now developed dealing with various aspects of the Dutch Disease. At the analytical level, existing models from the theories of international trade, open-economy macroeconomics and natural resource depletion have been extended to study the effects of a resource boom and to examine the possible rationales for government intervention. At a more applied level, a great many case studies have examined the steps in adjustment to changes in the price or availability of natural resources in individual countries. However, these two strands of literature have been inadequately integrated until now. This volume presents the proceedings of a conference, held at the Centre for Economic Policy Research in London in June 1985, which attempted to bridge this gap between theory and applications.

The opening chapter, written by the editors, sets the scene for the later applied studies with a synthesis of recent theoretical writings on the Dutch Disease. The concluding section of this chapter summarizes the principal implications of the theoretical models. This is followed by eight chapters which consider the experiences of specific countries from different perspectives. The book concludes with a round-table discussion which summarizes the main conclusions reached as well as pointing to the many questions that remain unresolved.

Chapter 1 examines the effects of natural resource discoveries using a series of models, each of which was designed to focus on a specific issue. In the simplest static model, a resource boom affects the economy in two ways. The first is the 'spending effect': higher domestic incomes as a result of the boom lead to extra expenditure on both traded and non-traded goods. The price of traded goods is determined by international market conditions and so does not rise despite the extra domestic spending; by contrast, the price of non-traded goods is set in the domestic market and does rise. The higher relative price of non-traded goods makes domestic production of traded goods less attractive, and so their output declines. A second effect emerges if, in addition, the booming sector shares domestic factors of production with other sectors, so that its expansion tends to bid up the prices of these factors. The resulting 'resource-movement effect' reinforces the tendencies towards appreciation of the real exchange rate (i.e., a rise in the relative price of non-traded goods) and a squeeze on the tradable goods sector, predictions which are common to most models of the Dutch Disease.

In addition to its effect on sectoral structure, a booming resource sector has often been identified as one of the causes of unsatisfactory macroeconomic performance. Chapter 1 identifies two cases in which a resource discovery can lead to unemployment. In the first case, unemployment may emerge if the rise in prices of non-traded goods requires a fall in workers' real wages but because of pre-existing contracts or trade union power real wages are downwardly sticky. The second case involves a purely nominal rigidity. The resource boom raises incomes and therefore the demand for money in real terms. In order to restore equilibrium in the money market and avoid unemployment, the real money supply must increase, which will not happen if the price level cannot fall and the nominal money supply is held constant. A moderately expansionary monetary policy which provides enough liquidity to accommodate the boom can avoid this type of unemployment.

Chapter 1 then turns to a model with two periods, in order to examine questions that arise from the intertemporal nature of resource booms. Policy-makers are often concerned that the industrial sector, if allowed to decline during a resource boom, will be unable to benefit from technological progress arising from 'learning-by-doing'. This learning effect can be modelled by assuming that second-period productivity in manufacturing depends on first-period output. There is then a case for a subsidy to manufacturing whether or not new resources are discovered. However, a resource boom may *increase* the optimal level of subsidy in certain cases. This is especially likely if there are capital market constraints which prevent the economy from smoothing consumption over time by acquiring foreign assets in the period when the natural resources are being exploited. A subsidized manufacturing sector thus acts as a surrogate for foreign assets and helps avoid the need for a sharp drop in consumption when the natural resource runs out.

In chapter 2, Alan Gelb addresses the recurring theme of how governments react to the increase in their revenues brought about by oil price increases. He first estimates the average size of the windfall gain from increased oil prices to seven developing countries in the 1970s. On average, the gain to these countries represented about one-quarter of non-oil GDP; about four-fifths of this windfall accrued to producer governments, whose reactions therefore primarily determined the ultimate effects of the price increase. The countries studied are very diverse, but their responses have much in common. They were dominated by the speedy use of about half the windfall to finance domestic, and overwhelmingly public, capital formation. This share was reduced by greater public and private consumption in the late 1970s, while the fraction invested abroad remained stable at a quarter.

What have been the effects of these investment programmes? Have they boosted growth in the non-oil economy? Very little, according to Gelb. Most infrastructure investments were subject to long gestation lags. The oil price shock itself rendered some of the initial capital stock obsolete. Much public investment was in large-scale, complex projects, which were prone to substantial cost overruns and disappointing operating performance. Accelerated public investment, entailing large recurrent expenditures, acquired a momentum that proved hard to restrain after oil revenues fell. Such downward inflexibility left these economies particularly vulnerable to the global recession of the 1980s, especially since their access to international capital markets tended to vary with the level of oil prices. Gelb argues that with hindsight these countries would have obtained greater benefits from their windfalls if they had limited domestic investment by applying market criteria more rigorously and had invested a higher proportion of the increased revenues abroad. This would have increased the volume of funds to be recycled by world capital markets, however, at a time when the markets' ability to cope with this process was in doubt. That could have created additional pressure to absorb the windfall domestically.

The importance of the government's use of windfall gains is also emphasized by Jeroen Kremers in chapter 3, which investigates the

4   J. Peter Neary and Sweder van Wijnbergen

extent of the Dutch Disease in the case which inspired the name, that of the Dutch economy following the exploitation of the Slochteren gas reserves in the 1960s. Some of the predictions of the Dutch Disease literature were in fact observed in The Netherlands during its natural gas boom, but the complex structure of the economy and the small share of gas output in gross domestic product suggest caution in attributing these developments to the gas boom alone. Resource-movement effects were slight, because the gas reserves were easy to exploit. Spending effects operated mainly through the government, which absorbed more than three-quarters of the revenue. However, the increased government revenues from gas merely reinforced an existing trend towards increased public consumption and transfer payments. There is little evidence of increased public or private investment to smooth the time path of consumption; Kremers suggests that the use of gas revenues to finance investment rather than current government spending might have helped to achieve this end.

During the 1970s there was a squeeze on profitability in the Dutch traded goods sector, due to a strong guilder, upward wage pressure and increasing energy prices. Profit margins absorbed the pressure at first, but significant effects on output and employment followed. Government support, sometimes in the form of subsidies, was provided to industry. Some of these industries now appear to have a healthy future; to this extent, the government support was successful. The decline in the traded goods sector also contributed to a sharp rise in unemployment. Policies to deal with this have been less effective. Unemployment benefits have been raised and public sector employment increased; at the same time, increases in social security contributions, minimum wages and labour market regulations have exacerbated the unemployment problem.

An economy with large reserves of an exhaustible resource is faced with important choices concerning the rate at which the resource is depleted and the size, composition and financing of its investment effort. This can only be analysed within an explicitly intertemporal framework, which Ricardo Martin and Sweder van Wijnbergen attempt to provide in chapter 4. Their framework is a long-run optimal growth model of the Egyptian economy. The economy is divided into three sectors: oil and gas, other traded goods and non-traded goods. Domestically produced traded goods are assumed to be imperfect substitutes for imported goods. Both oil and traded goods can be exported, but the latter face a downward sloping demand curve. The government is assumed to maximize the (discounted) stream of domestic consumption over time, subject to the economy's production possibilities and finite reserves of the natural resource. There are also limitations on the speed at which extraction capacity and domestic investment can grow, while foreign borrowing is constrained by an interest rate that increases with the amount borrowed.

In simulating the model, Martin and van Wijnbergen find that key features of the optimal development path for Egypt are relatively insensitive to changes in assumptions concerning future oil prices and oil discoveries. Much of current income arises from decumulation of exhaustible resources and from transfers such as workers' remittances and foreign aid. These may be only temporary, so it is desirable to achieve rapid structural adjustment via high rates of investment in the traded goods sectors. The analysis also generates time paths for shadow prices of goods and factors, which have more general implications for project analysis and foreign borrowing policies in other countries. For example, the existence of absorptive capacity constraints which are gradually relaxed over time implies that the accounting rate of interest (ARI) should be high while the constraints bind tightly and should decline over time. A constant ARI is commonly assumed in project evaluation, and this can lead to very misleading results. The optimal path of foreign borrowing depends on the trend in the relative price of consumption goods to foreign goods, since such borrowing must be repaid in terms of the latter. The optimal plan involves a gradual depreciation of the real exchange rate, which makes foreign borrowing more expensive in terms of consumption forgone to repay the loan.

The discovery of substantial reserves of oil has greatly increased the total wealth of Norway. At the same time, it has shifted the composition of Norway's national wealth towards oil, a riskier asset, thereby increasing uncertainty about the future path of national income. Methods of dealing with this increase in long-term uncertainty are examined by Iulie Aslaksen and Olav Bjerkholt in chapter 5. The planner's problem is formally modelled as one of maximizing the present value of consumption over a finite planning horizon, together with the present value of wealth at the end of the period. National income is viewed as the return on a set of assets, one of which is oil; the planner's decision resembles that of a private agent, who must allocate his portfolio among different assets. In each period the planner decides how much to consume and how to distribute total investment over a set of assets with different mixtures of risks and returns. Aslaksen and Bjerkholt assume that the rate of return on petroleum reserves equals the rate of growth of oil prices, net of marginal extraction costs. If national wealth is to be allocated optimally among the different assets, the rate of return on oil reserves, adjusted for risk aversion, should be equal to the common 'certainty-equivalent' rate of return on all other assets. Optimal consumption is then simply a linear function of total wealth, a result that depends on the assumption of an exponential utility function.

Aslaksen and Bjerkholt apply their theoretical framework to the Norwegian case, by considering a simplified planner's preference function. They base their estimate of the degree of risk aversion on a government advisory report and assume a rate of time preference of 1 per cent. The interrelated risk/return characteristics of a simplified asset menu are estimated from historical data. While the results are sensitive to the degree of risk aversion and depend on several simplifying assumptions, the analysis suggests that there are clear benefits to a rapid depletion policy, replacing oil resources by assets with a more certain return.

Can a simple computable general equilibrium model be used to analyse policy issues related to resource booms and slumps in a developing country? Lance Taylor, Kadir Yurukoglu and Shahid Chaudhry attempt this in chapter 6. The framework adopted is Keynesian but it also allows for the relative price effects, which the resource boom literature suggests are important. Data were taken from the national income accounts, budgetary statistics and the banking system, while estimates of the model's parameters were derived from various sources, including international evidence and expert opinion. The model was simulated over the late 1970s and early 1980s, to ensure that it replicated observed data accurately. It was then used to explore a variety of policy options, including devaluation of the exchange rate. These policy options were compared to a 'base' policy of modest fiscal contraction and increased foreign borrowing.

A policy of devaluation causes the federal government's oil revenues to rise in local currency terms, while the Nigerian constitution stipulates that 45 per cent of federal revenues be passed directly to state and local governments. Since the spending propensity of these bodies is close to unity, the authors argue that the expansionary fiscal consequences tend to offset the contractionary effects of devaluation arising elsewhere in the model.

The short-run consequences of a commodity export boom can differ greatly between developing and developed countries, because of differences in the structure of financial markets and the operation of monetary policy. A model with assumptions appropriate to developing countries is outlined by Sebastian Edwards in chapter 7 and applied to the Colombian experience of a coffee price boom. On the real side, the theoretical structure incorporates the spending effect of a price-based commodity export boom, which tends to raise demand for home goods. On the monetary side, the boom leads to a balance of payments surplus and an increase in international reserves. The increase in reserves is not sterilized; the monetary authorities do not attempt to control the supply of money, but rather base monetary policy on the exchange rate. As a result, the increase in foreign currency receipts automatically raises the domestic money supply. If this money-creation effect of the export boom is large enough, the real exchange rate may depreciate rather than appreciate; it may also overshoot its long-run equilibrium value.

Coffee accounts for about half of Colombia's measured exports, and receipts accrue mainly to private producers. Edwards argues that his model can be used to interpret the temporary coffee price boom of 1975–7, and the concern expressed by Colombian policy-makers over its monetary consequences. The Colombian experience was broadly in line with theoretical predictions. The analysis suggests that a key consideration was the extent to which the authorities allowed the domestic money supply to respond to a boom believed to be temporary.

Cross-country comparisons often highlight the processes at work in different countries and help to avoid invalid generalizations. This motivated Peter Forsyth in chapter 8 to compare the effects of the minerals boom in Australia with those of the exploitation of the North Sea oil reserves in Britain. A large proportion of North Sea oil revenues represented pure economic rents, and because of this rental component the spending effect was of primary importance in the UK case; in Australia, the movement of resources into the expanding minerals sector was more important, since the rental component of revenues was lower. North Sea oil was seen as likely to have a larger, more immediate impact on the United Kingdom than the longer-lasting mining boom on Australia. The Australian case demonstrated that such a mineral boom could give rise to considerable structural changes *within* the traded goods sector, with a much smaller effect on overall sectoral output patterns. A substantial part of the structural adjustment required by the boom will last only for the investment phase; costs of adjustment make it worthwhile to extend this phase, rather than attempt to complete it in a few years. Trade and capital flows also helped to smooth the adjustment.

The effects of the boom on government revenue have been important for the United Kingdom, but much less so for Australia. Forsyth presents a theoretical analysis which suggests that the optimal response to such a temporary revenue windfall includes some additional public investment, a lowering of other taxes and perhaps a rise in public consumption. Macroeconomic factors make it difficult to judge whether the UK government's response to its increased revenues has approximated the optimal one, or if not, whether private agents have taken compensating actions. It seems likely, however, that not enough of the windfall is being invested.

Forsyth also considers the sensitivity of the sterling exchange rate to oil price developments. Although the United Kingdom is no more than self-sufficient in oil in the long term, a rise in the price of oil has tended to strengthen sterling against most major currencies. This could be explained by the fact that most of Britain's trading partners are long-term oil importers, or by the use of higher discount rates in the foreign exchange markets than are used in the long-term calculations of the oil balance.

In the final paper of the conference, Peter Warr compares the qualitative predictions of the Dutch Disease literature with the experience of Indonesia. Since employment in the oil sector was less than 1 per cent of the total work-force, spending effects dominated resource-movement effects. Government expenditure grew rapidly, with about two-thirds of revenue coming from oil taxes. The predicted real appreciation (a rise in the price of non-traded relative to traded goods) did occur. The Indonesian exchange rate was tied to the US dollar, so domestic prices of traded goods could not adjust; therefore the real appreciation of the exchange rate caused by the oil price increase was brought about largely by increases in the prices of non-traded goods. By late 1978 the apparent decline in the profitability of the traded goods sector (excluding oil) was the subject of widespread public discussion in Indonesia. The large devaluation of November 1978 seems to have been motivated primarily by a desire to avoid an excessive contraction of these industries, a contraction that would need to be reversed when the oil ran out. This devaluation of the nominal exchange rate initially had the desired effect on the real exchange rate, but the effect was gradually eroded. The effects of these relative price changes on the structure of the economy are difficult to identify, but comparisons with neighbouring countries suggest that the growth of Indonesian manufacturing was slower than might otherwise have been expected.

The overall policy response in Indonesia seems to have been more successful than in some other oil-exporting developing countries. Indonesia spent a considerable amount of its windfall gain on investment and did not engage in excessive borrowing. Nevertheless, greater returns might have been achieved if more had been invested in overseas assets.

Peter Neary chaired the concluding round-table discussion, which opened with general overviews by four invited panelists. The first of these was Max Corden who began by distinguishing three main issues which had arisen during the conference: the cyclical nature of resource booms, structural adjustment aspects and optimal resource extraction issues. Concentrating (as had the conference) on the first two areas, Corden emphasized the links with earlier analyses of stabilization policy and structural change. The cyclical nature of booms raised normative questions concerning the appropriate policy response to a temporary boom, given certain asymmetric rigidities. On the analytical side, Corden argued that it was preferable to model government policy as endogenous rather than to specify arbitrary policy rules. Analyses of structural adjustment abstracted from these cyclical problems in order to focus on the long-run effects of a permanent resource boom on other sectors. The Dutch Disease literature differed from earlier analyses of the interaction between growth and trade, firstly by taking a more disaggregated approach and secondly by focusing on the implications for the returns to factors of production employed by the affected industries.

The next panelist, John Kay, argued that the empirical studies had reinforced the importance of the distinction between spending and resource-movement effects. This was illustrated by the differences that arose when the booming sector was an 'enclave' which did not compete for productive factors with the rest of the economy. He reviewed some of the microeconomic issues which arose in an enclave model, where most of the returns from the boom accrue to the government, raising its share of national income and so redistributing resources from the private sector to the government.

If the government captures rents from the resource through taxation, there is a reduction in the shadow price of government revenue, given that other taxes are distortionary. This means that the optimal level of provision of public goods rises; pressures to increase the actual scale of provision may also rise, since the political price of raising government revenue may fall even more. Subsequent discussion emphasized that there were many other factors influencing the optimal and actual levels of government spending, which also tended to change during a resource boom. For example, if public goods relied on non-traded inputs, the rise in the price of non-traded relative to traded goods would tend to reduce the socially optimal level of government spending. Reductions in distortionary taxes would also be an important part of the optimal policy package, so there could be no general presumption that an increase in the size of the public sector during a resource boom was desirable.

If the costs of adjustment and uncertainty about oil prices are large, one might expect markets or governments to develop means of dealing with them. Kay noted that this has not happened to any great extent.

There is no long and active futures market in oil, nor have western governments negotiated long-term supply contracts with each other.

The next panelist, Doug Purvis, noted that, with a variety of approaches, the empirical papers had each provided useful evidence on the issues and raised new questions for theorists. He singled out the problems of intertemporal optimization and uncertainty as particularly interesting. Greater attention would also have to be paid to the nature of the boom itself; price-induced booms had worldwide effects, while resource discoveries tended to be country- or region-specific. In order successfully to isolate the effects of the Dutch Disease itself, empirical studies also needed to take account of the short-run effects of macroeconomic policy.

It had been suggested that deindustrialization might not result from resource booms in LDCs, because the booms would allow greater foreign borrowing to finance investment in domestic industry. Purvis drew attention to Gelb's evidence, which showed that the constraints on foreign borrowing had indeed been relaxed, but that this had encouraged rather inefficient investments. These investments often involved attempts to incorporate the oil or gas enclave into the wider economy by building large 'downstream' projects such as petrochemical complexes or fertilizer plants, even when it would have been more beneficial to the economy as a whole to export the resource.

The last contributor to the panel discussion was David Newbery, who pointed out that oil could now be regarded as a commodity with an extremely volatile price. Estimates of the gains from the stabilization of other commodity prices had been small, even in models where macroeconomic consequences had been considered. The missing element in these models seemed to be a satisfactory theory of government behaviour. Many participants had stressed the importance of government responses to large increases in commodity prices. This consideration greatly strengthened the case for commodity price stabilization.

Newbery argued that the most important question concerning depletion policy for gas and oil is the timing of the required investment, which is large, risky and long-lasting. Once the investment has been made, the marginal costs of extraction are low, and it usually makes sense to extract the resource as fast as is technically possible.

In conclusion, the conference may be said to have succeeded in one of its aims, that of demonstrating the relevance of theoretical analyses of the Dutch Disease to the experiences of a variety of countries with natural resource based booms. At the same time, the range of experiences of the countries examined by the contributors and the diversity of analytical tools used to study them, defy any simple summary. In so far as one general conclusion can be drawn, it is that a country's economic performance following a resource boom depends to a considerable extent on the policies followed by its government. At a time when the world appears to be entering an era of falling rather than rising natural resource prices, it seems important to keep in mind the lesson that even small economies have considerable influence over their own economic performance; an influence that most of the contributions to this volume suggest they have rarely exercised wisely.

1

Natural resources and the macroeconomy: a theoretical framework*

J. PETER NEARY
and
SWEDER VAN WIJNBERGEN

1 Natural resources: disease or deliverance?

As noted in the Introduction, the objective of this volume is to attempt to bridge the gap between theoretical and applied studies of natural resource booms. With this in mind, the present chapter sets the scene for later empirical analyses by reviewing the theoretical models which have been used to analyse different aspects of the Dutch Disease.[1] To avoid unnecessary repetition, we concentrate throughout on the effects of natural resource discoveries. However, much of the analysis applies with only slight modifications to the effects on resource-exporting countries of exogenous increases in the prices they face.

The large-scale exploitation of natural resource discoveries is a real rather than a monetary shock to an economy, since its primary impact falls on the level of real income and on the intersectoral allocation of factors of production. Hence, it is natural to begin analysing the consequences of such discoveries with a real model which abstracts from monetary considerations. Further simplification is possible if we focus initially on the static effects of a resource boom. This is done in section 2, which uses a simple static framework to examine the consequences of a boom for relative prices, the size of the exposed traded sector and the level of unemployment. Next, section 3 introduces a two-period model, and examines the effects of a boom on the intertemporal allocation of resources. Monetary issues are then considered in section 4, which also looks at the implications of alternative macroeconomic policy responses and exchange rate regimes. Finally, section 5 concludes by attempting to summarize the implications of the different models considered for some of the most frequently asked questions about natural resource discoveries.

Two further general points should be made before we proceed. The first is that, although the initiating disturbance in all the models we consider is the discovery and exploitation of natural resources, we ignore the issues of optimal and competitive depletion rates which have been the focus of much recent work on the economics of exhaustible resources.[2] Rather than dealing with these longer-run issues, most of the literature we survey has concentrated on the short- and medium-run effects of asymmetric growth which takes place at an exogenous rate. It has thus taken the time path of extraction and revenues as given, and throughout the paper we follow it in this respect.

A second issue which should be clarified at the outset relates to the use of the term 'Dutch Disease' to describe the phenomena with which we are concerned. In fact, there is no presumption that the consequences of a natural resource discovery are harmful. On the contrary, its initial impact is beneficial and amounts to a Pareto improvement for the economy as a whole. Of course, legitimate grounds for concern may arise over the distribution of the gains, over the issue of whether transitional assistance should be offered to declining sectors and over the issue of the appropriate response to various market failures which may impede the smooth adjustment of the economy to its new equilibrium. However, as we shall have occasion to point out on a number of occasions, the case for treatment of the disease must be considered on its merits in each individual application.[3]

2 The static effects of a resource boom

The simplest general equilibrium model within which the static effects of the Dutch Disease can be analysed is one which distinguishes between two sectors, one producing a single non-traded good whose price is determined endogenously by the interaction of domestic supply and demand and the other producing a composite traded good whose price is fixed exogenously. We shall denote the output levels of these two sectors by x_n and x_m (m for 'manufacturing') respectively. In this model the natural resources sector is purely of the 'enclave' type, and does not directly compete with other sectors for factors of production. As a consequence, the resource boom operates in exactly the same manner as an exogenous transfer: it affects the domestic economy solely through a 'spending effect', whose consequences are examined in section 2.1. Section 2.2 moves on to consider the case where the expansion of the booming sector has a direct impact on domestic factor markets, and as a result the boom has an additional resource movement effect.[4] Finally, section 2.3 considers the case where domestic wages and prices do not adjust instantaneously to the boom, and shows that unemployment may result depending (among other things) on the degree of wage indexation.

2.1.   The spending effects of a boom

Equilibrium in this model can be characterized solely in terms of the market-clearing condition for the non-traded good. In obvious notation, this may be written as:

$$x_n(q) = c_n(q,y). \tag{1}$$

Here, x_n and c_n denote domestic production and consumption of the non-traded good respectively, and equilibrium in the market is brought about by adjustment of the price of non-traded relative to traded goods, q. This price is thus a key variable in this economy; its inverse, the price of traded relative to non-traded goods, is often referred to as the *real exchange rate*. While output of the non-traded goods depends solely on the real exchange rate, demand depends also on the level of real income (measured in terms of traded goods), denoted by y. This is fixed exogenously by the assumption of full employment, except that the effect of the boom is to increase it in a once-off fashion. The resulting excess demand for the non-traded good raises q, an outcome which we will refer to as a 'real appreciation'.

The implications of this disturbance for the pattern of output in the economy may be illustrated using the Salter (1959) diagram in figure 1.1. Non-traded goods output is measured along the horizontal axis and traded goods output (including both manufacturing and booming sector output) along the vertical axis. The curve TN is the economy's initial production possibilities frontier, depending on domestic technology and factor endowments. Before the boom, equilibrium is determined by the intersection of this curve with the highest attainable social indifference curve, I_0, at point A.[5] Since the boom is equivalent to a transfer, its effect is to shift the production possibilities curve vertically upwards to $T'N'N$ as shown. The initial real exchange rate equals the slope of the common tangent to the two curves at point A. If this were to remain unchanged, the production point would shift vertically upwards to point B: domestic output of both manufactures and non-traded goods remains unchanged but total domestic availability of traded goods is augmented

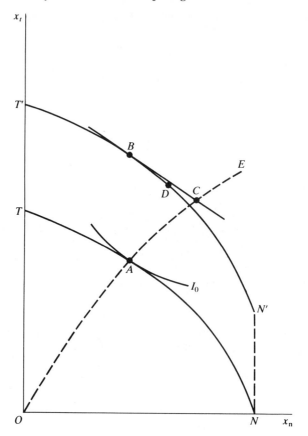

Figure 1.1   The spending effect of a resource boom.

by the extent of the additional resource output. With production and therefore domestic real income determined at B, desired consumption must lie along the price line tangential to B. Moreover, since relative prices are unchanged, it must take place at the point C where the price line intersects the income-consumption curve through A, OAE. (We assume that both goods are normal in demand, so that this curve is upward-sloping.) The resulting excess demand for non-tradables drives up their relative price until the new equilibrium at a point such as D is attained. The characteristics of this new equilibrium are obvious: domestic welfare has risen, but at the expense of a reallocation of production – the output of the non-traded good has risen whereas that of manufacturing has *fallen*. The spending effect of the boom thus

unambiguously gives rise to *both* deindustrialization and a real appreciation.

2.2 *The resource-movement effect of a boom*

Our next task is to examine how these results are altered if the booming
sector is not an enclave but requires a significant input of productive
factors which must be bid away from other sectors in the economy. The
answer to this question depends to a considerable extent on the detailed
production structure of the economy, and a great many different
specifications have been considered in the literature.[6] The simplest of
these, and probably the most appropriate to a relatively short time
horizon, is the so-called 'specific factors' model,[7] which assumes that
each sector uses a single specific factor as well as drawing on a pool of
intersectorally mobile labour. Under this specification, the output of
each sector depends on the real product wage it faces. Hence, equation
(1) must be replaced by the following:

$$x_n(q/w) = c_n(q,y). \tag{2}$$

where w is the wage rate, measured in terms of traded goods. This
model has two endogenous variables, q and w, and the additional
equilibrium condition comes from the requirement that the labour
market clear:

$$e_n(q/w) + e_m(w) + e_b(w,b) = L. \tag{3}$$

Here, L is the total available labour supply, assumed to be fixed, while
e_i is the labour demand function from sector i. In the two traded good
sectors, producing manufacturing and booming sector output respectively, these depend negatively on w, while in the non-traded good
sector it depends positively on q/w. In addition, the boom itself exerts a
direct influence on the demand for labour by the booming sector,
represented by the inclusion of the parameter b in that sector's labour
demand function.

The determination of equilibrium in this model may be illustrated by
locating the two equations (2) and (3) in (w,q) space, as illustrated in
figure 1.2. The non-traded goods market equilibrium locus, corresponding to (2), must be upward-sloping, since either an increase in q or a
decrease in w induces excess supply of the non-traded good. Moreover,
it must be more steeply sloped than a ray from the origin, since an
equiproportionate increase in w and q leaves supply unchanged but

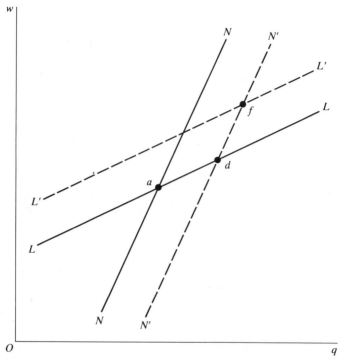

Figure 1.2   Spending and resource-movement effects of a boom.

discourages consumption so leading to excess supply. Similarly, the labour-market equilibrium locus, corresponding to (3), must also be upward-sloping, with either an increase in w or a decrease in q giving rise to unemployment. However, this curve must be less steeply sloped than a ray from the origin, since an equiproportionate increase in both variables leaves the non-traded sector's demand for labour unchanged but depresses that from the other two sectors, so giving rise to unemployment. The initial equilibrium is therefore as depicted by point a in figure 1.2, at the intersection of the non-traded goods market equilibrium locus NN and the labour market equilibrium locus, LL.

   The effects of the resource boom are now easily illustrated. We know, from section 2.1, that the spending effect generates excess demand for non-tradables, which must displace the NN locus rightwards to $N'N'$ as shown. If there were no resource-movement effect, the new equilibrium would be at point d, corresponding to point D in figure 1.1. In addition, the resource-movement effect displaces the LL locus: the increased demand for labour from the booming sector generates excess demand for labour at the initial point *a*, requiring either a rise in *w* or a fall in *q* if equilibrium is to be restored. The labour market equilibrium locus therefore shifts upwards to *L'L'* as shown, and so the final equilibrium is at point *f*. It is clear that, under the assumptions of the specific factors model, the resource movement effect reinforces the spending effect as far as changes in *q* and *w* are concerned. This means that the two principal conclusions of the last sub-section are unchanged: deindustrialization (since output and employment in manufacturing depend inversely on *w*) and a real appreciation (a rise in *q*) must follow the boom. The implications for the output of the non-traded good are ambiguous, however. This depends directly on the ratio *q/w*, and it is clear from the diagram that this may rise or fall, depending on which of the two effects dominates.

2.3   The effects of wage and price rigidities

So far, we have assumed that the wage rate and the price of the non-traded good are perfectly flexible, so that the economy moves smoothly and instantaneously to the new equilibrium. If this is not the case, then in the short run agents on the long side of either market will be rationed, in the manner familiar from the 'disequilibrium' or 'fix-price' macroeconomic literature.[8] It might be thought that the only disequilibrium regime that resource discoveries can induce is one of labour shortage, since we have seen in the last section that the wage rate may be expected to rise. However, as we shall see, this turns out to hinge crucially on the wage-setting mechanism.

For simplicity, we return to the case where the boom has a spending effect only. (The added complications from a resource movement effect will be noted briefly where appropriate.) To examine the consequences of wage–price rigidities, we first show how different exogenous values of the wage and the price of the non-traded good give rise to different disequilibrium regimes. We do this by dividing (*w,q*) space into different disequilibrium regions. This is done in figure 1.3, where the dashed curves represent the notional equilibrium loci from figure 1.2, where these differ from the effective equilibrium loci.

Consider first the labour market equilibrium locus. Since labour supply is exogenous, the notional locus is unaffected if households are rationed in the non-traded good market. (We assume throughout that no agents are ever rationed in the market for traded goods.) Since the booming sector does not use labour (given the assumption that there is no resource-movement effect), equation (3) need only be slightly modified as follows:

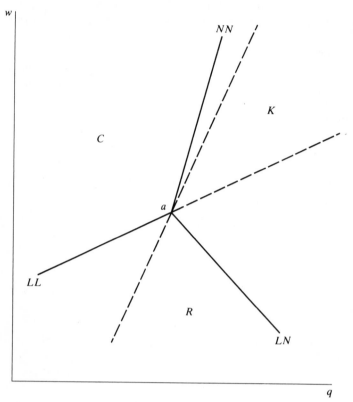

Figure 1.3   Disequilibrium regimes with wage and price rigidities.

$$e_n(q/w) + e_m(w) = L. \tag{4}$$

This curve is labelled LL, and extends to the left of point a in figure 1.3. To the right of that point, however, there is excess supply of the non-traded good. Domestic producers are rationed therefore, and scale down their labour demand in the face of the sales constraint they face. The labour market equilibrium locus in this region is therefore given not by (4) but by the following:

$$\bar{e}_n[c_n(q,y)] + e_m(w) = L. \tag{5}$$

The key feature of this effective locus is that, because employment in the non-traded good sector is now *demand*-determined, it depends *negatively* rather than positively on the relative price of the non-traded good, q. The locus is therefore downward- rather than upward-sloping in (w,q) space, and is denoted by the line LN in figure 1.3.

Consider next the equilibrium locus for the non-traded good market. We may confine attention to the case where unemployment prevails, since under excess demand for labour the effective non-traded good market equilibrium locus coincides with the LN curve just derived.[9] With unemployment, the locus is formally identical to (2), except that the level of income is no longer at its full employment level but is determined endogenously:

$$y = qx_n(q,w) + x_m(w) + v, \tag{6}$$

where v is the value of the natural resource discovery. This locus is labelled NN in figure 1.3. It may be checked that it is upward-sloping and more steeply sloped than the corresponding notional locus.

As a result of taking account of the spillovers between markets arising from wage and price rigidities, the diagram is partitioned into three regions, each corresponding to a different disequilibrium regime. Following Malinvaud (1977), these are labelled C for classical unemployment, K for Keynesian unemployment and R for repressed inflation. The next step is to investigate the effects of the resource discovery on the loci. Since we have excluded a resource-movement effect, it is clear from equation (4) that the LL locus is not affected. However, the same is not true of the NN and LN loci. The spending effect of the boom leads to a greater demand for the non-traded good and, in figure 1.4, the Walrasian equilibrium shifts to point d. This is, of course, exactly the same post-boom equilibrium as point d in figure 1.2. However, the new feature is that the economy does not immediately jump to d, but instead remains in the short-run at point a. Relative to the new equilibrium, this point is on the LL locus but to the left of the new $N'N'$ and $L'N'$ loci. Hence, the initial effect of the resource boom is to leave the labour market in equilibrium and to induce excess demand for the non-traded good.

The principal question of interest is how the economy will move from a to d, and, in particular, whether any unemployment will emerge during the adjustment period. Without specifying the dynamics of adjustment in detail, we may presume that the price of the non-traded good will rise in response to excess demand. However, the behaviour of the wage rate is more complex and depends on the wage indexation rule which is adopted. Following van Wijnbergen (1984b), we make the standard augmented Phillips curve assumption that real consumption wages can only be reduced by temporary unemployment. The crucial

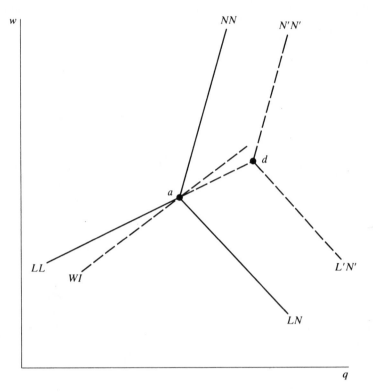

Figure 1.4   Effects of a boom with wage and price rigidities.

issue is, therefore, whether the real consumption wage at d is higher or lower than it is at a.

To answer this question, we add a further locus to the diagram, the wage indexation locus, labelled WI. Its slope is greater the larger the share of the non-traded good in the consumption basket of wage-earners. This may be seen most easily by assuming that the real consumption wage may be identified with the utility level of wage-earners, and by invoking their expenditure function:

$$w = E(p,q,u) \tag{7}$$

(p denotes the price of traded goods, which is fixed throughout). Equation (7) for the initial level of utility defines the WI locus. Figure 1.4 illustrates the case where it is more steeply sloped than the LL locus so that the movement from a to d requires a fall in the real consumption wage and transitional unemployment must result. It may be checked that this requires that the non-traded sector be 'more important' in demand than supply, in the sense that the share of its output in the consumption of wage-earners must exceed its contribution to a weighted average of the supply elasticities of the two sectors.[10] Conversely, if the non-traded good sector is less important in demand than in supply in this sense, the boom will raise the real consumption wage over time, and the economy enters a period of generalized labour shortage as it moves into the R region.

These results seem to accord well with some of the stylized facts of how different countries have responded to natural resource discoveries and increases in the prices of resources. Thus, the countries of the Persian Gulf, many of which import virtually all their consumption goods, experienced excess demand for labour after the oil price shocks. On the other hand, Latin American oil producers, with a long history of prohibitive tariff barriers making many of their consumer goods virtually non-traded, saw no employment benefits and in some cases (such as Mexico and Venezuela) increases in unemployment after the oil boom. Finally, it may be added that the addition of a resource-movement effect makes it more likely that labour shortage rather than unemployment will emerge, since, as already shown in figure 1.2, this provides a boost to the wage rate additional to that induced by the spending effect.

3   Intertemporal adjustment and public policy

It was argued in the Introduction that many aspects of the Dutch Disease can be satisfactorily examined in a static context. However, this is obviously not true of all. For example, issues arising from the finiteness of oil reserves or from the presence of learning-by-doing externalities in manufacturing require a dynamic perspective, and so it is necessary to develop a framework within which they can be analysed. In section 3.1 we outline the basic model of a two-period open economy producing traded and non-traded goods which is assumed to enjoy a resource discovery. We assume that there are no market imperfections or externalities, postponing consideration of these issues until sections 3.2 and 3.3.

3.1   *Intertemporal adjustment with no market imperfections*

We begin with the supply side of the economy. In the first period, technology and factor endowments are given and competition ensures that all factors are fully employed. In addition, we ignore for the present any supply-side or resource-movement effect of the oil discovery. The value of national output at domestic prices is therefore a function only of the relative price of the non-traded good, q. However, for later use it is convenient to make explicit the domestic price of manufactures, p, so that the value of national output is therefore written as $r(p,q)$.[11] While the capital stock in the first period is given by past decisions (and so there is no need to specify it in the function r), next period's capital stock is the outcome of current investment decisions. For simplicity, we assume that investment consists of manufactured goods only. The value of national output in the second period is therefore a function of the amount of capital invested in the current period, K, as well as of the future prices of the manufactured and non-traded goods, P and Q, respectively. We write this function as $R(P,Q,K)$.

The use of the revenue functions $r(p,q)$ and $R(P,Q,K)$ implies that factors of production are allocated efficiently within each period. But with no production externalities or wage–price rigidities, and with perfect foresight on the part of producers, factors will also be allocated efficiently *between* the two periods. The subsequent analysis is greatly simplified if we use this fact to define an intertemporal revenue function, which equals the present value of current and future national output:

$$\bar{R}(p,q,P,Q,\delta) = \underset{K}{\text{Max}} \; [r(p,q) - pK + \delta \, R(P,Q,K)]. \qquad (8)$$

where δ is the discount factor, equal to $1/(1+r^*)$, r^* being the exogenously given world rate of interest. It may be checked that the derivatives of $\bar{R}$ with respect to q and Q give the competitive non-traded good supply functions for the two periods:

$$\bar{R}_q(p,q,P,Q,\delta) = r_q(p,q) = x_n(p,q); \qquad (9)$$

$$\bar{R}_Q(p,q,P,Q,\delta) = \delta R_Q[P,Q,K(p,P,Q,\delta)] = \delta X_n(p,P,Q,\delta). \; (10)$$

Note that in deriving (10) we have made use of the fact that the first-order condition for maximization of (8) defines the optimal level of investment, K, as a function of p, P, Q and δ:

$$\delta R_K(P,Q,K) = p. \qquad (11)$$

Apart from permitting a more compact presentation of the model, the intertemporal revenue function yields an easy proof of the fact that optimal capital accumulation raises the own-price responsiveness of non-traded goods in the second period, i.e.[12]

$$\partial X_n(p,P,Q,\delta)/\partial Q > \partial X_n(P,Q,K)/\partial Q. \qquad (12)$$

This result (which is independent of the relative factor intensities of the traded and nontraded good sectors) will prove useful below.

Turning next to demand, we follow Svensson and Razin (1983) and van Wijnbergen (1984a) in characterizing this by a homogeneously separable expenditure function:

$$\bar{E}[m(p,q),\ \delta M(P,Q),\bar{U}] = \underset{z,Z}{\text{Min}}\ [mz+\delta MZ:\ \bar{U}(z,Z) \geq \bar{U}]. \qquad (13)$$

The terms z and Z denote period-specific sub-utility functions in the current and future periods respectively, and the functions m and M are per-unit utility expenditure functions for the two periods. Because of the assumption of homogeneous separability between periods, these functions may be interpreted as measuring the price level in each period. Differentiating (13) with respect to q and Q gives the demand (or consumption) functions for the non-traded goods in the two periods:

$$\bar{E}_q = \bar{E}_m\, m_q = c_n, \qquad (14)$$

$$\bar{E}_Q = \delta \bar{E}_M\, M_Q = \delta C_n \quad . \qquad (15)$$

We may now characterize an equilibrium of this model in terms of the market-clearing conditions for the non-traded good in the two periods:

$$x_n(p,q) = c_n\, [m(p,q),\delta M(P,Q),\bar{U}], \qquad (16)$$

$$X_n(p,P,Q,\delta) = C_n\, [m(p,q),\delta M(P,Q),\bar{U}]. \qquad (17)$$

In both these equations, the value of the household sector's lifetime utility is given by the intertemporal budget constraint, which requires the present value of expenditure to equal the present value of national output plus the oil wealth, $\bar{V}$:

$$\bar{E}\, [m(p,q),\ \delta M(P,Q),\bar{U}] = \bar{R}(p,q,P,Q,\delta) + \bar{V}. \qquad (18)$$

Because capital markets are assumed to be perfect (until section 3.3), the total differential of (18) takes a very simple form:

$$d \, \bar{U} = d \, \bar{V} \, / \, \bar{E}_{\bar{U}} \tag{19}$$

i.e., the change in lifetime utility as a result of the oil discovery equals the spending effect of the discovery (equal to the change in the present value of total income) multiplied by the marginal utility of income.

The determination of the equilibrium prices of the non-traded good in the two periods by equations (16) and (17) is conveniently illustrated in figure 1.5. Both the loci corresponding to the two equations must be upward-sloping. For example, a rise in q leads to excess supply of the non-traded good in the current period both because consumption falls and production rises; whereas a rise in Q has no effect on current production but encourages substitution towards consumption of both goods in the current period, and so generates excess demand for the current non-traded good.[13] In addition, the dominance of own over cross substitution effects ensures that the equilibrium locus for the current non-traded good market (labelled N_1) must be more steeply sloped than that for the future non-traded good market (labelled N_2), as shown.

The effects of a resource discovery are now easily derived. The effect on national welfare is given by equation (19) and is clearly positive. The resulting spending effect leads to excess demand for the non-traded good in both periods at initial prices, causing the two equilibrium loci to shift as shown. The outcome is a new equilibrium represented by point B. It is characterized by a real appreciation in both periods (i.e. a rise in the equilibrium values of both q and Q), and, with a normal price–output response, this increases the output of the non-traded good and reduces that of the traded good in both periods. Thus, the implications of the simple static model of section 2 – deindustrialization coupled with a real appreciation – continue to hold in our two-period extension.

One special case which is of some interest is where tastes and technology are identical in the two periods. With perfect foresight and perfect capital markets, the discovery has the same effect on demand in the two periods, and the only difference between periods follows from the fact that the capital stock can be optimally adjusted in the second period but not in the first. However, as already noted – *see* equation (12) – this leads to a larger supply response of the non-traded good in the second period, and so to a future appreciation which is *smaller* than that in the current period. In this case, therefore, the oil discovery leads to *overshooting* of the real exchange rate, in the manner to which Neary and Purvis (1983) have drawn attention. This case is illustrated in figure 1.5: point B lies below the ray OA, implying a larger rise in the real exchange rate in the short run than in the long run.

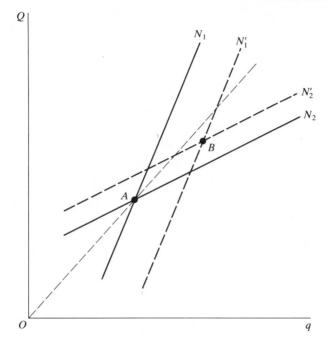

Figure 1.5   Effects of a boom on current and future real exchange rates.

Before leaving the undistorted case, we may note three additional points. First, a resource-movement effect of the discovery may easily be incorporated into the model by adding shift parameters to the period-specific revenue functions r and R. In this way it is possible to analyse the effects both of a permanent discovery (implying an equivalent shift in both functions) and a temporary one (implying a shift in r only). The implications of these extensions of the model are relatively straightforward (*see* van Wijnbergen, 1985).

Secondly, these results are completely independent of the time pattern of the oil revenues because of the assumption that capital markets are perfect. Even if the natural resource is fully exhausted in the first period, there will be no depreciation in the second, post-oil, period (relative to the real exchange rate which would have prevailed in that period if the boom had not taken place). Of course, this feature of the model depends crucially on the perfect capital market assumption and assumes that any excess of current revenues over the permanent income equivalent is used to accumulate foreign assets.

Finally, it should be stressed that, under the assumptions made so far, the real appreciation is an efficient response to the increase in oil revenues and is in no sense a symptom of 'disease'. On the contrary, the appreciation is essential to effect the allocation of factors of production out of the traded goods sector into the non-traded goods sector which is necessary to accommodate the natural resource boom. It is only a disease requiring treatment in the form of government intervention if there is some market failure preventing the appropriate adjustment or if there is some existing immovable distortion which is exacerbated by the natural resource boom. We now turn to consider some problems of this kind which may justify offsetting government intervention.

3.2   Learning-by-doing in traded goods production

A common concern of policy-makers in the presence of sudden increases in revenues from natural resource exploitation is that allowing the industrial sector to decline will prevent its benefiting from technological progress as a result of learning-by-doing. In this section we present a simple model which formalizes this idea.[14] We assume that technological progress takes place *only* in manufacturing and that it is external to the firm. In these circumstances, there is a case for subsidizing manufacturing whether or not it is threatened with being squeezed by another booming sector; the key issue rather is whether the boom justifies an *increase* in the optimal subsidy.

To capture the phenomenon of learning-by-doing externalities in manufacturing, we amend the second-period revenue function of the last sub-section to include the first-period output of manufacturing as one of its arguments. We also simplify by ignoring investment. Hence the value of national output in the second period is given by the following:

$$R = R(P,Q,x_m), \quad R_m > 0, \ R_{mP} > 0, \ R_{mQ} < 0, \tag{20}$$

where $R_m = \partial R/\partial x_m$, etc. and the signs of the cross-derivatives indicate that the externality benefits future manufacturing production. For analytical convenience we assume that the externality operates in a linear fashion, so that $R_{mm} = 0$. In turn, the output of manufacturing in the first period is itself given by:

$$x_m = r_p(p,q). \tag{21}$$

The subsidy to manufacturing output in the first period is denoted by s and is assumed to be financed by lump-sum taxation of consumers. The household sector's intertemporal budget constraint (18) must therefore be replaced by the following:

$$\bar{E}[m(p,q),\delta M(P,Q),\ \bar{U}]\bullet = r(p+s,q) + \delta R[P,Q,x_m] + \bar{V} - sx_m (22)$$

To determine the optimal subsidy, we differentiate equation (22) totally, holding $\bar{V}$ constant. This yields, after some simplifications:

$$d\ \bar{U} = (\delta R_m - s)\ dx_m/\bar{E}_{\bar{U}} \tag{23}$$

Hence the optimal subsidy is given by the following:

$$s^* = \delta R_m \tag{24}$$

This formula has a nice intuitive interpretation. Private producers will produce the socially optimal level of manufactured goods in the first period if they receive a subsidy equal to the marginal benefits generated by the learning-by-doing externality (R_m) discounted back to the present by the discount factor, δ.

Before the oil discovery takes place, we may view the model as a simultaneous system in which the market-clearing prices of the non-traded good in each period, q and Q, and the optimal subsidy level s^* are jointly determined. The three equations necessary to determine the values of these variables are the expression for the optimal subsidy, (24) and the market-clearing conditions for the non-traded good in each period, given by (16) and (17) with slight modifications. Strictly speaking, an algebraic analysis is required to solve this system. However, figure 1.6 allows us to deduce the effects of a resource boom on the optimal subsidy in a simpler manner.[15] The curve in the left-hand quadrant labelled OS illustrates the relationship between the optimal subsidy and the real exchange rate in period 2 implied by equation (24).[16] This curve is downward-sloping since a higher value of Q reduces the value of future benefits of the subsidy $(R_{mQ} < 0)$ and so reduces the optimal level of the subsidy. The curves in the right-hand quadrant have the same interpretation as those in figure 1.5, and the first-period equilibrium locus N_1 is unchanged. However, the second-period locus N_2 may be upward-sloping (as in figure 1.5) or downward-sloping (as illustrated in figure 1.6) since its slope now depends on two competing influences.[17] On the one hand, as in section 3.1, a higher value of q leads to excess supply of the non-traded good in period 1 and, since the goods in the two periods are necessarily substitutes in consumption, a rise in the future price Q works to restore equilibrium. This effect tends to lead to an upward-sloping locus. On the other hand, a higher value of q today tends to draw resources out of manufacturing today, leading to lower productivity in that sector tomorrow because of less learning-by-doing experience. This in turn will lead to a shift of resources out of manufacturing tomorrow, necessitating a lower value of Q.

The N_2 curve in figure 1.6 is drawn with a negative slope, implying that the learning-by-doing effect outweighs the intertemporal substitution effect. As a result, the effect of the boom on the future market-clearing value of Q is ambiguous. By the usual spending-effect mechanism, the boom shifts N_1 rightwards and N_2 upwards as shown. Since the OS curve is not itself affected by the boom, the direction of change in the optimal subsidy therefore depends solely in the change in Q: if, as in the case illustrated in figure 1.6, a *future real depreciation* (i.e. a fall in Q) is anticipated, then the optimal level of current subsidy to manufacturing *increases*. In this case, therefore, the term 'Dutch Disease' is indeed appropriate, in the sense that increased government intervention is justified by the natural resources boom.

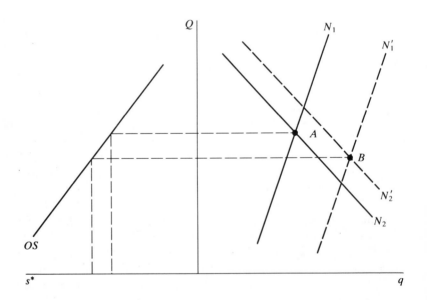

Figure 1.6 Determination of the optimal subsidy when manufacturing benefits from learning-by-doing.

3.3   *Imperfect capital markets*

A key assumption of the analysis so far is that of perfect capital markets. On the consumption side, this implies that the household sector is free to reallocate its spending between periods, so that the time profile of consumption is independent of the timing of the resource revenues. On the production side, it implies in addition that factors of production are allocated efficiently between as well as within the two periods. Since space precludes a consideration of all the issues which relaxing this assumption raises, we concentrate on the case where households do not have access to perfect capital markets. In addition, we simplify the model of section 3.1 by assuming that investment does not take place.

With households precluded from smoothing their income stream across periods, the single intertemporal budget constraint (18) must be replaced by two separate budget constraints, one for each period. (In effect, the prohibition of borrowing or lending amounts to fixing the current account exogenously at zero.) Suppose for concreteness that all the resource revenues accrue to households in the first period only. In the standard case of section 3.1, with no investment and no learning-by-doing externalities in manufacturing, the budget constraints therefore become:

$$e(p,q,z) = r(p,q) + v,\tag{25}$$

and

$$E(P,Q,Z) = R(P,Q).\tag{26}$$

Here, e and E are period-specific expenditure functions and z and Z are period-specific sub-utility functions.[18] Since only one of q and Q appears in each of equations (25) and (26), the diagrammatic analysis of this case is extremely simple. Instead of the configuration shown in figure 1.5, the N_1 curve is vertical, the N_2 curve is horizontal and only the former is shifted by the boom. In this case, therefore, the absence of any links between periods (either in the form of saving, investment or learning-by-doing) means that the real exchange rate adjusts fully in the period when the revenue from natural resource exploitation becomes available and subsequently returns to the level it would have reached in any case.

Of greater interest is the case where the learning-by-doing externality of section 3.2 coexists with imperfect capital markets. The budget constraints for the two periods now become:

$$e(p,q,z) = r(p+s,q) + v - sx_m \qquad (27)$$

and

$$E(P,Q,Z) = R(P,Q,x_m) \qquad (28)$$

In this case, the optimal subsidy may be derived by maximizing the direct utility function $\bar{U}$ which depends directly on z and Z. It can be shown that this leads to the following expression for the optimal subsidy:[19]

$$s^* = \lambda R_m, \quad \lambda = \frac{m\partial\bar{U}/\partial z}{M\partial\bar{U}/\partial Z} \qquad (29)$$

Here, λ is the ratio of the marginal utility of expenditure tomorrow to the marginal utility of expenditure today. In a perfect capital market λ would equal the world discount factor δ but with capital market imperfections that equality need not obtain. This formula should be compared with (24) in the last section: to induce private producers to produce the socially optimal level of manufactured goods in period 1, they should receive a subsidy equal to the marginal benefits generated by the learning-by-doing externality δR_m, corrected for any wedge between λ and δ caused by capital market imperfections. If there is no such wedge the formula simplifies to $s^* = \delta R_m$, as in equation (24). The presence of λ in (29) indicates that there is an intertemporal trade-off involved in s^*; an increase in s will lead to a decline in welfare today because of the increased static price distortion it causes today; but to an increase in welfare tomorrow because of the dynamic benefits associated with the larger future outward shift of the production function in manufacturing. If, at the margin, expenditure tomorrow generates less additional welfare than expenditure today because capital market imperfections prevent intertemporal arbitrage ($\lambda < \delta$), a smaller subsidy is called for than would otherwise be the case.

Now what happens when first-period oil revenues go up? We will use a diagrammatic representation of the equation system to help in the analysis. N_1 in figure 1.7 represents the first-period goods market schedule in (q,s) space where s denotes the *actual* subsidy level (by assumption s equals s^*, the *optimal* level, before the increase in oil revenues). z has been substituted out using (27). The N_1 schedule has a positive slope: a higher subsidy to manufacturing production draws resources out of the non-traded sector, reducing its output; a return to equilibrium requires a higher value of q.[20] Moreover, higher oil

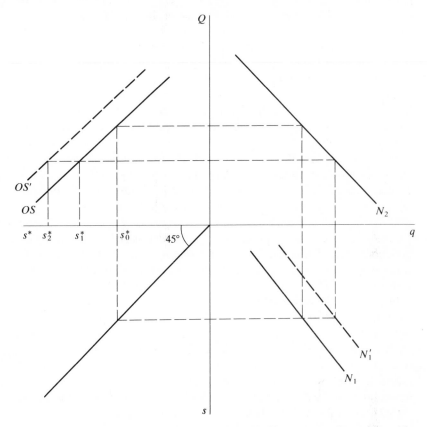

Figure 1.7 Determination of the optimal subsidy to manufacturing with imperfect capital markets.

revenues in period 1 will be spent partially on non-traded goods in period one, shifting the schedule rightwards (to N'_1 in figure 1.7).

The N_2 schedule represents non-traded goods market equilibrium in period 2. Except that Z has been substituted out using (28), this is the same N_2 schedule as in figure 1.6. Because of our assumption of an exogenous current account, the only intertemporal channel is that arising from learning-by-doing externalities. As we saw in section 3.2, this means that N_2 must have a negative slope. An increase in first-period oil revenues will not *directly* affect N_2 under our exogenous current account assumption.

Finally, the OS schedule represents equation (29) in (s^*, Q) space, where s^* is the *optimal* subsidy level. A higher value of Q in the second period implies a lower value of second period manufacturing output; therefore, given everything else, the value of the extra future productivity benefits of an additional unit of first-period manufacturing production declines and so does the optimal subsidy level: OS has a negative slope. First-period increases in oil revenues shift OS out under our exogenous current account assumption; more expenditure today for given expenditure tomorrow increases λ, the ratio of the marginal utility of expenditure tomorrow to that of expenditure today, because of the concavity of $U(Z,z)$. Since s^* equals λR_m, the OS schedule must shift out to OS'.

We now have all the building blocks in place to work through the effects of more oil today on the optimal subsidy to manufacturing. As argued above, higher oil revenues today will at least partially be spent on non-traded goods today, shifting the N_1 curve upwards and leading to a first-period real appreciation for standard Dutch Disease reasons. The resulting decline in manufacturing production will lead to a decline in second-period productivity in that sector as technological progress slows down. The resulting resource shifts into the non-traded sector will lead to a real depreciation in period 2 (i.e., a fall in Q).

For a given location of the OS schedule, this in itself would be enough to increase the optimal subsidy level: the negatively sloped OS schedule tells us that a lower second-period exchange rate (and so a higher value of manufacturing output in period 2) calls for higher first-period subsidies: the post-oil-increase optimal subsidy s^*_1 exceeds the pre-oil-increase one s^*_0. Moreover, we have already seen that higher oil revenues today will increase λ, the social discount factor, shifting out the OS schedule. This leads to a further increase in the optimal subsidy to s^*_2.[21]

We therefore have a clear-cut result: if the current account cannot be or is not used to smooth expenditure, subsidies to the non-oil traded goods sector should be increased if that sector shows the potential of significant learning-by-doing induced increases in productivity external to the firm. In this sense the Dutch Disease is indeed a disease.

4   The monetary consequences of a resource discovery

So far, we have considered only the aspects of the Dutch Disease that concern the allocation of real resources. However, especially in the short run, many of the important policy issues which arise in this context involve monetary considerations. In this section we turn to consider some of these issues, assuming for simplicity that the real side of the economy is characterized by the static model of section 2. In section 4.1

we assume that both the wage and the price of non-traded goods are flexible, while in section 4.2 we consider the consequences of wage and price rigidities, thus presenting an analysis which complements in many respects the disequilibrium analysis of section 2.3 above.

4.1   Monetary adjustment with flexible wages and prices

Since the real side of the model is essentially identical to that in section 2, the market-clearing condition for non-traded goods is little changed from equation (1). However, some amendments are necessary. First, since we are now concerned with the price level as well as with relative prices, we make explicit the nominal prices of traded and non-traded goods. We denote these by e and q respectively: since the domestic price of traded goods is linked directly to their world price, we may set world prices equal to unity and identify e with the *nominal* exchange rate (the domestic currency price of a unit of foreign exchange). We also allow for a real-balance effect on spending. Letting the parameter b represent the resource movement effect, the non-traded good market equilibrium condition may therefore be written as:

$$x_n(q/e,b) = c_n(q,e,y,M/P). \tag{30}$$

P is the domestic price level, which is homogeneous of degree one in the prices of traded and non-traded goods:

$$P = P(q,e). \tag{31}$$

Equation (30) is represented by the line NN in figure 1.8. Obviously, a rise in q induces an excess supply of the non-traded good while an increase in e gives rise to excess demand. Moreover, with a fixed nominal money supply, an equiproportionate increase in q and e leads to excess supply of the non-traded good by reducing the value of real money balances and so depressing spending. The non-traded good market equilibrium locus is therefore upward-sloping and less steeply sloped than a ray from the origin, as shown.

The determination of equilibrium is completed by adding the equilibrium conditions for the monetary sector. In this sub-section we simplify by assuming that money is the only asset and that velocity is constant. Hence, the requirement that the domestic money supply be willingly held is expressed by equating demand and supply:

$$M/P = \alpha y. \tag{32}$$

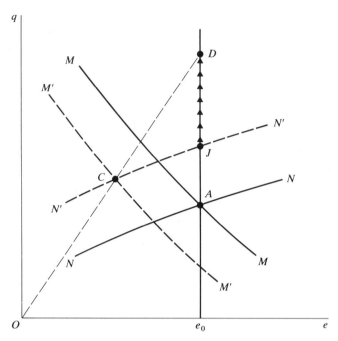

Figure 1.8   Real and monetary effects of a boom under fixed and floating
exchange rates.

Note that we assume that the resource boom affects money demand
directly through its effect on y: this gives rise to what we call the *liquidity
effect* of the boom (although the mechanism involved may just as well be
thought of as emanating from a wealth effect). Equation (32) is
represented by the locus MM in figure 1.8: from (31), an increase in
either nominal price raises the domestic price level P and so gives rise to
excess demand for money by reducing the real value of the given supply.
This locus is therefore downward-sloping as shown. If the exchange rate
is flexible (and assuming that the domestic money market always
clears), equilibrium must lie along this locus at all times. A rise in q must
be accompanied by a fall in e if the domestic money supply is to be
willingly held when the level of income is given at its full employment
level. Alternatively, under a fixed exchange rate, equilibrium in the
short run may be at (for example) a point above MM, reflecting a
shortfall of actual holdings of real money balances below desired
holdings. This disequilibrium must be offset by a build-up of foreign
exchange reserves to augment the domestic money supply. Hence, all

points above MM correspond to situations of balance of trade surplus and points below MM correspond to a deficit.

With the initial pre-boom equilibrium determined at point A, where the MM and NN loci intersect, we are now in a position to consider the consequences of a natural resource discovery. As far as the NN locus is concerned, we know already that both the spending and resource movement effects lead to excess demand for the non-traded good at initial prices. Hence, this locus shifts upwards to $N'N'$. The rise in real income also raises money demand and, if the domestic money supply is not changed, the price level must fall to restore money market equilibrium. The resulting liquidity effect therefore shifts the MM locus inwards to $M'M'$. Precisely what happens now depends on the exchange rate regime pursued by the authorities and we consider in turn the two extreme cases of floating and fixed exchange rate regimes.

If the nominal exchange rate is allowed to float freely, the new equilibrium must be at point C, where $M'M'$ and $N'N'$ intersect. The fact that a real appreciation has taken place is reflected in the greater slope of the ray OC relative to the ray OA. Under floating exchange rates, the mechanism whereby this comes about is through a *nominal* appreciation (a fall in e), so that the domestic prices of traded goods unambiguously fall. By contrast, the domestic nominal price of the non-traded good may either rise or fall, although we postpone considering the possible implications of this until the next sub-section.

What happens if the nominal exchange rate is not free to change but instead remains equal to its initial value e_0? On impact, with a constant nominal money supply, the shifts in the two equilibrium loci are as just described. Hence, the nominal price of the non-traded good rises to eliminate the incipient excess demand and equilibrium moves in the short run to point J. The change in the relative price of the non-traded good, and hence the degree to which the real side of the economy adjusts, is less than that required for long-run equilibrium, since the spending effect is dampened by the leakage into hoarding which is reflected in a balance-of-payments surplus. Since desired money balances are now greater than actual, the equilibrium at J cannot be permanently sustained. Over time therefore, the trade surplus leads to a build-up of foreign exchange reserves, and so, provided the authorities do not attempt to sterilize this inflow, the domestic money supply gradually increases. This causes both the $M'M'$ and the $N'N'$ loci to drift upwards, and so the equilibrium point moves upwards from point J as indicated by the arrows. Since the long-run equilibrium is independent of nominal variables, and in particular is independent of the exchange-rate regime pursued, this process can only end when the post-boom equilibrium real exchange rate represented by the slope of the line OC is attained. This occurs at point D, where the two loci once again intersect, the surplus is eliminated and the economy reaches its new long-run equilibrium.

The implications of this comparison between exchange rate regimes are clear: a fixed exchange rate delays the real effects of the boom and gives rise to inflationary rather than deflationary pressures. The required increase in the relative price of non-traded goods is brought about by a rise in their nominal price rather than by a *fall* in the nominal prices of traded goods. This may to some extent suggest that a strategy of permitting some nominal appreciation may be desirable, since experience in many countries suggests that the domestic inflation induced by a boom under fixed exchange rates may pose political problems which are just as severe as those arising from the required change in the structure of the economy.

Of course, the assumption made so far – that the domestic monetary authorities adopt a neutral stance – has been made for analytic convenience only, and the consequences of alternative assumptions can easily be examined in the diagram. For example, if the authorities are committed to a fixed nominal exchange rate but are concerned about its inflationary consequences, they may attempt to sterilize the inflow of foreign exchange reserves. This amounts to what Corden (1981) has called a policy of 'exchange-rate protection': the central bank acts to suppress the real appreciation, so protecting the traded goods sectors and mitigating the extent of deindustrialization. The cost of such a policy does not arise from a divergence between home and foreign relative prices (as with orthodox tariff protection). Rather, to the extent that the policy is successful, it arises from a continuing shortfall of aggregate consumption below the new level of national income, which is reflected in an ongoing balance of payments surplus.

4.2   *Sticky prices and the adjustment problem*

So far in this section we have assumed that prices and wages adjust instantaneously, so as to ensure the continual clearing of domestic goods and factor markets. We have already seen in section 2.3 that *real* wage stickiness can impede the adjustment process, irrespective of monetary conditions. We therefore concentrate in what follows on nominal rigidities. If we confine attention to rigidities in the domestic price of the non-traded good, then the discussion of figure 1.8 has already drawn attention to the fact that, under fixed exchange rates, the effect of the boom is to put upward pressure on q. Shortages in the home market may result in the short run therefore, especially if the authorities attempt to enforce price controls. Probably of greater policy concern, however, is the fact that the boom may require a *fall* in the domestic price of the non-traded good if the exchange rate is flexible. If the price of the non-traded good is sticky, then in this case the boom can paradoxically lead to domestic excess *supply*.

Figure 1.9 illustrates this possibility. The shifts in the *MM* and *NN* schedules are similar to those in figure 1.8, except that now it is assumed that the adjustment to the new long-run equilibrium under flexible exchange rates at point *C* requires a fall in *q*; in other words, the shift in the *MM* schedule as a result of the liquidity effect is assumed to dominate that in the *NN* schedule as a result of the spending and resource movement effects. Since in the short run the price of the non-traded good is sticky, the domestic price of tradables, that is to say, the nominal exchange rate, must bear all the brunt of adjusting to

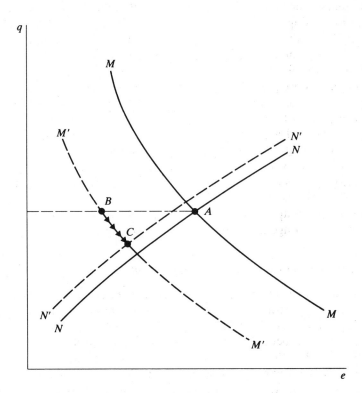

Figure 1.9   With sticky prices, a resource boom may lead to exchange rate overshooting and transitional unemployment.

ensure that the money market clears at the new higher level of real income. In other words, the nominal exchange rate *overshoots* its new long-run equilibrium value as a result of the boom.\Immediately after the boom, therefore, the equilibrium jumps from A to B, which lies on the post-boom money market equilibrium locus, $M'M'$. At this point, there is excess supply of the non-traded good and (assuming this feeds into the labour market) unemployment. Over time, the excess supply of the non-traded good drives down its price. The economy therefore gradually moves towards the new long-run equilibrium as shown by the arrows. The consequences for the real economy of moving along this path are clear: because both the real and the nominal exchange rates overshoot their final equilibrium values, manufacturing profitability and output fall even more in the short run than in the long run. Since this temporary recession emanates from a 'distortion' represented by the sticky price of the non-traded good, we may conclude that, in this case, flexible exchange rates exacerbate the Dutch Disease.

Finally, it may be noted that the overshooting result we have derived here continues to hold when we adopt a more sophisticated approach to modelling financial markets. For example, allowing for perfect international capital mobility, so that home and foreign bonds are perfect substitutes, does not significantly affect the analysis. It also continues to apply when exchange rate expectations are assumed to be formed rationally, although the degree of exchange rate overshooting in that case is somewhat less.[22] We may therefore conclude that the result appears to be relatively robust.[23]

5   Conclusion

In this paper we have examined the effects of natural resource discoveries in a variety of theoretical models representative of those in the now extensive literature on the Dutch Disease. Each model has been deliberately simplified as far as possible in order to focus on one or two particular issues. Rather than summarizing each of the models in turn, we conclude by considering their implications for some of the practical policy questions which typically arise in discussions of the effects of natural resource discoveries.

5.1   Is deindustrialization inevitable?

Deindustrialization, in the sense of a decline in output and employment in the exposed manufacturing sector, is indeed a feature exhibited by all the models we have considered. However, it is important not to be misled by labels. The key features of the sectors that may be expected to decline are that they are exposed to foreign competition and have little or no ability to set their own prices. Thus, export-orientated agricultural or even service sectors may be squeezed; and, conversely, industries that cater for the home market as a result of trade protection or that possess monopolistic price-setting powers in their export markets may benefit from the rise in home demand. Moreover, it should be stressed that deindustrialization is in general a symptom of the economy's adjustment to its new equilibrium. It certainly does not provide prima facie grounds for diagnosing a 'disease' that requires corrective action (*see* 5.4 *below*).

5.2 *Is a real appreciation inevitable?*

The models we have considered are also unanimous in predicting that a resource boom will give rise to a real appreciation, in the sense of an increase in the price of non-traded relative to traded goods. Once again, it is important not to be misled by labels, since a *nominal* appreciation (i.e. a rise in the external value of the home currency) is neither necessary nor sufficient for a real appreciation.[24]

5.3 *Can a resource discovery generate unemployment?*

Obviously, a necessary condition for this is that there be some degree of wage rigidity. In addition, two other issues are crucial. The first is the weight of non-traded goods in the consumption basket of wage-earners. If this is sufficiently large (in a sense made precise in section 2.3), then real wage stickiness will give rise to transitional unemployment following a resource boom. A second issue is the degree of monetary accommodation. Even if wages are merely sticky in nominal rather than real terms, unemployment may still ensue in certain cases, if the monetary authorities fail to provide adequate liquidity (*see* section 4.2).

5.4 *Is intervention at the industrial or sectoral level justified?*

This might alternatively be expressed as 'Does the Dutch Disease call for a cure?'. As has been repeatedly stressed, the fact that resource exploitation is likely to lead to deindustrialization and a real appreciation does not in itself provide any justification for offsetting intervention. On the contrary, these responses represent general equilibrium adjustments which are *necessary* if the economy is to enjoy the fruits of its increased wealth. Of course, on both allocative and distributional grounds, transitional adjustment assistance to the declining sectors may be justified. However, permanent subsidies are only justified if there is some market failure which implies a divergence between private and social valuations. Moreover, if such a market failure is present, then intervention is likely to be justified whether or not the economy enjoys a resource boom. In such cases, the relevant question is therefore whether the boom *raises* the optimal level of subsidy and, as we have seen (in section 3), this is more likely to be the case if capital market imperfections prevent intertemporal smoothing of consumption.

5.5   *What is the appropriate stance of macroeconomic policy?*

The conduct of macroeconomic policy is one of the most controversial issues in economics as a whole and raises questions that go far beyond the issue of natural resource discoveries. In so far as general conclusions can be drawn, there seems to be a clear presumption that maintaining a fixed exchange rate is likely to require an increase in the domestic price level in order to effect the necessary changes in relative prices (section 4.1). On the other hand, it is also possible that a policy of floating exchange rates without moderate monetary accommodation may lead the boom to subject the economy to a deflationary shock, with unfavourable consequences for output and employment in the short run (section 4.2).

5.6   *What happens when the oil runs out?*

The finite nature of reserves does not of itself pose additional problems if capital markets are sufficiently flexible and private agents are sufficiently well informed that they can carry out the necessary intertemporal smoothing of consumption without assistance. Of course, if industry is subject to significant learning-by-doing the 're-entry' problem when the resource revenue comes to an end may be considerable. In the case considered in section 3, this was seen to justify subsidies to manufacturing, and in certain circumstances the optimal degree of subsidization may rise as a result of the natural resource boom.

It should be added that even the stable of models we have considered is highly incomplete. Many other issues need to be taken into account to enhance our understanding of the process of structural change resulting from natural resource discoveries and no doubt further theoretical work will emerge to fill this gap. However, probably the greatest need in the present state of our knowledge is not for further theoretical elaboration but for detailed consideration of individual country experiences with resource exploitation with a view to ascertaining the usefulness of the theoretical models already developed. It is with this process that many of the other contributions to this volume are concerned.

NOTES

* Helpful comments from John Black and other participants at the conference are gratefully acknowledged.

1 For other surveys of the theoretical literature, see Corden (1984), Neary (1984) and van Wijnbergen (1985). The present chapter draws in part on the latter two papers.

2 See Dasgupta and Heal (1978).

3 For these reasons, we are attracted by the more neutral French term for these phenomena: 'Syndrome Hollandais'.

4 The terms 'resource-movement effect' and 'spending effect' of a natural resource discovery were introduced by Corden and Neary (1982).

5 For convenience, we use social indifference curves as a shorthand way of summarizing aggregate demands, and ignore the well-known difficulty that changes in income distribution are likely to shift them, except under restrictive assumptions.

6 Examples include Snape (1977), Corden and Neary (1982), Long (1983) and Cassing and Warr (1985). A general production structure allowing for any number of goods and factors is outlined in the appendix to Neary (1984).

7 See Jones (1971).

8 See Barro and Grossman (1971) and Malinvaud (1977). The present application draws on Neary (1980) and van Wijnbergen (1984b).

9 This follows from the assumptions that all of the output of the non-traded good sector is used for current consumption and that some of the labour market rationing falls on firms in that sector. If either of these assumptions does not hold, the two loci do not coincide and the region between them corresponds to a regime of 'underconsumption' or simultaneous excess demand for labour and excess supply of the non-traded good. Since points below and to the right of A are irrelevant to the effects of natural resource exploitation, we do not consider these issues further. For a fuller discussion, see Neary (1980) and van Wijnbergen (1984b).

10 This result is derived in Neary (1984) and van Wijnbergen (1984b).

11 We follow the convention throughout of using lower case notation for period 1, upper case notation for period 2 and a superimposed bar to denote variables that refer to both periods.

12 This is an example of the Le Chatelier principle and is proved by totally differentiating (10):

$$\bar{R}_{QQ} = \delta[R_{QQ} - R_{QK}R_{KK}^{-1}R_{KQ}] > \delta R_{QQ} \tag{12a}$$

The non-traded good is relatively capital-intensive in the second period if R_{QK} is positive, but (since this equals R_{KQ}) the inequality holds irrespective of the sign of this term.

44   J. Peter Neary and Sweder van Wijnbergen

13 Homogeneous separability of $\bar{E}$ guarantees that the non-traded good in the current and future periods are net substitutes: $\bar{E}_{qQ} = \delta\bar{E}_{mM}m_qM_Q > 0$.
14 This section is based on van Wijnbergen (1984a).
15 Details are given in van Wijnbergen (1984a).
16 This equation is independent of the first-period relative price, q, because of the assumption that period 1 manufacturing output affects period 2 national income in a linear fashion: $R_{mm} = 0$.
17 Note, however, that it must always be flatter than N_1 in stable configurations, at least in the neighbourhood of equilibrium.
18 The manner in which this specification is consistent with homothetic separability of the utility function $\bar{U}$ is spelt out in van Wijnbergen (1984a).
19 For details, see van Wijnbergen (1984a).
20 The N_1 schedule also depends on Q, so that complete graphical analysis is not possible. A similar remark applies to N_2, which depends on s as well as s^*. The algebraic analysis in van Wijnbergen (1984a) takes account of these interactions and shows that the diagrammatic analysis gives the correct conclusions.
21 Finally, when the actual subsidy s is set at its new optimal level, the N_2 curve will also shift, leading to a series of second-round effects. It can be shown that these will not reverse the result of an increase in s^* following an increase in first-period oil revenues.
22 See Eastwood and Venables (1982), Buiter and Purvis (1983), Neary (1984) and Neary and van Wijnbergen (1984).
23 The Dutch Disease has also been examined in models which allow for imperfect asset substitutability or controls on capital markets by Giavazzi, Sheen and Wyplosz (1984) and Pesaran (1984).
24 It should be noted that quite plausible theoretical examples of a resource discovery which gives rise to 'proindustrialization' or to a real depreciation have been uncovered (see Corden and Neary, 1982). However, these typically assume more than one intersectorally mobile factor (and so are less appropriate to a short-run horizon) and require that the resource-movement effect dominate the spending effect. Moreover, to date no convincing model has been constructed which predicts that a resource boom will generate both proindustrialization and a real depreciation.

REFERENCES

Barro R. and H. I. Grossman (1971) 'Output and Employment in General Disequilibrium', *American Economic Review*, **61**, 82–93.
Buiter W. H. and D. D. Purvis (1983) 'Oil, Disinflation and Export Competitiveness: a Model of the Dutch Disease', in J. Bhandari and B. Putnam (eds) *Economic Interdependence and Flexible Exchange Rates*, Cambridge, Mass.: M.I.T. Press.
Cassing J. and P. G. Warr (1985) 'The Distributional Impact of a Resource Boom', *Journal of International Economics*, **18**, 301–19.
Corden W. M. (1981) 'Exchange Rate Protection', in R.N. Cooper et al. (eds) *The International Monetary System under Flexible Exchange Rates: Global, Regional and National*, Cambridge, Mass.: Ballinger, pp. 17–34.
Corden W. M. (1984) Booming Sector and Dutch Disease Economics: Survey and Consolidation', *Oxford Economic Papers*, **36**, 359–80.

Corden W. M. and J. P. Neary (1982) 'Booming Sector and De-Industrialisation in a Small Open Economy', *Economic Journal*, **92**, 825–48.

Dasgupta P. and G. M. Heal (1978) *Economic Theory and Exhaustible Resources*, Cambridge: Cambridge University Press.

Eastwood R. K. and A. J. Venables (1982) 'The Macroeconomic Implications of a Resource Discovery in an Open Economy', *Economic Journal*, **92**, 285–99.

Giavazzi F., J. Sheen and C. Wyplosz (1984) 'Sterling and the Fiscal Aspects of North Sea Oil', University of Essex, mimeo.

Jones R. W. (1971) 'A Three-Factor Model in Theory, Trade and History', in J.N. Bhagwati et al. (eds) *Trade, Balance of Payments and Growth: Essays in Honor of C.P. Kindleberger*, Amsterdam: North-Holland, pp. 3–21.

Long N. V. (1983) 'The Effects of a Booming Export Industry on the Rest of the Economy', *Economic Record*, **59**, 57–60.

Malinvaud E. (1977) *The Theory of Unemployment Reconsidered*, Oxford: Basil Blackwell.

Neary J. P. (1980) 'Non-Traded Goods and the Balance of Trade in a Neo-Keynesian Temporary Equilibrium', *Quarterly Journal of Economics*, **95**, 403–29.

Neary J. P. (1984) 'Real and Monetary Aspects of the "Dutch Disease"', in D. C. Hague and K. Jungenfeld (eds) *Structural Adjustment in Developed Open Economies*, London: Macmillan.

Neary J. P. and D. D. Purvis (1983) 'Real Adjustment and Exchange Rate Dynamics', in J. Frenkel (ed.): *Exchange Rates and International Macroeconomics*, Chicago: Chicago University Press.

Neary J. P. and S. van Wijnbergen (1984) 'Can an Oil Discovery lead to a Recession?: A Comment on Eastwood and Venables', *Economic Journal*, **94**, 390–5.

Pesaran M. H. (1984) 'Macroeconomic Policy in an Oil-Exporting Economy with Foreign Exchange Controls', *Economica*, **51**, 253–70.

Salter W. E. G. (1959) 'Internal and External Balance: The Role of Price and Expenditure Effects', *Economic Record*, **35**, 226–38.

Snape R. H. (1977) 'Effects of Mineral Development on the Economy', *Australian Journal of Agricultural Economics*, **21**, 147–56.

Svensson L. and A. Razin (1983) 'The Terms of Trade and the Current Account: the Harberger-Laursen-Metzler Effect', *Journal of Political Economy*, **91**, 97–125.

van Wijnbergen S. (1984a) 'The "Dutch Disease": A Disease After All?', *Economic Journal*, **94**, 41–55.

van Wijnbergen S. (1984b) 'Inflation, Employment and the Dutch Disease in Oil Exporting Countries: a Short-Run Disequilibrium Analysis', *Quarterly Journal of Economics*, **99**, 233–50.

van Wijnbergen S. (1985) 'Oil Discoveries, Intertemporal Adjustment and Public Policy', in O. Bjerkholt and E. Offerdal (eds) *Macroeconomic Prospects for a Small Oil Exporting Country*, The Hague: Martinus Nijhoff.

DISCUSSION

A trade theoretic perspective   RONALD W. JONES

However it was introduced into our language, the phrase 'Dutch Disease' is now widely recognized in our profession as that curious phenomenon whereby new discoveries or favourable price changes in one sector of the economy seem to cause distress in other sectors despite an overall benefit to the country as a whole. In their paper, Neary and van Wijnbergen have succeeded in the bold venture of surveying several aspects of this disease, including macroeconomic features and the peculiar problems associated with natural resources as well as issues involving international trade. In commenting on their paper I restrict my remarks to trade theoretic issues and use their discussion primarily as a point of departure in assessing how the Dutch Disease phenomenon is intimately linked to the basic concept of comparative advantage.

The Neary–van Wijnbergen discussion points to a variety of trade models explored in the literature (e.g. *see* Corden and Neary, 1982), ranging from the specific factors model they use in the present work to three-sector versions of Heckscher–Ohlin theory. I find it useful to start at an earlier stage in the pantheon of models – with the labour-only Ricardian model. Furthermore, I postpone explicit concern with non-traded commodities. Having local resources used in part to produce commodities not tied to world markets is a centre-piece of their discussion; these activities are not, however, necessary in allowing Dutch Disease phenomena.

In such a simple Ricardian world each country can rank the productivity of its (labour) resources in earning dollars at going world prices for all (traded) commodities. Generally any one small price-taking country need produce only one commodity – the one with the highest value per unit input – and can rely on trade to satisfy a variety of consumption needs. Now suppose a 'boom' takes the form of raising labour's productivity in a commodity previously imported, to such an extent that value per unit of labour input now exceeds that in the traditional export sector. The consequence is severe: the law of comparative advantage is ruthless in casting aside an industry in which labour has lost none of its absolute productivity vis-à-vis other countries. The essence of comparative advantage is that a sector is locally viable only if it retains its productive superiority compared with other sectors of the economy.

The Dutch Disease is writ large even in (or especially in) this most basic setting.

Sector-specific and/or Heckscher–Ohlin models are usually favoured in discussing the phenomenon since they allow more than one traded activity to survive in the brisk climate of free trade. For example, in a two-sector specific factors model a boom (productivity increase) in the import-competing sector can cause labour to be reallocated from the traditional export sector and switch the trade pattern without completely wiping out the former export sector.

The role of a non-tradable good has been emphasized in the Dutch Disease literature. Although initially not sharing in the expansion in the booming sector (by assumption), its fate differs from that of the traditional export sector in that its price can adjust upwards. In the specific factors model the non-tradable shares in the cost push represented by the increase in the wage rate, but local demanders absorb some of this in a price rise. In addition, the domestic welfare gains can be expected to spill over into an outward shift in demand for non-tradables, serving further to raise their price. Some attention in the specific factors framework has been paid to the question of whether the price of the non-tradable might be bid up even more than the wage rate. If so, this sector actually expands and the return to specific capital in non-tradables would unambiguously rise. In either case, the increase in the price of non-tradables is passed on (in part) in a further wage increase, which serves increasingly to squeeze returns in the traditional tradable sector.

Several points have been stressed in the more detailed analytical literature on the Dutch Disease in the presence of non-tradables. First is the possibility just mentioned that the non-traded sector might actually expand. Furthermore, the return to the fixed factor in non-tradables might rise by more than the return to capital specific to the booming sector. Indeed, a sufficient rise in wages could actually depress the rate of return to this factor. The ultimate abuse to the factor specific to the booming sector cannot altogether be ruled out: its return might fall by more than that in the traditional sector if the relative share of labour in the booming sector is sufficiently high.

Discussion of the Dutch Disease is not limited to cases of resource discoveries. Instead, as in the case of energy in the seventies, significant worldwide price rises might confer large real income gains on energy-exporting countries. Although this case is in some respects similar to that of technical progress or a resource discovery in the booming sector, in other respects it differs, e.g. in triggering substitution effects in demand as relative prices change. The role of non-traded goods is clear in this scenario, and suggests, at least to my mind, a replacement of the Corden–Neary (and, by extension, the Neary–van Wijnbergen) terminology of resource–movement effect and spending effect by the more old-fashioned distinction between substitution and income effects.

To be more explicit, suppose the price of a certain exportable (B) is driven up by conditions in world markets, relative to the (given) price of other tradables (T). The earlier argument concerning the fate of non-tradables (N) in the specific factors context can be extended generally to the three-commodity case with smooth substitutabilities in production and consumption. A rise in p_B, denoted in relative terms by $\hat{p}_B$, leads either to:

$$\hat{p}_B > \hat{p}_N > \hat{p}_T \ (=0) \tag{1}$$

or to:

$$\hat{p}_N > \hat{p}_B > \hat{p}_T \ (=0) \tag{2}$$

In both cases the rise in price in the booming exportables sector confers gains to the community as a whole which help to raise the price of non-tradables. If substitution effects are relatively strong compared with income effects, the rise in p_N is kept below the rise in p_B (case 1). However, case (2) illustrates the price of non-tradables rising even more (relatively) than the price in the booming exportable sector, an outcome possible if substitution effects both in demand and supply are relatively weak. (The argument is spelled out for the case of a rise in import prices in Jones, 1974.)

Must a boom in one tradable sector create a Dutch Disease contraction in other traditional tradables? The one-factor Ricardian model is indeed severe in this respect – only one industry need survive. In a model with more than one factor but only two traded goods, technical improvement in one may or may not require a contraction in the other at constant prices. But a price rise in a booming sector, or an expansion in a resource used only there, must drag resources away from the other sector at given world prices. The possibility of a complementary relationship between outputs in the booming sector and a traditional sector requires the existence of more than two tradables. One such example was provided by Gruen and Corden (1970). To paraphrase their construction, suppose the booming sector requires labour and capital. Furthermore, let the supply of capital be fixed; the booming sector can draw labour from the rest of the economy, consisting of two other sectors, each requiring labour and land. At initial prices the Rybczynski effect declares that one of these sectors loses resources but the other actually expands. That other sector does not suffer a Dutch Disease contraction.

This discussion has presupposed that the booming sector produces a final consumption good. If, instead, the booming sector produces an input required by the traditional tradable sector, will the latter be favourably affected? Did increased energy production in Canada or the United Kingdom provide the means whereby traditional industry in these countries could expand? The negative response is linked to the tradability of energy on world markets. Unless the traditional export sector can obtain its energy requirements at lower prices (as it might if government intervenes or if such energy is non-traded), it does not directly benefit from the local energy boom. Instead, increases in prices of other inputs, such as labour, will produce a Dutch Disease result. It emerges that a likely scenario to produce joint expansion in a booming sector and a traditional export sector is for the former to provide an input to the latter at a lower cost. But even then, their joint use of other resources casts the two sectors in the role of substitutes instead of complements.

As these remarks suggest, the role of international trade is crucial. A boom in an input-producing sector that is non-tradable may well encourage output expansion in traditional tradables employing this input. But if the input is traded and its price is prevented from falling, traditional tradables (as an aggregate) are adversely affected in the Dutch Disease manner. If traditional tradables use other specific inputs that are themselves traded on world markets, one aspect of the Dutch Disease is avoided – the return to these specific factors is not driven down (in the small-country case). However, a different aspect of Dutch Disease is exacerbated – the fall in output levels is greater if some inputs flee the country. The phenomenon of cross-hauling of international capital flows is closely related to Dutch Disease: a boom in one sector may attract capital from abroad while, via its effect on local input prices, it drives out other traded inputs as their returns threaten to fall. (For details see Caves, 1971; Jones, Neary and Ruane, 1983.)

Cross-hauling is not an inevitable consequence of a boom. Indeed, elements of positive externalities and increasing returns to scale may well provide the basis for a non-Dutch Disease outcome. In such a scenario a boom in one sector attracts resources into industries capable of supplying this sector and induced expansion in 'social overhead capital' (or public inputs) may encourage development in a wider range of industries. However, the doctrine of comparative advantage still operates to ensure that establishment of a new exportable base co-exists with greater levels of net importables in other sectors, and these may traditionally have enjoyed export markets.

REFERENCES

Caves R. E. (1971) 'International Corporations: the Industrial Economics of Foreign Investment', *Economica*, **38**, 1–27.
Corden W. M. and J. P. Neary (1982) 'Booming Sector and De-industrialisation in a Small Open Economy', *Economic Journal*, **92**, 825–48.
Gruen F. H. and W. M. Corden (1970) 'A Tariff that Worsens the Terms of Trade', in I. A. McDougall and R. H. Snape (eds) *Studies in International Economics: Monash Conference Papers*, Amsterdam: North-Holland, pp. 55–8.
Jones R. W. (1974) 'Trade with Non-Traded Goods: the Anatomy of Inter-Connected Markets', *Economica*, **41**, 121–38.
Jones R. W., J. P. Neary and F. Ruane (1983) 'Two-Way Capital Flows: Cross-Hauling in a Model of Foreign Investment', *Journal of International Economics*, **13**, 357–66.

An international macroeconomic perspective
WILLIAM H. BRANSON

This paper presents a series of models illustrating different problems that could result from a resource discovery. I will begin with comments addressed directly to these models, before moving on to some more general remarks.

Some interesting insights can be gained by comparing the two-period models of section 3 of the paper with their static counterparts in section 2. In the two-period model, the increase in wealth caused by the resource discovery leads to a spending effect which is spread out over time. Hence there is a rise in P_n/P_t (a real appreciation) in both periods. The possibility of capital accumulation may give rise to overshooting of the real exchange rate. The long-run rise in P_n/P_t will lead to a higher long-run capital stock in non-tradables; this takes time, so P_n/P_t overshoots.[1]

The sticky price analysis seems to provide little support for demand expansion policies. The general result that unemployment emerges if the weight of non-traded goods in wage-earners' consumption exceeds their contribution to output can be illustrated by the extreme case in which the non-traded good is the wage good: the real product wage is then constant in the non-traded sector, but rises in tradables, so total employment falls.

A learning-by-doing model is used to analyse whether manufacturing should be subsidized during an oil boom to ensure that it still exists when the oil runs out. This analysis assumes the existence of a single manufacturing sector, and excludes the important possibility (to which I will return) that a rather different manufacturing sector may be required when the oil runs out. The way in which learning-by-doing is modelled is that current output affects future productivity. If this effect is strong enough, the optimal subsidy to manufacturing increases after an oil discovery. If capital market imperfections prevent some firms from borrowing to support present production, the case for government intervention (to improve access to capital or else subsidize) is stronger still. Similar arguments will apply for the case of scale economies in manufacturing. If assumptions on lump sum taxes and/or subsidy disbursement costs are removed, there may be a role for tariffs in the optimal policy package.

The monetary analysis of a resource boom suggests that if the money supply is held fixed there will be a nominal as well as real appreciation. This may be such as to require a fall in the price of non-traded goods. If this price is sticky a policy of some monetary accommodation would seem appropriate. In terms of figure 1.9 this would involve shifting the MM curve to intersect the (new) $N'N'$ curve at the existing price of non-traded goods; this would allow an immediate movement from old to new long-run equilibrium. The monetary analysis could also be used to show the possibility of an announcement of a future resource boom precipitating an anticipatory recession.

The use of a series of models to analyse different problems and effects makes it difficult to see how the various effects might interact. It may well be possible to integrate the models of this paper into a more general one in order to examine these interactions.

Moving on to more general cases, one must be careful in selecting an appropriate model to consider these issues in an LDC context, where *expansion* of the manufacturing sector is seen as essential for development. If this view is correct, there may be a case for increased infant-industry protection (promotion?) as a result of a resource boom. The sector-specific factors associated with agriculture, manufacturing and natural resources are often thought of as land, capital and resources. Ronald Findlay, in a comment at a National Bureau of Economic Research conference on trade, held in Kuala Lumpur in January 1984, suggested that the Corden–Neary paradox model, in which manufacturing is labour-intensive and agriculture is capital-intensive, may be more appropriate. If so, it means that a resource boom has still stronger deindustrializing effects.

It is possible to view current US experience in a Dutch Disease framework. The boom has been in the bond-producing sector, due to a decision to shift consumption towards the present. The spending effect has led to real appreciation and reduced employment in manufacturing. The appreciation is thought to be temporary, and a major policy issue is whether it will be possible to re-establish pre-existing industries when the dollar depreciates. The Neary–van Wijnbergen paper sidesteps this issue by assuming a single manufacturing sector. If, instead, learning-by-doing operates at industry level, it is possible that during the period of deindustrialization competitors will learn by doing to such an extent that it will not be possible to re-establish certain industries that existed before the appreciation. If so, it may be necessary to establish new industries in which we have no previous learning-by-doing experience. So it seems possible that the Neary–van Wijnbergen approach does not address the aspect of the problem that is most worrisome for policy-makers.

Neary and van Wijnbergen present models of one (small) country with a resource discovery. In this case, income and other effects lead to a rise in the P_n/P_t ratio, and this generates various problems associated with the Dutch Disease. This leads me to wonder whether a several-, or at least two-country model might give different results. Consider a world resource discovery shared by two countries. In this case the resource price P_r would fall relative to both P_t and P_n. There would be no particular prediction for the movement of P_n/P_t, and no general tendency for a Dutch Disease problem to appear.

Now suppose the two countries are in a setting where resource discoveries are random events. In this case, it might be natural for each to share in all discoveries via some kind of insurance scheme. The result would then be similar to the two-country resource discovery described just above. This line of analysis suggests that the Dutch Disease problem arises from countries trying to appropriate all the gains from their random resource discoveries instead of sharing them. In doing so, they may deindustrialize themselves in a self-defeating resource boom.

NOTE

1 I like the mention of the Le Chatelier principle in note 12; I have long argued that all overshooting models are specific examples of this general principle.

A natural resources perspective   PARTHA DASGUPTA

The Neary–van Wijnbergen paper is a characteristically interesting contribution. It presents an excellent survey of the various theoretical explanations that have been offered for the Dutch Disease. Being a novice in this area I had no idea that Holland had unwittingly given rise to a research boom. So I want to join and offer another explanation, which is based on the idea that resource management poses a portfolio problem for a nation. A slight advantage this approach has over those that Neary and van Wijnbergen survey is that it accounts for time rather explicitly. It suffers from drawbacks as well, not for reasons that David Newbery suggested at the conference, but for reasons I will let the reader figure out for himself.

Consider a dominant exporter of an exhaustible natural resource. It can do three things with the resource. It can leave it underground, it can extract it and feed it into domestic production of goods and services, and it can extract it and export it. As regards savings and investment the country can invest in building up domestic capital and it can hold foreign assets. As regards the latter, assume that the country in question is small in the international capital market. The question relevant for us is whether it will wish to build up domestic capital over time, or whether it will, over the long haul, wish to live off foreign assets. In dynamic equilibrium the nation will clearly allocate in such a manner that the domestic rate of return on investment equals the international interest rate at every moment. The latter is exogenously given, and fixed. So we must analyse what policy will keep the domestic rate of return pegged to it. Now, resource input into domestic production (as well as resource exports) must peter out to zero in the long run, because the resource is exhaustible. It follows that whether or not domestic capital is accumulated along an equilibrium path depends on domestic substitution possibilities between durable capital and resource input when the latter is vanishing small. *And it also depends on domestic technological progress.* Some years ago Robert Eastwood, Geoffrey Heal and I experimented with a model of this kind, assuming a Cobb–Douglas production function for the domestic economy. We found tht, if the rate of Harrod–Hicks neutral technical change is sufficiently high, domestic capital will indeed be accumulated along an equilibrium path. Not so if there is insufficient technical progress. In this case deindustrialization is the right way to proceed.

REFERENCE

Dasgupta P., R. Eastwood and G. Heal (1978) 'Resource Management in a Trading Economy', *Quarterly Journal of Economics*, **92**, 297–306.

2

Adjustment to windfall gains: a comparative analysis of oil-exporting countries

ALAN H. GELB*

1 Introduction

Developing countries with only a limited range of exports – typically primary products – face greater oscillations in their terms of trade than more diversified advanced economies. Mineral exports tend to be among the most volatile and, since such highly specialized exporting countries tend to have high ratios of exports and imports to GDP, mineral exporters are prone to exceptionally large fluctuations in national income. Because a large proportion of natural rent on rich mineral deposits usually accrues to producer governments, the conduct of fiscal policy is central in determining the use of resources from favourable but temporary movements in the terms of trade and their ultimate benefit to producing economies.[1]

The external shocks experienced by oil producers over the past decade have been exceptional, even by the standards of monoexporters. After slumping slightly in real terms over the 1960s, world oil prices quadrupled over 1973–4, then decreased slightly in nominal dollar terms over 1975–8. They then redoubled in 1979–80, peaking at around US $35 per barrel. As the world economy moved into recession and conservation measures in the major consuming countries began to affect the demand for (particularly petroleum-based) energy, prices fell by $6–8 per barrel. Although the appreciation of the US dollar compensated exporters, new sources of supply, notably the North Sea, came on stream. Output increased rapidly in Mexico and energy sales from the Soviet Union to Europe rose. These developments placed additional stress on traditional exporters who saw their sales contract during 1980–3, in some cases to little over half of their peak levels, as shown in tables 2.1 and 2.2. The slowly declining OPEC share, apparent before 1979, accelerated, so that by 1982 the cartel accounted for only 64 per cent of total crude oil exports.

A small group of producers – the capital surplus exporters such as Saudi Arabia and Kuwait – have exceptionally large oil reserves with low recovery costs, small populations and underdeveloped non-oil economies. With very limited absorptive capacity, such countries faced, in the first instance, a portfolio-choice problem: whether to store their major asset in the ground or to deplete reserves more rapidly and accumulate assets abroad.[2] These exporters are not considered in this paper, which focuses on a sample of countries – Algeria, Ecuador, Indonesia, Nigeria, Trinidad and Tobago, and Venezuela – with smaller reserves and projected oil incomes insufficient to shoulder the burden of development for more than perhaps two more decades, a short period in historical perspective. Mexico, Iran, Cameroon and Gabon also fall into

Table 2.1   Oil exports and prices, 1960–83

Year	Total exports of crude oil (mbd)	Posted price 34' Saudi light (US$/barrel)	Price index of manufactures imported by developing countries	Deflated price of 34' Saudi light
1960	n.a.	1.80	33.1	5.44
1965	12.9	1.80	34.0	5.29
1970	22.4	1.80	38.1	4.72
1971	25.5	2.06	41.2	5.00
1972	28.0	2.48	45.2	5.48
1973	31.6	3.36	54.0	6.22
1974	31.3	11.65	67.7	17.21
1975	28.5	11.32	76.9	14.72
1976	32.1	11.51	78.3	14.70
1977	33.0	12.40	84.8	14.62
1978	31.8	12.70	100.0	12.70
1979	33.5	16.72	111.6	14.98
1980	29.9	28.66	120.8	23.73
1981	25.8	32.50	115.1	28.23
1982	22.4[a]	34.00	112.8	30.14
1983	n.a.	29.50	109.2	27.02

mbd, million barrels per day.
[a] estimated.

Sources: OPEC, *Annual Statistical Bulletin*, various issues.
World Bank, United Nations, *Statistical Bulletins*, various issues.

Table 2.2   Percentage shares in world exports of crude oil, 1967–82

Year	Algeria	Ecuador	Indonesia	Iran	Nigeria	Trinidad & Tobago	Vene-zuela	OPEC
1967	4.8	—	1.9	13.5	1.8	0.2	10.5	89.6
1970	4.2	—	2.7	14.1	4.5	0.1	7.1	86.3
1971	2.8	—	2.6	15.6	5.8	0.1	6.9	86.3
1972	3.6	0.2	2.9	16.1	6.3	0.1	7.6	86.1
1973	3.2	0.6	3.2	16.7	6.3	0.2	6.7	87.3
1974	2.8	0.5	3.3	17.1	6.9	0.3	5.6	87.0
1975	3.1	0.5	3.5	16.5	6.0	0.5	5.2	84.4
1976	2.9	0.5	3.8	16.2	6.3	0.4	4.3	85.6
1977	3.2	0.4	4.1	15.1	6.3	0.4	4.1	83.9
1978	3.2	0.4	4.1	14.2	5.8	0.5	4.0	82.0
1979	2.8	0.4	3.3	7.1	6.5	0.4	4.2	80.2
1980	2.4	0.4	3.5	2.7	6.6	0.4	4.3	76.7
1981	2.0	0.4	4.1	2.8	4.8	0.4	4.9	71.6
1982	1.0	0.4	3.9	7.3	4.4	n.a.	4.7	63.9

Sources: OPEC, *Annual Statistical Bulletin*, various issues.
For Trinidad, UN, *World Energy Supplies 1961–70*.
UN, *Yearbook of World Energy Statistics*, various issues.

this category. The main questions addressed are: (a) How large have been the windfalls from oil over the past decade? (b) How have they been used? (c) What has been the impact on non-oil-producer economies? In particular, has oil laid a basis for self-sustaining growth at a higher rate than would otherwise have been possible? This appears to have been the main goal of all producer governments considered. Or, have the difficulties of economic management through fluctuating income severely reduced the benefits of oil windfalls, and resulted in increased oil dependence of producing countries?

In section 2 a methodology is developed to measure the gains which accrued to exporters from higher oil prices after 1973. Since about four-fifths of the windfalls were received by producer governments, the fiscal response has been central in accounting for its uses, which are discussed in section 3. Although the set of countries is quite heterogeneous in terms of income per head and the emphasis of development policy, a dominant common feature has been the speedy use of oil rents to fund domestic, and overwhelmingly public, capital formation.

The impact of these massive public investment plans on the non-oil economies of producers is addressed in section 4. In general, the patterns of real exchange rate movements confirm the conventional Salter-Swan model of adjustment. Nevertheless, there are some important divergences from the expected pattern of sectoral shifts which suggest that the 'Dutch Disease' (sharp relative contraction of non-oil tradables) may not be inevitable with (*a*) suitably productive investment programmes in the non-oil traded sectors or (*b*) measures to curtail private consumption and investment expenditures. The latter policy appears to have a high cost in terms of the efficiency of resource allocation, however. Overall, the growth impact of oil-led investment expenditures has been disappointing during 1972–81, partly because of lower quality of capital formation. But simple models of the growth process suggest that even under favourable conditions, investments on the scale of 1974–81 could not have satisfied expectations of a rapid economic transformation raised by the windfalls.

A further drawback to accelerated investment programmes is the difficulty of adjusting to their curtailment. The results of simulations with more complex models which are briefly reported, suggest that the costs of inappropriate time-phasing of expenditure out of oil windfalls can more than outweigh the gains from the windfalls themselves. This question is addressed in section 5, which briefly reports on the impact of the oil slump. Section 6 concludes by assessing the record of the past decade relative to three objectives of oil governments: growth, the extension of national control and reduced oil dependence.

2   Dimensions of the oil windfall

Windfalls from higher oil prices, their use and effects can be measured in a number of ways, which all involve measuring deviations from some counterfactual scenario of what would have transpired in their absence. This section develops a decomposition of the evolution of broad demand and oil/non-oil income-aggregates to assess the windfall and its use. Section 4 decomposes the major sectoral components of the non-oil economy to assess the impact on production structure of the oil shocks.

The approach begins by estimating the increase in domestic income resulting from an enlarged current-value oil sector relative to the non-oil economy. For reasons of cross-country data comparability, such computations are better performed with the economy partitioned into mining and non-mining, rather than oil and non-oil segments. Since non-oil mining is very small in most countries, this has only a minor effect on the results.

The national income accounting identity may be written:

$$R = Y + Z - C - I \tag{1}$$

where R, Y, Z, C and I represent the resource (trade and non-factor service, or NFS) balance, non-mining output, mining, consumption and investment, all at current market prices. A base period, denoted '0' is taken as the average of 1970–2. Respectively, p, pz, pc and pi are deflators for non-mining output, mining, consumption and investment. In each period t the quantity–price structure of the economy may be summarized by a state vector (r, z, c, i, qz, qc, qi), where the qs represent deflators relative to that of the non-mining economy and r, z, c, and i represent the (nominal) resource balance, mining sector, consumption and investment relative to non-mining GDP. From (1):

$$r_t = 1 + z_t - (c_t + i_t) \tag{2}$$

The counterfactual scenario, h, used below assumes (*a*) no changes in relative deflators from the base period; (*b*) a constant mining sector share in output and (*c*) a constant ratio of total absorption to output. The composition of absorption, is however, known to change systematically with growth of income per head, so that C_t^h and I_t^h (the superscript h denotes counterfactual values) are adjusted within their overall constraint in line with the projections of Chenery and Syrquin (1975), with real non-mining output level taken as the indicator of growth.[3] In the hypothetical scenario:

$$r_0 = 1 + z_0 - (c_t^h + i_t^h)$$
$$c_t^h + i_t^h = c_0 + i_0 \tag{3}$$

Adjustment of the oil exporter may then be written as:

$$(R_t - R_t^h)/Y_t^h = (Z_t - Z_t^h)/Y_t^h - (C_t - C_t^h)/Y_t^h - (I_t - I_t^h)/Y_t^h \tag{4}$$

Right hand terms may be further broken down into public and private components of consumption and investment. Each term may be decomposed again into price and quantity effects, using the average of actual and projected weights to minimize cross-effects and residual terms.[4]

Scaling all base year deflators to unity yields:

$$\frac{Z_t - Z_t^h}{Y_t^h} = (z_t/qz_t - z^h).(qz_t + 1)/2 + (qz_t - 1).(z_t/qz_t + z^h)/2 \tag{5}$$

Other terms may be similarly decomposed. The first term on the right hand side of (5) (the 'real effect') indicates the extent to which changing real mining output relative to the non-mining economy contributed to changing the value share ('value effect') of mining relative to non-mining GDP. The second term, the 'price effect' indicates the contribution of relative price changes to changes in value shares.[5]

Before analysing the results during 1973–81, table 2.3 provides an indication of the base absorption structures of seven oil economies, and compares these to Chenery–Syrquin norms for countries at a similar level of non-mining income per head. Iran, Algeria and Venezuela, with large, long-established oil sectors (and considerable remittance income in the second case), stand out as most mineral-dependent. Ecuador (the newest producer) was least dependent on oil in terms of absorption, but already had a higher share of oil in total exports than Indonesia, which benefited from aid inflows and non-oil mineral exports, notably copper. The breakdown of extra absorption indicates particularly strong investment biases in Algeria, Venezuela, Trinidad and Tobago, and high private relative to public consumption in Ecuador, Nigeria and Indonesia.[6]

Tables 2.4 and 2.5 show the estimates of windfalls and their uses during 1974–8 and 1978–81 respectively. Considering only windfalls for the moment, the mean windfall during 1974–8 was 24 per cent of non-mining income (22 per cent excluding Iran) and 23 per cent during 1979–81. Particularly after 1979, slower real growth of oil sectors reduced the impact of the price windfall by about one-quarter on average, and almost eliminated it in Venezuela. The second oil price rise impacted on relatively smaller oil sectors than the first, which helped to mute its impact.

Figure 2.1 indicates the (unweighted) average time profile during 1973–81 of the windfall as measured above for six countries expressed each year relative to their non-mining economies. In 1974 the average windfall peaked at 33 per cent of non-mining income but by 1978 had contracted to 15 per cent. The second oil price increase raised the windfall to 27 per cent of non-mining output in 1980 before declining sales began to reduce it. The combination of slumping prices and contracting sales during 1982–4 appear to have halved the windfall gain.

3   Use of the windfall

3.1   *The fiscal response*

With little direct linkage between the oil sector and the rest of a developing economy and upward adjustment of OPEC tax and royalty

Table 2.3 Composition of absorption: 1970–2 in relation to the Chenery–Syrquin norms[a]

	Algeria	Ecuador	Indonesia	Iran	Nigeria	Trinidad & Tobago	Venezuela
Private consumption							
Actual/non-mining GDP	64.5	75.5	83.5	72.2	80.2	80.9[a]	62.8
Norm	66.0	68.0	75.0	64.0	70.0	78.0	62.0
Public consumption							
Actual/non-mining GDP	18.0	10.6	9.8	23.4	8.6	n.a.	16.4
Norm	14.0	14.0	12.0	14.0	14.0	n.a.	15.0
Investment							
Actual/non-mining GDP	40.8	20.6	17.5	27.0	22.1	31.0	36.6
Norm	20.0	19.0	15.0	22.0	17.0	22.0	23.0
Absorption							
Actual/non-mining GDP	123.3	106.7	110.9	122.7	111.0	111.9	115.8
Norm	100.0	101.0	102.0	100.0	101.0	100.0	100.0
Breakdown of extra absorption (%)							
Private consumption	−6	132	96	36	102	24[b]	5
Public consumption	17	−60	−25	41	−54	n.a.	9
Investment	83	28	28	44	51	76	86
Memo: share of oil in exports							
1972 (%)	79	77	51	90	82	78	91

[a] Values are %.
[b] Includes public consumption.
n.a. : not available.

rates to reduce the share of rent accruing to the oil multi-nationals, the above fluctuations in relative mining value-added were mainly reflected in fiscal revenues. The impact is shown in tables 2.6, 2.7 and 2.8. For the six countries of figure 2.1, central government revenues jumped from 20 per cent of non-mining GDP to 37 per cent (42 per cent including Iran) with the first oil price increase.[7] This implies that, on average, about four-fifths of the windfall as previously measured accrued to producer governments. Iran, for which data after 1977 are limited, experienced a particularly large windfall, 36.7 per cent of non-oil GDP between 1974 and 1977, which was reflected in fiscal revenues.

Although there were significant differences in non-oil fiscal perform-ance between countries, almost all the increase in the ratios of fiscal revenues to non-mining income is attributable to increased taxes and royalties on oil, except in Algeria where non-oil taxes, particularly on domestic goods and services, were unusually high and buoyant. Tables 2.7 and 2.8 present estimates of the elasticity of non-oil taxes to growth of the non-oil economy over the first and second oil price shocks. Although most exporters relaxed import restrictions after 1974, the rapid increase in imports made possible a substantial rise in trade taxes which was compensated (except in Algeria) by a cut in the tax burden levied on domestic goods and services. Underlying this policy was the widespread desire to moderate inflationary pressure caused by acceler-ated public spending out of oil receipts. On average, non-oil taxes remained fairly steady as a proportion of non-mining income over the first oil price rise. They decreased slightly with the second because import volumes and trade taxes did not continue to expand.

Producer governments therefore did not transfer windfalls to the private sector by sharply cutting non-oil taxes, although in some cases non-oil tax efforts slackened.[8] Neither did most governments attempt to restrain private competition for scarce domestic resources through raising them. Except for Algeria, however, non-oil taxes were extremely low by international standards, frequently around half the levels 'normal' for countries at a comparable level of development as derived from cross-section regressions.[9] None of the countries with weak fiscal systems took advantage of fiscal respite to set in place non-oil tax systems capable of raising revenues efficiently for the post-oil boom period.

Levels of development and income per head vary significantly over the above producers. So do the economic role of government and the weight of the public sector in the economy. All countries had extensive and growing public involvement in the hydrocarbon industry during the 1970s, with virtually total nationalization in Algeria and Venezuela.

Table 2.4 Oil windfalls and their use, 1974–8[a]

	Algeria	Ecuador	Indonesia	Iran[e]	Nigeria	Trinidad & Tobago	Venezuela	Unweighted mean
Domestic oil windfall	27.1	16.8	15.9	36.7	22.8	38.9	10.8	24.1
Real	-4.8	9.2	1.6	-22.8	-2.3	2.3	-20.5	-5.3
Price	31.9	7.6	14.3	59.5	25.1	36.6	31.3	29.5
Absorption effects								
Trade & NFS	-4.3	3.5	5.3	17.0	2.8	27.2	-1.0	7.2
Current balance	-9.5	2.7	2.1	24.6	5.6	27.2	3.8	8.1
Non-oil growth effect	-7.4	15.9	-2.4	12.2	-1.5	-7.8	5.9	2.1
Allocation effects								
Values								
Private consumption	3.6	-0.9	2.1	-7.0	2.9	7.1[c]	1.9	1.4
Public consumption	1.4	5.5	2.4	10.2	4.2	6.9[d]	1.6	3.6
Private investment	—	3.8	-1.7	6.7	-6.6	-2.6	3.3	0.4
Public investment	26.4[b]	4.8	7.9	10.0	19.5	7.3	4.9	11.5
Prices								
Private consumption	-0.9	0.0	-1.1	-6.2	1.2	-18.4	-10.1	-5.1
Public consumption	-0.2	0.3	0.7	2.3	-0.1	—	3.5	0.9
Investment	4.1	4.3	-0.5	7.3	3.8	0.0	4.4	3.3

Real								
Private consumption	4.6	−0.9	3.3	−0.8	1.7	25.6[c]	12.1	6.5
Public consumption	1.6	5.2	1.7	7.9	4.3	—	0.8	3.1
Private investment	—	0.4	−1.3	2.5	−9.5	−2.6	1.8	−1.2
Public investment	22.2[b]	3.9	8.0	6.9	18.6	7.3	2.6	9.9
Real allocation plus growth effects								
Private consumption	0.0	1.0	−1.5	7.6	0.5	19.4[c]	15.8	8.0
Public consumption	0.3	6.9	1.5	13.2	4.2	—	1.8	4.0
Private investment	—	3.2	−3.4	4.5	−9.8	−4.6	3.3	−1.0
Public investment	1.91[b]	4.5	7.9	8.4	18.5	5.5	3.3	9.6

[a] Percentage of non-mining GDP.
[b] Includes small private investment on which accurate data are not available.
[c] Includes public consumption.
[d] Central government recurrent expenditure effect. Not included in mean.
[e] 1974-7.

Note that the average ratios presented are unweighted means of ratios for the individual countries. They thus represent the magnitude and use of the windfall for a representative country. This differs from the overall, aggregate magnitude and use of the windfall because the non-mining economies of the countries differ greatly in size.

Table 2.5 Oil windfalls and their use, 1979–81[a]

	Algeria	Ecuador	Indonesia	Nigeria	Trinidad & Tobago	Venezuela	Unweighted mean	(Mexico)
Domestic oil windfall	29.7	22.1	22.7	21.9	34.7	8.7	23.3	3.5
Real	-17.6	10.8	-2.5	-6.1	-7.4	-28.0	-8.5	
Price	47.3	11.2	25.2	28.0	42.1	36.6	31.7	
Absorption effects								
Trade & NFS	8.9	4.7	9.6	0.1	16.8	1.1	6.9	-1.8
Current balance	-0.6	-1.2	6.1	3.9	19.2	7.0	5.7	-0.2
Non-oil growth effect	-6.7	21.2	-3.5	-29.8	0.6	-6.6	-4.1	
Allocation effects values								
Private consumption	4.6	1.1	1.2	4.1	8.6[b]	9.4	4.8	-2.9
Public consumption	3.2	6.1	3.7	5.6	—	0.7	3.2	2.3
Investment	12.9	10.3	8.1	12.1	9.3	-2.5	8.4	5.9
Prices								
Private consumption	-2.2	0.0	-9.3	-4.1	-18.2[b]	-14.7	-8.1	-12.7
Public consumption	-0.1	0.1	0.3	0.6	—	0.4	0.2	1.4
Investment	4.4	6.3	-0.5	4.8	-2.6	1.1	2.2	18.7
Real								
Private consumption	6.8	1.1	10.5	8.2	26.7[b]	24.1	12.9	-0.1
Public consumption	3.3	6.0	3.4	5.0	—	-0.3	2.9	1.0
Investment	8.6	4.0	8.6	7.3	12.0	-3.5	6.2	4.1
Real allocation plus growth effects								
Private consumption	2.7	16.7	7.7	-15.3	27.2	20.0	9.8	
Public consumption	2.5	6.8	3.0	2.3	—	-0.7	2.3	
Investment	5.6	15.0	7.9	0.4	12.2	-6.0	5.8	

[a] Percentage of non-mining GDP.   [b] Includes public consumption.

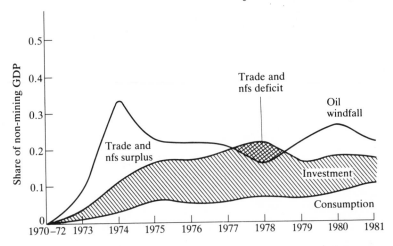

Figure 2.1   The oil windfall and its use, 1973–81. (Unweighted average: Algeria, Ecuador, Indonesia, Nigeria, Trinidad and Tobago, and Venezuela.)

Salient features of the development of this sector and moves to assume national control over it are summarized in table 2.9. These preceded the oil price increases, although the latter sometimes allowed the process to accelerate through providing more revenues to producer governments.

Moving away from the hydrocarbon sector, at the one extreme central government and public enterprises are estimated to account for about 90 per cent of domestic Algerian investment. At the other, the role of the Ecuadorian public sector outside the traditional functions of administration, defence and providing physical and human infrastructure has been quite limited. These differences in the public role across countries reflect both the varying ideological tendencies of successive governments and historical accident. For example, the extensive involvement in agriculture of Algeria's socialist government and (conservative) Indonesia's considerable public sector holdings in timber and plantation crops both stemmed from the departure of colonial proprietors, French and Dutch respectively, at independence. Public oil income had sometimes led the state's role to cumulate over a long period even in countries with a basically private-sector orientation.[10]

Nevertheless, all the oil exporters saw an unparalleled growth in the size of the public sector after 1973 and most experienced a considerable extension of its role, towards direct participation in industrial production. Although most governments expanded their activities in virtually all directions, there were considerable differences of emphasis between

Table 2.6 Structure of taxes and government expenditure, 1974–8[a]

	Algeria	Ecuador	Indonesia	Iran[b]	Nigeria	Trinidad & Tobago	Venezuela	Unweighted mean
Total revenue	59.9	12.9	23.1	71.1	27.7	55.9	42.1	41.8
Non-oil direct taxes	6.2	1.4	1.8	0.5	0.1	5.2	1.3	2.4
Domestic indirect taxes	14.1	2.3	3.3	1.7	0.6	3.0	1.6	3.8
Trade taxes	4.2	5.8	2.5	4.3	3.9	4.4	2.6	4.0
Total	24.5	9.5	7.6	6.5	4.6	12.6	5.5	10.2
Expenditure	71.5	14.4	25.0	71.6	24.2[c]	36.7	32.0	39.8
By function								
Admin. and defence	6.5[d]	4.9	9.9	23.6	9.1	5.8	5.0	9.2
Social	9.8[d]	4.8	2.7	10.1	4.3	11.0	9.6	7.4
Economic	2.0[d]	3.7	8.2	20.5	8.8	15.6	10.6	9.9
By economic classification								
Current	27.0	n.a.	14.5	49.3	13.6	21.1	20.5	24.4
(Wages and salaries)	(10.0)	n.a.	(4.1)	(16.4)	(4.1)	10.9	(11.2)	(9.4)
Subsidies & transfers	10.5	n.a.	5.1	13.1	3.4	3.1	5.8	6.8
Investment	44.5	n.a.	10.6	22.3	12.4	15.6	11.9	14.7
Net lending	29.0	n.a.	1.8	—	7.2	6.0	13.8	9.6
Memo:								
Total revenue 1970–2	32.6	14.2	15.6	31.7	12.3	19.9	25.2	
Total revenue 1979–81	57.4	14.2	30.9	n.a.	n.a.	57.2	36.3	

[a] Percentage of non-mining GDP.
[b] 1974–7.
[c] Expenditure and expenditure categories, 1975–8.
[d] Current expenditures.
n.a. Not available, or not available in compatible form.

Sources: International Monetary Fund, Government Finance Statistics and World Bank.

Table 2.7 Elasticity of taxes and government expenditure to non-mining output, 1974–8/1970–2

	Algeria	Ecuador[b]	Indonesia[b]	Iran[c]	Nigeria	Trinidad & Tobago	Venezuela	Mean
Total revenue	1.84	0.91	1.48	2.24	2.25	2.81	1.68	1.88
Non-oil direct taxes	1.15	1.00	1.25	1.00	—[e]	1.48	1.11	1.16
Domestic indirect taxes	1.25	0.85	0.92	0.72	0.20	0.71	0.90	0.80
Trade taxes	1.56	0.78	0.92	0.90	1.78	1.26	1.57	1.25
Total	1.26	0.83	0.99	0.85	0.83	1.13	1.20	1.02
Expenditure	1.78	1.02	1.34	1.90	2.24[f]	1.70	1.29	1.62
By function								
Admin. and defence	1.18[g]	1.32	1.25	1.92	1.44	0.89	1.16	1.31
Social	1.05[g]	1.04	1.69	1.53	4.78	1.23	1.09	1.77
Economic	—[a,g]	0.93	1.44	1.60	4.19	3.71	1.20	1.86
By economic classification:								
Current	1.36	n.a.	1.43	1.98	1.63	1.34	1.11	1.47
(Wages and salaries)	(0.98)	n.a.	(1.11)	(1.24)	(1.11)	(1.10)	(1.07)	(1.10)
Subsidies & transfers	2.19	n.a.	1.02	2.67	3.78	n.a.	1.38	2.20
Investment	2.15	n.a.	1.53	1.74	4.96	2.89	1.83	2.52
Net lending	2.74	n.a.	1.28	n.a.	3.00	n.a.	7.26	3.57

[a] Negligible expenditure 1970–2.
[b] 1974–8/1973.
[c] 1974-7/1970–2.
[d] 1974–8/1972.
[e] Negligible in 1972.
[f] 1975–8/1972.
[g] Current expenditures only.
n.a. Not available, or not available in compatible form.

Sources: International Monetary Fund, Government Finance Statistics and World Bank.

Table 2.8 Elasticity of taxes and government expenditures to non-mining output, 1979–81/1974–8[a]

	Algeria	Ecuador	Indonesia	Trinidad & Tobago[b]	Venezuela	Mean
Total revenue	0.95	1.10	1.34	1.02	0.86	1.05
Non-oil direct taxes	1.11	1.29	1.00	1.63	0.92	1.19
Domestic indirect taxes	0.80	1.17	0.78	0.80	0.96	0.90
Trade taxes	0.69	0.76	0.88	0.86	0.93	0.82
Total	0.86	0.94	0.87	1.16	0.93	0.95
Expenditure	1.01	1.19	1.28	1.18	0.97	1.13
By function						
Admin. & defence	0.89	0.94	1.46	1.90	0.94	1.23
Social	1.07	1.46	1.26	0.92	1.05	1.15
Economic	0.90	0.91	1.22	0.99	0.72	0.95
By economic classification						
Current	0.99	—	1.15	1.23	1.13	1.13
(Wages & salaries)	(1.20)	—	(1.10)	(1.11)	1.03	(1.11)
Subsidies & transfers	0.80	—	1.42	3.10	1.16	1.62
Investment	1.04	—	1.46	1.10	0.68	1.07
Net lending	0.99	—	1.06	1.50	0.50	1.01

[a] Excludes Iran and Nigeria, for which data are not available.
[b] 1979–81/1976–7.

Sources: International Monetary Fund, Joint Finance Statistics and World Bank.

countries. Algeria and Trinidad and Tobago with large gas, relative to oil, reserves, placed high priority on their development, the former for sale in primary form (liquefied and piped) and the latter through gas-based industrialization led by steel, fertilizers and chemicals. The Algerian public investment programme displayed perhaps the strongest bias towards heavy industry, which together with hydrocarbons, accounted for almost half of all investment. Venezuelan public investment emphasized the development of metals industries, notably steel and aluminium. Nigeria initially concentrated on providing universal primary education and developing road networks. Higher-level educational expansion, a major steel complex and a new federal capital were among its later goals. Ecuador's public programmes tended to be infrastructural, and commodity production was mainly encouraged by credit and subsidy concessions to the private sector. Indonesia pursued a strategy relatively balanced between physical infrastructure, education, agricultural development and capital-intensive industry where a $20 billion pipeline of projects including fertilizers, LNG and steel had been generated by the early 1980s. Nevertheless, more than any other exporter, it ensured that a high proportion of development spending was directed towards irrigation and infrastructural improvements in rural areas. The goal of rice self-sufficiency and the critical importance of rural reconstruction for the economic stabilization which followed the Sukarno era were responsible for this distinctive priority pattern.

Over the period of the first oil price increase, net lending by government and public investment outlays grew over twice as fast as the non-oil economies of the respective countries, as shown in table 2.7. Current expenditures grew less rapidly, with the notable exception of subsidies and transfers. This category, which will be discussed further below, continued to expand after 1979 while the relative growth of investment and net lending slowed. Correspondingly, the growth of economic spending initially exceeded that of social categories but this was reversed during the second oil price rise.

3.2 Overall use of the windfall

Returning to figure 2.1 and tables 2.4 and 2.5, we now consider the overall uses of the windfalls, which include both first and subsequent (multiplier) rounds of expenditures. During 1970–2 current account deficits in the six countries of figure 2.1 had averaged 5.1 per cent of non-mining GDP. In these years, deficits were especially high in Trinidad and Tobago (14.5 per cent) and Ecuador (6.9 per cent) because of large investment expenditures needed for oil extraction and

Table 2.9 Hydrocarbon industries in the oil exporters

Country	Start of production	Major companies	Extension of national control	Gas reserves and development	Domestic energy pricing
Algeria	1956, French discover oil in commercial quantities	Total, ERAP (French) plus Mobil, Philips, Shell	After 1965, a determined drive towards complete state control of hydrocarbon sector and replacement of foreign nationals by Algerians. 1963 SONATRACH, the state hydrocarbon company, was established. 1971, nationalization of all non-French foreign operations, and assumption of 51% public share in French interests. SONATRACH controlled 70% of crude oil production, 100% of exploration, refining and marketing. Foreign companies could participate in exploration programmes. 1980, $3 per barrel exploration fee levied on contract crude oil customers	Major emphasis on gas exports in industrial sector plans. First LNG and later piped; SONATRACH world leader in LNG exports (approx. 1 tcf per year) although pricing disputes held output well below capacity levels in some periods	

| Ecuador | Minor production since 1911, large deposits found by Texaco in 1967 | Anglo-Ecuadorian Oilfields (BP subsidiary) to 1963. Texaco-Gulf Consortium 1964 then became the major producer | 1945 constitution asserted state ownership of all minerals. 1971 Hydrocarbons Law created state oil company CEPE. 1972 military government of General Rodriguez Lara extended state control, Anglo-Ecuadorian interests transferred to CEPE. 1974 CEPE purchases 25% of Consortium. 1976 CEPE buys out Ecuadorian Gulf's 37.5% share. Exploration diminishes; 1978 Hydrocarbons Law amended to increase incentives for private investment | Estimated reserves 4 tcf. Not a major focus of development | State electricity company (INECEL) heavily subsidized. Gasoline prices among lowest in world but were raised from $0.18 to $0.60/gallon in 1981. About 20% of locally sold gasoline may have been exported illegally |

continued

Table 2.9 *continued*

Country	Start of production	Major companies	Extension of national control	Gas reserves and development	Domestic energy pricing
Indonesia	Oil discovered in 1883, commercial production by 1890	Royal Dutch/Shell, later Caltex	State oil company Pertamina formed in 1968 by merger of three locally owned companies. Largely autonomous until 1975. Foreign companies still produce 90% of oil, under contract of work, production sharing and technical assistance programmes. Although 1971 'Pertamina Law' made the company responsible for all petroleum activities, control is mainly pragmatic and orientated towards raising revenues.	Gas reserves estimated at 24 tcf. Output expanded rapidly, to 0.5 tcf in 1980. Major LNG investments together with Japan are an important part of hydrocarbon development	Domestic energy use, notably kerosene and diesel fuels, heavily subsidized
Iran	Oil discovered 1908 by BP	BP sole developer until 1951. Consortium after 1954 also included Shell, Gulf, Mobil, Exxon	1951, Prime Minister Mossadegh nationalized all petroleum resources and established the National Iranian Oil Company, NIOC. 1954 consortium deemed owner of fixed production assets and Iran owner of oil reserves. '50% tax principle' established. The 1960s saw a number	400 tcf reserves. Ambitious programme to export gas to Soviet Union and Europe via IGAT I and IGAT II pipelines in 1970s, curtailed after 1978	

			foreign companies. 1973 NIOC took over all operations but the consortium was allocated a marketing function. After 1978 trend to reduce foreign participation in energy industries		Some subsidization of petroleum products also of other energy forms
Nigeria	Oil discovered in 1956, exports began in 1958	Shell/BP partnership and other major companies	Political and economic significance of oil was recognized in mid-1960s. 1969 Petroleum Decree established State's option to part ownership of hydrocarbon industry to 51%. National oil company, the NNOC established in 1971. 1973, the ultimate objective was announced to be a nationalized industry. NNOC began production-sharing. 1974, public equity share in all oil operations increased to 55%, 1979 to 60% and BP's crude oil and marketing interests were nationalized. 1977 new incentive package to accelerate exploration.	Gas reserves about 75 tcf. Plans for major LNG facility at Bonny Island, for gas use in steel production and for power generation	

continued

Table 2.9 *continued*

Country	Start of production	Major companies	Extension of national control	Gas reserves and development	Domestice energy pricing
Trinidad & Tobago	Oil discovered in 1857; in 1913 Shell became first producer	Shell, Texaco and others	1969 Petroleum Act and 1970 Petroleum Regulations laid regulatory foundation. 1970 Trinidad–Tesoro (50.1% government owned) was established. Bought out Shell; 1974 established National Petroleum Marketing Company. 1976 bought out Texaco's marketing operations. 1979 National Energy Corporation NEC established. 1980 onwards, drive to increase public control of hydrocarbons, but 1981 amended Petroleum Act to increase private incentives to production and exploration	Estimated reserves: 12 tcf 'probable', 21 tcf 'possible'. Output about 0.5 tcf. Shift to gas-based industry is a central part of development strategy which implies continuing good relationships with private capital and expertise	Domestic petroleum prices subsidized, domestic sales of natural gas underpriced

Venezuela	By 1928 leading exporter and second largest producer in the world	Standard Oil of New Jersey (Exxon), Shell, Gulf, Texaco, Mobil, Sun and others	Gradual process of increasing domestic control and knowledge of industry over 40 years, culminated in nationalization of oil in 1976. 1935–48, extension of regulation and establishment of the '50% tax principle'. 1960, state-owned CVP established, to receive all future oil concessions with foreign investment to be through service contracts. 1971 Hydrocarbons Reversion Law called for reversion of existing concessions to state ownership in early 1980s. 1974 President Carlos Andres Perez called for early reversion. 1976 total nationalization, under Petroleos de Venezuela (PDVSA, formerly CVA)	Proven reserves 42.3 tcf, nationalized in 1971. Gas for domestic use plays a role in the heavy industrial strategy developed after 1974	Domestic petroleum and energy prices heavily subsidized throughout period

Sources: US Department of Energy, *Energy Industry Abroad*, September 1981.
US Office of International Affairs, Department of Energy, *The Role of Governments in the Energy Industry*, October 1977.
US Government, 'Indonesia's Petroleum Sector', Jakarta, June 1982, mimeo.
World Bank, various reports.

higher spending in anticipation of increased revenues. As indicated in
figure 2.1 and table 2.4, on average during 1974–8 about one-quarter of
the windfall was saved abroad through reducing these trade (and
current) deficits and one-quarter was consumed in value terms. Slightly
over half of the increase in consumption relative to non-mining value-
added was public, slightly under half private. The remainder of the
windfall was used for domestic investment. Although non-oil private
investment boomed in certain countries, notably in Venezuela during
1976–8, increased investment outlays were overwhelmingly public.
From 1974 to 1978 public investment absorbed about half the windfall
on average, less in Iran and Trinidad and Tobago which ran large
surpluses for very different reasons, but far more in Algeria. Taking
advantage of its improved creditworthiness, Algeria absorbed the entire
first windall in investment and borrowed abroad to finance a small rise in
public and private consumption relative to non-oil output and to
compensate for a fall in remittance income. By 1977 Algerian investment had reached the remarkable figure of 73 per cent of non-mining
GDP; virtually all of this was public.

The use of the windfall of 1979–81 was similar, except that private
consumption increased its share of the windfall at the expense of
domestic investment which accounted for only one-third of the second
windfall. For comparison, estimates are also presented for Mexico. An
exporter of more recent vintage, it experienced only a small oil windfall
in 1979–81. But rather like Algeria during 1974–8, it borrowed abroad
against future oil earnings to boost expenditures by a further 1.8 per
cent of non-oil GDP. The increased expenditures were mostly in the
form of public investment. Development expenditure for the Mexican
oil sector itself accounted for 2 per cent of non-oil GDP.

4   Some consequences of increased domestic expenditures

The standard Salter–Swan neoclassical model of adjustment predicts
several consequences of an oil-led boost in domestic expenditures.[11]
First, real exchange rates will appreciate. Secondly, this is associated, in
the medium run at least, with a shift in production structure towards the
non-traded sectors, an effect commonly termed the 'Dutch Disease' and
leading to greater dependence on oil for foreign exchange. Thirdly,
increased domestic investment should raise growth. This might have an
ameliorative effect on the real exchange rate and sectoral composition
of non-oil output depending on the efficacy and distribution of capital
formation and the factor intensity of various sectors.

For a number of reasons oil economies may deviate from these stylized patterns. Price controls and import liberalization can limit appreciation of the real exchange rate by deflecting demand onto imports. Measures to dampen multiplier effects out of increased government spending can constrain resource pulls towards the non-traded sectors. If traded sectors are able to respond strongly to investments financed by oil revenues, product market pulls towards the non-traded sectors may be counterbalanced, particularly if labour markets are slack so that expanding non-traded sectors do not draw labour from the traded sectors. Finally, the overall impact of higher public spending on growth may be low if the quality of investment projects declines with accelerating spending, or if subsidies and other expenditures drain resources from the public investment programme.

4.1 The real exchange rate

The extent of real appreciation after 1972 for the above set of countries is shown in table 2.10. Relative to their average levels during 1970–2, trade-weighted real exchange rates (defined as the ratio of the domestic price levels of the oil exporters to those of their trading partners) converted at average exchange rates were 10 per cent higher during 1974–8, 21 per cent higher over 1979–81 and almost 40 per cent higher during 1982–3. It should, however, be noted that in the 1970s the unit value of manufactures imported by developing countries (MUV index) rose relative to the price levels of most countries, largely because of oil and other primary intermediate price shocks. This relative price shift implied lower real appreciation relative to the MUV index, and limited the tendency for consumption and investment prices to fall relative to the cost of domestically produced non-oil commodities as would be normal with real currency appreciation. Purchasers were thus cushioned from increased import price shocks by their own real exchange appreciation. For this reason, the 'price effects' of tables 2.4 and 2.5 are not overall negative in 1974–8, and in real terms, domestic purchasers apparently gained little from appreciation. During 1979–81 domestic purchasers appear to have gained, on average, about 6 per cent of non-mining GDP through relative cheapening of imports, although there is not a close relationship on a country by country basis with the real exchange rate movements of table 2.10.

The two notable exceptions to the path of real exchange appreciation were Algeria and Venezuela, which limited appreciation until the end of the 1970s despite large increases in domestic expenditures. Price controls played a major role in both cases. There was great scope in

Table 2.10   Real exchange rate movements, 1974–83

	Trade-weighted real exchange rate[a]			Non-mining output deflator relative to unit value of manufactures imported by LDCs (MUV)[a]		
	1974–78	1979–81	1982–83	1974–78	1979–81	1982–83
Algeria	90.8	103.3	121.7	88.3	92.1	
Ecuador	106.4	112.7	120.0	91.8	101.0	
Indonesia	133.8	129.5	140.2	115.6	103.2	
Iran	100.4	119.2	151.1			
Nigeria	131.0	170.0	209.1	98.9	108.0	
Trinidad & Tobago	101.4	107.7	138.8	88.0	104.2	
Venezuela	97.6	103.2	124.7	81.6	93.4	
Mean[c]	110.2	121.1	139.1	94.0	100.3	
Memo: USA	92.3	93.4	105.2	82.1[b]	82.9[b]	98.2[b]

[a] Averages. Base = 1970–2.
[b] Wholesale price index relative to MUV deflator.
[c] Excluding Iran.

Sources: International Monetary Fund, International Financial Statistics.
World Bank and United Nations, Monthly Bulletin of Statistics.

Venezuela for the relaxation of import controls which allowed demand to spill over on to foreign goods. Algeria, a centralized socialist economy, followed a distinctive strategy of syphoning off private purchasing power through the accumulation of non-oil balances on a massive scale (see Conway and Gelb, 1984).

4.2   Growth

The impact of expanded investment on growth has been, at first sight, disappointing, as shown in table 2.11. Excluding Iran, where data are limited, only Ecuador proved able significantly to accelerate the growth rate of its non-mining economy during 1972–81 relative to performance during 1967–72. On average, non-oil economies[12] were 4.1 per cent smaller during 1979–81 than they would have been had they maintained their 1967–72 growth trajectories, as shown by the growth effect of table 2.5.

Table 2.11 Growth trends (%) in the oil exporters, 1967–81

| | Non-mining GDP | | Domestic investment | | Goods and non-factor services | | | |
| | | | | | Exports | | Imports | |
	1967–72	1972–81	1967–72	1972–81	1967–72	1972–81	1967–72	1972–81
Algeria	9.5	8.6	16.7	10.8	5.7	–1.0	11.6	10.8
Ecuador	4.7	7.6	3.2	10.2	15.9	6.0	6.0	9.7
Indonesia	8.5	8.2	24.3	13.0	15.7	4.3	16.7	19.1
Iran[a]	10.1	13.3	10.2	21.1	12.9	–0.3	17.7	23.7
Nigeria	9.2	5.3	–[b]	8.7	–[b]	–4.2	–[b]	15.3
Trinidad & Tobago	5.3	5.4	6.1	9.3	2.5	–6.5	6.6	8.4
Venezuela	6.5	5.1	11.9	3.5	–1.3	–8.7	7.7	12.8
Unweighted mean[d]	7.3	6.7	12.4	9.3	7.7	–1.7	9.7	12.7
Memo: middle income oil importers	5.8[c]	5.1[c]	8.2	5.6	6.7	4.0	7.4	1.5

[a] 1967–72 and 1972–7.
[b] Deflated data unreliable before 1970.
[c] GDP.
[d] Excluding Iran.

Source: World Bank.

Combining the real allocation plus growth terms in tables 2.4 and 2.5 permits an assessment of how the various components of absorption have changed relative to a scenario combining (*a*) non-mining growth at the rates of 1967–72 and (*b*) the hypothetical structure of relative prices and demand composition. This is shown in tables 2.4 and 2.5 for 1974–8 and 1979–81 respectively, as the sum of real allocation plus growth effects. On average real private consumption and public investment were considerably larger than their scenario values for 1974–8, as was public consumption. The means presented in table 2.5 suggest a further rise in consumption aggregates but a substantial cut in investment over 1979–81.

On closer examination, the growth record is less adverse than it appears from historical trends. Before 1972 Indonesia, Nigeria and Algeria had all been in recovery phases, the first two from internal disturbances and the third from a protracted war of independence. Ecuador and Trinidad had been stimulated by oil development and the prospect of growing export revenues. The non-oil growth performance of the sample was therefore exceptional during 1967–72. At 7.3 per cent it was some 1.5 per cent higher than the average growth of GDP in middle income developing countries. Average non-oil growth after 1972 was still 0.9 per cent more rapid than that of oil-importing developing economies through the favourable period of the 1960s. Much of this was, however, demand-led rather than supply-generated, in the sense that non-oil growth responded to increased absorption after 1974 but slowed after 1978 despite the expectation that large investments undertaken in 1975–8 would begin to contribute to output.

How much extra growth could have been expected from investments on the scale undertaken by the oil exporters? A single-sector Cobb–Douglas neoclassical model of the non-oil economy approximately parameterized to fit stylized growth and savings rates suggests that the real investment effects in table 2.4 could have added about 1.4 percentage points to non-oil growth with constant quality of investment, even assuming inelastic labour supply (immigration was significant in Venezuela and Nigeria) and disembodied technical change.[13] Actual performance for 1972–81 appears to have fallen well short of this.

4.3 *The 'Dutch Disease': Structural change in the non-oil economy*

Growth of income per head is associated with a shift from primary production to industry and services, and from the sectors conventionally considered as tradable – agriculture and manufacturing – towards services and construction.[14] This tendency might be weaker in constant

Table 2.12 Sectoral structure and the Dutch Disease

Initial conditions: 1972

Sectoral shares in non-mining GDP and modified Chenery–Syrquin norms (%)

	Algeria		Ecuador		Indonesia		Iran		Nigeria		Trinidad & Tobago		Venezuela	
	Act.	Norm	Act.	Norm	Act.	Norm	Act.	Norm	Act.	Norm	Act.	Norm	Act.	Norm
AG	11.0**	25	23.0	26	45.1	46	21.8	18	39.2	38	5.8*	16	7.6*	14
MA	15.8*	20	20.4	19	11.0	11	18.5*	25	5.1**	15	22.0	26	19.5*	27
CO	13.4**	5	4.8	5	4.3*	3	6.3	6	10.7**	4	8.0*	6	6.0	7
SE	59.8	50	51.8	50	39.7	40	53.3	51	45.0	43	64.2	52	66.9*	52
(MI)	17.9	4	2.0	4	12.1	6	28.5	3	15.1	5	8.8	2	20.5	2

Dutch Disease index

	Algeria		Ecuador		Indonesia		Iran		Nigeria		Trinidad & Tobago		Venezuela	
	18.2		1.6		0.9		2.7		8.7		14.2		13.9	

Average annual share change at constant prices

	Algeria		Ecuador		Indonesia		Iran		Nigeria		Trinidad & Tobago		Venezuela	
AG	-0.38	-0.82	-0.91	-0.77	-1.50	-1.31	-1.44	-1.02	-1.90	-0.67	-0.31	-0.49	-0.10	-0.32
MA	0.52	0.28	0.37	0.27	0.77	0.34	0.34	0.49	0.48	0.11	-1.03	0.20	-0.04	0.06
CO	0.82	0.09	-0.12	0.07	0.26	0.10	0.13	0.06	0.53	0.03	0.37	0.05	0.02	0.03
SE	-0.98	0.45	0.68	0.44	0.48	0.86	1.04	0.40	0.88	0.53	0.99	0.35	0.13	0.24

Change in Dutch Disease index over a decade

	Algeria		Ecuador		Indonesia		Iran		Nigeria		Trinidad & Tobago		Venezuela	
	-7.0		+0.5		-2.4		+5.7		+8.5		+10.5		-1.3	

Change in Dutch Disease index measured in current prices over a decade

	Algeria		Ecuador		Indonesia		Iran		Nigeria		Trinidad & Tobago		Venezuela	
	-3.5		+12.5		-0.4		+12.7		+2.4		+4.7		-3.2	

Act.: Actual.
* More than one standard deviation from norm.
** More than two standard deviations from norm. Following results of Chenery and Syrquin (1975), standard deviation is approximated by 0.25 norm.

price, however, since growth of income per head is also associated with a rise in the price of non-traded relative to traded goods.[15]

To assess the impact of oil windfalls on economic structure, the non-oil economy is decomposed into four major sectors: agriculture, manufacturing, construction and services. Norms for shares in output (SN_i) are derived from Chenery and Syrquin (1975) as are changes in norm shares due to increased real non-mining output per head. These are compared with constant-price shares (S_i) for the sample after 1972.[16] The 'Dutch Disease index', DD is defined as:

$$DD = (SN_{ag} + SN_{ma}) - (S_{ag} + S_{ma})$$

DD therefore measures the shortfall in the share of non-oil tradables relative to their 'normal levels'.

Results shown in table 2.12 indicate that Algeria, Trinidad and Tobago and Venezuela had the most severely skewed economies in sectoral terms before the oil price rise. The exceptional Algerian value of DD reflects disruption of agriculture and manufacturing by the war of independence as well as the effect of oil exports and remittances. Indonesian and Ecuadorian sectoral structures were almost normal, as, surprisingly, was that of Iran.

Table 2.12 also shows the average annual changes in norm and actual shares for 1972–81, and the implied change in DD over a decade. Algeria, Indonesia, and Venezuela managed to strengthen their non-oil tradable sectors as measured by a declining Dutch Disease index. The first two initially had severely distorted economies, however, and as noted above in connection with real exchange rate movements were able to limit domestic market forces by price controls, import liberalization (Venezuela) and constraints on private spending (Algeria). Only Ecuador, Indonesia and Venezuela managed to raise domestic food and agricultural supply per head over the 1970s, the latter from an extremely small base (during 1970–2 Venezuelan agriculture represented only 8 per cent of non-mining GDP). Despite a policy objective common to all governments, that of reducing dependence on oil, the volume of non-oil exports contracted in all countries except in Ecuador (which saw a large shift towards processed products and manufactures) and Indonesia, which maintained a fairly strong non-oil export performance across a wide range of traditional and non-traditional commodities despite real appreciation. Overall export volumes contracted, on (unweighted) average, by 1.7 per cent annually during the period 1972–81.

The most marked sectoral shifts to the non-tradeds occurred in Nigeria and Trinidad. Nigeria's agricultural decline was particularly rapid, reflecting public neglect, labour market pressures from construction and the spread of education and a number of other factors.[17] Trinidadian industry was affected by the decline of petroleum refining, and agriculture (particularly sugar) contracted despite mounting subsidies as labour moved off the land into construction and other public works programmes.[18] Iran, too, experienced a rapid decline in the share of its agricultural sector during the period for which data are available.

The table also indicates changes in the 'Dutch Disease index' on the basis of current-price data. As expected, there is a more pronounced tendency towards the construction and service sectors in four of the seven countries (mainly because of higher construction and lower manufacturing deflators). The exceptions are Nigeria, Venezuela, and Trinidad where deflator increases attenuate sharp real declines in agriculture and manufacturing. The sign pattern of resource allocation shifts as measured by DD remains unchanged.

4.4 The efficiency of public investment programmes and the growth of subsidies

As noted above, in addition to expanding their traditional functions, governments typically channelled windfall gains into industry, especially petrochemicals and heavy metals. They also invested heavily in physical infrastructure, notably to develop their transport and communications systems. Public projects tended to be large and complex and frequently were highly capital-intensive. In fact, among a sample of the top 19 developing countries with investments in projects exceeding $100 million each, all but five were oil exporters.[19] The dimension of that part of the investment programmes of the above set of countries which consisted of such large projects may be seen from table 2.13, which is mostly based on a sample of some 1,600 large projects in the developing countries during 1970–9. Iran, which ranked an overall second after Saudi Arabia, included in its investment programme 108 projects averaging over one billion dollars each. The total capital cost was equivalent to over one and a half times its 1977 GNP or ten times its 1977 oil windfall as previously computed. Venezuela's investment programme, which in contrast to Iran's placed heavy emphasis on metals (notably steel and aluminium), represented five times its 1980 oil windfall or half its 1980 GNP. The large projects identified in table 2.13 represent, on average, very roughly 4½ years' average oil revenue for 1974–81. The poorest producers, Indonesia and Nigeria, were somewhat less inclined to mortgage oil for large projects but their investments of this type were still considerable.

Table 2.13 Macroprojects in oil-exporting countries[a]

Country	No. of projects included	Cost ($b)	Average cost ($m)	Cost/ 1980 GNP	Cost/ 1980 oil windfall	Rank among developing countries	Project sector (%)			
							Hydro-carbons	Metals	Other industry	Infrastructure
Iran	108	119.6	1,107	1.57[c]	10.2[c]	2	30	7	9	54
Algeria	69	38.7	561	1.07	4.2	5	36	7	33	23
Venezuela	27	27.4	1,015	0.51	5.4	10	33	41	7	19
Mexico	59	26.0	441	0.18	5.1	.2	46	17	12	25
Nigeria	19	14.4	758	0.17	0.9	15	26	11	16	47
Indonesia	44	14.4	327	0.23	1.1	16	41	18	16	25
Trinidad & Tobago[b]	7	6.9	983	1.35	4.5	—	61	29	—	—

[a] Projects with costs exceeding $100 million.
[b] Gas-based industrial projects only. Includes Tenneco–Midcon LNG project proposed for 1988.
[c] 1977 GNP and oil windfall.

Sources: Murphy (1983) table 2.5; Auty and Gelb (1984).

The larger public projects had a greater tendency to overrun initial estimates both in terms of cost and time, as shown in table 2.14. One third of the largest projects in the sample on which the table is based experienced cost overruns which averaged 109 per cent. Overruns on the smaller projects were less frequent and more modest at 30 per cent. Delays of between 1 and 2 years plagued half the troubled projects; a further 25 per cent experienced delays of 3–4 years. These estimates greatly understate the true extent of cost and time overruns since many projects were not completed by 1980; many are still under construction, a number may never reach completion.

The tendency to overrun initial estimates and the poor operating performance of many plants once installed reflects a variety of factors, none specific to oil-exporting countries but all accentuated by the scope and pace of their investment growth.[20] First, projects were, in many cases, inadequately prepared and assessed. In no country does there appear to have been systematic assessment of relative costs and benefits across a spectrum of potential projects. Secondly, larger projects tended to be more complex, both technologically and in terms of the organization necessary to integrate the project with its necessary infrastructure. Some involved state-of-the-art technology which, in certain cases, was installed without the involvement of an experienced expatriate operating company. With little detailed knowledge of the industry or plant in question, public financing agencies were also sometimes slow to detect and correct emerging problems in construction, start-up and operation. Thirdly, about half of the purchasing power of oil relative to domestic

Table 2.14   Cost and time overruns in macroprojects

	Project size ($ m)			
	100–249	250–499	500–999	1000+
Percentage of total projects with cost escalations, completion delays or post-ponements/suspensions	21	28	38	47
Average cost escalation (%)	30	70	106	109
Percentage of total projects with:				
Cost escalation	10	18	28	34
Completion delay	11	14	16	16
Postponement/suspension	7	10	13	20

Source: Murphy (1983), p. 19.

construction costs was eroded by increases in the latter during 1973–8. Increased construction costs were a major factor in real appreciation of the exchange rate. As noted above, international inflation in traded manufactured goods was also high. Finally, certain industrial investments of the oil producers were severely affected by the global recession in the 1980s, as described below.

An additional claim on public resources came from the expanded programmes of subsidies and transfers which were usually directed towards holding down the rate of inflation and supporting loss-making firms. As noted above, between 1970–2 and 1974–8 fiscal subsidies and transfers expanded, on average, twice as rapidly as non-mining GDP and between 1974–8 and 1980–1 they rose about 1.6 times as rapidly. Producer governments were reluctant to raise domestic oil prices, choosing to pass part of the windfall on to domestic consumers in the form of lower prices. In at least three cases, domestic oil prices were set at roughly the cost of production so that government derived no revenue from that part of oil output consumed at home. Several producers, notably Ecuador and Indonesia, raised domestic prices of oil derivatives in the early 1980s but they still remained below world levels. As domestic oil consumption grew more rapidly than non-oil economies the implicit fiscal burden on the state increased.[21] Energy subsidies in 1980 were estimated to be equivalent to almost 10 per cent of household income in Ecuador, while fiscal subsidies rose sharply in Trinidad and Tobago, to around 7 per cent of GDP or 11 per cent of non-mining GDP by 1981.

Such estimates do not include the subsidies implicit in loans made to loss-making (usually public) firms, nominally for investment, and in guarantees enabling them to access commercial sources of finance. It is difficult to estimate these subsidies (since many such firms would probably have been unable to borrow from commercial sources at any price without support), but they appear to have been considerable and to have been accorded to some extremely unprofitable firms. For example, by 1983 it was estimated that the production costs of Caroni Sugar in Trinidad were five times those of efficient world-scale producers, despite the fact that some of the latter, notably in Australia, had unit labour costs several times higher.

In addition to supporting firms, some oil-producing governments stimulated employment directly through public works programmes. The INPRES programmes in Indonesia and the Special Works (DEWD) programmes in Trinidad and Tobago gave work to some 2.5 per cent of the two countries' respective labour forces. The impact of such programmes depends on their administration and on the extent to which labour is a major constraint to production, particularly in agriculture. While the impact of INPRES appears to have been beneficial in labour-surplus Java, the Trinidad programmes (which offered pay at least twice that in agriculture) contributed to accelerate a rapid movement off the land which led to a drop in agricultural output. Per capita food production and that of agriculture as a whole were both reduced by about 20 per cent from 1969/71 to 1982, during which time the population expanded by only 16 per cent. The main loser was sugar, which saw its output fall by 62 per cent.

The momentum of accelerated public investment (some of which implied large future recurrent obligations) and growing subsidies proved hard to curb when oil revenues fell, as they did in 1978 and after 1981. Central government deficits averaged 4.1 per cent of non-mining GDP in 1978 and, excluding Trinidad and Tobago where expenditures accelerated more slowly, current account deficits averaged 11.8 per cent of non-mining GDP. A number of exporters moved to slow domestic absorption of goods and services. Indonesia devalued by 50 per cent in November 1978, seeking to restore the domestic purchasing power of oil revenues and to promote non-oil exports.

These contractionary moves were interrupted by the second oil price increase which resulted in a current balance surplus of $11.8 billion in 1980 for the above six countries (excluding Iran). The second oil windfall was more abrupt than the first. As current-dollar commodity exports contracted by 21.6 per cent during 1980–2 and imports rose by 22.3 per cent, current balances shifted to a deficit of $19.6 billion by 1982. Of the current account deterioration between 1980 and 1982, 58 per cent may be attributed to decreases in merchandise export revenues and 36.8 per cent to increased imports of goods.

These swings in the exporters' current accounts usually mirrored developments in their respective public sectors. Ecuador's public sector, for example, ran surpluses of around 2 per cent of GDP in 1973–4, but these turned into deficits of 5 per cent of GDP in 1977–8. With the second oil price increase the deficit declined but with contracting revenues and mushrooming subsidies and interest payments it rose to around 8 per cent of GDP in 1982.

Economic management through the fluctuation in oil prices was rendered more difficult by the fact that access to international capital tended to vary with the level of oil prices, which affected future price and revenue expectations rather directly. As noted above, Algeria was able to boost the expenditure impact of increased oil revenues by half during 1974–8 through borrowing abroad, largely to finance a transition from an oil- to a natural gas-based hydrocarbon sector. Mexico augmented its comparatively small oil windfall (3.5 per cent of non-mining GDP for 1979–81) by two-thirds through financing a growing deficit on goods and non-factor services. In addition, Venezuela and Mexico were able to cushion the impact of growing private capital outflows by large public borrowings until the outlook in world oil markets deteriorated.

4.5   After 1981: the end of the oil boom?

The downturn in world oil markets after 1981 revealed the fragility of the development patterns of the oil exporters. Shifts in the allocation of resources towards the non-traded sectors which had cumulated over the 1970s could not be rapidly reversed and reluctance to devalue (plus the competitive devaluations of trading partners) caused real exchange rates to remain at an appreciated level during 1982–3, as shown in table 2.10. The massive infrastructural and educational investments which had been undertaken since 1974, whatever their implications for future productivity, did not represent an autonomous source of income to replace oil earnings. More seriously, the global outlook changed for a number of sectors – notably steel, aluminium and natural gas – which had featured prominently in investment programmes. For example, in 1980 the OECD was forecasting a doubling of global steel demand to 1400 million tons by the year 2000. More recent forecasts project a 20 per cent rise to only 900 million tons. This has serious implications, particularly for those countries with domestic markets too small to absorb full-capacity output of large capital-intensive plants, and which, like Trinidad and Venezuela, had gone forward without foreign partners to assure marketing outlets. Such countries would need to be competitive with the globally most efficient (or most highly subsidized) exporters, to overcome trade and transport margins and a preference for domestic supply in major markets. In the case of steel, this required a producer such as ISCOTT in Trinidad and Tobago to undercut US minimills by 15 per cent, although its production costs were some 50 per cent higher than their estimated level of $270 per ton in 1982.

As the pressure of demand slackened, the transient boom of the mid-1970s was followed by deceleration in non-oil growth, surplus capacity and slackening labour markets. A further factor decelerating demand was the tendency for private capital to flow abroad, particularly in those oil exporters with open capital markets such as Venezuela and Indonesia. During 1978–81 the total cumulative current balance deficits of the above six countries, at $4.8 billion, accounted for only 26 per cent of the deterioration in their net foreign assets (where the latter is defined as the change in external debt less that in currency reserves). Venezuela may have experienced an outflow equivalent to almost 10 per cent of GDP in 1982, impelled by a stagnant economy, interest rate ceilings and reluctance to adjust the exchange rate in line with perceived trends in world oil prices. During 1979–82 its non-oil economy virtually ceased to grow despite massive investments and considerable increases in the labour force which should have assured growth of at least some 4 per cent per annum, even in the absence of any productivity improvements.

Rapid expenditure of windfalls and borrowing against future oil incomes therefore has an additional cost. Expenditures will need to be cut back sharply when oil prices or exports decline. Unless prices and wages adjust flexibly (a proposition not supported by the real exchange rate measurements of table 2.10), the cost in terms of underused capacity of such rapid contractions in effective demand is likely to be large. Simulations with a multi-sectoral computable general-equilibrium model of Indonesia suggest that that they can outweigh the benefits of the windfalls themselves.[22]

5 Conclusion

The main objectives common to most oil-exporting governments were:

(a) growth and modernization of the non-oil economy;
(b) expansion of the sphere of national control;
(c) diversification away from oil as a sole source of foreign exchange.

Some governments also attempted to minimize inflation and other side-effects of accelerated domestic expenditures. Distributional concerns, though frequently expressed, appear in most cases not to have greatly influenced policy except in the context of objective (b) and through the introduction or increase of subsidy programmes.

The *ex ante* range of choice facing exporting governments was wide: saving abroad, domestic investment, public consumption or private consumption effected through transfers, subsidies or cuts in non-oil taxes. Results above indicate a clear choice: oil windfalls after 1973 were mostly transformed into domestic public investment with some spillover to public and private consumption which increased after 1978.

Considering (a), it is not yet possible to assess the impact of windfalls on producer economies since many investments, notably in transportation and education, would be expected to have long gestation lags. Overall, however, the yield on much domestic investment has probably fallen well short of that available abroad and its supply-side growth impact has been moderate, because it has generally not succeeded in providing an autonomous source of income and purchasing power to supplement or replace oil.

Domestic public investment was mainly large-scale and often in the form of complex projects. Exchange appreciation which raised the price of domestic capital goods, multiplier effects from investment expenditures, cost overruns, subsidy growth and the recurrent spending needs of much past investment all resulted in a tendency to overshoot available revenues when the latter fell. The result has been a pronounced and costly 'stop–go' rhythm through which economic management has been difficult. With hindsight, the oil exporters would probably have seen a larger benefit from their windfalls had they saved a higher proportion abroad and limited domestic investments through applying market criteria more rigorously.

In the petroleum sector at least, the oil exporters have greatly extended the scope of national control. Some, notably Nigeria, Indonesia and Trinidad and Tobago, promoted wide-ranging indigenization and nationalization programmes outside oil, often at high fiscal and economic cost.

Considering the final main objective, it appears that Indonesia has been the most successful in using oil revenues to strengthen agriculture and industry, as shown by both sectoral and export structures. Trinidad and Tobago and Nigeria saw their oil dependence increase dramatically. Most of the other countries were highly oil-dependent before 1972 and remain so. Even in those countries that have successfully promoted industry, a common problem is the *nature* of industrial growth, overwhelmingly import-orientated and dependent on oil exports for imported intermediates. Events of 1982–4 confirm that the goal of self-sustaining non-oil development is far from being attained.

NOTES

*   The World Bank does not accept responsibility for the views expressed herein which are those of the author and should not be attributed to the World Bank or to its affiliated organizations. The findings, interpretations and conclusions are the results of research supported by the Bank; they do not necessarily represent official policy of the Bank. The designations employed, and the presentation of material in this document are solely for the convenience of the reader and do not imply the expression of any opinion whatsoever on the part of the World Bank or its affiliates concerning the legal status of any country, territory, city, area or of its authorities, or concerning the delimitation of its boundaries or national affiliation.

The author would like to thank Shahrzad Gohari for her useful contribution to research project 672–49 on which this paper is based and Ann Meyendorff and Carlos Medeiros for able assistance.

1 Government may also absorb windfalls from non-mineral export revenues. For a review of the reaction of coffee and tea producers to the commodity booms of 1975–8, see Davis (1983).

2 Although the Hotelling rule predicts that unit natural resource rents should rise at the rate of interest, the medium-run fluctuations about any such long-run relationship have major consequences. An extra 250,000 barrels per day sold in 1981 with the proceeds invested in US government treasury bills would, by February 1984, have yielded approximately $4 billion, against an estimated value of $2.6 billion for the same volume of oil valued at February prices. The capital surplus countries are discussed in Hablutzel (1981).

3 This projection should not be taken to imply that countries would *actually* have followed such a pattern in the absence of terms of trade changes. For example, Venezuelan constant-price mining output would certainly have declined relative to the non-oil economy during 1972–8 for technical reasons. It rather provides a common basis for the comparative assessment of the impact and use of windfalls. No non-oil growth effect is attributed to the windfall, for reasons described below.

4 For an analysis of this (Tornquist–Theil) index as a discrete approximation to a Divisia index, see Diewert (1976).

5 Residuals are small and in results below have been subsumed into the price term.

6 This is against the expected tendency for mineral exporters described by Nankani (1979).

7 The unusual decrease for Ecuador is explained by (*a*) the fact that oil revenues also accrue to special funds outside government as defined here, and (*b*) the easing of certain non-oil taxes after 1974.

8 Measures to redistribute oil incomes directly to private individuals and firms have been implemented elsewhere. The state of Alaska responded to oil windfalls by abolishing all non-oil taxes and directly distributing profits from its Permanent Fund. The province of Alberta has made smaller direct transfers to its residents.

9 For cross-country tax norms see Tait, Gratz and Eichengreen (1979).

10 See Tugwell (1975), Bigler (1980) and Karl (1982) for analyses of the role of the Venezuelan state and the growth of the 'Third Sector' in the Venezuelan economy.

11 See, for example, Bruno (1976), Corden and Neary (1982), Gelb (1981).

12 Excluding Iran.

13 The investment effect in value terms would have added 1.8 percentage points but increases in the relative price of investment goods (particularly construction) lowered the average real investment effect from 12.0 to 8.6 per cent of non-mining output.

14 Changing patterns of output accompanying development are analysed by Chenery and Syrquin (1975).

15 Balassa (1964), Kravis, Heston and Summers (1978).

16 There are no cross-country constant price norms for sectoral structure. Constant-price data are preferable for the sample because of the untypical impact of oil booms on relative prices, particularly of construction. The effect of the bias introduced by comparing constant and current-price shares is to make it less likely that oil exporter economies will appear skewed towards non-tradeds.

17 For a discussion of Nigerian priorities and their impact on agriculture, see Bienen (1983).
18 See Auty and Gelb (1984).
19 Murphy (1983).
20 As witness the $8 billion cost of the trans-Alaskan oil pipeline versus its $900 million original budget, cost overruns can be large in developed countries also. Their peculiar significance for the oil exporters is due to the weight of large projects relative to the size of their economies.
21 Petroleum subsidies conceded by producer governments are usually implicit rather than fiscal because revenues forgone through pricing oil for domestic use below world prices are not included in fiscal amounts.
22 Gelb (1983).

REFERENCES

Auty R. and A. H. Gelb (1984) 'The Deployment of Oil Rents in a Small Parliamentary Democracy: the Case of Trinidad and Tobago', World Bank, February, mimeo.
Balassa B. (1964) 'The Purchasing Power Parity Doctrine: A Reappraisal', *Journal of Political Economy*, **72**, 584–96.
Bienen H. (1983) 'Oil Revenues and Policy Choices in Nigeria', World Bank Staff Working Paper no. 592.
Bigler G. E. H. (1980) 'State Economic Control versus Market Expansion: the Third Sector in Venezuelan Politics, 1928–78', Unpublished PhD dissertation, Johns Hopkins University.
Bruno M. (1976) 'The Two Sector Open Economy and The Real Exchange Rate', *American Economic Review*, **66**, 566–77.
Chenery H. and M. Syrquin (1975) *Patterns of Economic Growth 1950–70*, Oxford: Oxford University Press.
Conway P. J. and A. H. Gelb (1984) 'Oil Rents in a Controlled Economy: a Case Study of Algeria', World Bank, DRD Discussion Paper no. 92.
Corden W. M. and J. P. Neary (1982) 'Booming Sector and De-Industrialization in a Small Open Economy', *Economic Journal*, **92**, 825–48.
Davis J. M. (1983) 'The Economic Effects of Windfall Gains in Export Earnings 1975–78', *World Development*, **11**, 119–41.
Diewert W. (1976) 'Exact and Superlative Index Numbers', *Journal of Econometrics*, **4**, 115–45.
Garcia Araujo M. (1982) 'The Impact of Petrodollars on the Economy and the Public Sector of Venezuela', Paper delivered at the Tenth National Meeting of LASA, Washington, DC, March 4.
Gelb A. H. (1981) 'Capital Importing Oil Exporters: Adjustment Issues and Policy Choices', World Bank Staff Working Paper no. 475, August.
Gelb A. H. (1983) 'Oil Windfalls and Development: Exercises with a Model of Indonesia', mimeo.
Hablutzel R. (1981) 'Development Prospects of the Capital Surplus Oil Exporting Countries', World Bank Staff Working Paper no. 483.
Karl T. L. (1982) 'The Political Economy of Petrodollars: Oil and Democracy in Venezuela', Unpublished PhD thesis, Stanford University.

Kravis I. B., A. Heston and R. Summers (1978) *International Comparison of Real Product and Purchasing Power*, Baltimore, Md.: Johns Hopkins University Press.

Levy W. J. (1970) 'The Years that the Locust Hath Eaten: Oil Policy and OPEC Development Prospects,' *Foreign Affairs*, **57**, 287–305.

Morgan D. R. (1979) 'Fiscal Policies in Oil Importing Countries'. *International Monetary Fund Staff Papers* **26**, 55–86.

Murphy K. (1983) *Macroprojects in Developing Countries*, Westview Press.

Nankani G. (1979) 'Development Problems of Mineral Exporting Countries', World Bank Staff Working Paper no. 354, August.

Tait A., W. Gratz and B. Eichengreen (1979) 'International Comparison of Taxation for Selected Developing Countries: 1972–76', *International Monetary Fund Staff Papers* **26**, 122–56.

Tugwell F. (1975) *The Politics of Oil in Venezuela*, Stamford, Conn.: Stamford University Press.

COMMENT   SEBASTIAN EDWARDS

Alan Gelb has provided us with an interesting and informative paper. Gelb describes in detail the behaviour of six oil-exporting developing countries – Algeria, Ecuador, Indonesia, Nigeria, Trinidad and Tobago and Venezuela – following the oil shocks of the 1970s. He basically raises three questions:

(*a*) What was the size of the oil-related windfalls?

(*b*) How were these windfalls spent?

(*c*) What were the effects of these windfalls on the non-oil sectors of these economies?

The answers provided in the paper are:

(*a*) On average, for both shocks, the windfalls amounted to 24 per cent of output in the non-oil sector.

(*b*) On average, 25 per cent of the windfalls were spent. Gelb also finds that after the second shock in most of these countries government consumption increased quite substantially.

(*c*) In all these countries the non-oil sector did not perform well. More specifically, contrary to these countries' policy-makers' goals, the non-oil sector did not grow faster than its historical rate. Moreover, the share of the non-oil sector in production actually declined in most of these countries.

Gelb's overall conclusion is that – perhaps with the exception of Indonesia – these countries' performance fell way short of expectations.

What went wrong? Gelb argues that one of the clearer problems encountered by these countries is that they embarked on monstrously large public investment projects, with very low, or even negative, returns. With hindsight it appears that they would have done better by investing the oil windfalls abroad.

In general, I am quite sympathetic towards Gelb's conclusions. However, in the rest of this comment I would like to concentrate on a few points raised in Gelb's contribution which I think need some clarification.

The real appreciation that follows the oil boom constitutes a crucial element in Gelb's story, and in all Dutch Disease models. In most cases this real appreciation stems directly from the income effect generated by the boom. The price of oil increases, real income goes up, a proportion of this higher income is spent on non-tradables and a situation of an incipient excess demand for these goods emerges. In order for the non-tradable goods market to regain equilibrium its relative price has to go up, and the real exchange rate appreciates. In this story the extent of the real appreciation depends on the marginal propensity to spend on non-tradables. It is important to notice, however, that once substitution effects are allowed into the picture a richer set of possible results emerges. For example, if it is assumed that the excess demand for non-tradable goods depends both on the relative prices of non-oil tradables and oil, and if it is assumed that oil and non-tradables are complements, an oil boom can result in a real depreciation rather than a real appreciation. While this case is not necessarily a very relevant one from an empirical point of view, it is important to keep it in mind when evaluating the actual response of the real exchange rate to export booms.

An idea that is present in most of Gelb's analysis is that the real appreciation that accompanies the export boom is something *bad* and undesirable, that should be avoided. However Gelb does not spell out why this real appreciation is in fact such an undesirable event. In order to do this it would be necessary to introduce an explicit welfare criterion to evaluate exchange rate movements. In such a setting it would be necessary to point out what is assumed with respect to market failures, the existence of externalities, price rigidities and expectations formation. Central to any such story would be the distinction between temporary and permanent export booms.

If the increase of the commodity export price is permanent, the associated real appreciation will be a long-run equilibrium phenomenon. Under these circumstances there will be little reason to avoid it. On the other hand, if the export boom is only temporary (or if it is perceived to be temporary), it is easy to tell stories where it will be desirable actually to avoid the real appreciation, or at least reduce its magnitude. In this case, then, the crucial question relates to the possible ways to avoid this real appreciation. Some alternative ways to do this include reducing the proportion of the windfall spent on non-tradables, controlling the monetary consequences of the boom and, possibly, using nominal devaluations (as Indonesia did in 1978 and 1983).

Gelb's paper, and most of the discussion in this conference, has focused on the real appreciation and 'Dutch Disease' consequences of commodity export booms. There are, however, a variety of other important instances where this type of phenomenon is present. Perhaps the most important one is related to the effects of capital inflows on the real exchange rate. Among these cases it is worth mentioning the exchange rate deprotection that usually follows the liberalization of the capital account of the balance of payments. In that regard the recent experiences of the countries of the Southern Cone of Latin America are particularly relevant. In the 1970s Argentina, Chile and Uruguay embarked on major economic liberalization reforms. As part of these programmes in all these countries the capital account was liberalized, and capital was allowed to move freely in and out of the country. Following these reforms all three countries were flooded with foreign capital. As a consequence of this massive inflow of capital – a fraction of which was used to finance the expansion of the non-tradable sector – the real exchange rate experienced a steep appreciation, and the traditional tradables sector was greatly hurt.

3

The Dutch Disease in The Netherlands

JEROEN J. M. KREMERS*

In 1977 *The Economist* warned that, in the absence of a gradual adjustment to the post-gas era, the Dutch might 'wake up one morning in the twenty-first century with a monumental hangover'. Today it appears that this may not be necessary. After 15 years of a tendency towards gas-fuelled economic intemperance, The Netherlands seems to be in the process of regaining its traditional sobriety. The decline of the market sector, the stagnation of production growth and accelerating unemployment are bringing The Netherlands down to earth.

On balance, the huge natural gas discoveries of the late 1950s have benefited the country. It has built up an excellent infrastructure, some industrial sectors are very strong, and living standards are high, both for the economically active and for the economically non-active. However, in the sense that the Dutch economy has needed and still needs a sound dose of corrective medicine, the gas boom indeed represents a Dutch Disease to The Netherlands. In the following both the disease and the medicine will be studied against the background of the theoretical literature.

Three conclusions may be worth mentioning at the outset. First, the availability of natural gas has had a profound impact on the Dutch economy as a whole and on its sectoral structure in particular. Secondly, the theoretical framework of this book is valuable for understanding the Dutch experience. Thirdly, question marks must be placed against some of the policies adopted by the Dutch to cope with the gas boom.

There is one point that has to be emphasized. In this paper I concentrate on the impact of natural gas discoveries on the Dutch economy. I shall adduce empirical evidence which appears to be in remarkable accordance with strands of Dutch Disease theory. Thus the temptation exists to assign too much significance to gas as the exclusive *cause* of present economic difficulties. However, these difficulties are very much the result of a long-drawn process which originated before the gas boom. The increasing economic involvement to which Dutch society has invited its government is a central element in this process. Here I shall highlight the contribution of natural gas to it.

The setup of the argument is as follows. Section 2 contains a brief classification of the relevant theoretical issues. The way in which gas revenues have been spent is the subject of section 3, and section 4 focuses on the consequences for the sectoral structure of the Dutch economy. In section 5 the policy responses are evaluated, and section 6 concludes. Preceding all that, section 1 sets out some key characteristics of the Dutch economy.[1]

1   Characteristics of the Dutch economy

A main feature of the Dutch economy is its great openness. International trade amounts to more than 50 per cent of GNP. Trade contacts extend to all areas of the world, with a strong but recently decreasing concentration on within-EC trade. Germany accounts for about 30 per cent of Dutch exports, Belgium for almost 20 per cent. The balance of traded goods normally shows a deficit, whereas services score surpluses (figure 3.1). Exports are relatively concentrated in agriculture, mineral fuels, lubricants and related materials and chemicals. The country reveals comparative advantage in production using relatively little but highly skilled labour, in its natural resources (agriculture and, temporarily, energy), in its history in trade and in its location at the crossroads of Europe (WRR, 1980, p. 50; Koekkoek and Mennes, 1984). Much more about developments in the sectoral structure will be said below.

The public sector is deeply involved in economic life. It takes up a large and until recently increasing share of value-added in the private sector, both for spending and for redistributive purposes. Regulatory powers of government are considerable and are regularly used to guide the private sector in areas such as prices and incomes policy, industrial policy and sometimes even monetary policy. Because of the country's pluriform history and its sympathy with minorities, decisions are preferably taken by agreement of all those involved.

During the 1950s and early 1960s wage increases lagged behind the rapid growth of productivity. Later, the 1960s also accommodated a considerable wage explosion, which set in motion a trend rise of the share of labour in net value-added (see figure 3.6 and table 3.3). The exploitation of vast natural gas reserves occurred in a period of rapid growth, with an increasing share in world trade and low unemployment

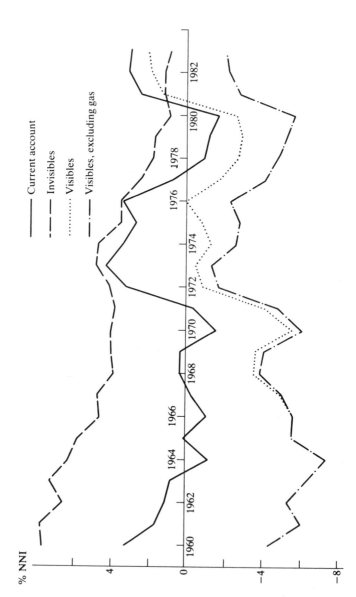

Figure 3.1 The Dutch current account, 1960–83.
Source: Central Economic Plans, 1979, 1984; Wieleman, 1982.
Note: Gas revenues do not include energy import substitution.

(figure 3.2). Before the gas started to come on stream, virtually no energy was home-produced. It was estimated that the gas reserves would satisfy total national energy requirements for several decades (Lubbers and Lemckert, 1980).

Initially, depletion policy aimed at rapid exploitation of the gas. World energy prices were expected to fall, and cheap and clean nuclear energy was expected to become available in the near future. Therefore, an aggressive pricing policy was adopted on the Dutch household and business markets, and soon substantial export contracts were signed.

Two justifications were given for exporting gas at prices below its oil equivalent at the world level. First, it had to be sold off fast and in large quantities, so that markets had to be conquered rapidly by aggressive pricing. Second, the conversion from other energy sources to gas in the importing countries (mainly Germany, Belgium, France and Italy) involved adjustment costs which had to be reflected in prices. This meant that for The Netherlands the opportunity cost of gas was temporarily below the world energy price level, which gave the Dutch economy a comparative advantage in energy during the 1960s. Later, the advantage diminished as export markets had been created and conversion had taken place. However, for contractual reasons export price rises kept lagging behind those of world equivalents, so that some of the advantage has remained until today.

In the course of the 1970s the picture changed drastically. Rocketing world energy prices, an Arab oil boycott of The Netherlands, the revealed vulnerability of a country without energy reserves, general concern at the finiteness of natural resources and a disappointing lack of progress on nuclear energy resulted in a reversal of the depletion policy. Domestic prices were moved up to world levels as much as possible. The strategy shifted from high speed depletion to long-term conservation. No new export contracts were engaged upon, house insulation and economy in energy consumption were promoted. By that time the consequences for the current account had become so enormous, that from this perspective also it was considered wise to cut back on gas exports and smooth its effects over time. Imports of energy reverted to an upward trend. Still, the experience of how to cope with a natural gas boom had only just begun.

2   The relevant theoretical issues

While discussing the impact of the gas boom on the Dutch economy, one can in the first place distinguish between resource-movement and

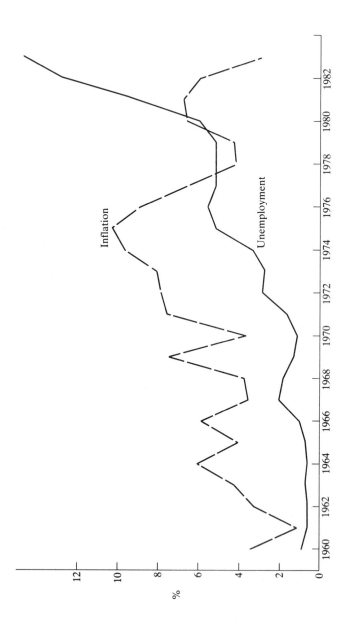

Figure 3.2   Unemployment and inflation in The Netherlands, 1960–83.
Source: ABN, *Economic Review*.
Note: Inflation as annual % change CPI; unemployment as % dependent labour force.

spending effects (see, for example, Neary, 1985; Corden and Neary, 1982).

Resource movement effects occur if the booming sector directly draws inputs away from the rest of the economy. As it happens, the exploitation of Dutch gas has required limited inputs. The gas sector does not provide much employment. Even though unemployment was low in the 1960s, we may for the purpose of this paper, assume that the labour requirements of the gas sector were negligible (Wieleman, 1982, p. 82). They never put pressure on other sectors.[2] A similar case can be made for capital inputs. Although investment costs constitute the major component of gas production costs, they do not seem to have put any pressure on Dutch capital markets. Total annual investment in the gas sector has never exceeded a few per cent of national investment, and could increasingly be financed from gas revenues. The spending effects of capital goods purchases themselves will be discussed below. On the financial side, it must also be remembered that The Netherlands has a small and very open economy with, in principle, free international movement of capital. Potential capital market pressure could have been offset from abroad. Therefore, the Dutch Disease in The Netherlands may be studied in a model without inputs to the booming sector.[3]

The spending effect involves a variety of issues. In theory it can be separated from the optimal depletion problem, but in practice this may not be possible. Consider this issue first. As a useful benchmark, Buiter (1983) formulates a concept of the net worth of the public sector, in which the present discounted value of future gas revenues accruing to the government would be one constituent asset. As the result of an intertemporal optimization problem (e.g. maximize intertemporal citizens' utility subject to the intertemporal public budget constraint – which contains the present value of gas – and the dynamic model of the economy), government normally ought to smooth the benefits of the gas boom over time. In a world of rational expectations, perfect financial, factor and product markets, and sufficiently operative intergenerational chains, the problem of maximizing the present value of future gas revenues can be solved separately from the overall government optimization problem. These conditions are sufficient but not necessary for the optimal depletion and general optimal budgetary policy problems to be solvable in a recursive way. If these conditions are not satisfied, it will in general depend on the specific features and parameters of the economy's model whether a recursive solution is feasible.

In the Dutch natural gas case, it was not possible to plan general macroeconomic policy conditional on an optimal solution of the depletion problem. The two were interrelated in a complicated way (see, for example, Withagen, 1982). To see this, recall that initial depletion policy was aiming at rapid exploitation. Since the export strategy required gas export prices to be below import prices of alternative sources of energy, it was attractive to absorb a large part of the gas reserves in the domestic economy. However, the absorptive capacities of the economy and of export markets were limited. It was decided to increase both. On the export side this was effected by aggressive pricing, and a similar strategy was followed with respect to domestic energy consumption. These two aspects of depletion policy were thus conditioned by short-run economic considerations. Influences also ran in the opposite direction. The originally low household prices changed the pattern of energy consumption and thus affected general macroeconomic relationships. Furthermore, government charged industry low energy prices to promote rapid depletion. This changed the industrial structure in favour of energy-intensive production and exports, another macroeconomic effect. Thus, optimal gas revenue generating and spending policies were intimately linked. Against this background, section 3 will give further quantitative insight into the way revenues have been spent. The conditioning role of depletion policy will have to be kept in mind.

The conventional Dutch Disease entails a relative decline of the traded goods sector in favour of the non-traded goods sector. This occurs in combination with an increase in the price of non-traded relative to that of traded goods, or a real appreciation of the currency. It hinges on the presumption that the energy boom results in an improvement of the energy balance of trade, and that at least part of the gas revenues are spent on non-traded goods. On the basis of the description of spending patterns in section 3, section 4 evaluates the extent to which the tradables sector has been affected by the gas boom in The Netherlands. Section 5, as remarked, comments on the appropriateness of policy reactions. In that context, not only spending policies are of relevance. Dutch monetary policy includes both domestic monetary conditions and balance of payments developments within its competence, and therefore has to be taken into account.

Before first proceeding to a description of spending patterns, two important divergences of Dutch experience from standard theoretical models remain to be emphasized. First, Dutch Disease theory tends to ignore the impact of the booming commodity as an intermediate input. In The Netherlands, the role of gas as a partly non-traded input is of great importance. This has tended to reinforce the contractionary impact of the oil price rises on the tradables sector, since that sector had meanwhile become more energy intensive (Corden and Neary, 1982, pp. 840–1). It has also been instrumental in Dutch sectoral policy, as we shall see below. Secondly, The Netherlands has experienced a great deal of inflexibility in real wages and prices. This has profound implications for the issues involved (van Wijnbergen, 1984b,c,d), and will be given ample attention in sections 4 and 5.

3 Spending the gas revenues

The share of government in actual gas revenues has risen from 65 to more than 75 per cent between the 1960s and today. At the margin, government's share is over 85 per cent. The remainder accrues to the oil companies.

It is difficult to trace the way in which the latter category has been spent, although initially a large part must have been devoted to exploitation investments. That investment demand was to quite an extent met by imports (Wieleman, 1982, p. 129). Relatively speaking, however, the amounts were still small.

Before concentrating on the way government spent its share in the revenues, it must be noted that *actual* revenue does not necessarily equal total *potential* revenue. The latter is the economically relevant concept. Since government has major power over price setting, any pricing below the revenue maximizing level can be counted as a subsidy to energy costs. It is difficult to determine whether particular pricing policies have been adopted for reasons of general macroeconomic and industrial policy, or in order to maximize revenues.

Pricing policies have roughly been as follows (for details, see Lubbers and Lemckert, 1980; Wieleman, 1982). Domestic prices, both for households and for industry, have always been above export prices. Gas export prices have always been below world energy equivalent prices.[4] Before 1973, domestic prices were far below world levels, partly in order to induce substitution towards gas. Agriculture and some parts of industry enjoyed substantially lower prices than households. For the pre-1973 period the policy stance taken was apparently to set gas export prices with a view to revenue maximization (i.e., fast depletion). Household and business prices were below those of world equivalents. Reasons for the low domestic prices were partly of the revenue maximization type (i.e., the stimulation of substitution), and partly of a general macroeconomic character. To the extent that the latter were significant, it seems that government has spent part of its potential revenue in this fashion as a transfer to households. The relatively low business prices must be seen as part of general industrial policy. In order to promote the utilization of the Dutch comparative energy advantage (recall that the gas was expected to be replaced soon by other energy sources) in the form of an investment for the future, government stimulated energy-intensive production by spending part of the potential gas revenue on low energy pricing for business. In combination with direct public investment, this led to rapid growth of energy-intensive industries such as chemicals, oil refining, steel and horticulture.

As explained in section 1, after the 1973/4 oil shock the depletion, pricing and spending policies changed. Slow depletion became the motto, and domestic prices went up to world levels. The argument of a Dutch comparative energy advantage lost ground as conversion towards gas had taken place and markets had been gained. Thus the opportunity cost of Dutch gas moved closer to the world energy price level. Low energy prices for industry would now be similar to a plain subsidy to industry, linked to the relative energy-intensity of the recipient's production. In the 1960s, as the comparative energy advantage was significant since foreign conversion and market penetration were still taking place, industrial prices were low partly in order to exploit this advantage. In the 1970s, as the advantage diminished, industrial prices rose accordingly. Although on theoretical grounds this may seem sensible, it represented a serious problem for the energy-intensive sectors set up in the 1960s.

Returning to the analysis of actual gas revenues, the government's share, amounting to approximately three quarters, remains to be accounted for. Since these revenues were treated as current government receipts, it is difficult to trace their specific destination. Table 3.1 gives an impression of the significance of gas revenues in the budget, and of general public financing patterns. It appears that after the first oil crisis gas revenue became a substantial element in government receipts (from 3 per cent of total receipts just before the first oil crisis up to 17 per cent in 1982!). These revenues have not been set aside for investment. Over the relevant period, net public capital spending as a percentage of national income has declined somewhat. Taxation has stayed roughly constant (it increased up to 1980 but has fallen since), so that current spending has increased. Indeed, the bulk of growth can be found in net income transfers, wages and purchases of goods and services. Except for expenditure on education, which is included in the last category and may be considered investment in human capital, most of the increase was therefore spent on consumption.

Resuming, it appears that before the first oil price rise part of potential gas revenue was invested by means of direct investment (note 2) and low energy prices for agriculture and industry. Not much was

Table 3.1   Budget of total government (excluding social security), 1965–82

	1965/9	1970/4	1975/9	1980	1982
	(average % of net national income)				
Wages, purchase of goods and services	16.7	17.5	19.0	19.2	18.7
Interest payments	3.0	3.3	3.4	4.1	5.7
Price subsidies (house rent, etc.)	1.0	1.5	2.3	2.7	2.5
Net income transfers	3.5	4.3	8.4	9.5	10.5
Net current spending	24.2	26.6	33.1	35.5	37.4
Taxation	26.8	29.0	29.4	30.0	27.4
Gas revenues	0.2	1.0	3.2	4.5	6.1
Investment income	1.7	1.7	1.9	2.1	2.7
Current receipts	28.7	31.7	34.5	36.6	36.2
Net investment	4.6	4.0	3.1	2.8	2.6
Net capital transfers	0.8	0.9	1.6	2.8	2.6
Net loans	3.7	2.7	2.1	2.5	2.7
Net capital spending	9.1	7.6	6.8	8.1	7.9
Budget deficit ($-$)	-4.6	-2.5	-5.4	-7.0	-9.1
Memo: Social security contributions (*not* included in taxation)	14.0	17.5	19.7	20.2	22.1

Source: Central Planning Bureau, *Macro Economische Verkenningen, 1983.*

spent on consumption yet, but total gas revenues were still limited. After the first oil crisis, as revenues increased, it is evident that a large part thereof was spent on income transfers and consumption. Of course, if income recipients are sufficiently rational, the fact that government spent a large part of the revenues on income transfers does not necessarily mean that it indirectly spent it on consumption. Private individuals might increase their savings when faced with such windfall incomes. However, household savings have remained fairly stable at around 10 per cent of net national income (Eizenga, 1983). It seems, therefore, that consumers have not been all that rational, or at least that their effective time horizons have prevented them from being so. Figure 3.3 shows the pattern of consumption.

In addition, net public capital spending decreased somewhat, and on top of that the public sector started to run larger budget deficits just as

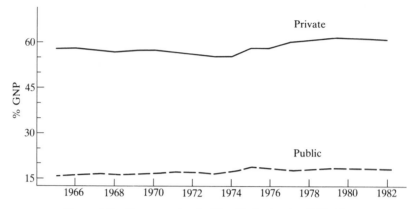

Figure 3.3   Consumption in The Netherlands, 1965–82.
Source: De Nederlandsche Bank, *Kwartaalconfrontatie Middelen en Beste-dingen*.

gas revenues approached their maximum. A channel by which some of the gas proceeds may have been saved is through the balance of payments. This channel will be highlighted in section 5. For now, the general conclusion is that gas revenues have tended to be put to consumption purposes. A mix of traded and non-traded goods was purchased.

4   Gas and sectoral structure

The core of the Dutch Disease literature focuses on the decline of the tradables relative to the non-tradables sector, assuming that no compensating action is undertaken by the government. Table 3.2 shows the broad line of developments in sectoral structure in The Netherlands. This table is in volume terms. It appears that the output of manufactures has grown somewhat more rapidly than that of services in 1963–73. In value terms services have grown slightly faster, because prices of services have tended to rise more (*Central Economic Plan*, Appendices D5/6). The latter development has become much more pronounced in the period after the first oil price rise (1973–8), as services grew relative to manufacturing both in value and in volume terms.

The pattern of services vs. manufacturing up to about 1977 was not peculiar to The Netherlands. Albeit taking off from different starting levels, similar developments occurred in other EC countries (EC, Basic Statistics). Belgium's experience is very similar to the Dutch, even

Table 3.2 Production volume: composition and growth by sector, 1963–83

	Share 1980 %	1963/73	1974/8	1979/83
		(average *annual* % change)		
1 Agriculture	4.2	3.5	2.7	4.5
2 Animal Products	0.3	4.0	1.0	3.0
3 Other Food	2.0	3.5	2.4	2.3
4 Beverages, Tobacco	1.6	7.5	3.2	4.3
5 Textiles, Clothing, Footwear, Leather	0.9	−0.5	−5.5	−4.7
6 Paper and Printing	2.4	4.0	4.2	−0.4
7 Wood and Construction Materials	1.6	5.0	−0.4	−4.2
8 Chemicals, Plastics, Rubber	2.8	12.0	2.7	2.7
9 Basic Metals	0.9	9.5	−0.8	−1.4
10 Metal Products, Precision Instruments	3.9	5.5	1.0	−0.6
11 Electrical Equipment	2.6	8.0	2.6	3.4
12 Transport Equipment	1.3	5.0	−3.2	0.1
13 Oil Refining	1.4	9.0	−1.9	−3.3
2–13 Manufacturing	21.7	6.5	0.9	0.3
14 Mining (including Natural Gas)	6.9	11.0	0.8	−2.4
15 Electricity, Gas and Water	2.6	13.5	4.2	0.5
2–15 Industry	31.2	7.0	1.1	−0.3
16 Construction	8.5	3.0	0.0	−4.4
17 Owner-occupied Dwellings	6.0	3.0	2.4	4.0
18 Distribution	15.2	5.5	4.3	−0.9
19 Sea and Air Transport	1.3	2.5	2.8	0.1
20 Other Transport and Communication	6.5	6.0	3.6	2.3
21 Banking and Insurance	5.8	8.0	4.1	2.8
22 Medical and Veterinary Services	6.9	6.0	4.7	2.7
23 Other Services	14.4	3.0	3.0	1.3
17–23 Services	56.1	5.0	3.8	1.4
Total private sector	100.0	5.7	2.9	0.8

Source: Own calculations based on Central Planning Bureau, *Central Economic Plans*, 1979, 1984.

though Belgium has not enjoyed an energy boom. This changed around 1978. The decline of Dutch manufacturing accelerated, and the international discussion of the Dutch Disease began (*The Economist*, 1977; OECD, 1978).

The crucial separation in that literature does not run between services and manufacturing. It is drawn between traded and non-traded goods. Most Dutch manufacturing is indeed involved in exporting, or is at least exposed to import competition.[5] It is difficult to divide total services into traded and non-traded services. An attempt has been made by the Scientific Council for Government Policy (WRR, 1980, p. 42). They select as internationally orientated services the categories 18, 19 and 20: Trade, Transport and Communication. Agriculture should also be counted as a tradables sector, whereas Electricity, Gas and Water and Construction are largely non-traded.

The following picture emerges. Before the first oil crisis the output of tradables as well as non-tradables grew considerably. Beverages and Tobacco, Chemicals, Basic Metals and Oil Refining were particularly successful. Textiles and Clothing lost ground as import penetration was high in this sector (Kol and Mennes, 1980, Table 2). Notice that the successful sectors tended to be energy-intensive and labour-extensive, whereas the opposite was true of declining sectors. Services show a general growth. Agriculture and Construction lost some ground, while Electricity and Gas thrived.

After the oil price explosion of 1973/4 these patterns change. First, there is an across-the-board decline in growth rates. The decline is generally stronger in tradables than in non-tradables. Exceptions on the tradables side are Agriculture, Food and Beverages, and traded services. Non-tradables appear more sheltered from decline. The post-1979 period presents basically similar developments, except that the traded services join in the general decline of tradables. The decline was least in Agriculture, Food and Beverages, Chemicals and Electrical Equipment.

The Dutch experience is thus characterized by a squeeze on tradables in favour of non-tradables. What are the main causes of this development? Is it the standard Dutch Disease case of a boom in a tradables sub-sector, which squeezes traded production by raising the relative price of non-traded goods? One major ingredient has already been identified above: a significant part of gas revenues was spent on non-tradables. The next question is whether this fed through via an appreciation of the real exchange rate to a loss of domestic and export markets. Events on the export side will now be examined in some detail. Since those on the import competing front are very similar, they will be treated only briefly afterwards.

Some insight into Dutch export performance is given by figures 3.4 and 3.5. The steady gain in market share, which had already started before 1965, came to a sudden halt in 1973/4. Both graphs in figure 3.4 are in volume terms so as to eliminate some of the effects of price fluctuations following the oil crises.[6]

The dramatic loss of market share (about 15 per cent in 5 years) of course stimulated research and discussion in The Netherlands (Gerards and Jager, 1980; Groot and Janssen, 1980; Brakman et al., 1982). Two strands of that literature are of relevance here. The first concentrated on the role of the exchange rate in the market loss. The second argued that changes in the product composition of Dutch exports, brought about by the availability of cheap gas in the 1960s, may have played a special role in the overall export performance.

The upsurge of the guilder after the collapse of the world's system of stable exchange rates in the early 1970s is shown in figure 3.5. There has been little formal empirical research into the relationship between natural gas and the exchange rate. The guilder rate is very much a result of exchange rate policy, which links the guilder to the Deutschmark (section 5). The Central Bank has always commented that this policy has been successful thanks to the availability of gas with its present and

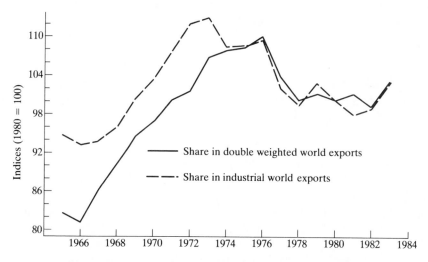

Figure 3.4   Dutch goods export market shares, 1965–83.
Source: *Central Economic Plan*, 1984; IMF *International Financial Statistics*.
Note: Double weighting refers to geographical and product composition weighting of Dutch goods exports, and is applied in order to remove these effects so as to leave only the price competitiveness effect.

Figure 3.5   Dutch price competitiveness and the exchange rate, 1965–83.
Source: *Central Economic Plan*, 1984.
Note: Double weighting: see note to figure 3.4.

expected future effects on the current account.[7] I shall adopt that relationship in this paper, forgoing any attempt to determine exactly how much of the appreciation is due to gas and how much to other causes. This also implies that I shall not examine in detail the exact timing of appreciations (cf. Sheffrin and Russell, 1984), or the determinants of the long-run equilibrium value of the guilder. The actual upsurge of the guilder continued throughout the 1970s, and came to an end only in 1979 as the upward move of the dollar began.

The price variable which is relevant for export competitiveness is not the nominal exchange rate, but the relative price which Dutch exporters charge on foreign markets. In order to concentrate on these price effects, figure 3.5 shows the relative effective export price, weighted by the geographical distribution and product composition of Dutch exports. The weighting is meant to remove effects on export performance which are due to the particular composition of the markets on which the Dutch operate, and the particular set of products they sell. One should, however, not grant the resulting double weighted statistics too much significance in *explaining* export performance. That is because some of the market gains or losses to be explained are already reflected in the statistic via their presence in the weights. Double weighted variables will only be used in a *descriptive* fashion.[8]

Keeping this *caveat* in mind, figures 3.4 and 3.5 do appear to express the main conclusions of the Dutch discussion on export performance.[9] Up to 1973, Dutch exports gained market share because of generally positive influences from all three factors: geographical distribution, product composition and price competitiveness. The price factor tended to be dominant, which can be recognized in the similar slopes of both market share curves in figure 3.4.

After 1973, price competitiveness continued to exert a positive influence up to 1976, whereupon it suddenly turned to the opposite. The deterioration in price competitiveness hampered exports in the mid-to-late 1970s. Later, there was a distinct improvement of the price factor, but the earlier adverse circumstances remained a handicap for Dutch exporters.[10] Losses of competitiveness and market share have lagged effects as well. The decline between 1973 and 1977 was partly due also to stagnation in the EC, which is the main trading area of The Netherlands, and to the German recession in particular.

The contribution of the product composition of exports requires separate attention. The reactions of different product categories to oil price rises vary greatly. Strong reactions and heavy fluctuations occur, especially in energy-intensive sectors. This is connected to large-scale international inventory movements in sectors such as primary energy, chemicals and oil products. The Dutch relative concentration in these sectors made a substantial positive contribution to export shares just before and during the oil crises, but a negative contribution just afterwards. Apart from the temporary fluctuations, it seems that in volume terms the typical energy-intensive sectors have not prospered in the 1970s and early 1980s. In value terms they did better, despite major price substitution effects away from these products on the demand side. Still, the energy-intensity of Dutch industry (excluding gas of course) has *with hindsight* not been beneficial during that period.[11] In the next section this will be evaluated from a policy point of view.

The relationship between price competitiveness and *import* competition was similar to that in the export field, although the nominal effective appreciation relative to import competitors was smaller than that relative to export competitors (De Nederlandsche Bank, *Quarterly Statistics 1981*, No. 1). As the mirror image of increasing export market shares, import penetration was already rising in the 1960s (Groot and

Janssen, 1980; Kol and Mennes, 1980). This was not discouraged by the government, since it was seen as part of a general movement towards an improved international allocation of production. For example, labour-intensive sectors such as textiles were slowly, reluctantly, but steadily given up to the low-wage countries. These ideas were particularly alive in the 1960s as The Netherlands enjoyed virtually full employment.

Increasing imports were not only a consequence of price effects. The expansionary fiscal policy stance (table 3.1) fed through to imports of a mainly consumptive nature. For example, a major factor behind the deteriorating invisibles balance (figure 3.1) was the sharp rise of foreign travel by Dutch citizens.

Figure 3.5 leaves one puzzle. Despite a continuously hardening guilder, price competitiveness for prolonged periods improved rather than deteriorated. This begs the question of export price setting.[12] In order to see the significance of this question, return for a moment to the standard theory of the Dutch Disease. As an optimal reallocation of resources, the tradables sector declines relative to the non-tradables sector. This is brought about by a relative price rise of non-traded goods, which initially entails a higher traded product wage (so lower profitability in that sector), and a lower non-traded product wage (higher profitability). This stimulates the shift of labour from tradables to non-tradables. If wages and prices are flexible, they will adapt so as to bring about an equilibrium with full employment, a larger non-tradables sector with more employment and a smaller tradables sector with less employment than before the gas boom. If, however, wages and prices are *not* sufficiently flexible, there exists a risk that profitability in the traded sector will *decline* more than necessary, and that profitability in the non-traded sector will not *rise* enough to absorb all the labour shed in the tradables sector (van Wijnbergen, 1984b,c,d).

Broadly speaking, this is indeed what has happened in The Netherlands. The findings of Driehuis' (1975) study of wage formation in The Netherlands can be summarized as follows (see also van den Beld, 1978). In the 1960s, wages became virtually completely indexed to the Consumer Price Index (CPI), which contained indirect taxes and the cost of household energy consumption. Increments in direct taxes and employees' social security contributions tended to be passed on in higher wage claims throughout the economy. In the generally central-ized wage bargaining process, an aggregate indicator of labour produc-tivity played a central role. This put upward pressure on product wages in all but the most productive sectors. Even productivity in the natural gas sector, where employment is minimal and production very high, was a constituent of the productivity indicator. In addition, employers' contributions to social security increased steadily, thus contributing to the rise in total labour costs.

This process, which originated in the 1960s, remained in operation throughout most of the 1970s. The implications for the diagnosis of unemployment, and for the medicine one could successfully prescribe, will be further analysed in section 5. Here, the consequences of the rigidities for profitability will be described.

If there are upward pressures on labour costs, which cannot be passed on in higher sales prices, there are several possible consequences for a firm faced with this problem. First, it can make labour-saving invest-ments so as to increase labour productivity and decrease unit labour costs. Second, if an increasing labour share in value-added causes the firm to incur losses, it can absorb these losses by borrowing or by temporarily eating into its reserves. These two strategies will only be followed if the firm expects a future reversal of these temporarily adverse circumstances. If a firm does not have sufficient confidence in the likelihood of sound returns in the future, or if the short-run liquidity pressure caused by the lack of profitability becomes too heavy, then it will go out of business or leave the country.[13]

In order to get some insight into what has happened to profitability in Dutch manufacturing, I follow Sachs (1983), and decompose changes in the labour share of value-added into three components:

$$\dot{s}_L = (\dot{w} - \dot{p}_c) - (\dot{y} - \dot{l}) + (\dot{p}_c - \dot{p}_y) \tag{1}$$

where s_L denotes the labour share, w the nominal hourly wage rate, p_c the CPI, l total hours worked, y net value added and p_y the value added deflator. Dots denote annual rates of change. The first term gives an impression of developments on the wage formation side. The second expresses the contribution of labour productivity. The third, which I call the 'composite term', is a variable which covers 'changes from several sources: supply shocks, in which input prices change in real terms; changes in indirect tax rates; changes in exchange rates, which vary prices of non-traded goods relative to manufacturing tradables; and demand shifts away from or toward manufacturing' (Sachs, 1983).

In the Dutch case, the composite term covers selling-price pressure from foreign competition due to the rising guilder, influences from changing demand patterns and indirect taxes. Of course, only part of these phenomena is caused by the impact of gas on spending behaviour and the exchange rate.

The result of the decomposition is shown in figure 3.6. The trend rise of real labour costs (deflated by the CPI and including employers' social security contributions) throughout the 1960s and 1970s was initially compensated by improving labour productivity. In combination with a moderate upward trend in the composite term, the labour share in value-added increased slowly but steadily. It would be interesting to follow Sachs (1983) and decompose the three factors in figure 3.6 into

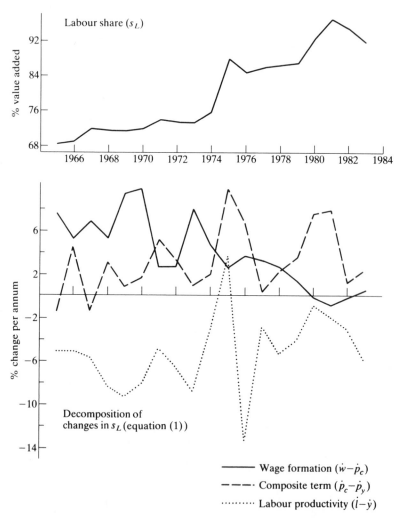

Figure 3.6 Labour's share in Dutch manufacturing value-added, 1965–83.
Source: *Central Economic Plans*, 1979, 1984; own calculations 1965–73.
Note: Definition of labour share: see table 3.3.

trend and cycle components. Since, however, the Dutch economy has experienced more than moderate structural change over the 1970s, this would be a difficult venture. For now, I try to interpret the actual patterns as shown in the figure.

The improvement of labour productivity in the 1960s was a result of labour-saving investments. However, in 1975 the labour share jumped by more than 10 per cent. This was caused by a combination of cyclical capacity underutilization, labour cost rises and an increasing influence from the composite term. This reflects rapid structural change in the real and nominal economy, consisting partly of the effects addressed in this book. Until 1979, the labour share remained fairly stable at 85 per cent. A slowdown of the improvements in labour productivity and an intensified cost/price squeeze were responsible.

Table 3.3   Labour's share in value-added, 1964–83

	1964/8	1969/73	1974/8	1979/83
	(average % of total value-added)			
Manufacturing	72.5	74.5	84	92
Services	75	78.5	79	74

Labour's share equals total labour cost including employers' contributions to social security and imputed income of self-employed, divided by net value-added at factor cost.

Source: Central Planning Bureau, *Central Economic Plans*, 1979, 1984.

The second oil crisis brought another jump, this time to a historic high of 96 per cent.[14] A productivity slowdown and the composite term are to blame. Labour cost restraint was not sufficient to keep the share from rising. Only as productivity increased and cost–price squeeze effects declined by 1982/3 was there some improvement in profitability.

Returning to the options open to firms faced with increasing costs and decreasing sales prices, the following rough sketch seems to capture the Dutch experience. In the 1960s and 1970s, a period of an optimistic business outlook, rising labour costs were met by labour-saving investment.[15] Some erosion of profit margins began, but this was accepted against a background of general optimism. Since profit margins were used as a buffer, and at the same time net investments were still made, this affected the financial structure of the business sector.

Though not the sole reason, the slow process of profit erosion added to an almost continuous rise of the share of debt capital in total capital (figure 3.7; see also den Dunnen, 1981a; Wellink, 1982). As can be seen from table 3.4, labour was shed while production still grew.

The process continued in 1974–83, although with a shift of emphasis. With the optimism concerning future demand prospects fading and financing becoming more and more of a problem, net investment declined.[16] Firms started to leave the market, production growth stagnated, and more labour was shed (see also figure 3.2). Market exit often meant going abroad, as we shall see in section 5 where international capital movements appear in the analysis.

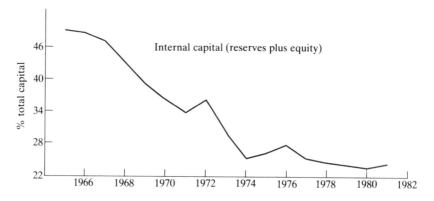

Figure 3.7   The financial structure of Dutch industry, 1965–81.
Source: Central Bureau of Statistics, *Statistisch Zamboek*.
Note: Industrial firms on Amsterdam Stock Exchange, excluding Internationals.

I have emphasized the impact of Dutch Disease type of developments (in combination with expectations of future sales) on the profit and financial position of business for two reasons. First, this phenomenon introduces lags into the channels through which usual Dutch Disease patterns operate. Although we have already observed the usual changes in sectoral structure occurring in the 1970s, there may be more to come. Second, concern for the financial state of the private sector has been one of the factors determining the policies of De Nederlandsche Bank, an aspect of the Dutch Disease in The Netherlands to which we shall turn in the next section.

Table 3.4 Employment: composition and growth by sector, 1963–83

	1980 share %	1963/73	1974/8	1979/83
		(average *annual* % change)		
1 Agriculture	6.8	−3.0	−1.7	−1.1
2 Animal Products	1.2	1.0	−2.0	−3.0
3 Other Food	2.7	−1.5	−2.9	−1.2
4 Beverages, Tobacco	0.5	−1.5	−2.3	−2.6
5 Textiles, Clothing, Footwear, Leather	1.7	−6.0	−9.2	−8.8
6 Paper and Printing	2.7	0.5	−1.3	−1.4
7 Wood and Construction Materials	2.2	−1.0	−3.0	−4.9
8 Chemicals, Plastics, Rubber	2.7	1.5	−3.2	−1.4
9 Basic Metals	1.0	3.5	−1.6	−2.4
10 Metal Products, Precision Instruments	5.0	0.5	−1.9	−2.8
11 Electrical Equipment	2.7	1.0	−2.1	−2.1
12 Transport Equipment	1.7	0.0	−2.2	−3.2
13 Oil Refining	0.2	0.5	−1.5	1.9
2–13 Manufacturing	24.3	−0.5	−2.7	−2.8
14 Mining (including Natural Gas)	0.2	−13.0	−9.2	2.7
15 Electricity, Gas and Water	1.2	1.5	0.0	1.3
2–15 Industry	25.7	−1.0	−2.8	−2.5
16 Construction	11.0	1.0	−0.7	−5.2
17 Owner-Occupied Dwellings	—	—	—	—
18 Distribution	18.8	1.5	−0.3	−1.2
19 Sea and Air Transport	1.0	−5.0	−1.2	−1.1
20 Other Transport and Communication	6.8	1.0	0.7	0.4
21 Banking and Insurance	4.2	4.0	2.1	1.1
22 Medical and Veterinary Services	7.6	6.0	3.9	2.3
23 Other Services	18.1	2.0	1.3	1.0
17–23 Services	56.5	2.0	0.9	0.3
Total private sector	100.0	0.5	−0.3	−1.1

Source: Own calculations based on Central Planning Bureau, *Central Economic Plans*, 1979, 1984.

Jeroen J. M. Kremers

5 Monetary and fiscal policy

In previous sections I have presented the basic economic problems of
The Netherlands: stagnating growth, unemployment and major shifts in
sectoral structure. I have shown that natural gas has had an impact via
two channels. First, via spending effects, which have affected demand
conditions and the real exchange rate. Secondly, via its direct influence
as an intermediate input. Thus the gas seems to be jointly responsible
for the present economic difficulties, of which the origins – it must be
emphasized – lie already in the pre-gas era (wage formation, public
sector behaviour). In this section, I concentrate on policy measures.
Since the major issues concerning the consequences of natural gas in
The Netherlands lie in the field covered by the fiscal policy-maker, I
shall avoid going into too much detail on monetary policy.

5.1 *Monetary policy*

Monetary policy has only a relatively modest role to play in The
Netherlands (den Dunnen, 1973, 1979, 1981a,b). This stems from the
size and openness of the economy. The country is highly dependent on
international trade, and is a supporter of stable exchange rates. It
participated in the 'snake' and is now a member of the EMS. Except for
short-run divergences, this renders monetary conditions dependent on
developments in Germany (see Budd and Warburton, 1981).

The actual attachment of the guilder to the Deutschmark is tighter
than imposed by the EMS. This is a Dutch policy choice. It has been
made in order to provide a stable environment for trade (notice that
Belgium, the second Dutch trading partner, is also in the EMS), and
also to limit the import of inflation by associating with a major
low-inflation economy (figure 3.2 and Kessler, 1980).

In the Dutch Disease context, two aspects of monetary policy require
attention. The first relates to the money supply, the second to the
exchange rate. It has been argued that a resource boom which is met by
a restrictive monetary policy may lead to a recession (Buiter and Purvis,
1983; Neary and van Wijnbergen, 1984). Neary (1985) has called the
mechanism giving rise to this the liquidity effect of a resource boom.
Essentially, if the nominal stock of money remains constant, the
spending effect of the boom is dampened by the increased demand for
real balances. The exact channels depend on the exchange rate regime
and on price and wage adjustment mechanisms.

In The Netherlands, the first oil shock was accommodated by a rising money supply. This may have had a stimulative impact, as witnessed by the temporary increase in output growth after 1975 (figure 3.8). In contrast, the second oil shock was met by contractionary policy. A recession followed, to which monetary policy may have contributed. In both cases, however, fiscal policy worked in similar directions, so that the separate influence of monetary policy should not be overestimated. The exact extent to which these cyclical money supply and output patterns were related remains under discussion (compare, for example, the views of den Dunnen, 1981b, Graph 3, and Bomhoff, 1983, Para. 2.4). In any case, the money supply policy of De Nederlandsche Bank has usually operated carefully and gradually. Rigorous formal empirical evidence with respect to its role in the Dutch Disease context is lacking. Nevertheless, the major choices presented by the gas boom have been made by the fiscal policy-maker.

Before proceeding to those choices, the Central Bank's exchange rate policy requires attention. This policy has been a contentious issue. This is not the place to go into the intricacies of the exchange rate debate.[17] The aspects which are relevant in the resource boom context have been analysed theoretically by Corden (1981a,b). One of the ways to protect the tradables sector from pressure caused by appreciation is simply to prevent the appreciation itself from occurring. Corden calls this exchange rate protection: spend gas export revenues to finance a balance of payments surplus and build up a reserve of foreign assets.

It is clear that such a policy on a large scale is unsustainable in the long run.[18] However, if exchange rate pressure is expected to be only temporary because of the finiteness of the resource boom, it may be sensible to protect the tradables sector during this period of pressure by keeping the exchange rate down and investing in foreign assets. There are sound practical arguments for the possible superiority of that form of protection over alternative forms such as tariffs, quotas and subsidies (administration, reversibility and international commitments; *see* Corden, 1981a).

It is difficult to determine to what extent Dutch exchange rate movements and policy reactions have been connected with the gas boom. The link with the Deutschmark has been the overriding policy goal. Pleadings in favour of guilder depreciation to boost competitiveness have always been countered on two grounds. First, depreciation in the heavily indexed and very open economy was feared to lead to inflation. This would worsen rather than improve competitiveness.[19] Moreover, the real inroads on profitability in the business sector were considered to be the combined responsibility of the fiscal policy-maker

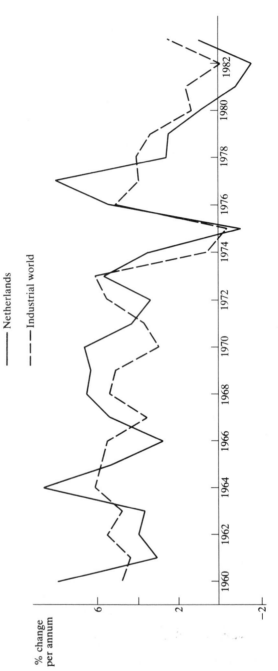

Figure 3.8 Real growth of Dutch and industrial world GDP, 1960–83.
Source: IMF, *International Financial Statistics*.

and the wage formation process. Secondly, depreciation would affect international confidence in the guilder. This confidence is deemed to allow The Netherlands relatively low interest rates, which are considered desirable in view of the financial state of the business sector alluded to above (Duisenberg, 1982).

All this seems to lead to the conclusion that *reverse* exchange rate protection may have been pursued. However, that has not generally been so. Over the 1970s, the guilder depreciated somewhat relative to the Deutschmark. The *effective* appreciation is the result of a collective appreciation of the 'snake' and later the EMS currencies relative to the dollar and others. Periods of upward pressure were followed by periods of downward pressure on the guilder. Thus, only short-run (stabilization) exchange rate protection may to some extent have been provided by De Nederlandsche Bank.

As remarked above, it is difficult to attribute exchange rate and policy developments explicitly to the gas boom. In practice, a resource boom does not result in a surplus *per se*, but rather adds to surpluses and reduces deficits that follow from the general course of events. Figure 3.1 indicates that the positive contribution of gas revenues to a fluctuating current account has increased steadily over the 1970s. During the period of substantial surpluses of the mid-1970s, both the government and De Nederlandsche Bank stimulated a compensating outflow of capital (*see below*). This may create the misleading impression that much of the gas revenues has been invested via the balance of payments, not in foreign reserves but by capital exports. In order to see the falsity of that impression, reconsider briefly the broad lines of spending effects during the 1970s.

Most of the gas revenue accrued to the government. Within the fiscal budget, on balance this came down to growing income payments and transfers. That development was enhanced by increasing budget deficits. There is no evidence that income and transfer recipients have smoothed the gas benefits over time by investing in assets with future returns.[20] On the contrary, the ratio of saving (both private and public) to national income has declined until recently, and consumption has increased accordingly (figure 3.3). The current account surpluses of the mid-1970s, which by definition equal the balance of national saving and national investment, were to a large degree a reflection of stagnating domestic investment (figure 3.9). There is no sign of a significant channelling of gas revenues via government income and transfer payments through increased national saving to investment in foreign assets. At best, therefore, the capital outflow of 1972–77 would *temporarily* have replaced some domestic investment.[21]

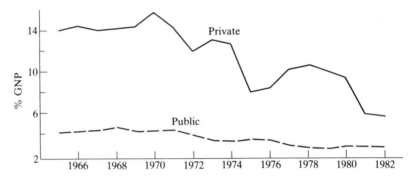

Figure 3.9   Net investment in The Netherlands, 1965–82.
Source: De Nederlandsche Bank, *Kwartaalconfrontatie Middelen en Bestedingen.*
Note: Net investment including Dwellings and Stock changes.

However, the actual form of capital outflow was somewhat of a mixed blessing. A brief look at international financial flows will clarify this point (for details, *see* van Nieuwkerk, 1981; van Nieuwkerk et al., 1982). The current account surplus of 1972–7 was largely reflected in net private capital outflows. These were the outcome of diverging developments. The net outflow was triggered off in 1972/3 by restrictions on foreign purchases of guilder securities in The Netherlands. Subsequently, during 1974–5 Dutch direct investment abroad increased, but only temporarily. The net outflow was sustained from 1975 until 1977 by a *permanent* reduction of foreign direct investment in The Netherlands. Net capital outflows declined by 1977, partly because Dutch direct investment abroad had returned to previous levels. However, the main factor in the 1977 decline in capital outflow was a trend rise in purchases of guilder securities by foreigners after the abolition of restrictions.

Of all the securities available, purchases of bonds increased, whereas those of equity decreased. A large part of the bonds were government securities, issued to finance rising budget deficits. Finally, there was a trend rise in short-run foreign liabilities of Dutch commercial banks, which had already started to increase around 1971.

In conclusion, and admittedly as a rough sketch, it seems that apart from an outflow of foreign direct investment, one underlying current of international financial flows consisted of a substitution of debt capital for risk capital by foreign investors in The Netherlands. Secondly, the rise in the short-run foreign liabilities of commercial banks is interesting in connection with changes in the financial structure of Dutch business in the direction of debt financing. To the extent that the banks have acted as intermediaries in this process, it does not seem surprising that the major Dutch commercial banks have recently suffered from domestic rather than South American or East European defaults. From a national perspective, it is fairly immaterial whether the banks or the business firms have gained from such a scheme. Finally, the shedding by foreigners of risk-bearing involvement in The Netherlands is compatible with the declining profitability described in previous sections of this paper (and with evidence in McKinsey & Co., 1978).

Of course, a net capital outflow remains a net capital outflow, however one may care to look at it. Still, the underlying causes and patterns must affect one's judgement of how successfully gas revenues have been invested abroad. Recall that gas export revenue has been rising continuously, so that its investment abroad should not necessarily have coincided with current account surpluses originating from other sources. There is no evidence that a substantial part of gas revenues has systematically been invested, either abroad or domestically.[22]

5.2 *Fiscal policy*

Most of the picture of the Dutch Disease in The Netherlands has been presented above. This sub-section evaluates the response of the authority responsible for spending the lion's share of gas revenues. It is difficult to evaluate the exact effects of natural gas on the economy. Ideally, we should like to be able to peel the gas effects off observed economic developments, and infer what would have happened had the gas been unavailable. This is impossible, due to widespread simultaneity of which the major threads have been sketched above.

One thing we can do, however, is derive the optimal response of policy to the availability of gas from an application of Dutch Disease theory to actual circumstances in The Netherlands, and contrast the benchmark policy with that actually pursued. If actual and benchmark policies have diverged, theory may offer predictions of the consequences. Should these predictions happen to correspond to what has occurred in reality, then this may lend support to the applicability of the theory and yield some indication of the effects of natural gas on the Dutch economy.

The choice of a social welfare function, which must precede any statement about the optimality of particular policies, is a normative one. I adopt a social welfare function which attaches similar weights to the wellbeing of present and of future generations. Although not all individuals may support such weighting, one can argue that a responsible government should cater for future as well as for present generations.

124 **Jeroen J. M. Kremers**

Thus the usual smoothing arguments following from public sector permanent-income accounting apply (Buiter, 1983). Of course, the results derived from a more myopic social welfare function are likely to be quite different. That may well explain part of the differences between long-term optimal policies and actual Dutch policies.

To begin with, assume the point of view of the policy-maker of the 1960s. The intricacies of the relationship between optimal depletion and spending policies have been explained above. From the perspective of the 1960s, depletion and part of spending policies seem to have been in accordance with intertemporal smoothing prescriptions. Government made the necessary exploitation investments before any revenue accrued, which entails some smoothing. Still, these investments are different in kind from investments that are made while revenues are streaming in, since they are necessary for there ever to be any revenue at all. Dutch governments of those days invested more than that minimum, by directly founding and supporting new industries and by charging low energy prices. In retrospect one may view the initial rapid depletion policy and the stimuli for energy-intensive production as rather unfortunate. From the perspective of the time at which decisions had to be taken, both were sensible. Moreover, it appears that a number of energy-intensive industries which the government helped through the 1970s are now doing very well indeed.

Such is not true, however, of the radical changes in general budgetary policy in the 1970s, of which the origins go back to the late 1960s. From 1960 up to the early 1970s, budgetary policy was executed along the lines of Structural Budget Policy prescriptions (Dixon, 1972; Burger, 1975; Diamond, 1977; den Dunnen, 1981b). This can be summarized by the objective of a long-run rate of growth of the budget deficit in line with the long-run growth of national income, while short-run deficits absorb cyclical shocks in taxation. In principle, therefore, expenditure was kept on trend. Discretionary changes in expenditure were allowed only if financed entirely and immediately by taxation, so that the long-run path of the deficit was unaffected. This policy was designed to exert an automatically stabilizing influence on the economy. The practical use of it made The Netherlands one of the very few countries where budgetary policy has been conducted along *ex ante* and fairly stable rules over a prolonged period of time.[23]

Officially, the policy was abandoned in the 1979 Budget. In practical terms, this had already happened before the mid-1970s. The prime reason was the fact that government spending had to a considerable degree become endogenous to the economic process, whereas Structural Budget Policy requires that expenditure be under control.

The origins of the loss of control lie in the late 1960s. Government started to endogenize spending by initiating an ambitious welfare programme, indexation and legal measures such as minimum wages (CED, 1982; Halberstadt et al., 1982a,b; van der Wielen, 1983). This was done in a period of economic optimism, generated by prosperous growth and expectations of future gas revenues. Research in progress indicates that the shocks to the economy around the 1973/4 oil crisis first brought the effective abandonment of Structural Budget Policy out in the open (for an early result, see Kremers, 1983). Up to then, it still looked as if government could set expenditure at its discretion. The fact that discretion was increasingly slipping was initially veiled by rapid economic growth and the gas revenues.

The mechanisms installed in the late 1960s implied important restrictions on the degrees of freedom of future policy-makers. Because of their substance and open-endedness, the discounted value of those policies later proved a liability that exceeded the discounted value of normal revenues (Le Blanc Committee, 1983). For a correct assessment of Dutch Disease type of developments in The Netherlands, the endogeneity of budgetary policy must not be lost sight of. It has been argued that government embarked on a misguided expansionary fiscal policy in the mid-1970s (e.g., van Wijnbergen, 1984c). Although policy indeed became increasingly expansionary, it was to some extent simply the continuation of a pattern rooted in the 1960s.[24]

The expansionary policy stance was defended on the basis of the view that The Netherlands suffered Keynesian unemployment, due to deficiencies on the demand side. Before examining the appropriateness of the policy itself, first recall how it was executed (section 3 and table 3.1). While relying heavily on boosting consumption demand, special support for industry was provided but at the cost of public saving and investment.

Van Wijnbergen (1984b,c,d) analyses the consequences of a resource boom in a model with real wage rigidity.[25] He finds a considerable risk that under circumstances such as the Dutch an economy will move into a situation of classical unemployment, which is not due to demand deficiencies but rather to a lack of profitability in the business sector. In reality of course unemployment is unlikely to occur in such pure forms. The Netherlands definitely suffered a lack of effective demand due to the world recession of 1974/5. Still, that recession was immediately followed by an international upswing in which The Netherlands did not fully take part. Furthermore, even without the expansionary policy, consumption would have remained fairly strong. Domestic demand slackened because of collapsing investment, which was by itself a *result*

Table 3.5 The shift from private to public sector in The Netherlands, 1963–83

	1963	1973	1983
Distribution of income generated in the market sector	(% of value added by the market sector)		
a Market sector payments and transfers to the public sector[a]	38	48½	50½
b Disposable income of the market sector	62	51½	49½
labour income	50½	42½	36
capital income[b]	11½	9	13½
Public sector expenditure and revenues, on a trans-actions basis (after deduction of relevant taxes and social insurance contributions)	(% of value added by the market sector)		
1. Expenditure			
a Expenditure on incomes			
Wage and salary bill[c]	14½	21	24½
Benefits under General Old Age Pensions Act and General Widows' and Orphans' Pensions Act	5	7½	9
Benefits under unemployment schemes	1	1½	6
Benefits under other schemes covering loss of income	3	7½	11½
Minus taxes and social insurance contributions in respect of expenditure on income[d]	−4	−10½	−17½
Net expenditure on incomes	19½	27	33½
economically active persons	11½	14½	15
economically non-active persons	8	12½	18½
b Expenditure on goods and services[e]	13	11½	13
c Corrections to income distribution[f]	4	4	5½
d Interest payments on national debt	2½	3	6½
e Income transfers abroad (net)	—	—	½
f Other expenditure[g]	3½	4	3
Total (*a* to *f*)	42½	49½	62
2. Receipts from the market sector	38	48½	50½
3. Financial deficit (−) (2 − 1)	−4½	−1	−11½

continued

[a] Taxes and social insurance contributions, personal sector income transfers, public sector factor income (including natural gas revenues). Capital transfers to industry and cost-price-reducing subsidies, as well as receipts on account of corrections to income distribution, have been deducted from the payments and transfers.

	1963	1973	1983
Income recipients in the public sector and in the market sector		(000)	
1. Economically active persons in the public sector[h]			
a Public authorities and social insurance funds	490	570	690
b Semi-public sector	115	250	380
Total (a + b)	605	820	1,070
2. Economically non-active persons in the public sector receiving benefits under:			
a General Old Age Pensions Act and General Widows' and Orphans' Pensions Act	995	1,285	1,555
b Incapacity for work benefit schemes	120	280	590
c Sickness benefit schemes	170	290	245
d Unemployment benefit schemes	75	115	575
e Early retirement schemes			25
f Sheltered Employment Act, Painters, Sculptors and Allied Artists Regulation, and social assistance[i]	30	100	145
Total (a to f)	1,390	2,070	3,135
3. Income recipients in the public sector (1 + 2)	1,995	2,890	4,205
4. Income recipients in the market sector[h]	3,560	3,575	3,240
5. Total number of income recipients (3 + 4)	5,555	6,465	7,445
economically active persons	4,165	4,395	4,310
economically non-active persons	1,390	2,070	3,135

[b] Disposable income also includes capital transfers to industry, such as subsidies under the Act on the Investment Account.

[c] Including the wage and salary bill of the semi-public sector (non-commercial services in the areas of health care, social welfare, culture and recreation). Excluding expenditure on account of schemes covering loss of income (such as sickness and incapacity for work benefit schemes) and corrections to income distribution (such as family allowances).

[d] Relevant direct taxes and social insurance contributions, and an imputed part of personal sector income transfers to the public sector.

[e] Including the semi-public sector's expenditure on goods and services bought.

[f] Comprises mainly family allowances (including those for public servants), student grants, tenant-related rent subsidies and part of social assistance payments.

[g] Comprises public sector lending (including public housing loans), and net capital transfers to the personal sector, pension funds and abroad.

[h] Excluding absence due to sickness expressed in man-years.

[i] Put at half the number of recipients of social assistance under 65 years of age living at home who periodically receive benefits (other than under Government group schemes).

Source: De Nederlandsche Bank, *Annual Report* 1983.

of the lack of immediate profitability and the lack of profitable demand prospects. Under these circumstances, expansionary fiscal policy boosting demand tends to put additional upward pressure on the real exchange rate, if non-tradables constitute a relatively large share of the demand boost. The formal analysis of van Wijnbergen shows that such demand policy will not facilitate the necessary adjustments of the economy, but only exacerbate the difficulties.

The temporary nature of the gas boom, the size of the Dutch economy and its dependence on international trade provide reasons for temporary government support to industry. The Dutch Disease literature stresses the optimality of a reallocation of resources from tradables to non-tradables, but this is of course very much a matter of degree. Especially when the boom is temporary one should be careful with such a reallocation, even if gas revenues are being invested abroad with high returns (which was not really the case in The Netherlands). For a small country, it is quite a risk to step out of rapidly developing industries if it would like to or might have to step back in later (this is the learning-by-doing argument of van Wijnbergen, 1984a). It depends on the exact policy objectives and on practical opportunities what type of support for industry is preferable. In The Netherlands, industrial policy has had some success. Though criticized for a lack of strategic coherence and a generally defensive attitude (WRR, 1980; Wagner Committee, 1981; Koekkoek et al., 1981), it has helped some sectors with a future through the difficult 1970s (Steel, Agriculture, Chemicals, Car Manufacturing). However, it has been argued to have been too late, too little, and to have been carried out at the cost of public investment.

If government is particularly concerned about employment, labour cost subsidies are an effective tool. Against this background, Dutch fiscal policy was ineffective in a double sense. Expansionary policy could have been expected to exacerbate the difficulties. In addition, it was accompanied not by labour cost *subsidies* mimicking the required wage adjustments, but if anything by *taxation* of work. Social security contributions rose rapidly, income differences and margins between remuneration for activity and non-activity declined. An abundance of regulations and the institution of a minimum wage operated in the same direction. Thus both the incentive to hire labour and the incentive to work were undermined (Corden, 1984, fn. 14). As a result, both the number of economically active and the number of economically inactive income-recipients in the public sector rose dramatically (table 3.5). Only *after* restoration of the supply side could expansionary policies have been expected to produce lasting positive results.

Taken together with the unfit financial state of the private sector, it has become clear that the fiscal policies initiated in the late 1960s are unsustainable. Present policy seems to be focusing on restoring balance to the public finances, and on the supply side of the economy. This is not the place for an evaluation of present policies, but a general acceptance of the unsustainability of past patterns seems an essential step towards restoring equilibrium. The role of natural gas in the process has been highlighted in this paper. The concluding section briefly strikes a balance.

6 Conclusion

I have argued that alternative ways of spending Dutch gas revenues would have been preferable in order to smooth the benefits of the gas windfall over time, and I have highlighted the role of the gas boom in recent adverse experiences. Nevertheless, it should be emphasized that the gas has helped The Netherlands to develop one of the most advanced welfare systems in the world. This paper has indicated some basic points on which developments may have gone too far, but in no way wishes to criticize the foundations of the system. On the contrary, it is well worth an effective defence which, as indicated in the introduction, will not have to wait until the next century. The fundamental problems of the Dutch economy now seem to be generally acknowledged, which should already lead some way to a solution.

Apart from agreement on the basic causes of the current difficulties, four more grounds for an optimistic conclusion can be mentioned. First, government has not supported too many 'sunset' industries; the Dutch economy now includes some very competitive sectors. Secondly, the welfare system itself is an important asset in cushioning the social consequences of the present difficult transitional period. Thirdly, large gas reserves are still available. Finally, there is one learning-by-doing argument which has been ignored in the Dutch Disease literature, and that is the experience of going through the Disease itself.

NOTES

* For valuable suggestions and comments I am grateful to J. Black, J. S. Cramer, J. Frijns, H. van Gemert, Th. van de Klundert, J. Muellbauer, J. P. Neary, D. Neven, F. Nivard, M. Scott, and participants of the Conference on Natural Resources and the Macroeconomy at the Centre for Economic Policy Research in London, June 1985. Errors are mine.

1 Detailed introductions can be found in den Dunnen (1981a), *The Economist* (1982) and Posthumus (1983).

2 On the contrary. As a result of the rapid conversion of energy consumption to gas, the government decided to close the country's coal mines. This cost about 50,000 jobs. Within a brief period, this would have added more than 20 per cent unemployment in the mining region of Limburg. The government used gas revenues to set up alternative employment. The main projects were DSM, now one of Europe's largest chemical companies, and Volvo Cars. The blow of the mine closures could thus be accommodated although the welfare system has had to carry a substantial part of the cost. (For an interesting account of this regional policy in English, see European Commission, 1978). Even though this employment effect is nothing like a 'negative resource allocation' effect, the assumption that the gas sector did not put pressure on the labour market seems warranted. The coal mine closures can be categorized as a direct substitution effect between gas and coal in household and business energy consumption.

3 Models such as that of Neary and Purvis (1983), in which the real exchange rate overshoots due to real inertia of factor movements, do not seem applicable here.

4 i.e., the world market price of oil of the same calorific content as some quantity of gas, plus a premium for some advantages of natural gas over oil.

5 Market penetration for industry as a whole (defined as the ratio of imports over domestic absorption) has increased from 42 to 50 per cent in 1970–82. Penetration in 1978 was more than 25 per cent for each subsector of industry, except Animal Products (18.3 per cent) (Kol and Mennes, 1980).

6 The volume of gas exports is included. Without gas, the basic patterns are very similar, except that after 1980 somewhat higher gains are made (De Nederlandsche Bank, *Annual Report* 1982, p. 57). Of course market shares in value terms also have their significance, especially as far as profitability is concerned. This issue will be followed up shortly.

7 The current account effects of the gas which are shown in figure 3.1 do not contain direct energy import-substitution effects. Weitenberg (1975) and Brouwer (1979) show that import-substitution effects far exceeded gas export revenues in the 1970s.

8 In addition, effective exchange rates can differ by sector. Anema and Jepma (1978) calculate that the effective rate using the relevant sector weights for Fuels and Lubricants increased by 2 per cent between 1971 and 1976, whereas the increment for Beverages and Tobacco amounted to 23 per cent. The other sectors cover the range in between. For analysing sectoral performance, the aggregate numbers appear of limited value.

9 The test statistics quoted in the three mentioned papers do not give much insight into the econometric rigour of the empirical results. It seems likely that in this type of macroeconometrics simultaneity, exogeneity and dynamics are major issues. I shall only quote results which the three studies have in common, and which in broad lines seem supported by evidence from other sources.

10 If one excludes gas, the improvement in price competitiveness after 1978 is less marked (figure 3.5), and some share of the world market is regained (figure 3.4, and note 6).

11 Notice in table 3.2 how remarkably well Dutch Chemicals have fared in the 1970s. Adverse developments occurred mainly in Steel, Transport Equipment and Oil Refining. All these sectors, including Chemicals, suffered from overcapacity.

12 The argument that follows goes through for import competition as well.

13 The two important variables are therefore total value-added and its distribution. As argued below, expectations of future growth in value-added kept business investment going in the 1960s, whereas they had a negative impact after the early 1970s. Apart from distributive aspects, the gas also affected value-added directly via asymmetric effects of exchange rate appreciation on export and import prices. The latter tended to decrease more slowly than export prices increased in the first half of the 1970s, making imports of raw materials relatively expensive and thus reducing value-added (de Ridder, 1978; Kessler, 1980). This was reversed in the second half (De Nederlandsche Bank *Quarterly Statistics*, December 1981, p. 7).

14 The UK, in a similar energy position to The Netherlands, seems to have experienced similar jumps of the labour share in manufacturing value-added after the two oil crises (Buiter and Miller, 1983). Because of differences in measurement and institutions, international comparisons should be made with care. The level of the labour share in Dutch manufacturing exceeded that of any major OECD country in the 1960s, and its subsequent rate of growth exceeded those in the countries with the highest initial levels (Sachs, 1983; Duisenberg, 1984). Van Laer (1981) argues that the non-labour share in Dutch manufacturing was less than half that in the UK in 1976–80 (both excluding the energy sectors).

15 As explained above, gas was sold cheaply as an input to industry. This not only changed the sectoral structure, but also the production process in general. In a three-factor model, Magnus (1979) shows that energy was a substitute for unskilled labour and a complement to capital in Dutch enterprises (excluding the energy sector itself) during the period 1950–78. If this was also true for manufacturing (which seems most likely), it helps explain high labour productivity growth in an environment of high labour and low energy costs. In view of the figures in table 3.4, it seems that government has indirectly been stimulating the movement of labour out of manufacturing into services. Indeed, van Gemert et al. (1983) argue that whereas the reaction to the availability of domestic energy of a shift away from manufacturing into services is by itself a normal phenomenon, the intensity of that reaction has been particularly strong in The Netherlands. The OECD is the reference group.

16 Instead of increasing capacity, firms improved utilization rates.

17 A survey of the exchange rate debate has been provided by Szasz (1981). The original of Kessler (1980) offers a defence of the Central Bank's policy in English by one of its directors (paper presented at the Conference on Employment Policy and Employment Theory, Groningen, 1980). See also den Dunnen (1979, 1981a,b) and the Bank's annual reports.

18 Moreover, Corden (1981a) shows that there are superior ways of protecting a lagging tradables sector. Essentially, this follows from the fact that exchange rate protection not only benefits the lagging tradables sector, but also boosts the booming sector.

19 Central Bank President Dr Zijlstra warned that depreciation would be a mixed blessing, comparing the freedom gained by depreciation with the freedom of a helter-skelter with uniform acceleration (cf. the experience of Indonesia, van Wijnbergen, 1984b, and model results for The Netherlands, Knoester, 1980, pp. 162–7).

20 An exception is the temporary boom on the housing market.

21 An exception is the period 1973–4, when there was a temporary increase in the private savings ratio. This led to increased direct investment abroad, but the amounts involved – though substantial in absolute terms – are minor compared to

total gas revenues. In 1974–5, the Dutch direct investment capital outflow was sustained by the collapse of domestic investment.

22 The fact that in 1978/9 The Netherlands was the largest foreign investor in the US (*The Economist*, 1982; Atkinson and Hall, 1983), was more the result of a geographical reallocation of Dutch foreign investment from the EC to the US and of a general withdrawal of foreign direct investment from The Netherlands than anything else (van Nieuwkerk et al., 1982).

23 The German Konjunkturneutrale Öffentliche Haushalt and the American High Employment Budget are comparable, but tend to be used more as indicators than as *ex ante* rules (Sterks, 1984). The Medium Term Financial Strategy of the UK has not yet been used over a prolonged period of time.

24 A variety of constructions served to give what were later realized to be largely autonomous developments an appearance of discretion. In the Budget, expected positive effects of macroeconomic policy were already recorded as revenues before they actually occurred ('inverdieneffecten'). A calculated normal degree of future underexhaustion of budget expenditure was entered as additional revenue ('onderuitputting'). Substantial heads of expenditure were debudgeted. Rates of growth were consistently overpredicted, and gas revenues were more and more treated as current receipts rather than temporary windfalls. All this illustrates a failure to cope with increasing pressure on the Budget.

25 The Dutch Disease literature has formulated the relevant phenomena in an elucidating framework, but not all the ideas themselves are novel. Though in a different terminology, Professor Stevers has been analysing Dutch difficulties exactly along these lines since 1970 in his annual comments on the Budget (Stevers, 1979). It seems hard to argue that policies failed because of a lack of analytical insight at the time.

REFERENCES

Anema W. J. and C. P. Jepma (1978) 'De effectieve wisselkoers als maatstaf voor de opwaardering van de gulden' ('The Effective Exchange Rate as an Indicator for the Appreciation of the Guilder'), *Economisch Statistische Berichten*, **63**, 792–6.

Atkinson F. and S. Hall (1983) *Oil and the British Economy*, London: Croom Helm.

Beld C. A. van den (1978) 'De-industrialization in the Netherlands?', in F. Blackaby (ed.), *De-industrialization*, London: Heinemann, pp. 124–40.

Bomhoff E. J. (1983) *Monetary Uncertainty*, Amsterdam: North-Holland.

Brakman S., C. J. Jepma and S. K. Kuipers (1982) 'The Determination of the Netherlands' Export Performance during the Late 1970s. A Matter of Competitiveness or Export Structure?', *De Economist*, **130**, 360–80.

Brouwer M. (1979) 'Het aardgas en onze economie, zegen of vloek?' ('Natural Gas and our Economy, Blessing or Curse?'), in J. J. Klant et al. (eds), *Samenleving en onderzoek*, Leyden: Stenfert-Kroese, pp. 293–309.

Budd A. P. and P. Warburton (1981) 'Monetary Policy and Exchange Rate Policy in The Netherlands', London Business School, Econometric Forecasting Unit Discussion Paper 91, September.

Buiter W. H. (1983) 'Measurement of the Public Sector Deficit and its Implications for Policy Evaluation and Design'. *International Monetary Fund Staff Papers*, **30**, 306–49.

Buiter W. H. and M. H. Miller (1983) 'Changing the Rules: Economic Consequences of the Thatcher Regime', *Brookings Papers on Economic Activity*.
Buiter W. H. and D. D. Purvis (1982) 'Oil, Disinflation and Export Competitive-
ness: a Model of the Dutch Disease', in J. Bhandari et al. (eds), *Economic
Interdependence and Flexible Exchange Rates*, Cambridge, Mass.: MIT Press.
Burger H. (1975) 'Structural Budget Policy in The Netherlands', *De Economist*, **123**,
329–51.
CED (Commissie Economische Deskundigen SER) (1982) *Rapport economische
groei en financiering publieke sector* (Economic Growth and Financing the
Public Sector), The Hague: SER Publication 21, November.
Corden W. M. (1981a) 'Exchange Rate Protection', in R. N. Cooper et al. (eds),
*The International Monetary System under Flexible Exchange Rates: Global,
Regional and National*, Cambridge, Mass.: Ballinger, pp. 17–34.
Corden W. M. (1981b) 'The Exchange Rate, Monetary Policy and North Sea Oil:
the Economic Theory of the Squeeze on Tradables', in W. A. Eltis et al. (eds),
The Money Supply and the Exchange Rate (Supplement to *Oxford Economic
Papers* – New Series 33), pp. 23–46.
Corden W. M. (1984) 'Booming Sector and Dutch Disease Economics: Survey and
Consolidation', *Oxford Economic Papers*, **36**, 359–60.
Corden W. M. and J. P. Neary (1982) 'Booming Sector and De-industrialisation in a
Small Open Economy', *Economic Journal*, **92**, 825–48.
Diamond J. (1977) 'The New Orthodoxy in Budgetary Planning: a Critical Review of
Dutch Experience', *Public Finance*, **32**, 56–76.
Dixon D. A. (1972) 'Techniques of Fiscal Analysis in The Netherlands', *Internation-
al Monetary Fund Staff Papers*, **19**, 615–46.
Driehuis W. (1975) 'Inflation, Wage Bargaining, Wage Policy and Production
Structure: Theory and Empirical Results for The Netherlands', *De Economist*,
123, 638–79.
Duisenberg W. F. (1982) 'Interest Rates in The Netherlands', De Nederlandsche
Bank *Quarterly Statistics*, December, pp. 97–102.
Duisenberg W. F. (1984) 'De positie van Nederland in international verband' ('The
Position of The Netherlands in an International Perspective'), *Economisch
Statistische Berichten*, **69**, 84–7.
den Dunnen E. (1973) 'Monetary Policy in The Netherlands', in K. Holbik (ed.),
Monetary Policy in Twelve Industrial Countries, Federal Reserve Bank of
Boston, pp. 282–328.
den Dunnen E. (1979) 'Postwar Monetary Policy', *De Economist*, **127**, 21–79.
den Dunnen E. (1981a) 'Dutch Economic and Monetary Problems in the 1970s', in
A. S. Courakis (ed.), *Inflation, Depression and Economic Policy in the West*,
London: Mansell, pp. 181–201.
den Dunnen E. (1981b) 'Long-term Fiscal and Monetary Policies in The Nether-
lands', De Nederlandsche Bank, mimeo.
The Economist (1977) 'Business Brief: the Dutch Disease', 26 November.
The Economist (1982) 'Ruffles on the Calm: a survey of the Dutch Economy', 30
January.
Eizenga W. (1983) 'De ontwikkeling van de besparingen in Nederland' ('The
Development of Savings in The Netherlands'), Leyden University, Centre for
Research in Public Economics Report 83.07.
European Commission (1978) *Regional Development Programmes for The Nether-
lands, 1977–1980*, Regional Policy Series No. 8, Brussels.

134 Jeroen J. M. Kremers

van Gemert H. G., R. J. de Groof and A. J. Markink (1983) 'Werkgelegenheidsstructuren, groei en energie' ('Employment Structures, Growth and Energy'), *Maandschrift Economie*, **47**, 3–14.

Gerards J. and H. Jager (1980) 'De structurele ontwikkeling van de Nederlandse uitvoer' ('The Structural Development of Dutch Exports'), *Economisch Statistische Berichten*, **65**, 64–9.

Groot W. and J. J. L. M. Janssen (1980) 'Goederenuitvoer en -invoer' ('Exports and Imports of Goods'), *Economisch Statistische Berichten*, **65**, 119–25.

Halberstadt V., B. le Blanc, K. Goudswaard and D. Meys (1982a) 'Budget Cutting Policies: Recent Experiences in The Netherlands', Leyden University, Centre for Research in Public Economics Report 82.20, June.

Halberstadt V., K. Goudswaard and B. le Blanc (1982b) 'Current Control Problems in Public Expenditure in Five European Countries', Leyden University, Centre for Research in Public Economics Report 82.28, November.

Kessler G. (1980) 'De invloed van het Nederlandse monetaire beleid en wisselkoersbeleid op de ontwikkeling van de werkgelegenheid' ('The Employment Effects of Dutch Monetary and Exchange Rate Policies'), *Maandschrift Economie*, **45**, 53–80.

Knoester A. (1980) *Over geld en economische politiek* (On Money and Economic Policy), Leyden: Stenfert-Kroese.

Koekkoek K. A., and L. B. M. Mennes (1984) 'Revealed Comparative Advantage in Manufacturing Industry: the Case of The Netherlands', *De Economist*, **132**, 30–48.

Koekkoek K. A., J. Kol and L. B. M. Kennes (1981) 'On Protectionism in The Netherlands', World Bank Staff Working Paper 493, October.

Kol J., and L. B. M. Mennes (1980) 'Nederlandse industrie en internationale concurrentie' ('Dutch Industry and International Competition'), *Economisch Statistische Berichten*, **65**, 1210–16, 1233–8.

Kremers J. J. M. (1983) 'Public Debt Creation in The Netherlands, 1953–1980', *De Economist*, **131**, 196–216.

Laer E.E. van (1981) 'Enkele macro-economische effecten van energiebaten' ('Some Macroeconomic Effects of Energy Revenues'), *Economisch Statistische Berichten*, **66**, 1184–91.

Le Blanc Committee (Studiegroep Begrotingsruimte) (1983) *Zevende Rapport*, The Hague: Staatsuitgeverij.

Lubbers R. F. M. and C. Lemckert (1980) 'The Influence of Natural Gas on the Dutch Economy, in R. T. Griffiths (ed.), *The Economy and Politics of The Netherlands since 1945*, The Hague: Martinus Nijhoff.

Magnus J. R. (1979) 'Substitution between Energy and Non-energy Inputs in The Netherlands 1950–1976', *International Economic Review*, **20**, 465–84.

McKinsey & Co. (1978) Aantrekkelijkheid van Nederland voor buitenlandse beleggers ('The Attractiveness of The Netherlands for Foreign Investors'), October.

Neary J. P. (1985) 'Real and Monetary Aspects of the Dutch Disease', in K. Jungenfeld and D. Hague (eds), *Structural Adjustment in Developed Open Economies*, London: Macmillan.

Neary J. P. and D. D. Purvis (1983) 'Real Adjustment and Exchange Rate Dynamics', in J. A. Frenkel (ed.), *Exchange Rates and International Macroeconomics*, National Bureau of Economic Research, pp. 285–308.

Neary J. P. and S. van Wijnbergen (1984) 'Can an Oil Discovery lead to a Recession? A comment on Eastwood and Venables', *Economic Journal*, **94**, 390–5.

Nieuwkerk M. van (1981) 'De financiering van het betalingsbalanstekort' ('Financing the Balance of Payments Deficit'), in E. den Dunnen et al. (eds), *Zoeklicht op beleid*, Leyden: Stenfert-Kroese, pp. 241–68.

Nieuwkerk M. van, N. P. Driesprong and A. C. J. Stokman (1982) 'Aspecten van de Nederlandse betalingsbalans' ('Aspects of the Dutch Balance of Payments'), *Economisch Statistische Berichten*, **67**, 1224–7, 1254–9, 1280–3, 1278–9.

OECD (1978) *Economic Survey of the Netherlands*, Paris.

Posthumus G. (1983) 'The Netherlands: Financial-Economic Adjustment Policies in the 1970s', in M. de Cecco (ed.), *International Economic Adjustment: Small Countries and the European Monetary System*, Oxford: Blackwell.

Ridder P. B. de (1978) 'Wisselkoers, concurrentiepositie en werkgelegenheid' ('The Exchange Rate, Competitiveness and Employment'), *Economische Statistische Berichten*, **63**, 198–202.

Sachs J. D. (1983) 'Real Wages and Unemployment in the OECD Countries', *Brookings Papers on Economic Activity*, **1**, pp. 255–304.

Sheffrin S. M. and T. Russell (1984) 'Sterling and Oil Discoveries: the Mystery of Nonappreciation', *Journal of International Money and Finance*, **3**, 311–26.

Sterks C. S. M. (1984) 'The Structural Budget Deficit as an Instrument of Fiscal Policy', *De Economist*, **132**, 183–203.

Stevers Th. A. (1979) *Na Prinsjesdag in de Volkskrant* (Comments on the Budgets of the 1970s), Leyden: Stenfert-Kroese.

Szasz A. (1981) 'Het wisselkoersdebat' ('The Exchange Rate Debate'), in E. den Dunnen et al. (eds), *Zoeklicht op beleid*, Leyden: Stenfert-Kroese, pp. 303–23.

Wagner Committee (Adviescommissie inzake het industriebeleid) (1981) *Een nieuw industrieel elan* (*A New industrial Elan*), June, mimeo.

Weitenberg J. (1975) 'De betekenis van het aardgas voor onze economie' ('The Significance of Natural Gas for our Economy'), *Politiek Perspectief*, July/August, 77–88.

Wellink A. H. E. M. (1982) 'Enkele aspecten van de huidige investeringsproblematiek' ('Some Aspects of the Current Investment Problem'), in *De economie van het aanbod*, Preadviezen van de Vereniging voor Staatshuishoudkunde, Leyden: Stenfer-Kroese, pp. 49–80.

WRR (Scientific Council for Government Policy) (1980) *Plaats en toekmost van de Nederlandse industrie* (The Position and Future of Dutch Industry), The Hague: Staatsuitgeverij.

Wieleman F. G. M. (1982) 'De economische betekenis van nederlands aardgas' ('The Economic Significance of Dutch Natural Gas'), Erasmus University Rotterdam, Institute for Economic Research Discussion Paper 8218/G, October (abbr. *Economisch Statistische Berichten*, **67**, 1012–6).

Wielen H. van der (1983) 'The Public Sector's Interaction with the Market Sector in The Netherlands', in C. L. Taylor (ed.), *Why Governments Grow – Measuring Public Sector Size*, Beverly Hills, Sage, pp. 60–72.

van Wijnbergen S. (1984a) 'The "Dutch Disease": a Disease After All?', *Economic Journal*, **94**, 41–55.

van Wijnbergen S. (1984b) 'Inflation, Employment and the Dutch Disease in Oil-exporting Countries: a Short-run Disequilibrium Analysis', *Quarterly Journal of Economics*, **99**, 233–50.

van Wijnbergen S. (1984c) 'Oil Discoveries, Intertemporal Adjustment and Public Policy', University of Warwick, Development Economics Research Centre Discussion Paper 46, May.

van Wijnbergen S. (1984d) 'Government Deficits, Private Investment, Employment and the Current Account under Different Employment Regimes: an Intertemporal Disequilibrium Analysis', University of Warwick, Development Economics Research Centre Discussion Paper 47, May.

Withagen C. (1982) 'The Exploitation of Dutch Natural Gas: an Alternative Approach', *De Economist*, **130**, 71–100.

COMMENT   JEAN M. G. FRIJNS

The paper by Jeroen Kremers is an attempt to confront the theoretical results of the Dutch Disease literature with the actual growth path of the Dutch economy during the period that gas revenues boomed. From his rather complete description of the structural changes in this economy he concludes that these appear to be in remarkable accordance with strands of Dutch Disease theory. I tend to agree with this conclusion though in my opinion this disease can only to a small extent be attributed to the additional wealth effect of the higher oil and gas prices. Much more important were the economic effects of a booming government sector. To highlight this point I will limit myself to a much more sketchy picture than the one presented by Jeroen Kremers.

I will distinguish three sub-periods: 1963–73, 1973–9 and the period from 1980 onwards. The second sub-period most clearly shows the characteristics of what has been labelled Dutch Disease; economic growth in the latter sub-period has been dominated by other factors such as depressed world demand, restrictive fiscal policy, etc.

The first sub-period, 1963–73

The Dutch economy enjoyed high growth rates in this sub-period with booming investment rates in the intermediate industries (refining, chemicals and base metals) leading the way. In the Rotterdam seaport region a vast petrochemical complex was built up in this period. (See, for example, van den Beld and Middelhoek, 1971), who constructed a two-sector model of the Dutch economy to demonstrate the resource-movement effects of this booming sector. Also important was the discovery of a vast natural gas field near Groningen; however, initially gas was more important as a cheap energy input than as a cash-cow: on average annual government revenues from gas amounted to less than 0.5 per cent of GDP. On the energy-consuming side, gas was mainly used as a substitute for coal, not for oil. In fact national oil consumption increased sharply between 1963 and 1973, thus leaving the country quite vulnerable to the oil price shocks in 1973 and 1974.

A further consequence of the high growth rates during the sixties was an increase in labour market tensions leading to rising wage claims and even higher wage expectations.

The sub-period 1974–9

The oil price shock in 1973–4 hit the Dutch economy hard, given the important role of oil as an intermediate input. In addition, workers did not show much restraint in their wage claims but instead tried to pass on the higher costs of living (gasoline, electricity, etc.) into higher wages. The linking of gas prices to the oil price further increased energy and labour costs. I agree with Jeroen Kremers that these consequences of higher oil and gas prices have been often overlooked: for the Dutch economy this is especially important, since taken as a whole higher gas revenues are to a large degree matched by higher costs of imported oil. In fact, during the seventies the Dutch manufacturing sector surely suffered from a severe supply-side shock, in the form of higher energy prices, as sketched by, for example, Bruno and Sachs (1985).

The linking of gas prices to the sharply increasing oil price implied higher gas revenues for the government. Furthermore, total gas exports increased by 60 per cent between 1973 and 1979, thus adding to total government revenues. The share of gas taxation in GDP rose from 1 per cent in 1973 to 3.5 per cent in 1979. Kremers notes that these revenues were not set aside for investment. Worse than that: the deficit of the central government, which was zero in 1973, rose quickly to a level of almost 4.5 per cent of GDP in 1979. Further, in addition to the higher 'tax burden' in the form of higher domestic gas prices, the share of conventional taxes and social security contributions in GDP increased from 42 per cent to 46.5 per cent. Given the strictly temporary character of the higher gas revenues it is difficult to interpret this increase in government expenditure as an optimal reaction to the gas price boom.

Thus the picture of a booming government sector emerges, financed not only by higher gas revenues but also by large government deficits and higher tax rates. With respect to the spending effects it does not matter much whether additional government expenditures or income transfers are financed by gas revenues or by larger deficits.

Higher tax rates and a more generous social security system shifted the labour supply curve to the left and led through decreasing mobility of labour to an increase in the natural rate of unemployment. Over the period 1973–9 both an increase in registered unemployment and an outward shift of the unemployment–vacancies curve could be observed. Vacancies remained high throughout this period and were concentrated in the manufacturing sector. Substantial expansion of public sector employment contributed to the persistence of labour market tensions.

Thus the process of wage formation was characterized by strong upward pressures as workers tried to pass on higher tax rates, social security contributions and energy prices in a labour market characterized by excess demand, especially in the sub-markets for skilled workers. This led to a substantial redistribution of factor income in favour of labour, as is shown in table 3A.1.

The important point of this labour market performance is that it was not due to an exogenous supply shock but that, to a large degree, it can be explained as an *endogenous* reaction to the energy price shock and government policy. Thus it forms an integral part of the Dutch Disease phenomenon leading to a process of *deindustrialization*.

The period 1974–9 witnessed a rather sharp deindustrialization process: the growth rates of production and employment in the manufacturing sector were low, relative both to those of the manufacturing sector in other OECD countries and to total GDP growth. Even more important was the dramatic and sustained fall in *profitability* of the manufacturing sector. Jeroen Kremers rightly stresses this point as one of the most intriguing phenomena. In the traditional Dutch Disease literature this is just a transitory phenomenon, necessary to bring about a reallocation of labour from the tradables sector to the sector producing non-tradables. However, Dutch experience suggests that this is a long-lasting process.

Table 3A.1   Real national income and real disposable income in the private sector

	1972–5	1976–9
	average annual % changes	
Real national income per worker in the private sector	2.8	2.6
Real disposable income per worker in the private sector[a]	−0.4	1.0
Real disposable wage income in the private sector	2.6	2.2

[a] Net of taxes and social security contributions.

Source: *Centraal Economisch Plan*, 1985.

Following Kremers this might be explained by increasing labour market rigidities and the usual decision lags at firm level which imply that initially profit margins are used as a buffer. Another factor, which is not mentioned by Kremers, is government policy with respect to ailing industries. Rather substantial amounts of money were poured into these industries, like the shipbuilding industry, in a vain attempt to protect employment. Furthermore, investment and other subsidies were used to soften the consequences of the seemingly inevitable erosion of profit margins.

Thus one is tempted to conclude that rigidities in the structural adjustment process, which is not an uncommon characteristic of many European countries, seriously aggravate the Dutch Disease. What is initially perceived as a transitory shock gradually deteriorates into a long-lasting decline in profitability with serious consequences for investment and the growth of production capacity. Thus the Dutch Disease may lead to a classic unemployment regime, as van Wijnbergen (1984) has already noted.

Kremers suggests that 'the expansionary policy stance was defended on the basis of the view that The Netherlands suffered Keynesian Unemployment, due to deficiencies on the demand side'. I do not agree with this opinion. In fact the prevailing view in the mid-seventies, held for example, by the Central Planning Bureau, the Nederlandsche Bank and government officials, was that real wage rates were too high, thus endangering future employment growth. These results were confirmed by the VINTAF model of the Central Planning Bureau, which was published in 1975.

Kremers discusses monetary policy briefly without reaching strong conclusions. I agree with him that the exchange rate policy of the Nederlandsche Bank comes down to preserving the link with the Deutschmark. This has been quite successful, even in the turbulent years 1973 and 1974 when the Deutschmark and the guilder appreciated against most other currencies, and most notably against the US dollar. The link with the Deutschmark helped to contain inflation. On the other hand, real interest rates were not very low; in general they were 0.5–1 percentage points higher than the corresponding German rates. The real appreciation, predicated by the Dutch Disease literature, was only partially reflected in a nominal appreciation. Also important were the steadily rising relative price of Dutch exports in foreign markets, e.g. relative to German producers, as Kremers correctly points out, and the deteriorating terms of trade between the manufacturing sector and the industries specialized in non-tradables.

Putting things together, the disappointing performance of the Dutch economy in this sub-period has to be attributed not only to the spending effects of the increased gas revenues but also to the supply-side consequences of the oil price shock, to the spending effects of an increase in the government deficit and to labour market policies in general (including tax rates and social security contributions). The negative effects of the oil price shock could to a large degree have been avoided if the additional gas revenues had been used for a reduction of tax rates and other policy measures which would have increased labour supply and reduced labour market rigidities (See, for example, Frijns, 1982).

The sub-period 1980–5

The second oil price shock resulted in a further increase in gas revenues; the share of gas taxation in GDP reached an all-time high in 1982 (5.5 per cent of GDP). On the other hand, depressed world demand, low investment rates (possibly as a delayed reaction to the low profitability) and initially high family savings resulted in negative GDP growth rates in the years 1980–2. Combined with a demographically determined upswing in labour supply, unemployment rates rose sharply. At the same time serious attempts were made to reduce the growth in government expenditure and social security outlays. This policy of fiscal restraint has been pursued in more recent years when world demand picked up, so that since then the government deficit, tax rates and social security contributions have been falling. Together with the very high unemployment rates this has resulted in very modest nominal and real wage claims.

As a consequence, the overall economic picture has been dominated less by the spending effects of increased gas revenues and accompanying high real wage claims and more by depressed domestic demand, increasing current account surpluses and a restoration of profitability. Needless to say, the growth rate of production in the manufacturing sector once again exceeds the growth of production in the non-tradables industries. This underlines the basic truth that structural changes in a diversified economy, as the Dutch economy is, do not depend solely on a single factor such as increasing gas revenues.

REFERENCES

Beld C.A. van den and A. J. Middelhoek (1971) 'Evaluation of Seaport Projects', Central Planning Bureau, Occasional Paper No. 3.

Bruno M. and J. Sachs (1985) *Economics of Worldwide Stagflation*, Oxford: Basil Blackwell.

Centraal Economisch Plan (1985) The Hague: Staatsuitgeverij.

Frijns J. M. G. (1982) 'Energiebaten in een Twee-Sectoren Model', ('Energy Resources in a Two-Sector Model'), Central Planning Bureau, mimeo.

VINTAF (1977) 'Een Macro Model voor de Nederlandse Economie op Middellange Termijn', ('A Medium Term Macro Model of the Dutch Economy'), Central Planning Bureau, Occasional Paper No. 12.

van Wijnbergen S. (1984) 'Inflation, Employment and the Dutch Disease in Oil-Exporting Countries; a Short Run Disequilibrium Analysis', *Quarterly Journal of Economics*, **99**, 233–50.

4

Shadow prices and the intertemporal aspects of remittances and oil revenues in Egypt*

RICARDO MARTIN and
SWEDER VAN WIJNBERGEN

1 Introduction

In 1974, 6 per cent of total expenditure in Egypt was financed from oil revenues and remittances. Ten years later this share had risen to no less than 40 per cent, with the by now well-known consequences for the real exchange rate (see figure 4.1). However, although oil revenues and remittances are currently large in comparison to the non-oil economy, this situation is projected to change almost as rapidly as it came about. The transition to a non-oil economy is an issue of considerable concern to Egyptian policy-makers and international lending agencies alike.

The particular intertemporal structure of the anticipated time path of remittances and oil revenues gives rise to a series of questions. The first one deals with the intertemporal allocation of expenditure. How much of current income should be saved for future use; of those savings how much should be allocated to investment, and in which sector, and how much should go to accumulation of foreign assets, reduction of foreign borrowing, or even retirement of foreign debt? In fact, what is the optimal extraction pattern of oil itself? These issues are dealt with at length in Dervis, Martin and van Wijnbergen (1984), and we will only touch upon them here to the extent that they are influenced by the intertemporal pricing patterns to which we turn next. This will in particular be the case for optimal borrowing strategies.

The second set of questions concerns shadow prices, and that is our main concern in this paper. We will focus on three major prices: the shadow price of foreign exchange or the real exchange rate, the Accounting Rate of Interest (or, after a trivial transformation, the

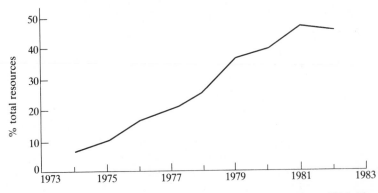

Figure 4.1 Share of exogenous resources in total resources, 1974–82.

relative price of future goods in terms of current goods), and the shadow price of natural gas.

The time path of the real exchange rate is clearly important for projects requiring non-traded inputs or producing non-traded goods. In addition, however, we will demonstrate that *changes* in the real exchange rate have major implications for optimal borrowing strategies. This aspect is stressed in some recent theoretical work (Martin and Selowsky, 1981; Dornbusch, 1983; van Wijnbergen, 1984); this paper is, to our knowledge, the first attempt to quantify it.

Many factors influence the time path of the real exchange rate. The anticipated decline in oil revenues exerts downward pressure on future exchange rates through standard 'Dutch Disease' or transfer problem arguments (see Corden and Neary, 1982; van Wijnbergen, 1984, 1985). Also, anticipated changes in energy prices will play a role, since energy intensity differs between traded and non-traded goods sectors. Finally, as capital is accumulated in the process of development, the aggregate capital–labour ratio will increase. This will also influence the real exchange rate to the extent that traded and non-traded goods have different capital intensity. All these factors will be taken into account in the model presented in the next section.

The importance of the accounting rate of interest (*ARI*), or the social valuation of future goods in terms of current goods, needs little explanation. No project analysis can be undertaken at all without it. Standard practice notwithstanding, it is not really possible to calculate the *ARI* without explicit forward-looking intertemporal optimization, to determine current and future value of capital. Formally the *ARI* equals the rate at which that value declines over time. The results of our paper strongly indicate that the common practice of assuming a constant period-to-period *ARI* can be very wrong, especially during a process of structural change such as during sudden increases or anticipated decreases in oil revenues. Two factors are important for the time pattern of the *ARI*. First a savings or absorptive capacity constraint whose tightness declines over time (cf. Little and Mirrlees, 1974). The second factor is a changing real exchange rate: a *gradual* depreciation (appreciation) of the real exchange rate raises (lowers) the *ARI* (*see* Dornbusch, 1983, and Martin and Selowsky, 1984).

The final shadow price we look at is the shadow price of natural gas. This is an interesting problem in Egypt, because Egypt has reserves too small to warrant the fixed costs of a liquefaction plant. Without such a plant (or a pipeline), natural gas is a non-traded good, whose shadow price determination is complicated by intertemporal aspects: less gas now means more tomorrow, since the total stock is fixed. The problem is made more interesting because reserves are large enough to warrant extraction rates so high that gas on the margin is an imperfect substitute for fuel oil. Once again an explicit intertemporal optimization approach is necessary to solve satisfactorily for shadow prices.

In this paper we present a simple intertemporal optimization general equilibrium model, which can be used to derive those shadow prices.

Before we introduce the model, we should note that the level of aggregation chosen is far too high to be of direct use for actual project analysis, other than by determining the aggregate shadow prices discussed above. On the other hand, the level of aggregation that would be useful for evaluation of real world projects is so low that a proper intertemporal optimization approach would become impossible because of the sheer size of the problem. In the project of which this paper is one of the products, we have chosen a two-stage approach. A simple highly aggregated model plus rigorous intertemporal optimization was used to derive the basic shadow prices that any detailed analysis would require as an input. The main focus was on shadow prices that either are expected to change over time under the impact of declining oil revenues (the real exchange rate) or that are explicitly intertemporal (the *ARI*). In a second stage those prices were used as an input in a purely static, but much more disaggregated analysis (Page, 1982).

The model is highly stylized as far as *intra*-temporal detail is concerned. Apart from oil and gas, we only distinguish foreign and domestic traded goods, and non-traded goods, all three of which are imperfect substitutes for each other in production and consumption. This will allow us to discuss both the real exchange rate and the terms of trade. The intertemporal choices to be made concern the optimal rate of oil and gas extraction, the intertemporal allocation of consumption (how much to save?) and the optimal allocation of savings over physical capital accumulation and claims on the rest of the world, i.e., an optimal strategy for foreign borrowing. A useful way of looking at this problem is as a portfolio problem: what is the optimal allocation of wealth, at each point in time, over oil and gas, physical capital and foreign assets (i.e., minus net foreign debt)? This problem is solved simultaneously with the optimal savings problem, i.e., how much of current income should go to current consumption and how much to accumulation of wealth? The model parameters are derived from Egyptian data, in a manner described elsewhere (Dervis, Martin and van Wijnbergen, 1984). The optimization problem is then solved numerically. The dual solution to this optimization exercise yields shadow prices. Finally, we test the sensitivity of the results by reoptimizing for different values of exogenous variables, especially oil prices, and for different parameter values characterizing preferences (curvature of the utility function, rate of time preference and so on).

The remainder of the paper is organized as follows: in section 2 we present the basic model and discuss some of the first order conditions characterizing the optimal solution to the dual optimization problem. These give us value and time path of the shadow prices we are interested in. In section 3 we present the result for the real exchange rate and the *ARI*, and discuss their implication for optimal debt accumulation under various oil price scenarios. In section 4 we discuss the shadow price of natural gas. Section 5 offers some conclusions and suggestions for further research.

2   The model

This section describes the optimizing growth model used in the paper. The starting point is the standard traded/non-traded open economy model augmented with an exhaustible resource sector. It also incorporates, however, some extensions and special features to reflect important aspects of reality that we wanted to introduce into the analysis. The features are the following:

1   There is an explicit input–output structure and commodities are required as inputs in production as well as for final use.
2   Domestically produced tradables and tradables produced in the rest of the world are imperfect substitutes. While the world price of

imports is exogenously given to the Egyptian economy, the proportion of imports in total domestic demand for tradable intermediate and consumer goods is responsive to the relative price of imports in terms of domestically produced tradables.

3   There is no such substitution possibility for investment goods; imported capital goods remain a fixed proportion of total investment.

4   Domestically produced tradables can be used in the domestic economy or they can be exported. The world price of Egyptian exports (excluding oil, Suez, remittances) does depend, however, on their volume. The relative price of exports (terms of trade) will fall with increases in volume, although we assume a high demand elasticity so that large increases in exports can occur with relatively minor declines in price.

5   We distinguish oil from natural gas. Gas can substitute for oil as a source of energy only up to a certain point. Also gas is treated as non-tradable. For Egypt, LNG exports are not considered a viable alternative even with optimistic reserve estimates.

6   The production of oil in any period is endogenous. However, production costs depend on the ratio of the flow of extraction to the stock of proved reserves. Since production costs are to a very large extent borne by foreign oil companies who 'recover' their costs by getting a share of total production, rising production costs in the oil sector are reflected by a rising share of the foreign oil companies. Moreover, proved reserves are updated every time period, by adding new discoveries and subtracting current production levels. New discoveries are exogenously projected so that total reserves are also exogenously given to the model.

7   The production of gas is treated somewhat differently in that investment costs are borne by Egypt, rather than foreign companies and per unit production costs are assumed constant. There is therefore a standard capital-output ratio reflecting the need for domestic investment in the gas sector.

8   The marginal efficiency of total economy-wide investment declines if investment grows too rapidly. While there is no 'absolute' absorptive capacity constraint that constitutes a rigid upper bound for investment in any period, the productivity of investment falls if it exceeds a certain critical level determined for every period by the rate of technical progress, the rate of growth of the labour force and the level of investment in previous periods.

A complete description of the model and associated dual equations is contained in the Appendix. Here we will only highlight three points.

The objective function is the discounted sum of the social value of *per capita* consumption over the planning period. The social value of an additional unit of consumption declines as society gets richer. In addition, in order to give equal weights to present and future representative families (before discounting), the social value of consumption is multiplied by the total population in each period.

The capital stocks are constrained to be at least equal to their steady state values at the end of the planning period.[1] The long planning horizon (30 periods), made this an acceptable approximation to an infinite horizon model, given the turnpike property of the model when defined in labour efficiency units.

For oil, the cost of production depends critically on the relationship between the stock of reserves and the flow of extraction. Given a certain number of fields and certain levels of reserves, there is an upper limit on how much oil or gas can be produced without endangering the long-term productiveness of the fields. Nevertheless, with the aid of secondary and tertiary recovery techniques, oil production can be maintained at high levels even in old fields with small reserve-to-production ratios. The model captures this relationship by linking cost recovery share of the foreign oil companies to the production–reserve constellation. Capital expenditures in the oil sector are overwhelmingly financed by the oil companies. The companies then recover their costs 'in kind' by getting a certain amount of cost-recovery oil in addition to their contractual share in profit oil. Attempts to push production beyond 'normal' levels will run into diminishing returns to the Egyptian economy, reflected in a steeply increasing cost-recovery share. In the gas sector, the same kind of relationship does in fact exist between reserve levels and production flows but there is somewhat greater flexibility. There are also important institutional differences. The foreign companies' role is minor and domestic investment is required to expand productive capacity. These considerations as well as computational constraints have led us to drop the variable production costs specification for gas and use a specification based on a simple capital-output ratio plus quantity constraints on annual output.

3 The real exchange rate and the accounting rate of interest

The model and associated optimization problem outlined in section 2 was solved under a variety of assumptions about future oil price scenarios, about the parameters measuring time preference and curvature of the utility function, about average and marginal cost of foreign borrowing and so on. For a complete description of all policy experiments, *see* Dervis, Martin and van Wijnbergen (1984). The dual to the solution provides information about shadow prices. In what follows we first discuss the time pattern of the real exchange rate and then the *ARI*; the final subsection discusses the implications of changes in the shadow price of foreign exchange for the optimal time path of foreign debt.

3.1   *The real exchange rate*

The available reserves of oil and gas, plus expected path of remittances from abroad, still allowed some room at the beginning of the planning period, to expand the ratio of those 'external' resources to domestic value-added. Soon, however, this ratio will fall (see figure 4.2). The behaviour of the real exchange rate reflects these changes: the price of non-traded goods in terms of imports and exports falls steadily, after increasing in the initial years. That change is required, of course, to give the incentives in production and consumption to adapt to a situation where imports are financed by non-oil exports, instead of remittances and oil revenue.

The total real devaluation is 10–15 per cent. This may not seem very much, given the magnitude of the required reallocation in the economy implied by figure 4.2. The reasons are twofold. First, even when capital is not shiftable once it is installed, a model with perfect foresight can anticipate the need for future reallocation of production, so that any change in the ratio of value-added for traded and non-traded goods would depend only on differences in capital intensity, which in our model are not high. Non-traded goods are assumed to be more labour-intensive. The corresponding Rybczynski effect, thus, also contributes to a lower devaluation over time. In fact, as figure 4.3 shows, the ratio of value-added for traded and non-traded goods hardly changes after the initial jump in reaction to the initial reallocation of capital.

The second point to consider is that traded goods are considerably less energy-intensive than non-traded goods (which includes things like transportation, power generation, etc.). With an increasing price of energy, as postulated in the model, the price of non-traded goods in terms of traded goods, P_n/P_t, must increase just to maintain the same levels of incentive for other factors of production in the sector. This is also the reason for the temporary decline in P_n/P_t in the 1990s; this is the period of natural gas and cheap energy (see section 4).

The wide gap between the price of exports and the domestic price of exportables implicit in figure 4.3, is the direct consequence of the

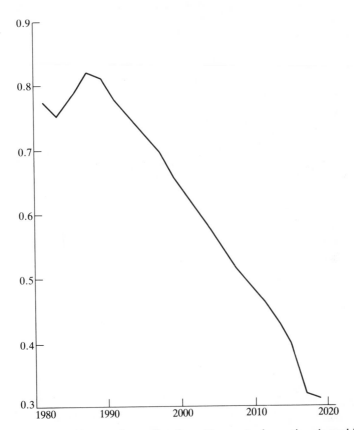

Figure 4.2   Ratio of income from oil and remittances to domestic value-added, 1981–2019.

assumption that the volume of exports cannot be expanded without reducing the unit value obtained from them. This can be interpreted as the cost of penetrating new markets, increasing transportation costs as products are sold in more distant countries, etc. Under these conditions it is optimal to create a wedge (an 'optimal tariff') between international and domestic prices: the latter should be equal to the marginal revenue from exports, which is lower than the price paid by foreign consumers.

3.2   *The accounting rate of interest*

Two major factors dominate the behaviour of the *period-to-period ARI*.[2] The first one is that absorptive capacity constraints rule out an

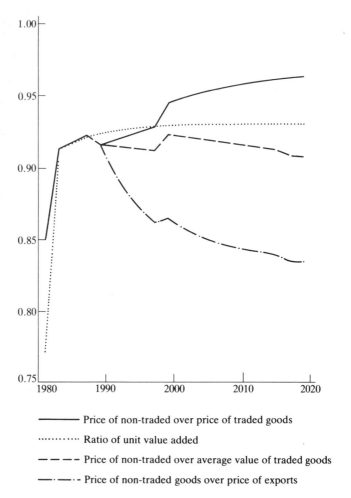

Figure 4.3   Real exchange rates: price of non-traded goods in terms of various traded goods, 1981–2019.

immediate jump of the level of investment from the current level to the one indicated by a proper intertemporal optimizing analysis. This constraint will be relaxed over time which in turn leads to a value of capital (in terms of 'real consumption') that falls over time and accordingly a higher *ARI* now than later on, after the absorptive capacity (AC) constraint ceases to be binding. The existence of AC constraints (and their anticipated relaxation over time) indicates that less investment should be undertaken than without those constraints; it is very important however, that this does not simply imply the use of a higher *ARI* for all projects. This would not only lead to less investment but would also unduly bias its composition towards quick-yielding projects. What such a situation will lead to is a high period-to-period *ARI* initially but a lower one later on. It cannot be stressed enough that the use of simple internal rate of return criteria in such circumstances is extremely misleading.

The value of capital goods in this model has two components: the first major component is simply the discounted value of all future output to be produced by the 'marginal' machine. The second is related to our assumption that the absorptive capacity constraint is related to past capital accumulation. More investment now will accordingly relax the AC constraint in the future. Accordingly, if the AC constraint is anticipated to be binding tomorrow, capital formation will be more useful than when it is not because of this externality. In our model *all* capital formation has this property; in the real world this is, of course, not the case. Accordingly, we separated these two components of the value of capital and also derived an *ARI* that does *not* incorporate this externality (*ARI** in figure 4.4). Clearly, *ARI* > *ARI** because the value of this externality declines over time. This does not mean that when two projects with identical cost–benefit structure but the first one with this externality (road building project) and the second without (sweet factory) are compared, the first one has to be rejected because of the higher *ARI*. One should also incorporate the higher value of its output: during the period of binding capacity constraints capital goods (roads) are more valuable than consumption goods (sweets). It is easy to show with the numbers coming out of this exercise that when two of these projects have exactly the same net benefits over time the road project will nevertheless have a higher net present value, the higher *ARI* and similar net benefit streams notwithstanding. The valuation difference dominates the *ARI* difference. In our case the value of capital *including* this externality (roads), expressed in terms of capital *excluding* this externality, falls from 1.5 to 1 between now and 1990.

The second factor determining the *ARI* is the existence of a major temporary component in current income (oil revenues). This leads to temporarily high savings and investment programme. The implication of that is, once again, *not* a lower *ARI* for all projects, but a period-to-period *ARI* that is low during the period of high but declining oil revenues and high after revenues have stopped flowing in. A 'flat' *ARI* pattern would again produce a biased composition of aggregate investment, in this case against quick-yielding projects.

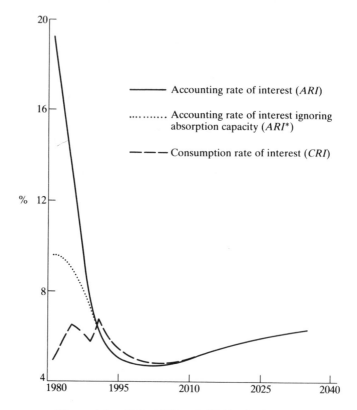

Figure 4.4   *ARI, ARI** and *CRI* in the base run.

The combined result of the gradually relaxed AC constraints and the decline of oil revenues gives a U-shaped *ARI* pattern (figure 4.4).

The consumption rate of interest (*CRI*) pattern does not follow the *ARI* pattern exactly because the relative value of capital in terms of the price of a 'representative' bundle of consumption goods changes over time. Initially the value of capital falls faster than the value of an additional unit of consumption because of the gradual relaxation of the absorptive capacity constraints and the rapid accumulation thereafter so that the *CRI* is lower than the *ARI* during that period (see figure 4.4). After about 12 years, however, there are no significant changes in the relative value of capital goods in terms of consumption goods so from there on the *CRI* equals the *ARI*.

After the effect of the binding absorptive capacity constraint has died out, the *CRI* also follows a U-shaped pattern because of the currently high but declining pattern of oil revenues. The story is really the same as the one told for the *ARI* but seen from a different angle. Remember that the only endogenous component in the *CRI* is the growth rate of per capita consumption. This growth rate is falling initially, in line with the gradual decline in oil revenues, making for a gradually declining *CRI*. After the oil has run out, the decline stops and the growth rate gradually climbs back up towards its steady state value, which is reflected in a gradual increase in the *CRI* in the second half of the planning period.

Let us consider the variant of no absorptive capacity constraints. The impact of the AC constraint on the *ARI* is most clearly seen by comparing the base run time pattern of the *ARI* with that obtained in the first variant presented: this is a run made under the assumption that there is *no* absorptive capacity constraint at all, resources devoted to capital formation lead one for one to increases in the capital stock. The *ARI* is more than 8 per cent lower in the first period, a difference that takes about 10 years to fade away. From there on the *ARI* is the same (figure 4.4). Of course Tobin's *q*, the value of capital over its reproduction costs, is always equal to one in this run. There are some relative price changes between capital and consumption, but not enough to drive a significant wedge between the *CRI* and the *ARI*. Initial investment is unbelievably high, the optimization exercise indicates that in the absence of AC constraints a full 54 per cent of GDP should be devoted to capital formation in the first period. Absorptive capacity constraints bring that down to a more realistic 29 per cent. The value of capital is naturally much lower initially, in fact only half of the value in period 1 in the base run. One-third of that difference is caused by the lower future marginal productivity in period 2 and later (the capital stock is bigger in those periods because of the high initial investment). The remaining two-thirds of the difference is due to the fact that new capital has beneficial effects in the base run because it loosens up future AC constraints, benefits that are absent in this variant.

3.3 *Optimal foreign debt, oil prices and the time pattern of the real exchange rate*

The time path of per capita debt in the base run is straightforward, an increase initially before oil income reaches its peak in 1990 and a gradual decline thereafter. Our main interest however, is not so much in that base run; of more interest is the sensitivity of optimal borrowing strategies to changes in the external environment, such as, say, a drop in oil prices.

The 'base run' oil price scenario used in the base case was rapidly made obsolete by the events of late 1982/early 1983. We therefore present an alternative run under the assumption of a substantial downward shift in the entire schedule of oil prices.

The welfare effects of such a relative price change (oil is cheaper in terms of everything else) depend on one's *net* export position in oil; the situation is complicated in the case of Egypt because it is a net exporter for the next decade at least, but will turn into a net importer after that. The question then comes down to whether the benefits of lower oil prices during the future net importer phase outweigh the losses during the current net exporter phase. An alternative but equivalent way of looking at it is by looking at the gross flows (oil output and oil use) and seeing what changes in the value of those flows do to the value of the assets making up Egypt's wealth: oil in the ground, physical capital and labour stock. The value of oil in the ground, according to the model, falls by nearly 25 per cent, the *rent* on a barrel of oil kept in the ground falls from \$14.60 to \$11.16. On the other hand, lower oil prices lead, *ceteris paribus*, to more value-added left over to pay capital and labour. The value of capital (discounted value of all its future marginal products) indeed increases by slightly above 5 per cent as derived from the dual of the optimal solution under the new price scenario. The entire path of the marginal product of labour ('shadow wage') also shifts up around 5 per cent. The net effect cannot be signed on a priori grounds; the numerical outcome indicates that future benefits in fact dominate current losses: the discounted utility of current and future consumption in fact increases under the low price scenario, although not much – by 1.5 percentage points.

The higher marginal productivity of capital at lower oil prices calls for more investment, although that increase is kept in check during the initial few periods by the absorptive capacity constraints. Over the first 6 years investment should, at lower oil prices, be about 2 per cent higher than in the base run, a difference that will increase as AC constraints cease to be binding further in the future.

Current GNP falls by one percentage point (in fact the growth rate will also be lower by an average 1.5 per cent over the first 6 years), and investment should go up; should one conclude that since wealth has in fact increased a little bit, aggregate consumption should also rise, necessitating an increase in the optimal CA deficit and an increase in foreign debt? Higher or equal wealth coupled with lower current income would argue yes; however, the gradually increasing loss in oil revenues leads to a gradually increasing real depreciation in comparison with the base run, indicating that loans taken out now will have to be paid back in traded goods that are becoming more and more expensive. This argues for less borrowing rather than more and a 'tilt' of the consumption pattern towards less consumption now and more in the future, and accordingly less foreign borrowing and a lower CA deficit.

The numerical solution indicates that the second ('cost of borrowing') effect dominates, the increasing real depreciation over the first couple of years calls for a slowdown in consumption and initial *decrease* in the CA deficit that is gradually reversed over time. From the period where the real exchange rate starts catching up again (the level remains permanently below the base run path, but the difference starts to decrease again from 1990 onwards), foreign borrowing increases above the base run level, as the real cost of borrowing and wealth effects now work in the same direction (see figures 4.5 and 4.6).

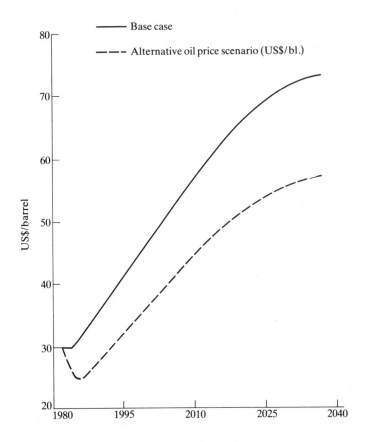

Figure 4.5   Different oil price scenarios, 1981–2038.

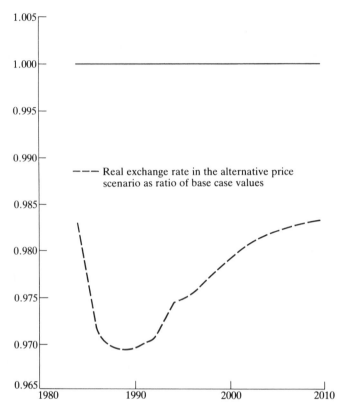

Figure 4.6   The real exchange rate (P_n/P_t) under different oil price scenarios.

The accompanying optimal current account deficits are presented in table 4.1.

In looking at those numbers one should take the indicative nature of such results into account, the patterns produced by these runs will come out under a wide variety of assumptions, but specific numbers are rather sensitive to things we do not know much about.

Finally, it is maybe worth while to point out that the lower oil prices call for a significant shift towards non-oil exports, which should be substantially higher in the low oil price scenario (nearly 30 per cent), necessitating both a decline in consumption and a shift away from traded goods (hence a real depreciation). Clearly the composition of investment also has to change in favour of capital in the traded goods sector.

Table 4.1 Optimal per annum current account deficits (US$b) under the base run and an alternative oil price scenario

Case	1981–2	1983–4	1985–6	1991–2
Base run	3.46	2.22	1.88	1.81
Alternative oil price scenario	2.05	1.60	2.48	3.27

4   The shadow price of natural gas

There are two interesting shadow prices for each of our exhaustible resources, oil and gas:[3] the price to the user (including costs of extraction and delivery), and the value of the stock in the ground (rent to reserves). In the case of oil, since it is a fungible, tradable good in a market in which Egypt is only a small actor, the shadow price to the user is just the international price. This price is distributed between cost of extraction (paid to the oil companies as a share in the output), and rent to reserves, mainly as a function of how future extraction costs are expected to increase as the reservoirs are depleted. In addition, during the first few periods, in which output is still limited by the speed with which oil can be extracted from the existing fields, part of the price is imputed as rent to those limiting factors.

For natural gas the situation is more complicated, since reserves are not large enough to justify the construction of the liquefaction plant needed to make it an exportable commodity. On the other hand, there are many uses in which natural gas and oil products (fuel-oil) are almost perfect substitutes (e.g., a power plant can operate as efficiently burning oil as using natural gas, once it is converted). For other uses, e.g., transportation, substitution is more difficult. In this exercise we made the admittedly extreme assumption that gas and oil are perfect substitutes for up to 50 per cent of total energy use, and that gas cannot substitute for oil at all above that cut-off rate. The cut-off rate increases to 60 per cent over the first 10 years, to account for the gradual conversion of equipment as gas become more abundant. The result of these assumptions is that the price of natural gas will be given by its oil equivalent (i.e., by international prices) only in periods in which the substitution possibilities have not been exhausted, be it because gas output, or deliveries, cannot be increased, or because the opportunity cost of reserves (i.e., the value of future rather than current use) is high enough to make it desirable to limit current production. In all other periods, the shadow price of gas will be below the price of oil (in energy equivalent units).

Figure 4.7 shows the resulting time path for the price of gas and reserves. The most significant result is that for a period of about 10 years, starting in the late 1980s, the price of gas is below its oil-equivalent by 25–30 per cent. In earlier periods the capacity for production and distribution is too limited to exhaust substitution possibilities for oil in the range where it can do so without declining efficiency. Later, the rapid growth of the economy, and consequent increase in total energy demand, once again make the production capacity of gas a binding constraint. At the very end, capacity is not binding and the price of gas equals extraction costs plus rent to reserves,

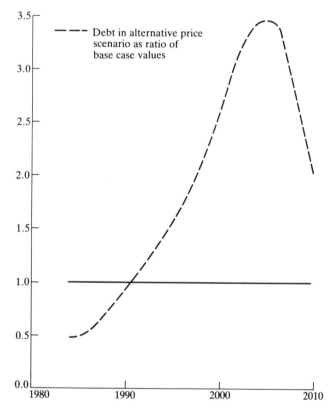

Figure 4.7   Optimal borrowing levels (commercial debt) under a different oil price scenario.

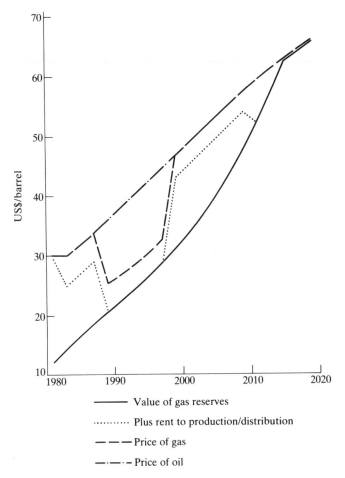

Figure 4.8   Decomposition of the price of gas, 1981–2019.

without any rent to production/distribution constraints. It is that final period which determines the rent to reserves over the entire planning horizon and, thus, the rent to capacity constraints when those constraints are binding or the price of gas when they are not. This is so because the rent must be constant in discounted value (as required by the Hotelling equation) along an optimal extraction path. *When* should reserves be exhausted, and at *what rate* they should be discounted are endogenous variables in the model: and it is difficult to see how they could be determined other than by an optimizing model as used in this paper.

5   Conclusions

One of the main conclusions of this paper is that the static approach to shadow pricing that is standard in applied work, and the resulting use of a relative shadow price structure that is constant over time, can be extremely misleading. This approach is especially inappropriate when significant structural change is anticipated in an economy; declines in remittances and in revenues from oil that are predicted to take place in Egypt over the next decade, were shown to have significant implications for the level and time pattern of the real exchange rate.

Also, the existence of absorptive capacity constraints now, and anticipated gradual depreciation of the real exchange rate in the future, were shown to lead to a pronounced time pattern in the period-to-period *ARI*. The practical importance of a time pattern in the period-to-period *ARI* is difficult to underestimate. The standard practice of using a flat *ARI* profile over the entire planning horizon might lead to the correct volume of investment, but will introduce potentially severe bias in the composition of the portfolio of accepted projects.

Gradual exchange rate changes were also shown to have a major impact on the time pattern of the optimal level of foreign debt. A downward shift in the schedule of oil prices (rather similar to what actually happened in 1984 and 1985!) produces negative income effects now but positive income effect from the mid-nineties onward, when Egypt will be a net importer of oil. This suggests, as it turns out incorrectly, that Egypt should borrow more initially after a downward shift in oil prices. However, the lower oil price schedule also produced an increasing gradual depreciation, which raises the cost of foreign debt (one borrows in terms of goods that are becoming more and more expensive over time). This substitution effect was shown to *reverse* the optimal current account response to lower oil prices: Egypt should reduce external deficits after a downward shift in oil prices.

All this demonstrates, in our view, the usefulness of an explicitly intertemporal optimization approach to the derivation of such crucial shadow price variables as the real exchange rate, the *ARI* and the valuation of capital goods. Computational and informational limitations necessitate a high level of intratemporal aggregation if sufficient attention is to be paid to intertemporal issues. The alternative that is followed in practice, however, i.e., to ignore intertemporal aspects altogether, is surely inferior. Anyhow, the results of a highly focused intertemporal exercise can be (and have been, in our case) used in more traditional, static and low level of disaggregation analyses.

The intertemporal approach advocated in this paper at least allows us to explore the implications of what we know about future structural change for shadow prices needed for project analysis now. However, there is of course much that we do not yet know about future developments, and a great deal of uncertainty about precise values and timing of events we can with reasonable confidence expect to take place. That points to what we see as the major shortcoming of this work – its assumption of perfect foresight. Although sensitivity analysis with respect to assumptions about exogenous future variables can provide some information (and we have done such sensitivity tests), that is no substitute for explicit incorporation of the effect of uncertainty about future events on the value of current shadow prices. Extending the current methodology to take into account such uncertainty is surely the most promising direction for future research.

Appendix   Summary of the Model

A.1   *Variables*

(i) Primal (activity level)

C_{it} = Final consumption of good i
X_{it} = Gross domestic output of good i
K_{it} = Capital stock used to produce good i
L_{it} = Employment in sector i
E_{it} = Exports of good i
M_{it} = Imports of good i
F_t = Net exogenous inflows of foreign exchange (aid, remittances etc.)
Z_{it} = Intermediate use of good i
Y_{it} = Effective investment in sector i
H_{3t} = Maximum production of oil per period
H_{4t} = Maximum production of gas per period
I_t = Total investment
Y_t^* = Level of investment at which absorption capacity becomes a binding constraint
H_{Et} = Level of exports at which price starts to decline
U_t = Utility level (i.e. real consumption) in period t
R_{3t} = Reserves of oil at the end of period t
R_{4t} = Reserves of gas at the end of period t
CD_t = End of period commercial debt
CAD_t = Current account deficit

DSR_t = Debt service ratio in period t

r_t = Cost of borrowing

All the above variables are measured in per capita terms.

L_t = Labour force in period t

(ii)   Coefficients

a_{ij} = Unit requirement of good i to produce good j

PW_{it} = International price of good i

ρ_i = Substitution parameters

δ = Discount rate

ϕ = 1 + elasticity of the marginal utility of income

g = 1 + rate of growth of the labour force

g_i = 1 + rate of labour augmenting technical change, $i = 1,2$

α_i = Share parameters in the production functions

b_i = Capital–output ratio in sector i

S_i = Share of sector i in the production of new capital

d_i = 1 − depreciation rate

η = Price elasticity of exports

(iii)   Dual (shadow prices)

λ_t = Marginal utility of real consumption

p_{it} = Unit value of final good i

v_{it} = Unit value added in sector i

r_{it} = Marginal productivity of capital in sector i

q_{it} = Unit value of capital goods in sector i

s_{3t} = Unit value of reserves of oil

s_{4t} = Unit value of reserves of gas

p_{It} = Unit value of investment goods

w_t = Marginal productivity of labour

The sectors are:

1 – Traded goods (exported and used domestically)

2 – Non-traded goods

3 – Oil and gas sector

4 – Gas sector (measured in tons of crude equivalent)

5 – Non-competitive imports

Sector 6 is used as an aggregation index for sectors 1 and 5, defining a composite *importable* good, which is used in consumption and production.

A.2   *Objective function*

$$v = \sum_{t=1}^{T} \delta^{-t} L_t U_t^{\phi}$$

$$(\lambda_t) \quad U_t = (\gamma_2 C_{2t}^{-\rho_u} + (1 - \gamma_2)C_{6t}^{-\rho_u})^{-1/\rho_u} \tag{1}$$

A.3 Constraints

(i) Production functions

$$(\nu_{1t} \geq 0) \quad X_{1t} \leq A_1(\alpha_1 K_{1t}^{-\rho_1} + (1 - \alpha_1)(L_{1t}g_1^t)^{-\rho_1})^{-1/\rho_1} \tag{2}$$

$$(\nu_{2t} \geq 0) \quad X_{2t} \leq A_2(\alpha_2 K_{2t}^{-\rho_2} + (1 - \alpha_2)((1 - L_{1t})g_2^t)^{-\rho_2})^{-1/\rho_2} \tag{3}$$

$$(\nu_{3t} \geq 0) \quad X_{3t} \leq \min \{K_{33t}/b_3, H_{3t}\} \tag{4}$$

$$(\nu_{4t} \geq 0) \quad X_{4t} \leq \min \{K_{34t}/b_3, H_{4t}\} \tag{5}$$

$$K_{33t} + K_{34t} = K_{3t} \tag{6}$$

(ii) Material balances

$$(p_{1t} \geq 0) \quad Z_{1t} + E_{1t} + S_1 I_t \leq X_{1t} \tag{7}$$

$$(p_{2t} \geq 0) \quad C_{2t} + S_2 I_t + a_{21}X_{1t} + a_{22}X_{2t} + a_{23}X_{3t} \leq X_{2t} \tag{8}$$

$$(p_{3t} \geq 0) \quad E_{3t} + a_{31}X_{1t} + a_{32}X_{2t} \leq X_{3t} + X_{4t} \tag{9}$$

$$(p_{Gt} \geq 0) \quad X_{4t} - a_{41}X_{1t} - a_{42}X_{2t} \leq 0 \tag{10}$$

$$(p_{6t} \geq 0) \quad C_{6t} + a_{61}X_{1t} + a_{62}X_{2t} + a_{63}X_{3t} \leq A_6(\alpha_6 Z_{1t}^{-\rho_6} + $$
$$(1 - \alpha_6)Z_{5t}^{-\rho_6})^{-1/\rho_6} \tag{11}$$

$$(p_{5t} \geq 0) \quad M_{5t} = Z_{5t} + S_5 I_t \leq \Pi_{1t}E_{1t} + \Pi_{3t}E_{3t} + F_t - $$
$$\theta(R_{3,t-1})\Pi_{3t}X_{3t} \tag{12}$$

In the version with endogenous foreign borrowing, (12) is replaced by

$$(p_{5t} \geq 0) \quad M_{5t} \leq \Pi_{1t}E_{1t} + \Pi_{3t}[E_{3t} - \theta(R_{3,t-1})X_{3t}] + F_t - $$
$$r_t CD_{t-1}/g + CAD_t \tag{12a}$$

$$r_{t+1} = ELIBOR(t)/[1 + A_0\psi(- A_1 CD_t)] + $$
$$A_2 DSR_t/\min(0.001, DSUB-DSR_t) \tag{12b}$$

r_{t+1} is the cost of borrowing; $ELIBOR(t)$ is the LIBOR rate (6 per cent per annum in section 5.3); $\psi(\ )$ is the cumulative normal distribution and A_0, A_1, A_2 are parameters (equal to 0.03, 0.7 and 0.0 in the runs reported here).

The debt service ratio (DSR_t) is defined as real amortization (considering a 5 per cent rate of world inflation and an average maturing of loans of 20 years) plus interest, divided by total export revenues.

The change in the stock of debt from period to period is given by:

$$(q_{7t} \geq 0) \quad CD_t = CD_{t-1}/g + CAD_t \tag{12c}$$

since CD_t, like all other variables in our model, is defined in per capita terms.

(iii)   Investment

$$(q_{it} \geq 0) \quad K_{it} = d_i K_{i,t-1}/g + Y_{i,t-1}/g \quad i = 1,2,3 \tag{13}$$

$$(p_{It} \geq 0) \quad \sum_{i=1}^{3} Y_{it} = \left\{ \begin{array}{ll} I_t & \text{if} \quad I_t \leq Y_t^* \\ g(I_t, Y_t^*) & \text{if} \quad I_t > Y_t^* \end{array} \right. \tag{14}$$

Where $Y_t^* = 1.2 \sum_{i=1}^{4} Y_{i,t-1}$

and $g(..) = Y_t^* + \dfrac{1}{\alpha}\{1 - \exp[-\alpha(I_t - Y_t^*)]\}$

This allows for an annual increase in investment of 10 per cent before the efficiency of investment starts to decline. After that, the marginal efficiency declines to 10 per cent when $I_t = 2y_t^x$.

$$(q_{Rt}^0) \quad R_{3,t-1} = R_{3,t}/g - X_{3t} \tag{15}$$

$$(q_{Rt}^G) \quad R_{4,t+1} = R_{3,t}/g \tag{16}$$

(iv)   Terminal conditions

$$(q_{iT} \geq 0) \quad K_{iT} \geq K_{iT}^* \quad i = 1,2 \tag{17}$$

The terminal capital stocks are those obtained from the steady-state solution of the model, which exist when all variables are defined in terms of efficiency units of labour. With endogenous borrowing, there is also a condition on terminal debt:

$$(q_{7T} \geq 0) \quad CD_T \leq CD^*_T \tag{17a}$$

where CD^*_T is a value which produces approximately the same debt/GNP ratio that Egypt had at the beginning of the planning period.

A.4 First order conditions for maximization

The dual equations (first order conditions for maximization) are:

(i) Allocation of consumption

$$(C_{2t} \geq 0) \quad \lambda_t \gamma_2 (U_t/C_{2t})^{1+\rho_u} \leq p_{2t} \tag{18}$$

$$(C_{6t} \geq 0) \quad \lambda_t (1 - \gamma_2)(U_t/C_{6t})^{1-\rho_u} \leq p_{6t} \tag{19}$$

(ii) Value-added

$$(X_{1t}) \quad v_{1t} = p_{1t} - p_{2t}a_{21} - p_{3t}a_{31} - p_{6t}a_{61} \tag{20}$$

$$(X_{2t}) \quad v_{2t} = p_{2t} - p_{2t}a_{22} - p_{3t}a_{32} - p_{6t}a_{62} \tag{21}$$

$$(X_{3t}) \quad v_{3t} = p_{3t} - p_{2t}a_{23} - p_{6t}a_{63} - q_{3t} - p_{5t}\Pi_{3t}\theta_t \tag{22}$$

$$(X_{4t}) \quad v_{4t} = p_{4t} - p_{2t}a_{24} - p_{Gt}a_{64} - q_{4t} \tag{23}$$

$$\text{where } p_{4t} = p_{3t} - p_{Gt} \tag{24}$$

(iii) Optimal production conditions

$$(L_{1t}) \quad w_t = v_{it}(1 - \alpha_i)(A_i g_i^t)^{\rho_i}\left(\frac{X_{it}}{L_{it}}\right)^{1+\rho_i} \quad i = 1,2 \tag{25}$$

$$(K_{it}) \quad r_{it} = v_{it}\alpha_i A_i^{\rho_i}\left(\frac{X_{it}}{K_{it}}\right)^{1+\rho_i} \quad i = 1,2 \tag{26}$$

$$v_{3t} = v_{31,t} + v_{32,t} \tag{27}$$

$$v_{4t} = v_{41,t} + v_{42,t} \tag{28}$$

$$(K_{3t}) \quad r_{3t} = v_{31,t}/b_3 = V_{41,t}/b_4 \tag{29}$$

(iv)   Value of the stock of capital and value of reserves

$$(K_{it}) \quad q_{it} = r_{it} + d_i q_{i,t+1}/g \quad i = 1,2,3 \tag{30}$$

$$(R_{3t}) \quad s_{3t} = s_{3,t+1}/g + f_{56}\Pi_{3t}E_{36}\theta'_t \tag{31a}$$

where $\theta'_t = \partial\theta(R_{3t}, X_{3t})/\partial R_{3t}$ is the increase in the share of foreign oil companies as extraction costs increase due to depletion of reserves

$$(R_{4t}) \qquad s_{4t} = s_{4,t+1}/g \tag{31b}$$

(v)   Value of new capital

$$(Y_{it} \geqslant 0) \quad q_{it}/g + p_{I2,t+1}\frac{\partial g_{t+1}}{\partial Y_t} \leqslant p_{It} \quad i = 1,2,3 \tag{32}$$

with $p_{It} = p_{i1,t} + p_{I2,t} \tag{33}$

and $g_{t+1} = g(I_{t+1}, Y^*_{t+1})$ the absorption constraint function defined in equation (14).

$$(I_t \geqslant 0) \quad p_{I1,t} + p_{I2,t}\,\partial g_t/\partial I_t \leqslant S_1 p_{1t} + S_2 p_{2t} + S_5 p_{5t} \tag{34}$$

(vi)   Exports

$$(E_1t) \quad p_{1t} = \begin{cases} p_{5t} \text{ if } E_{1t} \leqslant H_{Et} \\ p_{5t}(E_{1t}/H_{Et})^{\eta-1} \text{ otherwise.} \end{cases} \tag{35}$$

$$(E_{3t}) \quad p_{5t}\Pi_{3t} = p_{3t} \tag{36}$$

(vii)   Aggregation of imports and traded goods

$$(Z_{1t} \geqslant 0) \quad \alpha_6 p_{6t} A_6^{\rho_6}(X_{6t}/Z_{1t})^{1+\rho_4} \leqslant p_{1t} \tag{37}$$

$$(Z_{5t} \geqslant 0) \quad (1 - \alpha_6)p_{6t}A_6^{\rho_6}(X_{6t}/Z_{5t})^{1+\rho_6} \leqslant p_{5t} \tag{38}$$

A.5   *National aggregates*

Per capita gross national product is given by any of the following expressions:

$$Y_t = v_{1t}X_{1t} + v_{2t}X_{2t} + (v_{3t} + S_{3t})X_{3t} + (v_{4t} + S_{4t})X_{4t} +$$
$$(p_{5t}\pi_{1t} - p_{1t})E_{1t}$$

$$Y_t = (r_{1t}K_{1t} + r_{2t}K_{2t} + r_{3t}K_{3t}) + w_t + v_{32,t}H_{3t} + S_{3t}X_{3t} +$$
$$v_{42,t}H_{4t} + S_{4t}X_{4t} + (p_{5t}\Pi_{1t} - p_{1t})E_{1t}$$

$$Y_t = (p_{2t}C_{2t} + p_{4t}C_{4t}) + (s_1p_{1t} + S_2p_{2t} + S_5p_{5t})I_t +$$
$$(p_{1t}E_{1t} + p_{3t}E_{3t} - p_{5t}M_{5t})$$

The first expression is the usual definition as sum of value-added in all sectors plus rents (plus the implicit optimal tariff to exports). The second expression defines income as factor payments to capital, labour and rents in the oil and export sector. Finally, we show the decomposition into consumption, investment and current account surplus.

NOTES

* This paper draws extensively on joint work with Kemal Dervis, reported in Dervis, Martin and van Wijnbergen (1984). The views expressed in this paper do not necessarily reflect those of the World Bank or its affiliated institutions.

1 There is a constant rate of population growth, and all technical change is assumed to be labour-augmenting, so that the steady rate is defined in terms of labour efficiency units.

2 It is misleading to use a single *ARI* in an economy facing major future changes in income streams. We will discuss the pattern of the period-to-period $ARI(t)$. To discount back from t to 0, one forms the discount factor $[(1 + ARI(1)) (1 + ARI(2)) \dots (1 + ARI(t))]$.

3 In the version of the model with endogenous investment and foreign borrowing, both resources are combined into one, to reduce the number of state variables to consider. The numerical results reported below are based on the version with investment growing exogenously at its historical rate and no external borrowing (see Dervis, Martin and van Wijnbergen (1984) for details).

REFERENCES

Corden M. and J. P. Neary (1982) 'Booming Sectors and Deindustrialization in a Small Open Economy', *Economic Journal*, **92**, 825–48.

Dervis K., R. Martin and S. van Wijnbergen (1984) 'Policy Analysis of Shadow Pricing, Foreign Borrowing and Resource Extraction in Egypt', World Bank Staff Working Paper No. 622.

Dornbusch R. (1983) 'Real Interest Rates, Home Goods and Optimal External Borrowing', *Journal of Political Economy*, **91**, 141–54.

Little I., and J. Mirrlees (1974) *Project Appraisal and Planning for Developing Countries*, London: Heinemann.
Martin R. and M. Selowsky (1984) 'Energy Prices, Substitution and Optimal Borrowing in the Short Run', *Journal of Development Economics*, **14**, 331–50.
Page J. (1982) 'Shadow Prices for Trade Strategy and Investment Planning in Egypt', World Bank Staff Working Paper No. 521.
van Wijnbergen S. (1984) 'The Dutch Disease: A Disease After All?', *Economic Journal*, **94**, 41–55.
van Wijnbergen S. (1985) 'Oil Discoveries, Intertemporal Adjustment and Public Policy', in O. Bjerkholt and E. Offerdal (eds), *Macroeconomic Prospects for a Small Oil Exporting Country*, The Hague: Martinus Nijhoff.

COMMENT   ALASDAIR SMITH

This paper gives an admirable demonstration of the sensible and sensitive application of economic ideas to the analysis of the key intertemporal allocation decisions facing a resource-dependent country. It provides a nice blending of optimal growth theory and 'Dutch Disease' theory, and to say that the conclusions appeal to enlightened common sense is to pay tribute to the illumination the paper provides. There are, however, three questions – two general and one more specific – that can be asked about the exercise undertaken here.

The first general problem concerns the implication throughout the paper that the shadow prices derived here can be used in project evaluation. There is a distinction to be made between the shadow prices that describe the optimum of a social planning exercise and the shadow prices that should be used to guide piecemeal policy reform in a distorted economy (see Srinivasan, 1980, and Drèze and Stern, 1986). The importance of this in the present instance is that we can assert with a fair degree of confidence that whatever path is followed by the Egyptian economy over the next few decades it will not be the path mapped out by Martin and van Wijnbergen. It follows that the shadow prices appropriate for project evaluation on the actual path will be significantly different from the prices derived here. It may be that the principal conclusions of the paper, for example the conclusion about the time-varying nature of the accounting rate of interest, are quite robust to changes in the pattern of intertemporal allocation of resources, but this needs explicit argument.

A related issue arises in connection with the assumption made in the model that factors of production are intersectorally mobile. The effect of this assumption, as is well known in the literature on numerical general equilibrium models, is that relative goods prices have to change very little in order to bring about quite substantial intersectoral reallocations of outputs – the production possibility curve in the numerical model is very flat, in contrast with the curves typically shown in textbooks. Thus, though the paper makes reference to 'structural adjustment' as a key issue, structural adjustment is in fact a rather painless process in this model.

Now, for the purposes of a long-run modelling exercise, the assumption of intersectoral factor mobility seems an appropriate one, especially where the focus is on intertemporal allocation decisions; but this does create some difficulties in evaluating the practical implications of this kind of exercise. Figure 4.3 implies a very rapid reallocation of factors between sectors. Even if the short-run policy implications are not intended to be the central focus of the model, there is a sense in which they are bound to be the most significant implications. In a year's time or even in 6 months' time, we will have new predictions on oil prices, export prospects and so on, and the plan will be recomputed. Therefore the policy implications for this year – such as the policy prescription that investment should be concentrated only in tradables – have a quite different status from prescriptions for 1995, which are needed as part of the description of what we should be doing now, but which have probability zero of being the correct things to do in 1995 when (and if) we arrive there.

Moving now to a less fundamental issue, I am concerned about the way that capacity constraints on investment and oil-extraction are given a key role in keeping the model away from extreme solutions, such as selling all the oil in one year or as soon as physically feasible. The losses of rapid extraction are only the second justification that most of us would offer for restraint on such policies. The first is uncertainty, specifically the uncertainty about the future path of oil prices that should lead a risk-averse decision-maker to keep some oil in the ground as a form of portfolio diversification. Obviously sensitivity analysis with respect, especially, to alternative patterns of oil price changes goes some of the way to meeting concerns on this point, and in the paper we are given some of this, but the range of alternative oil price scenarios seems remarkably conservative.

REFERENCES

Drèze J. and N. H. Stern (1986) 'The Theory of Cost–Benefit Analysis', in A. Auerbach and M. Feldstein (eds), *Handbook of Public Economics,* volume 2, Amsterdam: North-Holland, forthcoming.
Srinivasan T. N. (1980) 'General Equilibrium Theory, Project Evaluation and Economic Development', in M. Gersovitz, C. Diaz-Alejandro, G. Ranis et al. (eds), *Development: Essays in Honor of W. Arthur Lewis,* London: Allen & Unwin, pp. 220–51.

5

Certainty equivalence methods in the macroeconomic management of petroleum resources

IULIE ASLAKSEN
and
OLAV BJERKHOLT

1 Introduction

For some petroleum-rich economies petroleum resources have turned out to be a mixed blessing in spite of the fact that OPEC I and OPEC II implied an increase in national wealth of tremendous proportions for these countries. The difficulties that arose were various, but can roughly be sorted into two types: adverse and unforeseen effects of using oil and gas revenues ('Dutch Disease') and difficulties in assessing long-term trends and adjusting the growth path of the economy accordingly. The distinction between these may be a little fictitious, as they are obviously interrelated, but one may consider extreme cases in one of which the sudden riches cause upheavals of an unprecedented nature while the future is all provided for. In the other extreme case the adjustment to the use of resource revenues is smooth and efficient, while looming in the future are problems when the resource wells run dry and the revenues are gone.

The methods discussed in this paper are applied to problems of the second kind: long-term uncertainty and how to adapt to it. The petroleum-rich country under consideration is Norway, both with regard to the application of such methods within the institutional context of long-term planning and in the empirical illustrations in section 4. The Norwegian background is described in section 2 and the formal optimization framework is set out in section 3. The general approach is inspired by Leif Johansen (1978, 1980), the mentor of Norwegian economists for 20 years until his untimely death in 1982.

2   Petroleum exploitation and the use of revenues under uncertainty: the Norwegian situation

Norway became a net exporter of crude oil in 1975 and of natural gas in 1977. The petroleum sector – production and pipeline transportation of oil and gas – now (1984) accounts for 19 per cent of GDP. Only few countries outside OPEC have a higher dependence upon the petroleum sector and very few industrialized countries have a higher dependence upon a natural resource.

At the same time as the petroleum sector rose from nothing to become considerably larger than the whole of manufacturing, i.e. from the early 1970s until today, uncertainty about economic development in Norway has been steadily increasing. The increased uncertainty has been manifest in increased fluctuations in macroeconomic aggregates, in enlarged uncertainty about the prospects for major industries, and in greater deviations between forecasts and actual developments. This can be seen partly as the result of the increasing role of a new industry with much uncertainty connected with it and partly as the result of increased uncertainty about world economic development in general. To a considerable degree petroleum activity and international economic development have pulled in opposite directions in their effect upon the industrial structure of the Norwegian economy. Petroleum activity has meant high revenues, high expected future revenues and a strong inclination to increase domestic demand, while the development in the industrialized countries has implied a reduction in growth potential through reduced growth in world trade. No wonder that *structural reallocation* has been *the* theme of economic policy debate in these years and *higher petroleum income* and *sluggish world economy* the main reference points as to what we can expect from the future.

Uncertainty about macroeconomic development is, however, nothing new in Norwegian economic history. By international standards Norway has had rapid economic growth over the past 100–150 years thanks to uncertain but profitable export-orientated activities such as timber export, pulp and paper, herring fisheries, whaling, and electrochemical and electrometallurgical processing. In spite of the openness of the economy cyclical disturbances in the post-war period have been smaller in Norway than in most countries. From the early 1970s the international picture changed with sluggish world trade, increased competition from newly industrialized countries and increased uncertainty about cyclical developments. Norwegian anticyclical policy in the 1970s, financed by drawing on future oil revenues, dampened the contractive effects of the international recession. Without the petroleum reserve the vulnerability of a small open economy would have been much more strongly felt.

The emergence of the petroleum sector represents in a way a step backwards in industrial structure with an increased emphasis on export of primary commodities. Never before has the future of the Norwegian economy been so dependent upon one single price as is the case today with the international crude oil price. On the other hand, the increased uncertainty has been amply rewarded. From the viewpoint of other small open industrialized economies the role of petroleum in the Norwegian economy may seem more like a sure card than an uncertain asset.

The dependence upon petroleum as a source of income differs from the primary commodity based sources of income of earlier times by the following characteristics:

1 The long-run time perspective of petroleum in the Norwegian economy.
2 The macroeconomic importance of petroleum activity, e.g. as a share of GDP.
3 The large resource base, as measured, for instance, by the value of unexploited petroleum resources as a share of national wealth.
4 The high rent share of gross value of petroleum production.
5 The high government share of petroleum rent.

In the national accounts petroleum rent is a component of national income. In a longer perspective the stock of unexploited petroleum – under the bed of the North Sea in the Norwegian case – can be more naturally viewed as a part of national wealth. In this perspective the production of oil and gas does not generate income, but represents the reduction of a large, yet limited, stock. The real source of income is the increase in value of these resources. A liquidated part of petroleum wealth, i.e. a produced and marketed quantity of oil or gas, can be consumed or invested in other assets such as domestic real capital or net claims on other countries. Optimal portfolios depend not only upon the relative rates of return, but also upon the uncertainty connected with portfolio alternatives and the degree of social risk aversion.

There are several factors that contribute to uncertainty in future oil and gas revenues: oil and gas prices (customarily quoted in US dollars); rates of exchange; resource base/level of production; costs of investment and production; and tax regimes.

The oil price is the prominent source of uncertainty. Gas prices may directly or indirectly be tied to oil prices. The volatility of the oil price need not be elaborated, and it is reflected in volatility of price forecasts. This could clearly be observed after OPEC II. The mainstream of international forecasters raised not only future prices but also the rate of growth of the oil price. Some leading forecasters' assessment of the oil price in 2000 is today only half of what was assumed when forecasts peaked in 1981. Such misjudgements may have grave consequences for governments!

The changes in rates of exchange in the period in which Norway has exported oil have been large also compared to annual changes in oil prices. The increase in the value of the dollar from 1982 has thus counteracted the fall in the oil price. The real value of a unit of oil for the Norwegian economy is, however, measured neither in dollars nor in Norwegian kroner but by the terms of trade between oil and an aggregate of imports.

In the formal framework below we consider the oil price – interpreted as its real value – as the only source of uncertainty. The resource base is assumed known, which, of course, it is not. It is, however, very large. Proved reserves amount to 2700 Mtoe, which means that the current level of production of 50 Mtoe can be maintained for 50 years. How much petroleum there is beyond proved reserves is anybody's guess. While the size of the oil and gas reservoirs is of great importance in really long-term considerations, uncertainty about the level of production is only of short-term interest. We remark only in passing that because the level of production determines the annual amount of revenues – and thus is of great political importance – it has in recent years been 'adjusted for uncertainty' in annual and quadrennial programmes of the Norwegian government (the formal procedure is set out in Revised National Budget 1984, Annex 1).

The fourth factor of uncertainty mentioned was costs of investment and production. We know little about future costs of production. This is in fact only the dual aspect of uncertainty about the resource base. A major uncertainty on the cost side is the probability of major breakthroughs in deep-sea technology. 'Tax regimes' were mentioned as the final factor of uncertainty. Tax rules are, of course, not uncertain for the government, but oil companies may consider future tax regimes as uncertain. For the government the uncertainty of the tax regime is its effect as incentive for exploration and investment and its efficiency in expropriating petroleum rent.

How can we deal with uncertainty about the oil price? Several characteristics distinguish the production and market conditions of petroleum from those of other export-orientated industries and explain why uncertainty in the oil sector is of greater macroeconomic importance. One reason is the large scale of individual projects. For instance the Troll field will alone require investments that in total amount to about one-third of the Norwegian GDP. Individual projects in aluminium, paper or shipping may also be uncertain, but the uncertainty is usually of much less importance at the macroeconomic level because each of these industries is small in the total economy and has little importance for government revenues.

In a systematic treatment of uncertainty in a long-term macroeconomic context we want to find out how uncertainty about future events should influence decisions made today. In the same perspective it is a point of importance to await as much information as possible before binding decisions are made. A *strategy* is in this context a decision rule that determines current policy measures as a function of the current values of state variables and the current set of information about future uncertain events. The strategy will thus determine how long-term policy should be adjusted as we go along and observe the realization of uncertain events.

In our formalization of the decision procedure we focus upon consumption as a measure of societal welfare. In the formal optimization procedure we maximize the utility of consumption (or more precisely the sum of discounted utility). The utility function we shall employ is, alas, rather arbitrarily chosen, at least with regard to empirical verification. An important feature of the utility function in this context is the degree of *risk aversion* it expresses. This can be expressed by means of *risk premium*. Let the utility function be $U(C)$ and the consumption C a stochastic variable with expectation $\bar{C}$ and variance σ^2. If the decision-maker is willing to pay a risk premium M for having the utility of expected consumption rather than the expected utility of consumption then we have

$$U(\bar{C}-M) = EU(C) \tag{1}$$

If M is positive then there is risk aversion, and the larger M the larger is the risk aversion. By a Taylor approximation of $U()$ we can from (1) find an approximate expression for the risk premium

$$M = -1/2\sigma^2 U''(\bar{C})/U'(\bar{C}) \tag{2}$$

For a given value of the variance the risk premium is proportional to $-U''/U'$ which is used as a measure of risk aversion, usually denoted as *absolute risk aversion.* Dependent upon the shape of the utility function risk aversion may be constant, increasing or decreasing with the level of consumption. The utility functions we shall apply are exponential functions. That implies constant absolute risk aversion. The advantage of this specification is the *certainty equivalence property* of the exponential utility function, whereby the stochastic optimization problem can be simplified to a non-stochastic optimization problem.

The uncertainty we shall consider apart from the oil price is uncertainty in rates of return of the other assets constituting national wealth. One of the main variables to be determined by the optimization is the rate of petroleum depletion. It will be determined as a trade-off between expected rates of return and degrees of uncertainty in oil price development compared to other rates of return. Optimal consumption is a function of current wealth and depends upon the parameters of the probability distribution and the risk aversion coefficient so that the effect of uncertainty is revealed. Uncertainty about future periods influences optimal consumption today through an income and substitution effect. A high expected oil price tomorrow implies higher optimal consumption today, while higher uncertainty of the future oil price implies lower optimal consumption. Such is the logic of our approach which we now will develop in more formal terms.

3 A multi-period optimization framework with stochastic rates of return

The optimization problem we shall consider below is the maximization of the sum of discounted utility from consumption over a planning horizon of length T, taking also into consideration the discounted utility of terminal wealth (which must be interpreted as derived from the consumption possibilities it represents beyond the planning horizon). The objective function can thus be written as

$$\sum_{t=1}^{T} U(C_t) (1+\delta)^{-t} + V(G_T) (1+\delta)^{-T-t} \tag{3}$$

where C_t is consumption in period t, G_T terminal wealth and δ the rate of time preference.

The objective function is assumed to be a sum-of-exponentials preference function

$$U(C_t) = -B \exp(-\beta C_t)$$
$$V(G_T) = -G \exp(-\gamma G_T)$$

The exponential coefficients, β and γ, are the constant absolute risk aversions of these functions.

National wealth consists of stocks of $n+1$ assets. At the beginning of each period the returns on the various assets are added up and distributed between consumption and accumulation in the same assets.

$$\sum_{i=0}^{n} r_{it} W_{it-1} = R_t = C_t + \sum_{i=0}^{n} I_{it} \tag{4}$$

All income is thus assumed to be capital income, accruing from investment undertaken one period earlier. In aggregated asset terms the budget equation can be written

$$W_{t-1} + R_t = G_{t-1} = C_t + W_t \tag{5}$$

where total wealth at the beginning of period t, G_{t-1}, consists of stocks of assets from the previous period plus capital income. The rates of return are stochastic variables assumed multi-normally distributed (see appendix). When decisions are to be made at the beginning of period t the rates of return dated t are known whereas uncertainty regarding future periods has to be taken into account. The decision problem at the beginning of each period is the distribution of total wealth and the level of consumption to be maintained in that period.

The optimization problem given by maximization of the expected value of (3) under the constraint (5) and given initial value of total wealth $\bar{G}_0$ can be approached by the method of stochastic dynamic programming which by the certainty equivalence property of the objective function can be simplified to non-stochastic dynamic programming. The solution is set out and explained in the appendix.

The framework can be extended to include natural resources among the assets although they are not usually counted as part of national wealth. The value of petroleum reserves can be measured as the product of the amount of reserves, S_t, and the price net of marginal extraction costs, $q_t = p_t - b_t$, where p_t is the current oil price and b_t is marginal extraction cost. The rate of return on petroleum reserves is equal to the rate of growth of the net oil price.

Introducing petroleum resources as an additional asset in (5) hence gives

$$W_{t-1} + R_t + q_{t-1}S_{t-1} + \left(\frac{q_t}{q_{t-1}} - 1\right) q_{t-1}S_{t-1} = G_{t-1}$$

$$= C_t + W_t + q_t S_t \tag{6}$$

By netting out petroleum terms (6) can be stated as

$$W_{t-1} + R_t + q_t X_t = C_t + W_t \tag{7}$$

where $X_t = S_t - S_{t-1}$

The stochastic assumptions concerning future oil prices are as follows. The oil price is assumed to be normally distributed with expected value π_t and variance σ_{pp}. Covariances between the oil price and the rates of return on non-oil assets are given by σ_{pj}, $j = 0, 1, \ldots, n$.

The solution of the general multi-period model is set out in the appendix. One property of the solution is the equalization of all certainty equivalent rates of returns. The corresponding equality for the certainty equivalent net oil price, $\bar{q}_{t+1}$, is

$$(\bar{q}_{t+1}/q_t) - 1 = \bar{r}_t \tag{8}$$

where $\bar{q}_{t+1} = \pi_{t+1} - b_{t+1} - K_t(\sigma_{pp}S_t + \sum_{j=0}^{n} \sigma_{pj}W_{jt})$

and $\bar{r}_t$ is the common certainty equivalent rate of return in period t. (8) implies that oil extraction should be determined by a modified Hotelling rule which is simplest in the case when there is one asset (no. 0) with a certain rate of return (i.e. $r_t = r_0$). Then it says that the certainty equivalent net oil price should grow at a rate of return equal to the certain rate of return.

In the appendix the solution is summed up in the form of *strategy functions*. The strategy function for optimal consumption is

$$C_t = b_{T-t}G_{t-1} + a_{T-t} \tag{9}$$

The optimal marginal propensity to consume b_{T-t} is dependent upon the risk aversion coefficients β and γ as well as the interest rate (certain rate of return) r_0. In the limiting case when $T-t \to \infty$, b_{T-t} approaches $r_0/(1+r_0)$ and is thus independent of γ as well as β.

The strategy functions for optimal wealth accumulation are

$$W_{it} = \frac{1}{\beta b_{T-t}} \left\{ \sum_{j=1}^{n} (\rho_j - r_0)\, \hat{\sigma}_{ij} + \hat{\sigma}_{pi}\, (\pi_{t+1} - b_{t+1} + (1+r_0)q_t) \right\} \tag{10}$$

and

$$S_t = \frac{1}{\beta b_{T-t}} \left\{ \sum_{j=1}^{n} (\rho_j - r_0)\, \hat{\sigma}_{pj} + \hat{\sigma}_{pp}\, (\pi_{t+1} - b_{t+1} - (1+r_0)q_t) \right\} \tag{11}$$

Hence, optimal oil extraction in period t is given by

$$X_t = S_t - S_{t-1} \tag{12}$$

We have thus obtained explicit solutions of optimal policy with intuitive interpretations, but only by making rather strong assumptions about the utility function, the stochastic parameters and the production structure for oil extraction.

4   Optimal depletion and wealth management under uncertainty: some illustrations

The two most important issues of economic policy in connection with petroleum activity in a country such as Norway are determination of the rate of depletion and the use of revenues. These two issues are decided in very different ways. The rate of depletion is normally under direct government control exercised mainly through leases and concessions. The use of revenues is typically not subject to separate political decisions, but is rather the result of current economic policy. The issue of the use of revenues is thus difficult to keep apart from macroeconomic planning and policy-making in general, just as petroleum revenues may not be distinguishable from other revenues. The question is how and to what extent political targets with regard to the use of revenues can and should become binding constraints on current economic policy decisions. Another question of equally great importance is what relation there should be between the rate of depletion and the use of revenues. Should the rate of depletion be determined by the intended use of petroleum rent or vice versa or neither? This issue has been referred to in Norwegian debate as the question of 'freewheeling' between depletion and use of revenues (*see*, for example, NOU 1983:27, which argues that the rate of depletion should be adjusted to a target for domestic use of revenues with a buffer fund as an intermediary).

What is really needed for economic policy purposes is a good answer to the question of how much use of petroleum revenues the medium-term economic policy should be based on. Preferably, the answer should be in a strategy form so that the dependence upon the current situation and new information is revealed. Such an answer must, however, be based on long-term optimization considerations with regard to the saving rate and the composition of wealth. It is to these issues that our approach with the concepts and tools of section 3 is addressed.

The determination of optimal wealth composition requires a comparison between expected returns and uncertainty of returns. In a long-term perspective the wealth concept should include all forms of capital accumulation: real capital, human capital, foreign assets and non-oil natural resources as well as petroleum wealth.

The rate of return on the latter is the annual increase in net oil price. Uncertainty connected with the future oil price creates considerable uncertainty about the future returns on stocks of unexploited petroleum reservoirs. If the return on total wealth can be increased by channelling petroleum incomes into other, less uncertain, assets, then depletion should take place as quickly as possible. More likely there will be a trade-off between reduced expected income and reduced uncertainty.

To approach these issues bold assumptions are needed. At the present stage the assumptions may be too bold to have great empirical relevance. They may, however, serve very well to illustrate where this approach may take us. The assumptions include an assessment of the policy-makers' preferences. After having formulated the preferences in terms of risk aversion we actually estimate the degree of risk aversion from a government advisory report. Another set of assumptions includes the stochastic structure and assessed values of parameters which we have roughly estimated from historical data. The stochastic assumptions about future oil prices are not corroborated. The macroeconomic structure of the economy is hardly visible in the optimization framework apart from definitional equations. So much for apologies.

We have approached the problem of assessing risk aversion coefficients and preferences by deriving the underlying preferences from macroeconomic projections in a report called the 'Perspective Analysis' (NOU 1983:37), published in 1983 by a government-appointed committee of experts relying to a great extent on the model tools and data sources used by the government for its projections. The committee stated views on the methodology of using macroeconomic models for long-term projections as well as presenting its own projections in the form of a reference path and alternative scenarios reflecting both uncertainty issues, policy alternatives and policy performance. All projections have been elaborated by means of the MSG model, originally constructed by Leif Johansen (1960, 1974). The MSG model is a large general equilibrium model which combines an overall macroeconomic framework with a considerable amount of detail.

The intended application of the stochastic optimization framework outlined in section 3 is mainly as a means of evaluating and corroborating long-term projections from the MSG model. Although stochastic elements are not included in the MSG model, the model is a valuable means for illustrating the wide range of possible long-term projections under alternative oil price assumptions. Model calculations are performed with alternative oil price scenarios and exogenously stipulated oil and gas production profiles. The consequences of alternative oil revenue scenarios are traced out by model calculations. These long-term projections illustrate the considerable impact on sectoral development and accumulated foreign reserves of alternative oil price assumptions. A consistent evaluation of these long-term equilibrium growth paths under uncertainty requires a stochastic optimization framework.

The projections of the Perspective Analysis were elaborated without the political commitments that are given to the projections presented in, for example, the quadrennial medium-term programme. However, for our purpose it may not be totally misleading to interpret them as reflecting current political preferences. The projections of the Perspective Analysis do not easily lend themselves to the assessment of preferences. Little is said about the evaluation of the alternative projections, and no precise guidelines are given for the trade-off between consumption and wealth accumulation.

Although no explicit welfare function or preference indicator has been applied in the elaboration of the projections, the various statements given in the report can be interpreted as expressions of a set of underlying preferences. The discussion of the policy choices between domestic use of oil revenues versus increased current account surplus has been our starting point for deriving the preferences.

The present analysis is based on the reference path and the four alternative projections which are summarized in table 5.1.

These alternative projections of the Norwegian economy toward year 2000 result in different states of the economy by the end of the planning period. In the highly simplified representation of these alternatives in our further discussion we ignore most structural and other aspects of the differences between these alternatives and focus on only two variables: consumption level (or rather increase over 1980) and wealth position. Figure 5.1 plots all five projections with regard to these two characteristics. These five projections illustrate a wide range of possibilities for the choice between consumption and accumulation of foreign assets. The two triangles in figure 5.1 indicate the feasible sets under the assumptions of either higher petroleum income (2.1 and 2.2) or sluggish world economy (3.1 and 3.2). Little is said about the choice between increased domestic use and increased capital exports in the case of higher petroleum income, and the choice between tight and lax policy in the case of a sluggish world economy.

Table 5.1   Selected results from the Perspective Analysis

Scenario	Total consumption (private and government) in 2000 as increase over 1980 (%)	Net foreign reserves in 2000 plus value of proved oil reserves in 2000 (billion kr)
1. Reference path	62.2	1419.6
2. Higher petroleum income		
2.1 Increased domestic use	82.8	1575.4
2.2 Increased capital exports	62.2	1811.8
3. Sluggish world economy		
3.1 Tight policy	50.5	1379.4
3.2 Lax policy	70.6	1204.9

Note: The figures are derived from NOU 1983:37, and unpublished material from the Ministry of Finance. The reference path is based on full employment and an increase in the production of oil and gas reaching 80 mtoe in year 2000. The crude oil price is in the reference path assumed to grow by 1 per cent per annum in real terms. Non-oil exports grow by less than 2 per cent per annum. In the two higher petroleum income scenarios the production of oil and gas is assumed to reach 90 mtoe in year 2000, while the crude oil price grows by 3 per cent per annum. In 2.1, the increased income is used to promote growth in domestic demand. Employment and the rate of technical progress increase, while in 2.2 the increased income is accumulated as foreign assets. The sluggish world economy scenarios depict developments where non-oil exports grow even less than in the reference path, only 1 per cent per annum. In 3.1 the balance of payments is maintained by means of tight demand management. Employment falls off compared with the reference path. In 3.2 on the other hand priority is given to employment. Private and government consumption are increased with adverse consequences for the balance of payments. This table reveals, in fact, little about the differences between the alternatives. The Perspective Analysis also presented three or four other alternative scenarios.

Based on the information provided in the report of the Perspective Analysis we have however adopted the following assumptions. Consider the following stochastic experiment with two possible outcomes: either the outcome of higher petroleum income is realized, where the feasible set is represented by the line segment between 2.1 and 2.2, or the outcome of a sluggish world economy is realized, where the feasible set is represented by the line segment between 3.1 and 3.2. These two outcomes are assumed to have an equal probability. The alternatives 2.1 or 2.2 and 3.1 or 3.2 thus represent extreme policies under each income

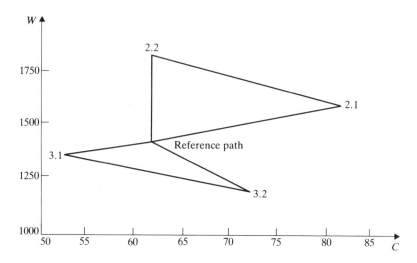

Figure 5.1   Selected projections from the Perspective Analysis.
C = Total consumption (private and government) in 2000 as percentage increase over 1980. W = Net foreign reserves plus value of proved oil reserves in 2000 (billion kroner).

scenario, and to reveal the optimal policy we state the following assumptions:

(a) Sluggish world economy: Given a feasible set of all points between 3.1 and 3.2 the best choice is to pursue a policy aiming at a result midway between the two extreme policies.

(b) Higher petroleum income: Given a feasible set of all points between 2.1 and 2.2 the best choice is to pursue a policy aiming at a result slightly closer to 2.1 than the midpoint.

(c) Reference path: The reference path is considered as the *certainty equivalent* of the stochastic experiment described above. Given the two optimal policies described in (a)–(b), the expected utility of these two outcomes is equal to the utility of the reference path.

These assumptions are formulated in view of a preference function given by

$$U(C,W) = -B\exp(-bC) - G\exp(-gW) \tag{13}$$

C = Total consumption (private and government) in 2000 as percentage increase over 1980.

W = Net foreign reserves plus value of proved oil reserves in 2000 (billion kroner)

To simplify the estimation of the risk aversion coefficients, the preference function (13) has been formulated as a static analogy to the multi-period preference function (3) of the dynamic optimization problem. In (13) preferences are attached to the percentage increase in consumption over the planning horizon, rather than the sum of discounted utility of consumption in each period. However, this reformulation does not alter the main conclusions for the trade-off between consumption and terminal wealth under uncertainty. The numerical estimate for the risk aversion coefficient b will differ from the risk aversion coefficient β of the multi-period preference function, and the appropriate estimate for β will finally be derived.

The wealth concept W defined as net foreign reserves plus the value of the oil reserves is highly tentative, to say the least. It does not properly reflect the concept of national wealth as defined in the optimization model. According to the preference function (3), consumption should be weighed against total wealth at the end of the planning period, i.e. production capital, financial assets and natural resources. The role of terminal wealth in the preference function is to represent production and income potential for future consumption beyond the planning horizon. The discussion of the Perspective Analysis is, however, more explicitly related to the trade-off between consumption growth and net foreign reserves at the end of the planning period. The point of foreign reserves in this connection seems to be as a safeguard against the risk inherent in the oil reserves. In order to accommodate the views expressed in the report as a guideline for our estimation of the risk aversion coefficients, the value of petroleum reserves and net foreign reserves are included in our wealth concept here while other assets are disregarded. This may be a dubious interpretation and inclusion of real capital would have given different estimation results.

The above assumptions (a)–(c) give three relationships to determine the parameters b, g and G/B. The level of utility is arbitrarily chosen by setting $B = 1$. Furthermore, the parameter values are adjusted to yield $G = B = 1$. The following parameter values are thus obtained:

$b = 0.1426$
$g = 0.00589$

Figure 5.2 shows the estimated preference function as represented by three indifference curves implicitly referred to in assumptions (a)–(c).

In order to apply the multi-period framework of section 3, we have to establish the correspondence between the preference function (3) of the dynamic model and the static analogy given by (13). In order to find the appropriate risk aversion coefficient in a dynamic context, we make the

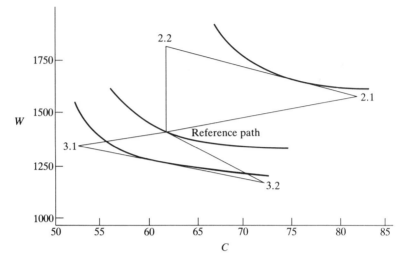

Figure 5.2   Indifference curves with $b = 0.1426$ and $g = 0.00589$.

assumption that the sum of discounted utility from consumption over the planning period is equal to the utility of the percentage increase of consumption. The annual growth rate of consumption in the reference path is 2.4 per cent. We assume that the time preference rate is 1 per cent. Given the estimate of $b = 0.1426$ an estimate of $\beta = 0.0352$ is thus obtained for the risk aversion coefficient of the dynamic model. The estimate of the risk aversion coefficient $g = 0.00589$ is calibrated in order to include the production capital. An estimate of $\gamma = 0.0027$ is thus obtained.

The model framework of section 3 requires a definition of assets constituting total national wealth. We shall distinguish between four assets apart from oil:

W_S = real capital in the sheltered sector (i.e., non-tradable goods production protected sectors)
W_E = real capital in the export sector
W_H = real capital in the import-competing sector
W_U = foreign assets

Foreign assets are assumed to yield a risk-free rate of return of 3 per cent. This is our r_0. The net oil price is measured in dollars per barrel and its expected value is assumed to increase by 2 per cent per annum through the whole period.

Table 5.2   Average rates of return: estimation period 1962–81

ρ_i	%
Sheltered sector (excluding government)	7.53
Import-competing sector	10.00
Export sector	5.45

The variance–covariance matrix for the estimated rates of return in the period 1962–81 is given in table 5.3 and the inverse variance–covariance matrix is given in table 5.4.

The choice of breakdown of non-oil national wealth is – as the other specifications of the model – rather tentative. A priori we would expect capital in the non-tradable sector to be a more certain asset (i.e., lower rate of return, but also lower variance) than investment in the tradable sectors.

For a small oil exporting country like Norway the oil price is exogenous, independent of domestic reserves and the rate of extraction.

Table 5.3   Variance–covariance matrix: estimation period 1962–81

$\sigma_{ij}, \sigma_{pj}, \sigma_{pp}$	Sheltered sector	Import-competing sector	Export sector	Real oil price
Sheltered sector	1.65685	−0.088861	−1.84331	−1.28275
Import-competing sector		2.30443	1.93291	−0.897742
Export sector			13.8807	0.621457
Real oil price				16.789

Table 5.4   Inverse variance–covariance matrix

$\hat{\sigma}_{ij}, \hat{\sigma}_{pj}, \hat{\sigma}_{pp}$	Sheltered sector	Import-competing sector	Export sector	Real oil price
Sheltered sector	0.756811	−0.037254	0.102251	0.052005
Import-competing sector		0.507531	−0.076836	0.027137
Export sector			0.096458	0.000218
Real oil price				0.064979

It may be less obvious that the stochastic rates of return on assets other than oil are independent of time and of the stocks of the respective assets, as assumed in section 3 above. In the following we assume that real capital by sector has constant expected rates of return as set out in table 5.2. This exceedingly simplified picture of a national economy can only be defended on the ground that it serves a higher purpose!

From these estimates and assumptions we can calculate a reference scenario based on the stochastic optimization model. There are many reasons why this reference scenario will not coincide with the reference scenario of the Perspective Analysis elaborated by means of the MSG model. The stochastic optimization model has hardly any macroeconomic infrastructure. The labour market, production structure and foreign trade are not explicitly dealt with. Asset composition can be changed in a frictionless way; we thus pay no attention to the transition problem of changing the asset composition from what is historically given. An additional problem is the more specific assumptions of the constancy of the parameters of the model estimated above. We have chosen, however, to interpret the scenario based on these assumptions as the appropriate scenario for the further analyses. In the reference scenario consumption increases smoothly and reaches a level in 2000 which is 74.4 per cent higher than in 1980. Investments in uncertain assets are declining throughout the planning horizon, whereas foreign debt is gradually reduced. Total wealth is increasing in early years and is decreasing thereafter. The development of total wealth is crucially dependent on the relationship between the risk aversion parameters and the risk-free rate of return. The parameters of our reference scenario give the condition

$$\beta/\gamma < (1+r_0)/r_0 \tag{14}$$

which entails a concave path of total wealth. If the inequality sign is reversed, total wealth increases along a convex path.

Optimal oil reserves in 1980 turn out somewhat lower than the actual level of oil reserves in 1980. An initial jump in the oil production profile to 161 Mtoe is thus necessary in order to reach the optimal path which starts at 106 Mtoe in 1981 and increases gradually to 123 Mtoe in 2000.

The scenarios of the Perspective Analysis which we are referring to illustrate the implications of tight and lax economic policy under alternative scenarios for uncertain future income. These policy alternatives are established by variations in the exogenous variables and government instruments in the MSG model. It is not obvious how a corresponding simulation of policy alternatives can be performed in the stochastic optimization model. However, different assumptions about the risk aversion parameters entail a different propensity to pursue a tight or a lax economic policy. Consider a situation where the government is more concerned about future consumption possibilities and wants to pursue a policy for increasing the national wealth at the end of the planning period. In a fully elaborated macroeconomic context this is aimed at by steering the exogenous variables so as to decrease current consumption and promote accumulation in foreign (and domestic) assets. In our model it is natural to express such a concern in terms of risk aversion: a policy which aims at reducing current consumption and increasing terminal wealth corresponds to a shift in the risk aversion parameters toward higher β and lower γ.

In order to realize the effect of risk aversion, it is elucidating to express a specified change in economic policy by the corresponding variations in the risk aversion parameters. In this empirical application we have intended to interpret the policy alternatives discussed by the perspective analysis in terms of risk aversion.

The alternatives 2.2 and 3.1 represent the tight policy alternative under each income scenario, whereas 2.1 and 3.2 represent the lax policy alternatives. By variations in β and γ we have established the scenarios of our model which correspond to these four policy alternatives. The results are presented in table 5.5.

Table 5.5   Selected results from the stochastic optimization model

Scenario	Total consumption in 2000 (billion kr)	Total wealth 2000 (billion kr)	Net foreign reserves 2000 (billion kr)
1. Reference path	490	5568	−1219
2. Higher petroleum income			
2.1 Increased domestic use	658	5561	−973
2.2 Increased capital exports	527	7846	−878
3. Sluggish world economy			
3.1 Tight policy	417	5619	−1218
3.2 Lax policy	492	4904	−1911

As the reference scenario of the stochastic optimization model deviates from the reference scenario of the MSG model, it has not been our intention to simulate the four alternatives (2.1, 2.2, 3.1, 3.2) exactly by appropriate adjustments of the risk aversion parameters. However, we have applied the same *criteria* for establishing our alternatives as those of the Perspective Analysis:

Tight policy in the high expected income scenario (= 2.2) and lax policy in the low expected income scenario (= 3.2) should aim at the same consumption in 2000 as the reference scenario

Tight policy in the low expected income scenario (= 3.1) and lax policy in the high expected income scenario (= 2.1) should aim at the same terminal wealth position as the reference scenario.

These criteria have been our guidelines for the choice of appropriate variations of the risk aversion coefficients. The numerical results can be summarized as follows:

An increase in β of 15 per cent corresponds to a tight policy whereby consumption is reduced according to this criterion. Since the terminal wealth position differs between the two income scenarios, it was furthermore necessary to reduce γ by 10 per cent to simulate 2.2 and to reduce γ by 5 per cent to simulate 3.1. Terminal wealth varies inversely with γ. Since 2.2 is the alternative of higher expected income than 3.1, it was necessary to reduce γ relatively more in the simulation of 2.2 to account for the large terminal wealth of this alternative.

In the simulation of the lax policy alternatives 2.1 and 3.2, β was decreased accordingly, i.e. by 15 per cent. Since the terminal wealth position of 2.1 should reflect the higher expected income as compared to 3.2, γ is increased by 20 per cent in 2.1 and decreased by 5 per cent in 3.2.

The variations in the risk aversion coefficients β and γ in the simulation alternatives are all within the range given by (14). Investments in uncertain assets decline monotonically in all simulation alternatives, as our assumptions about the risk aversion parameters entail that a conversion from uncertain assets into the risk-free alternative will take place. Thus foreign debt is reduced throughout the planning period in all alternatives. However, none of the alternatives implies positive net foreign reserves within a horizon of 20 years. The explanation is that initial optimal accumulation in the uncertain assets is substantially higher in all alternatives than the corresponding national accounts figures for 1979, which are used to determine initial wealth of the model. In order to realize the optimal solutions for consumption and investments in uncertain assets a substantial foreign debt has to be incurred initially and positive net foreign reserves will not be obtained within a time span of 20 years. This conclusion is crucially dependent on the constancy of the parameters other than the risk aversion coefficients. If e.g. the standard deviation of the oil price is increased by 25 per cent, the reference scenario will in fact come out with positive net foreign reserves in 2000.

Within each alternative oil production is fairly constant once the optimal path has been reached (see figure 5.3). In the alternatives of lax policy 2.1 and 3.2, the initial optimal value of the oil reserves is substantially higher than the initial estimate for the value of the oil reserves because of the reduction in the risk aversion coefficient β. As a consequence, the model gives negative oil extraction in 1980 (not shown in the figure). Similarly, a substantial peak occurs in initial oil production in the tight policy alternatives 2.2 and 3.1 because the initial

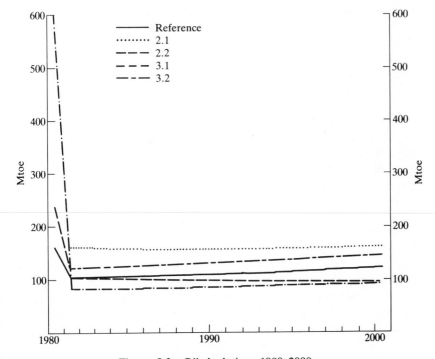

Figure 5.3   Oil depletion, 1980–2000.
Note: for scenarios 2.1 and 3.2 the first-year depletion is negative, about −320 Mtoe.

optimal value of the oil reserves is reduced due to the higher degree of risk aversion. However, from 1981 the oil production paths show that optimal oil production is higher in the lax policy alternatives and lower in the tight policy alternatives as compared to the reference scenario.

Although solutions with initial peaks in oil production or initial negative oil production are not exceptional in an optimization context, they can naturally not be implemented. In terms of policy guidelines, we can, however, interpret the initial negative oil production as an indication that oil production has been too high in the preceding periods and the remaining level of oil reserves is too small in 1980 as compared to the optimal oil reserves. If oil production is temporarily postponed for some years, the value of the oil reserves will gradually reach the optimal level, and thereafter oil production can follow the optimal path.

Accordingly, a solution with initial oil production which is higher than existing capacity suggests that actual oil production should gradually increase above the optimal level until the optimal reallocation of uncertain assets has taken place.

As a consequence of uncertainty, oil production in all alternatives is higher throughout the planning horizon than the projected oil production paths in the scenarios of the Perspective Analysis. However, in the alternatives of low risk aversion (2.1 and 3.2), optimal oil reserves are initially higher than the current estimate because it is more profitable to maintain uncertain assets. On the other hand, the optimal terminal oil reserves come out lower in *all* alternatives as compared to the projections of the Perspective Analysis. Thus the conclusion that uncertainty provides an incentive to increase oil production and convert the oil reserves into more certain assets, is near at hand. Our conclusion is in accordance with the present value calculations given in the report of the government-appointed committee on the future extent of petroleum activities on the Norwegian continental shelf (NOU 1983:27, annex 14). In these present value considerations uncertainty was not explicitly taken into account. However, it must be kept in mind that although a lower risk aversion implies higher oil production, it also indicates that the initial oil reserves should be higher.

In terms of risk aversion, we have thus established alternatives for economic policy corresponding to what is considered by the Perspective Analysis as a relevant feasible set. Starting from the given stochastic assumptions and with a given degree of risk aversion, the stochastic optimization model yields guidelines for policy implications under uncertainty, which can be applied for evaluating long-term macroeconomic projections for the MSG-model. Perhaps a lesson to be drawn is that moderate variations in the attitude toward risk may have fairly large impacts in terms of choices of economic policy.

Appendix   Solution of the multi-period optimization problem

Optimization criteria:

$$\underset{\substack{\text{Max}\\ \text{w.r.t. } W_{it}}}{\text{Max}} \quad E\left\{ \sum_{t=1}^{T} U(C_t)(1+\delta)^{-t} + V(G_T)(1+\delta)^{-T-1} \right\}$$

for all i, t

Constraint:

$$\sum_{i=0}^{n} (1+r_{it}) W_{it-1} = G_{t-1} = C_t + \sum_{i=0}^{n} W_{it}$$

Initial condition:

$$G_0 = \bar{G}_0$$

Stochastic assumptions:

The r_{it}'s normally distributed with expectations $\{\rho_i\}$ and variance–covariances $\{\sigma_{ij}\}$ and with stochastic independence between rates of return in different periods.

The optimization criterion given above is not well defined as the dynamic structure of the decisions is not revealed. A more precise formulation can be given using the notation of dynamic programming which is also the method we shall employ to solve the problem.

Dynamic programming formulation:

$$J_t(G_{t-1}) = \underset{\substack{\text{Max}\\ \text{w.r.t. } W_{it}}}{\text{Max}} \quad E_t\{U(C_t) + J_{t+1}(G_t)/(1+\delta)\} \tag{15}$$

for all $i, t = 1,2,\ldots,T$

$$J_{T+1}(G_T) = V(G_T) \tag{16}$$

Specification of utility functions:

$$U(C_t) = -B \exp(-\beta C_t)$$

$$V(G_T) = -G \exp(-\gamma G_T)$$

The specification of the utility functions and the stochastic assumptions imply that the problem can be transformed from a stochastic to a non-stochastic dynamic programming problem. This follows from $J_T()$ being an exponential function as we shall show below and the *certainty equivalence property of exponential functions,* namely

$$E \exp(-\alpha x) = \exp(-\alpha \tilde{x})$$

where $\tilde{x} = Ex - 1/2\alpha \operatorname{var} x$, whenever x is normally distributed. We use the tilde above a variable to indicate the application of this certainty equivalence operator. (The notation is not fully satisfactory but should cause no misunderstandings in this context.)

The dynamic programming formulation (15) can be rewritten in non-stochastic form on the assumption that $J_{t+1}()$ is an exponential function (which obviously is the case for $t=T$) as

$$J_t(G_{t-1}) = \operatorname*{Max}_{\text{w.r.t. } W_{it}} \quad \{U(C_t) + J_{t+1}(\tilde{G}_t)/(1+\delta)\} \tag{17}$$

for all i

First-order conditions:

$$U'(C_t) = [(1+\tilde{r}_{it})/(1+\delta)]J'_{t+1}(\tilde{G}_t) \qquad i = 0,1,\ldots,n \tag{18}$$

where the $\tilde{r}_i$'s are certainty equivalent rates of return defined as

$$\tilde{r}_{it} = \sigma\tilde{G}_t/\delta W_{it} - 1$$

It is immediate from the first order conditions that all certainty equivalent rates of return are identical.

$$\tilde{r}_{it} = \tilde{r}_t$$

By the envelope theorem we have

$$J'_t(G_{t-1}) = U'(C_t)$$

We can now easily prove that if $J_{t+1}()$ is an exponential function then $J_t()$ is also exponential. As $J_{T+1}()$ is defined by (16) as an exponential function, it would follow that $J_t()$ is exponential for all t. If $J_{t+1}()$ is an exponential function, then it follows from the first-order condition that $J_{t+1}(\tilde{G}_t^*)$ is proportional to $U(C_t^*)$ where $\tilde{G}_t^*$ and C_t^* are maximizing functions of G_{t-1}. Hence

$$\frac{J_t'(G_{t-1})}{J_t(G_{t-1})} = \frac{U'(C_t^*)}{U(C_t^*) + J_{t+1}(\tilde{G}_t^*)/(1+\delta)} = -K_t \tag{19}$$

is independent of G_{t-1} and $J_t()$ is exponential. The exponential coefficient K_t can be found recursively from (19) as

$$\beta/K_t = 1 + \beta/K_{t+1}(1+\tilde{r}_t) \qquad t = 1,2,\ldots,T$$
$$K_{T+1} = Y$$

Using K_t the certainty equivalent rates of return can be written out more explicitly as

$$\tilde{r}_{it} = \rho_i - K_t \sum_{j=0}^{n} \sigma_{ij} W_{jt} \qquad i = 0,1,\ldots,n \tag{20}$$

The whole model can now be solved recursively. The solution can be given in various forms. We are particularly interested in the solution given in the form of *strategy functions*, i.e. the solution of W_{it} and C_t given as functions of the state variable G_{t-1}. One of these functions follows of course from the others. Below are given the solutions for C_t and W_{it}, $i=1,2,\ldots,n$ in an almost explicit form.

Strategy function for consumption:

$$C_t = b_{T-t}G_{t-1} + a_{T-t} \tag{21}$$

where

$$b_{T-t} = \gamma \prod_{\tau=t}^{\tau=T} (1+\tilde{r}_\tau)/\left\{\beta + \gamma \sum_{\mu=1}^{T-t+1} \prod_{\tau=T-\mu+1}^{\tau=T} (1+\tilde{r}_\tau)\right\}$$

and $a_{T-t} = (1-b_{T-t})(a_{T-t-1} - (\tilde{r}_t - \delta_t^*)/\beta)$

with $a_{-1} = \ln(\beta B/\gamma G)/\beta$

b_{T-t} is in fact equal to K_t/β. a_{T-t} depends upon the remaining horizon $T-t$, the rate of time preference δ, the parameters of the preference functions and the stochastic structure. The rate of time preference and the stochastic parameters are subsumed in an *uncertainty adjusted rate of time preference*:

$$\delta_t^* = \delta + 1/2 \sum_{i=0}^{n} \sum_{j=0}^{n} (\rho_i - \tilde{r}_t)(\rho_j - \tilde{r}_t)\sigma_{ij}$$

Strategy functions for wealth accumulation:

$$W_{it} = \sum_{j=0}^{n} \hat{\sigma}_{ij}(\rho_j - \bar{r}_t)/K_t \qquad i=0,1,\ldots,n \tag{22}$$

where $\{\hat{\sigma}_{ij}\}$ is the inverse variance–covariance matrix. The solution is not quite explicit as $\bar{r}_t$ is also endogenously determined. A simplification which will be applied in the empirical illustration is to assume that asset 0 is risk-free, yielding a certain return r_0. Then the occurrences of $\bar{r}_t$ in (22) and in the expression for b_{T-t}, a_{T-t} and δ_t^* can be replaced by r_0.

The rationale for the utility of terminal wealth is that the terminal wealth represents consumption possibilities beyond the horizon given by T. This can be utilized to derive the parameters of $V()$, G and γ, from those of $U()$. The permanent consumption level that can be maintained beyond T on the basis of remaining terminal wealth is

$$C_t = \frac{r_0}{1+r_0} G_T \qquad t = T+1, T+2,\ldots$$

and the utility of beyond horizon consumption is

$$V(G_T)/(1+\delta)^{T+1} = \sum_{t=T+1}^{\infty} U(r_0 G_T)/(1+\delta)^t$$

It then follows that

$$\gamma = \beta_0/(1+r_0) \text{ and}$$
$$G = B(1+\delta)/\delta$$

For a more complete discussion see Aslaksen and Bjerkholt (1985). This approach follows Samuelson (1969) and Chow (1975).

REFERENCES

Aslaksen I. and O. Bjerkholt (1985) 'Certainty Equivalence Procedures in the Macroeconomic Planning of an Oil Economy', in O. Bjerkholt and E. Offerdal (eds) *Macroeconomic Prospects for a Small Oil Exporting Country*, The Hague: Martinus Nijhoff, pp. 283–318.

Chow G. C. (1975) *Analysis and Control of Dynamic Economic Systems*, New York: Wiley, chapter 8, pp. 197–201.

Johansen L. (1960) *A Multi-Sectoral Study of Economic Growth*, Amsterdam: North-Holland.

Johansen I. (1974) *A Multi-Sectorial Study of Economic Growth,* 2nd ed. Amsterdam: North-Holland.

Johansen L. (1978) *Lectures on Macroeconomic Planning,* Part 2. Amsterdam: North-Holland, chapter 8.

Johansen L. (1980) 'Parametric Certainty Equivalence Procedures in Decision-making under Uncertainty', *Zeitschrift für Nationalökonomie,* **40,** 257–79.

NOU 1983:27 'The Future Extent of Petroleum Activities on the Norwegian Continental Shelf'. Universitetsforlaget.

NOU 1983:37 'Perspektrivberegninger for norsk økonomi til år 2000'. Universitetsforlaget.

Revised National Budget 1984 Report to the Storting no. 88 (1983–84), Ministry of Finance.

Samuelson P.A. (1969) 'Lifetime Portfolio Selection by Dynamic Stochastic Programming'. *Review of Economics and Statistics,* **51,** 239–46.

COMMENT DAVID M. G. NEWBERY

This is a useful and stimulating paper on an important topic which has been somewhat neglected in recent discussions of the macroeconomics of natural resources. Oil wealth is a large fraction of Norwegian wealth – 71 per cent in 1980 (Aslaksen and Bjerkholt, 1985, table 5) – and its value will fluctuate with the price of oil. Since there is substantial uncertainty about future oil prices, the Norwegian economy therefore faces significant risk. The claim of this paper is that aggregate consumption and savings decisions ought to be influenced by the existence of this risk, as should the oil depletion plan.

Few would disagree that the problem is important, but most economists and policy-makers might be tempted to throw up their hands and claim that the problem is too difficult for quantitative analysis. It is the great merit of this paper that it presents a set of assumptions under which the problem can be solved quantitatively and, more usefully, in a way which allows one to engage analytically with the important issues. My first task is to explain the strategy adopted by the authors in a way which makes it more accessible. The second task is to point to the roles played by the various assumptions, so that one can judge whether they are acceptable, or whether they need modification. I shall argue that at least for some policy issues the assumptions do need modifying, but that the present model remains useful for its intuitive insights and as a benchmark against which to compare alternatives.

The key assumption, which simplifies the analysis and drives the results, is that the oil price follows a random walk with drift. In other words, if, as assumed, the trend rate of growth of the real oil price is 2 per cent per annum, and if the initial price of oil today is p_0, then the expected price in T years time is normally distributed with a mean value of $p_0(1.02)^T$ and a variance of $\sigma_{pp}T$, or, from table 5.3 of the paper, US\$16.8T/barrel. Put another way, the coefficient of variation of the estimated price of oil in 20 years time, starting from a 1980 price of oil of \$30/barrel, is 44.6 per cent. A 10 per cent fall in the current price of oil leads to all future expected prices falling by the same 10 per cent. A direct consequence of this is that if the current net price (i.e. the price net of extraction costs) falls by 10 per cent, then so does the value of oil wealth.

Given the assumption that oil prices follow a random walk, the choice of model is then fairly simple – it is an intertemporal version of the capital asset pricing model. An exponential utility function (i.e. one exhibiting constant absolute risk aversion) together with the assumption that asset returns are jointly normally distributed makes the certainty equivalent value of risky income or wealth a linear function of mean and variance. (For a discussion of the advantages and limitations of this approach, see Newbery and Stiglitz, 1981, pp. 85–9.) It makes asset demand functions linear, and consequently the optimal level of current consumption is a linear function of current wealth, as in equation (9):

$$C_t = b_{T-t}G_{t-1} + a_{T-t}.$$

From the numbers presented, the first term on the right hand side accounts for about 83 per cent of total consumption in 1980. Given the share of oil wealth in total wealth, then, the elasticity of consumption to the net price of oil is about 0.6. Thus a 10 per cent fall in the current price of oil should lead current desired consumption to be reduced by 6 per cent. Adjustment costs will reduce the speed with which this adjustment is made, but will not reduce the magnitude of the desired reduction. If one ignores the variances and covariances of the other components of Norwegian wealth, then one can quickly estimate the implied coefficient of variation of consumption from that of oil, and it will be about 8 per cent, which is obviously quite large and indicates the importance of oil risk to Norway.

The response of oil depletion to a change in next year's forecast price can be deduced from equations (11) and (12). Differentiate X_t with respect to next period's expected oil price, q_{t+1}, and insert the numerical values for the parameters, and one finds that a fall in the expected price of \$1/barrel leads to an increase in current extraction rates of about 41 Mtoe (using data from Aslaksen and Bjerkholt, 1985), or about 40 per cent of planned depletion rates, as shown in figure 5.3 of the paper. Roughly the same increase in current optimal depletion rates would follow from an increase in the current net price of oil, q_t, holding expected future prices constant. In a way, the interesting feature of these results is not so much that the response is so large, but that it is so small, for no constraints on the rate of extraction have been imposed. In the deterministic case a small deviation of current prices from the equilibrium price path would induce a potentially unbounded supply response, enough to ensure that the price never succeeded in deviating from its equilibrium. Here the presence of risk means that the oil producer hedges his bets by responding to some extent, neither reducing his supply to zero nor attempting to sell his entire portfolio in response to small price movements.

Nevertheless, the sensitivity of oil supply to price changes is still large, and constraints on supply would obviously limit the supply responsiveness in practice. But the moment one recognizes the importance of supply constraints, then one is also forced to question whether the extraction decision, and the extraction costs, have been appropriately modelled. The characteristic feature of deep off-shore oil production is that most of the substantial production costs are incurred as investment before any oil is extracted. The size of the investment influences the maximum rate at which the reservoir can be depleted, and once this decision has been taken, current extraction costs are very low. It then follows that if oil prices are expected to rise more slowly than the rate of interest (and the assumption in the paper of a trend rate of increase of real oil prices of 2 per cent per annum would seem consistent with this case), it is optimal to deplete at the maximum efficient rate (bearing in mind such physical factors as the reservoir dynamics). The interesting depletion decision is not how fast to draw down oil from presently producing fields, but rather, how quickly to exploit new fields, and what quantity of production capacity to install. It may be that the present model could be adjusted to deal with that problem, though one would have to model the investment costs rather carefully.

The main implication of assuming a random walk for oil prices is that the past history of oil price movements gives no information at all about the likely future course of oil prices (except for revealing the standard deviation of oil price changes). The same is often argued to be true of financial assets, and is a characterization of an efficient asset market, in which all predictable profit opportunities have been arbitraged away. To apply this same arbitrage argument to the oil market would require a fringe of competitive suppliers with similar cost conditions to Norway, and facing no constraints on varying their rates of production. Since supply constraints are in fact very important for the kind of fringe producers who might be expected to behave competitively, one should be wary of accepting the random walk hypothesis without careful examination of plausible alternatives. One useful test question to ask is whether a large fall in the current price of oil leads analysts to lower substantially their forecast price of oil in 20 years' time, or whether it might lead them to raise the forecast price. If the current fall reflects new information about reserves or the level of likely future demand, then a downward revision might well be appropriate, but a fall due to current market instabilities, or the fragmentation of OPEC, or a world recession, or a rise in current real interest rates, might, by increasing demand for oil without increasing forecast reserves, lead analysts to expect a tighter oil market in the future. If so, then oil prices in successive periods will not be uncorrelated, as assumed here. The great advantage of assuming that prices in successive periods are uncorrelated is that it simplifies the choice of assets – and in particular how much oil to hold in the ground, i.e. how much to deplete this period. If prices in different periods were negatively correlated then the portfolio problem would require that the choice of current and future oil stocks were taken simultaneously, greatly increasing the dimensionality of the problem. It might be interesting to explore a three period version to see whether the qualitative results for the depletion rule are greatly affected.

There are a number of other interesting methodological and calibration questions which throw further light on the way the model works. In this type of model the utility function plays two roles – it captures attitudes to risk and intertemporal consumption preferences. For tractability it is tempting to work with constant absolute risk aversion utility functions as these give rise to linear asset demand functions, and are thus easy to solve. They give rise to less satisfactory intertemporal consumption paths and I think one would be wary of taking them very seriously, except for the very near term. There is a deeper problem, and that is how to calibrate such a function. Obviously it should give plausible consumption and savings behaviour, but one then is forced to ask whether calibrating it to give such behaviour leads to plausible attitudes to risk. It is hard to interpret the values of constant absolute risk aversion, since these are not dimensionless, but from the data given one can calculate the implied value of the coefficient of relative risk aversion, which is dimensionless, and hence can be readily compared with values found from other empirical studies of behaviour under risk. The coefficient of relative risk aversion to variations in wealth, R (which is the form typically dealt with in the standard static framework), is, in the notation of the paper,

$$R = -GV''(G)/V'(G),$$

where $-V''/V'$ is γ, or 0.0027, and G is wealth, or 4596 billion 1980 Nkr in 2000. From these numbers $R = 12.3$, which seems rather high – numbers of between 1 and 2 being more plausible for an individual's attitude to risk. An alternative measure of attitudes to risk, which is theoretically less attractive but empirically more plausible, is the measure of partial risk aversion, P, where

$$P = -C \ U''(C)/U'(C),$$

and where U is the utility of current consumption, C. Binswanger (1981), who discusses this formulation, the empirical evidence for it and the theoretical objections against it, finds values of between 1 and 2 from his experimental studies, again for individuals. Using the data from the paper P would be about 7, and again rather high. The conclusion is that it is difficult to construct a utility function which exhibits plausible behaviour for intertemporal decisions and plausible attitudes to risk. The problem may lie in the different focus of optimal aggregate growth models and measurements of individual attitudes to risk – i.e. the problem may be one of aggregation. It may well be that most of the adverse consequences of varying aggregate consumption fall on a small subset of individuals, whose consumption fluctuates considerably more than the average or aggregate, and for whom the costs of risk are therefore substantially higher. It may therefore be quite reasonable to attribute rather higher levels of risk aversion at the aggregate level to capture the uneven way in which risks are borne within the population.

It should also be noted that the optimal consumption path is very sensitive to the rate of pure time preference and the rate of return on the safe asset. Apart from the problem that one might be loath to accept that foreign investment represented a way of avoiding all risk, this sensitivity to two numbers, neither of which is known with any precision, creates additional unease – not so much with this paper but with the present state of the theory of intertemporal decision-making.

Another aspect of model calibration which is slightly troubling is that the estimated variance–covariance matrix presented in table 5.3 suggests that the price of oil is positively correlated with the price of exports and negatively correlated with the sheltered sector – both very much at variance with the Dutch Disease story. Presumably these numbers were estimated from a period of Norway's history when her oil was as yet undiscovered. If so, then the numbers are not relevant to the present position and should be replaced with estimates derived either from an economy with a past history of oil wealth, or perhaps from a simulation of a model of the current Norwegian economy.

These comments may sound critical, but they are intended to clarify the kind of exercise with which we have been presented, and to suggest features that could probably be modified if they were thought to be unsatisfactory, though some of them will require theoretical advances as well as different functional forms. For some purposes the results of the paper are likely to be fairly robust – thus if one believes the random walk oil price hypothesis, then continuous and large adjustments in the level of desired consumption are an almost inevitable consequence of the sheer magnitude of Norway's oil wealth. At the other extreme, I think one would be least happy in accepting the implied depletion rule, though in part for reasons which are inevitably left out of this kind of exercise – such as the problem of absorptive capacity, the rationality of governments, the problems of macroeconomic adjustment and the lumpiness and irreversibility of oil investment decisions. Some of these issues have been dealt with elsewhere in this volume, and the others will doubtless continue to challenge Norwegian (and other) economists.

REFERENCES

Aslaksen I. and O. Bjerkholt (1985) 'Certainty Equivalence Procedures in the Macroeconomic Planning of an Oil Economy', in O. Bjerkholt and E. Offerdal (eds) *Macroeconomic Prospects for a Small Oil Exporting Country*, The Hague: Martinus Nijhoff, chapter 12.
Binswanger H. P. (1981) 'Attitudes Towards Risk: Theoretical Implications of an Experiment in Rural India', *Economic Journal*, **91**, 867–90.
Newbery D. M. G. and J. E. Stiglitz (1981) *The Theory of Commodity Price Stabilization*, Oxford: Oxford University Press.

6

A macro model of an oil exporter: Nigeria*

LANCE TAYLOR, KADIR T. YURUKOGLU and SHAHID A. CHAUDHRY

Macro forecasting models for developing countries put strong demands on theory and data. On the data side, available national accounts rarely permit econometric testing in the usual sense – with sufficient ingenuity any hypothesis can be 'verified' on a time series of 10 or 20 annual points. Theory is required to put such short series (plus cross-sectional information) into useful patterns. The accounting balances underlying national income estimates help in this process, by relating price and quantity variables therein. Starting from the national accounts in a base year, not many additional restrictions are required to fit the past to an alarming degree of precision. Prior judgement about how the economy operates must underlie the choice of restrictions appropriate to the problems at hand.

This paper is about a macro model for Nigeria. It relies on the substantial body of theory that has grown up in the past few years on mineral or oil-exporting economies.[1] The model was designed in the light of this theory to forecast and analyse policy changes for Nigeria in the short to medium run.

Through the 1970s, changes in the structure of the Nigerian economy followed the classical pattern for mineral exporters. Oil extraction uses minimal domestic inputs. Structural adjustment requires the absorption of the foreign resources that petroleum exports create into the national production and consumption economy. As in most mineral-exporting countries, the production pattern in Nigeria during the 1970s shifted towards non-traded goods – for its level of per capita income the country has a low share in GDP of both industry and agriculture. Some degree of market isolation for domestic agriculture persists because of bureaucratic and transportation bottlenecks, but agricultural exports declined from over a billion to less than a hundred million dollars a year with the arrival of oil. Domestic manufacturing is more directly open to foreign competition than agriculture, and consequently may benefit more from official protection.

Other results of the growth of oil exports were increased monetization of the economy, and a shift in relative prices towards home goods. Fiscal and monetary policies are not easily distinguished in a country like Nigeria since the federal deficit is largely financed by borrowing from the banking system or abroad. The ratio of money supply (M_2) to GDP rose from 12 to 33 per cent between 1972 and 1980. This growth in bank liabilities was partly related to oil – the share in GDP of the thoroughly monetized petroleum sector rose from 11 to 27 per cent over the same period. Even if oil exports boom again, however, fiscal expansion must be more restrained than in the past – the M_2/GDP ratio cannot maintain the growth rates of the 1970s. But in the early 1980s – with overt trade deficits – fiscal deficit spending is required to generate both aggregate demand and healthy money supply growth.

The shift in relative prices towards home goods had at least two important consequences. The adjustment was inflationary since the nominal wage or price of labour – at least partially a non-traded good – rose, fed in to further cost increases, and generated a price–wage spiral. The other outcome was an 'overvalued' real exchange rate, or a low relative price of non-petroleum traded goods. Attempts at altering this price structure will play a key role in Nigerian policy over the next several years.

When the model described here was put together in 1982 and 1983, the likely situation over the next few years was that oil exports would grow only slowly from their already low levels of 1981 and 1982. The current account was in deficit, and keeping its magnitude within limits imposed by available foreign finance was essential. For the longer term, altering the structure of the economy to permit effective import substitution and non-oil export promotion was of importance, since Nigerian oil reserves may allow only a decade or two of production in the 1.5–2 million barrel per day (mbd) range. Available policy tools are largely commercial (devaluation, tariffs and subsidies, quotas) and fiscal. It has already been noted that fiscal and monetary policies are closely linked. An additional institutional constraint is that the Nigerian constitution mandates that 45 per cent of federal revenues be passed directly to state and local governments. Since the marginal propensity to consume of these entities may safely be assumed to be one, the overall spending propensity of the consolidated government is quite high. This short-run manifestation of 'Please's Law' strongly influences the effectiveness of policy instruments, as discussed below.[2]

In what follows, section 1 describes how the model was constructed to marry weak data with macro theory. The following section discusses calibration, or how the numbers were adjusted to the model. A base run for the period 1981–6 is set out in section 3, and individual exogenous or policy-based perturbations to the base simulations are described in section 4. Possible effects of policy packages are outlined in section 5, and conclusions appear in section 6.

1   Model structure

As the foregoing sketch indicates, the structure of prices – of home goods versus traded goods, real versus nominal exchange rate, price relationships among various traded goods – is a key policy issue in an oil-exporting country. The other major issue is maintenance of aggregate demand.

It seems reasonable to approach these questions by using a price-sensitive Keynesian model, as set out in this section.[3] The usual way to build in price responsiveness is with neoclassical tools – the present model incorporates a combination of CES and Cobb–Douglas technology specifications on the supply side, a complete system of demand equations and price-elastic exports. It is possible that all this apparatus overstates the flexibility of the Nigerian economy – observations will be made on this issue as we go along. It seems unlikely, however, that at present the economy is strongly supply-constrained; hence the Keynesian orientation of the model.

We begin with a description of the model's within-period (of one year) price formation rules, its income-generation mechanisms and the circular flow of income back to production through the demand side. Monetary linkages and dynamics of change from one year to the next are then described. In practice, the model is a simple computable general equilibrium (CGE) system, and is readily solved. Indeed, in Lagos it was set up on an Apple microcomputer and is perhaps the first CGE model running on such a small machine.

The accounting is in terms of four producing sectors based on the usual disaggregation in the national income statistics – petroleum extraction, agriculture, manufacturing and 'home goods' (or the rest of the economy including construction). In addition, five major categories of imports are considered – intermediates into agriculture and manufacturing, capital goods, services and consumer imports of agricultural and manufactured goods. All are 'non-competitive' in the sense that their

204 L. Taylor, K. T. Yurukoglu and S. A. Chaudhry

prices from the world market do not directly determine values of comparable domestic goods from trade arbitrage and the 'Law of One Price'. However, demand levels for domestic and imported 'similar' products from agriculture and income are assumed to respond to relative prices, as discussed below.[4]

Internal price formation centres on the demand–supply balance for home goods. Demand faced by the sector rises with economic activity but is reduced by an increase in the home goods price. Within the model's solution period of one year, supply of home goods from both domestic production and imports is assumed to respond slightly to price. That is, imports of services go up when the home goods price rises relatively to import costs as figured above. The production of home goods also rises with the price level, from a base set by available credit and historical circumstances as discussed below. Market equilibrium is attained when the price adjusts to bring excess demand (demand less home production and service imports) to zero. A price-clearing non-traded sector is a central feature in most theoretical models of an oil-exporting economy.

Prices in manufacturing and agriculture are cost-based, with supply adjusting freely to meet demand. The manufacturing cost function is based on a combination of CES and Cobb–Douglas technologies, with constant returns to scale. Intermediate inputs (imported, and from the non-oil domestic sectors) trade off in a CES technology, with an elasticity of substitution of one-third to produce a generalized intermediate product.

The manufacturing producer price is a geometric mean of this input, capital costs with a pre-specified profit rate, and interest costs on credit from the banking system for working capital and wages. The chief exogenous items are the money wage and intermediate import costs as determined by a tariff and the exchange rate. Both wage and exchange rate are assumed fixed within the year, but they change between solution periods according to rules discussed below. To a large extent, the manufacturing producer price is a mark-up over these elements of prime or variable cost. If wages and exchange rates rise, then prices will follow in an inflationary spiral.

Price formation in agriculture is similar, except that decreasing returns to scale are assumed in a Cobb–Douglas technology, so the producers' price depends positively on the level of output, as well as on variable costs. The two main cost elements are the wage and interest on working capital. Also, the price level responds negatively to increased modern capital in agriculture (the accumulation mechanism is discussed below) and to the volume of a modern input package provided by the government.

The last price-determination rules apply in the petroleum sector. Here, the dollar price per barrel of exported oil (net of imports of grades of crude required to keep domestic refineries and the sales network operating) is fixed from the world market; the volume of exports is also predetermined. The internal sale price is a policy variable, and in general it differs from the world price. Internal oil demand is assumed to be sensitive to this price, as well as to real disposable income. The level of oil production is determined by demand, and profits on all sales accrue to the federal government, after deduction of foreign and domestic processing charges and intermediate input costs.

With these pricing rules in hand, the next step is to spell out income generation mechanisms and trace the circular flow of purchasing power from production around to demand.

As just noted, value-added in petroleum all goes to the federal government (the relatively small wage bill is ignored). Real federal outlays on current consumption and capital formation are predetermined policy variables, so there is no direct linkage from petroleum income to federal government demand. However in the Nigerian institutional set-up 45 per cent of all federal revenues are transferred automatically to the state and local governments. By assumption in the model, an increase in state and local revenue at the margin is spent 30 per cent on manufactured goods and 70 per cent on home goods, as current public consumption. Through this revenue transfer, about one-half of an increase in petroleum receipts is translated automatically into final demand. Increased oil exports mostly feed into the internal economy via this channel.

Income generated in agriculture and manufacturing leads to increased consumer demand after the usual leakages to private saving and taxes. Employment in the two sectors rises with their levels of production, with labour–output (and other input–output) ratios determined by marginal productivity relationships based on their combined CES and Cobb–Douglas technologies. These ratios are price-sensitive functions of real input costs.

Because of decreasing returns to scale in the short run, payments generated by marginal productivity rules do not exhaust the value of the product in agriculture. The accounting discrepancy is resolved by attributing all the value of output net of intermediate input costs to household income. Wage and profit income flows in manufacturing are treated separately for tax purposes, but an identical linear saving function from all disposable income regardless of source is assumed. One consequence is that demand retardation when real wages fall may be underestimated by the model, as discussed below.

Agriculture and manufacturing follow essentially Keynesian adjustment patterns (aside from decreasing returns) in that their levels of output change without restriction to meet demand. In the home goods sector, price is the main adjusting variable, combined with weak supply response. The value of home goods production is directly imputed as income, and constitutes the last important payment flow.

On the demand side of the model, domestic consumption of petroleum products depends on total disposable income generated from production (deflated by a price index), a time trend and the controlled petroleum price. Strictly speaking, some intermediate uses of petroleum are included in this demand concept, but accounting for them properly in input–output terms was not possible from existing data.

The total of consumer spending for non-petroleum products is computed by applying the saving and tax functions to incomes generated in production and then subtracting consumption of petroleum and an unclassified imports term. The sectoral breakdown of consumer spending is based on a tree-like demand structure.[5] At an aggregate level, consumers choose among agricultural, manufactured and home goods according to a linear expenditure system. As discussed in the following section, manufacturing demand is taken to be income elastic, agriculture inelastic and home goods in between. At a lower level, demands for agricultural and manufactured goods can be satisfied from either imports or domestic sources – the two sorts of goods substitute with constant elasticities of substitution. The elasticity for agriculture is assumed lower, to reflect Nigerian farmers' isolation from the world market. Food consumption subsidies and excise taxes make consumer prices for domestic agricultural and manufactured products differ from the corresponding producer prices; tariffs on the two kinds of imports enter into determination of their consumer prices as well.

Since the linear expenditure system is a complete set of demand equations, sectoral consumption values sum to total consumer expenditure generated from the production side. With 'adding up' thus assured, the model can be solved as a closed Leontief system (with endogenously varying prices), given a sectoral breakdown of exogenous final demands. The main items are public consumption by the federal government (recall that consumption by the states and localities is determined endogenously by the budget transfer process), and real gross investment by the federal and state governments and the private sector. Along with stock changes, investment is set exogenously on the assumption that it is controlled by government planning and credit allocation policy. Exports of agricultural and manufactured products are the remaining final demand items. The level of each export type is assumed to respond positively to the exchange rate, an index of world prices of similar commodities and a subsidy; and to respond negatively to the internal producer price. The response elasticities are set at 2.0 for agricultural exports and 1.5 for manufacturing.

The model as just described solves for all important price and quantity variables. An obvious question is, how does money fit into the system? The answer is that – one exception aside – financial magnitudes follow a posteriori from the real equilibrium.

The details go as follows: the real model generates the federal government's overall deficit and the surplus on the balance of payments. Added to the previous year's final stocks of credit to the government and foreign assets of the banking system, these flows generate two key items in the monetary balance identity:

> Money supply = Bank credit to the government + Net foreign assets of banking system + Net bank credit to the private sector − Non-monetary liabilities of the banking system.

The main policy variable here is bank credit to the private sector. Credit demands from agriculture and manufacturing rise with economic activity, as described above. Given overall supply, available credit to the home goods sector is determined residually. Through the home good supply function, a credit crunch leads to reduced output and a higher price level.

Total money supply is computed from the equation above when non-monetary liabilities of the banking system (combining the putative effects of monetary policy, some purely balancing items, and errors and omissions) are taken into acount. In the solutions below, supply is compared to current price GDP. Alternatively, it could be compared to money demand figured as a function of real GDP, the price level, interest rates etc. If supply in a model simulation departs excessively from its historical ratio to GDP or from projected demand, then the real part of the solution is suspect on financial grounds.

Within its solution period of one year, the model is a price-endogenous Keynesian system. An increase in aggregate demand – from higher investment or oil exports, for example – will lead to increased outputs in all sectors and higher producer prices in agriculture and (especially) home goods. There will be higher intermediate and consumer imports (as well as capital goods imports, if investment goes up). Money demand will rise, and money supply will adjust in the light of changes in the government cash deficit and the balance of payments. Since the money wage and nominal exchange rate are fixed within the year, the price increases mean that both the real wage and the exchange rate will fall.

Similar short-run scenarios can be sketched for other changes in policy or exogenous variables, as discussed in numerical terms in following sections. We close here with a description of how the solution proceeds from year to year. The main dynamic elements are the following:

1 Money wages in year $t + 1$ increase over those in year t in response to the cost of living increase from year $t - 1$ to year t: there is wage indexing with a one-year lag. The fraction of the previous year's inflation passed through to wage increases is treated as a policy variable. In most runs of the model, it is set at 90 per cent.

2 As discussed above, growth of the modern capital stock in agriculture is related to the previous year's increase in the government's modernized input package.

3 Also as noted above, capacity in the home goods sector grows between years t and $t + 1$ in response to the overall increase in economic activity between years $t - 1$ and t. This specification is in lieu of explicit accounting for capital stock accumulation and technical progress in the sector, which was not feasible with existing data.

4 Output in manufacturing is not capital-limited, but an annual increase of 3.5 per cent in total input productivity is assumed.

5 The main final demand items – federal government consumption, investment demand, stock changes and export and prices in the petroleum sector – are updated in light of probable policy changes and exogenous trends. As described in the numerical solutions, a number of policy variables such as the exchange rate, tax and tariff rates, the size of the agricultural input package etc. are also changed over time.

6 Domestic demand for petroleum is assumed to grow exogenously at one per cent per year, as well as responding to income and price changes.

2   The data base

Within a year, the model structure just discussed amounts to an accounting scheme augmented by behavioural relations. The accounting essentially is that of the national income statistics (set up consistently with consumer demand data and input–output relationships), coupled with budgetary data from the federal and state governments and their links to the banking system. Ideally, the national income, budgetary and monetary numbers should be mutually consistent and form a harmonious whole. They could then be used to set up a social accounting matrix for a base year of the model, which could serve both as a jumping off point for simulations forwards and backwards in time, as well as a basis for parameter calibration (as discussed below).[6]

In practical country applications, the three main data sources never completely harmonize and must be adjusted towards consistency according to *ad hoc* (though sensible) procedures. The data situation is worse in Nigeria than many other countries for which similar exercises have been done, and unusually heroic assumptions were required to produce a base year data set for 1981:

1 There is a great discrepancy between the magnitude of transfers to the state governments according to the fiscal statistics and public consumption according to the national accounts. The solution was to accept the fiscal estimates for 1981, and treat state spending incrementally around that level in subsequent years.

2 There are large discrepancies between national accounts and Central Bank estimates of the foreign current account. An unclassified imports category was used in 1981 to close the gap (and was treated as a policy variable in later years).

3 Pure algebra was used to bridge the national accounts and the sector's own estimates of oil production and value-added. Domestic 'consumption' of oil in the model incorporates both consumer and intermediate demands.

4 The national accounts are not input–output based. Intermediate flows for the agricultural and manufacturing sectors were estimated from secondary sources, and flows to home goods were simply ignored.

5 A number of other estimates – the breakdown of capital formation by government and private sectors, tariff and tax rates, etc. – were computed subject to control totals from the national accounts and other sources. Total private saving was determined residually.

When accounts were set up for the base year, the next step was to assign parameter variables consistent with prior knowledge about Nigeria (and other countries) and the 1981 data set. On the production side, Cobb–Douglas exponents were set equal to the appropriate input shares, and CES parameters were computed from the shares according to standard rules. For consumption, budget shares plus prior information on Engel elasticities and a 'Frisch parameter' suffice to determine all the parameters in the linear expenditure demand system. The substitution elasticities between domestic and foreign goods in consumption were based on (scant) international evidence. Marginal saving rates consistent with recent Nigerian experience were postulated – together with the 1981 saving level they sufficed to determine the saving function. Elasticity parameters for oil demand, export price-responsiveness, money demand etc. were based on expert opinion.

The remaining crucial parameters refer to supply and import responses to price changes in the home goods sector. The relevant elasticities determine macro price and quantity shifts resulting from a change in aggregate demand. That is, if home goods supply were completely inelastic to price, an increase in demand would call forth large price increases to cut the real wage and consumer demand for home goods until demand–supply balance was again achieved. If supply were highly elastic, output would rise to meet demand at a modestly higher price. In practice, the model was simulated over the late 1970s and early 1980s with different values of these parameters until it replicated observed price and output changes accurately. One hesitates to call such a procedure 'estimation' but at least it provided empirical backing for the elasticity parameters that were finally chosen.

The values for key parameters and policy variables are given in table 6.1. Some entries (such as demand elasticities in the linear expenditure system) will change slightly over time from their 1981 values. For the policy variables, the changes between 1981 and 1983 reflect government policy shifts in response to the fall in oil exports after 1980, essentially the imposition of tariffs and taxes, a reduction in federal spending and import controls. The data set underlying the model was set up in mid-1983 and 1983 variables are based on numbers available at that time. In particular, the import controls were assumed to hold imports after 1981 below their historical levels. Data for 1986 refer to the base simulation for the model, described in the following section.

3   A base run

When confronted with an unexpected balance of payments problem, the economic authorities in most countries follow two policy courses. They experiment with economic contraction, but rarely to the point where the trade deficit is reduced via slow (or negative) growth to its initial level.

They also usually impose restrictive commercial policy – devaluation, tariff hikes, import quotas and so on.

True to form, Nigerian policy-makers followed both courses in 1981 and 1982. They devalued by about 11 per cent, increased average tariffs by almost 10 per cent and reduced the share of the federal deficit in GDP by 1 per cent in a year of negative growth. Even if quotas on top of the other policies cut imports by 700 million naira (the assumption of the model), the current account deficit still increased by more than a billion dollars. What other options were left to pursue?

The base run of the model reported in table 6.2 presupposes further restrictive fiscal policy coupled with an additional option, increased foreign borrowing. As table 6.2 shows, the share of the federal deficit in GDP (at factor cost) is assumed to fall from 9.5 per cent in 1982 to 4.4 per cent in 1986. The *modus operandi* is a reduction in real federal investment spending (1981 prices) from 7.9 billion naira in 1981 to 3.5 billion in 1984, and 3 billion in 1985 and 1986. At the same time, federal current expenditures grow only about 1 per cent per year in real terms.

In the model, the outcome of these exertions is negative GDP growth through 1984, and an average growth rate of non-oil product of only 1.3 per cent per year, 1983–6. If import arrears of $6 billion run up in 1982 and 1983 are paid back at the rate of $2 billion per year in 1984–6, the net capital inflow required to support a reasonable level of reserves works out to be $14 billion over the three years. Oil exports slightly above the assumed levels of 1.0 mbd in 1983 growing to 1.3 mbd in 1986 would ameliorate this situation, but not to a significant degree.

Other points to note in table 6.2 include relatively stable ratios of (broad) money and private credit to nominal GDP – the fluctuations are in a range that could be offset by monetary policy in the form of trading assets between the central and commercial banks. The real naira/dollar exchange rate (taking into account foreign vs. domestic inflation) depreciates slightly, and the share of home goods in real non-oil GDP falls from 59 to 57 per cent. The reason is steady growth in manufacturing output, responding to the exchange depreciation, a high Engel elasticity and local productivity increases.

Because of the relatively tight fiscal policy, demand pressure against agriculture and non-traded goods is held down. As a consequence, inflation averages only 5.9 per cent per year in 1983–6. With 90 per cent of the previous year's inflation passed into money wage increases, the real wage falls by ½ per cent per year, on average.

Table 6.1   Main parameters of the model

Petroleum sector	
Income elasticity, domestic demand	1.0
Trend growth rate in domestic demand	0.01
Own-price elasticity, domestic demand	−0.3
Foreign component, petroleum processing cost	0.025
Domestic component, petroleum processing cost	0.053
Agricultural sector	
Income elasticity, consumption aggregate (in 1981)	0.6
Own-price elasticity, consumption aggregate (in 1981)	−0.452
Elasticity of substitution between imported and domestic consumer goods	0.3
Labour output elasticity	0.4
Input package output elasticity	0.05
Credit output elasticity	0.004
Price elasticity of exports	2.0
Manufacturing sector	
Income elasticity, consumption aggregate (in 1981)	1.5
Own-price elasticity, consumption aggregate (in 1981)	−0.874
Elasticity of substitution between imported and domestic consumer goods	0.7
Rate of factor productivity growth	0.035
Capital output elasticity	0.23
Credit output elasticity	0.02
Labour output elasticity	0.15
Intermediate input output elasticity	0.6
Elasticity of substitution among intermediates (σ)	0.3333
CES distribution parameters:	
Home goods	0.005
Imports	0.087
Agricultural goods	0.005
Manufactured goods	0.005
Profit rate	0.091
Domestic share of capital goods	0.712
Price elasticity of exports	1.5
Home goods sector	
Income elasticity, domestic demand (in 1981)	0.934
Own-price elasticity, domestic demand (in 1981)	−0.620
Credit output elasticity	0.02
Output price elasticity	0.15
Output wage elasticity	−0.05
Import price elasticity	2.0
Saving and income generation	
Capital income share of home goods value-added	0.17
Average saving rate in 1981	0.046
Marginal saving rate, non-wage income	0.09
Marginal saving rate, wage income	0.05
Pass-through coefficients for wage indexation	0.9

Tax and subsidy rates and exogenous prices	1981	1983	1986
Oil export price (dollars/barrel)	38.0	30.0	36.3
Domestic oil price (naira/barrel)	7.0	8.0	8.0
Interest rate	0.1	0.13	0.13
Exchange rate index	1.0	1.111	1.111
Tariff on intermediate imports	0.21	0.21	0.21
Corporate income tax rate	0.093	0.093	0.093
State government income tax rate	0.011	0.011	0.011
Subsidy rate on agricultural input package	0.158	0.426	0.463
Tariff on manufactured consumer imports	0.192	0.350	0.350
Tariff on agricultural consumer imports	0.200	0.300	0.300
Manufacturing excise tax rate	0.055	0.120	0.120
Agricultural exports subsidy rate	0.0	0.0	0.0
Manufactured exports subsidy rate	0.0	0.0	0.0
Exogenous final demand items[a]			
Oil exports (mbd)	1.15	1.0	1.3
Volume of agricultural input package	0.63	0.8	0.85
Unclassified imports (current naira)	2.13	1.0	1.0
Total capital formation	12.10	9.50	9.50
Federal government capital formation	7.92	4.0	3.0
State government capital formation	2.18	2.5	3.0
Stock changes, agricultural goods	0.2	0.2	0.2
Stock changes, manufactures	0.47	0.6	0.6
Federal government demand, manufactures	2.66	2.7	2.8
Transfers to state and local governments (current naira)	4.63	4.93	7.11
Net capital inflows ($b)	0.50	2.50	5.0
Import arrears ($b)	0.0	2.0	−2.0

[a] Billions of 1981 naira unless otherwise stated.

4   Changes in policy variables

In this section, results from eight runs of the model are presented, to show possible effects of policy changes. Results for 1986 from the runs appear in table 6.3.

Policy number one is a 30 per cent devaluation of the dollar/naira exchange rate (from 1.485 to 1.143) in 1984. As described above, devaluation increases government naira revenue from oil exports, much of which is spent by the states and localities. In 1984, for example, state and local spending rises by 590 million naira (prices of 1981) and real GDP by 1.36 billion. These effects cumulate to give an increase in the average growth rate of non-oil GDP of 1 per cent per year, 1983–6. By contrast, a run of the model in which nominal transfers to the states and

Table 6.2   Results from the base run, 1982–6

	1982	1983	1984	1985	1986	1983–6
Annual output growth (%)						
Total GDP	−2.4	−5.9	0.1	4.1	4.2	2.8
Non-oil GDP	−3.6	−7.0	−1.9	2.8	3.1	1.3
CPI inflation rate (%)	13.0	5.7	2.3	9.6	5.7	5.9
Annual real wage growth (%)	0.4	5.7	2.8	−7.0	2.9	−0.5
Exchange rate ($/naira)	1.485	1.485	1.485	1.485	1.485	
Real exchange rate index (naira/$)	1.127	1.149	1.219	1.157	1.170	
Oil exports (mbd)	1.011	1.0	1.1	1.2	1.3	
Oil export price ($/barrel)	34.57	30.00	31.00	34.00	36.30	
Domestic oil demand (mbd)	0.273	0.264	0.267	0.285	0.307	
Domestic oil price (naira/barrel)	7.5	8.0	8.0	8.0	8.0	
Average tariff rate (%)	10.8	16.7	17.4	17.2	17.6	
Non-oil exports (1981 naira)	0.74	0.72	0.77	0.75	0.74	
Foreign reserves (naira)	2.85	2.79	1.14	0.85	0.98	
Capital inflows ($)	0.5	2.5	4.0	5.0	5.0	
Arrears ($)	4.0	2.0	−2.0	−2.0	−2.0	
Current account surplus ($)	−6.98	−7.50	−5.75	−5.39	−4.74	
Federal deficit/GDP (%)	9.5	9.4	7.7	5.6	4.4	
Money supply/GDP (%)	38.2	44.8	43.8	36.3	34.1	
Private credit/GDP (%)	22.8	28.3	33.0	32.2	35.9	
Import ratio, agricultural consumption (%)	12.4	12.4	12.2	12.3	12.3	
Import ratio, manufacturing consumption (%)	58.3	59.1	56.9	56.7	55.4	
Intermediate imports/manufacturing output (%)	23.6	23.3	22.2	21.8	21.1	
Shares in real GDP (%)						
Petroleum	19.6	21.6	22.2	23.0	24.0	
Agriculture	23.0	23.3	22.7	22.7	21.8	
Manufacturing	8.9	9.1	9.2	10.0	10.3	
Home goods	48.5	46.0	45.9	44.3	43.9	

Note: Level variables are in units of one billion.

localities are held constant shows that devaluation *reduces* the growth rate from the base run by 1.1 per cent. The constitutional disposition of oil revenues evidently is of macroeconomic import in Nigeria.

As shown towards the bottom of table 6.3, the maxi-devaluation leads to some reduction in import penetration and mildly stimulates non-oil exports. The outcome is an improvement of the current account, by $800 million in 1984 and $1.14 billion in 1986. These relatively small gains stem from the expansionary effect of devaluation. When revenue transfers are held constant and devaluation is contractionary, the 1986 current account gain is $3 billion.[7]

Since it drives up the costs of both production inputs and imported items that enter the consumer price index, devaluation is inflationary. In 1984, the price index rises by 22 per cent and the real wage falls by 13.9 per cent. By contrast, in the base run, prices rise by only 2 per cent and the real wage goes up. These effects cumulate into 7 per cent higher inflation and 1 per cent slower real wage growth annually from 1983 to 1986.

Real wages are partially protected from inflation by indexation, but the same is not true of the real exchange rate. It appreciates in terms of a naira/dollar index from 1.344 in 1984 (1.219 in the base run) to 1.28 in 1986. Note that the initial gain in the real exchange rate is only about 10 per cent (far less than the 30 per cent nominal devaluation), and that this differential declines over time.

Finally, the money supply rises in 1986 from 18.9 billion naira in the base run to 20.7 billion in run number one. The cause is a reserve increase of 2.3 billion, which offsets reduced federal government borrowing from the banking system of 500 million. However, the money/GDP ratio *falls* from 34 to 31 per cent, due to faster growth and price inflation. This result suggests that devaluation might have to be coupled with expansionary credit policy (the ratio of private credit to GDP falls from 36 per cent to 30 per cent) to offset possible restrictive effects on output growth from the financial side of the economy.

Runs two through four show the effects of more detailed commercial policy interventions, in the form of higher tariffs or export subsidies.

In run two, tariffs are raised in 1984 on capital goods (5–15 per cent) and on intermediates (21–35 per cent). One immediate outcome is somewhat higher inflation – 1 per cent more per year (1983–6) in the consumer price index and 2 per cent in the manufacturing sector producers' price. Real GDP growth goes up slightly, as agriculture and home goods gain from substitution of demand away from manufactures.

Table 6.3   Model responses to policy shifts (results for 1986)

	Base run	Run 1 30% deval. 1984	Run 2 Raise input tariffs	Run 3 Raise final tariffs	Run 4 30% export subsidies	Run 5 Lower federal investment	Run 6 Lower agricultural input package	Run 7 Raise domestic oil prices	Run 8 Slower wage indexing
Annual output growth (%)									
Total GDP	2.8	3.6	2.9	2.8	3.4	2.1	2.6	2.4	2.9
Non-oil GDP	1.3	2.3	1.4	1.3	2.0	0.5	1.1	1.1	1.4
CPI inflation rate (%)	5.9	12.9	6.8	7.3	5.9	5.3	6.7	5.7	5.5
Annual real wage growth (%)	−0.5	−1.5	−0.7	−0.8	−0.4	−0.1	−0.8	−0.5	−1.3
Exchange rate ($/naira)	1.485	1.143	1.485	1.485	1.485	1.485	1.485	1.485	1.485
Real exchange rate index (naira/$)	1.170	1.280	1.129	1.147	1.176	1.200	1.138	1.174	1.187
Oil exports (mbd)	1.3	1.3	1.3	1.3	1.3	1.3	1.3	1.3	1.3
Oil export price ($/barrel)	36.3	36.3	36.3	36.3	36.3	36.3	36.3	36.3	36.3
Domestic oil demand (mbd)	0.307	0.313	0.306	0.307	0.312	0.299	0.303	0.258	0.308
Domestic oil price (naira/barrel)	8.0	8.0	8.0	8.0	8.0	8.0	8.0	14.0	8.0
Average tariff rate (%)	17.6	18.0	22.7	22.2	17.9	17.6	17.9	17.5	17.7
Non-oil exports (1981 naira)	0.74	0.80	0.71	0.73	1.10	0.76	0.72	0.75	0.76

Foreign reserves (naira)	0.98	3.30	0.72	1.65	1.68	3.08	1.68	1.32	1.10
Capital inflows ($)	5.0	5.0	5.0	5.0	5.0	5.0	5.0	5.0	5.0
Arrears ($)	-2.0	-2.0	-2.0	-2.0	-2.0	-2.0	-2.0	-2.0	-2.0
Current account surplus ($)	-4.74	-3.60	-4.89	-4.40	-4.23	-3.79	-4.47	-4.50	-4.65
Federal deficit/GDP (%)	4.4	3.0	4.3	4.0	4.4	3.1	4.0	4.0	4.3
Money supply/GDP (%)	34.1	30.9	32.9	33.7	35.9	34.6	33.3	33.6	34.4
Private credit/GDP (%)	35.9	29.7	35.0	35.3	35.5	37.4	35.5	35.4	36.2
Import ratio, agricultural consumption (%)	12.3	12.1	12.4	12.2	12.5	12.2	12.5	12.3	12.3
Import ratio, manufacturing consumption (%)	55.4	53.1	57.7	51.9	55.3	54.9	55.8	55.2	54.8
Intermediate imports/manufacturing output (%)	21.1	20.4	20.6	21.3	21.1	21.1	21.2	21.1	21.0
Shares in real GDP (%)									
Petroleum	24.0	23.6	24.0	24.0	23.7	25.0	24.1	23.5	23.9
Agriculture	21.8	21.5	21.8	21.7	21.8	21.9	22.0	21.9	21.9
Manufacturing	10.3	10.3	10.2	10.3	10.5	9.5	10.2	10.3	10.3
Home goods	43.9	44.6	44.0	44.0	44.0	43.6	43.7	44.3	43.9

Note: Level variables are in units of one billion and growth rates are annualized over the period 1983–6.

Non-oil exports fall, and import penetration of final goods goes up. The consequence is a deterioration in the current account of $150 million in 1986. The ratio of intermediate inputs to manufacturing output declines – this must be viewed as the major favourable response to this tariff increase.

Run three shows a better case for the balance of payments. Tariffs on consumer imports are increased, from 30 to 40 per cent for agricultural goods and from 35 to 50 per cent on manufactures. The outcome is reduced import penetration for manufactures. (Recall the assumption that the elasticity of consumer substitution is higher for manufactures than agriculture.) The current account improves by $340 million in 1986. At the same time, annual inflation according to the consumer price index rises by 1.4 per cent, as increased consumer prices are passed along into faster money wage growth.

In run four, 30 per cent subsidies are instituted for agricultural and manufactured exports in 1984. This policy can be viewed as an attempt at export-led growth. It is successful in the model because high price elasticities for non-oil exports are assumed – 2.0 for agricultural goods and 1.5 for manufactures. In practice, more detailed policy interventions would be required to generate the sorts of results the model gives – a 50 per cent increase in non-oil exports (to 1.1 billion naira) in 1986 over the base run.

If such an export increase could be engineered, its results would be highly favourable: 0.7 per cent faster non-oil real GDP growth, an improvement of $500 million in the current account in 1986, and negligible additional inflation. The reason for the last result is that export subsidies do not feed into the consumer price index and from there to wage inflation. This linkage is important for tariff increases and devaluation.

As discussed in section 3, the base run already assumes a degree of fiscal stringency. The policy is tightened in run five, in which real federal investment is cut by 500 million naira in 1984 through 1986. The results include slower non-oil GDP growth and lower inflation (by 0.8 and 0.6 per cent per year, respectively). The current account in 1986 improves by $950 million, and the federal deficit falls from 4.4 to 3.1 per cent of GDP. The multiplier of real non-oil GDP with respect to investment turns out to be 1.8, a reasonable value given the large import leakages in the economy.

Runs six through eight show the effects of policies aimed at rationalization of resource allocation. The agricultural input package is reduced by 200 million naira (1981 prices) in run six. As a consequence, current spending on agricultural subsidies falls by 320 million naira in 1986, and the government deficit declines from 4.4 to 4.0 per cent of GDP. At the sectoral level, the inflation rate of the agricultural producers' price rises from 5.6 to 7.6 per cent per year. Agricultural real output actually falls as demand shifts from the sector, and import penetration goes up. There is a loss of 0.2 per cent per year in real GDP growth.

In run seven, the internal oil price is raised from 8 to 14 naira per barrel, in two-naira steps beginning in 1984. In 1986, there is a fall in consumption by 50,000 barrels per day, and slightly lower overall aggregate demand.

Run eight is based on the assumption of lower pass-through of previous private inflation to money wage increases. The indexing coefficients are reduced from 0.9 in the base run to 0.6 in 1984 and 0.8 in 1985–6. Inflation drops by 0.4 per cent per year. Real GDP growth goes up by 0.1 per cent – a result that would reverse if the differential in the propensities to consume from wage and non-wage income is in reality wider than the 4 per cent assumed in the model. There is a small improvement in the current account, and the federal deficit as a share of GDP falls slightly. The real wage grows 0.8 per cent per year more slowly. Only the political process could decide whether or not such a shift in the income distribution outweighs gains on the inflation front.

5 Policy packages

The one-shot changes just discussed can be combined in policy packages. One that might be called 'conservative' as of summer 1983 would incorporate the following changes:

1 A 30 per cent devaluation in 1984, as in run one.
2 Higher input tariffs, as in run two.
3 Higher final goods tariffs, as in run three.
4 Fiscal stringency in the form of lower federal government investment, as in run five.
5 Reduced agricultural subsidies, as in run six.
6 Higher internal oil prices, as in run seven.
7 Less complete wage indexing, as in run eight.

Table 6.4 shows how the base run and this package compare over the period 1984–6.

The first thing to note is that the package does not significantly affect real output – expansion from the devaluation and contraction from reduced federal investment and the other policy changes balance off.

Table 6.4 Comparisons of the base run and a run with a 'conservative' policy package

	1984		1985		1986		1983–6	
	Base	Pkge	Base	Pkge	Base	Pkge	Base	Pkge
Annual output growth (%)								
Total GDP	0.1	2.0	4.1	2.5	4.2	3.5	2.8	2.7
Non-oil GDP	−1.9	0.7	2.8	1.2	3.1	2.5	1.3	1.5
CPI inflation rate (%)	2.3	24.3	9.6	12.6	5.7	7.3	5.9	13.3
Annual real wage growth (%)	2.8	−16.7	−7.0	6.1	2.9	2.6	−0.5	−3.2
Exchange rate ($/naira)	1.485	1.14	1.485	1.143	1.485	1.143		
Real exchange rate index (naira/$)	1.219	1.353	1.157	1.266	1.170	1.252		
Oil exports (mbd)	1.1	1.1	1.2	1.2	1.3	1.3		
Oil export price ($/barrel)	31.0	31.0	34.0	34.0	36.3	36.3		
Domestic oil demand (mbd)	0.267	0.251	0.285	0.250	0.307	0.256		
Domestic oil price (naira/barrel)	8.0	10.0	8.0	12.0	8.0	14.0		
Average tariff rate (%)	17.4	27.6	17.2	28.0	17.6	28.1		
Non-oil exports (naira of 1981)	0.77	0.89	0.75	0.80	0.74	0.78		
Foreign reserves (naira)	1.14	2.23	0.85	2.20	0.98	1.29		
Capital inflows ($)	4.0	3.5	5.0	3.5	5.0	2.5		
Arrears ($)	−2.0	−2.0	−2.0	−2.0	−2.0	−2.0		
Current account surplus ($)	−5.75	−3.12	−5.39	−2.50	−4.74	−1.86		
Federal deficit/GDP (%)	7.7	3.4	5.6	1.2	4.4	0.2		
Money supply/GDP (%)	43.8	31.6	36.3	29.9	34.1	26.2		
Private credit/GDP (%)	33.0	28.4	32.2	27.1	35.9	29.6		
Import ratio, agricultural consumption (%)	12.2	11.3	12.3	11.8	12.3	11.8		
Import ratio, manufacturing consumption (%)	56.9	50.8	56.7	51.8	55.4	50.9		
Intermediate imports/manufacturing output (%)	22.2	20.3	21.8	20.4	21.1	19.8		
Shares in real GDP (%)								
Petroleum	22.2	21.5	23.0	22.5	24.0	23.2		
Agriculture	22.7	23.2	22.7	22.5	21.8	21.4		
Manufacturing	9.2	9.4	10.3	9.9	10.3	10.3		
Home Goods	45.9	45.9	44.3	45.1	43.9	44.6		

The package, due to the devaluation, gives an initial output spurt in 1984, but this erodes in later years.

Second, inflation from devaluation and the minor policy shifts outweighs price deflation from the cut in federal spending. The annual rate of consumer price inflation goes up by 7.4 per cent in 1983–6.

As a consequence of the price jump in 1984, the real wage falls by almost 17 per cent. Contemporary experience in Brazil, Mexico and other countries suggests that a 20 per cent real wage cut may strain the social contract. Even with slower indexing, real wages begin to recover in the Nigeria simulations after 1984, but they still decline from 1983 to 1986 at 3.2 per cent per year.

The major gain from the 'conservative' policy package is improvement in the current account, by almost $3 billion in 1986. To maintain reserve levels comparable to the base run in 1986, $9.5 billion in net capital inflow in 1984 through 1986 is required with the policy package, as opposed to $14 billion in the base run. Since the level of economic activity varies little between the two runs, these trade gains come from reduced import penetration (mostly) and export promotion. Sector-specific policies and devaluation interact in producing these results.

On the financial side, the ratio of private credit to GDP declines with the inflation induced by the devaluation. The federal deficit also declines, from 4.4 per cent of GDP in 1986 in the base run to 0.2 per cent in the policy simulation. With less borrowing from the banking system by the government, the money supply is also restricted. The low value of 26.2 per cent for the ratio of money supply to GDP in the policy run for 1986 suggests that credit tightness should not be a major goal in the medium-term future if something like the policy package is put into effect.

For a summary view of these results, look at table 6.5. The changes induced by the 'conservative' package are presented for 1986, with a decomposition into shifts without the devaluation or the federal investment cut. The results again show that devaluation and fiscal stringency have offsetting effects on output growth, but that devaluation induces inflation. Together with the rest of the package, both policies reduce import penetration and lead to some export promotion.

On the basis of these results, the natural question to ask is whether trade improvement can be obtained with less inflation and real wage loss. The last column of table 6.5 shows results from an alternative package in which the 30 per cent devaluation in 1984 is replaced by a 10 per cent devaluation and export subsidies at the rate of 30 per cent. The GDP and current account stories are similar in the two runs, with the alternative package giving more export promotion (on the model's

Table 6.5   Changes from the base run in 'conservative' and 'alternative' policy packages

	Base run levels	Conservative packages			Alternative package with export subsidies and 10% deval.
		Entire package	Without deval.	Without investment cut	
Real output, 1986 (1981 naira)					
Total GDP	43.33	-0.15	-1.32	0.63	-0.11
Non-oil GDP	32.94	0.19	-0.94	0.93	0.22
Inflation rate 1983–6 (%)					
Annual CPI	5.9	8.6	1.6	9.4	4.1
Current account surplus, 1986 ($b)	-4.74	2.88	1.81	1.95	2.73
Annual real wage growth, 1983–6 (%)	-0.5	-2.7	-0.9	-2.8	-1.8
Non-oil exports, 1986 (1981 naira)	0.74	0.04	-0.03	0.01	0.35
Import ratio, agricultural consumption, 1986 (%)	12.3	-0.5	-0.1	-0.4	-0.2
Import ratio, manufacturing consumption, 1986 (%)	55.4	-4.5	-2.1	-3.8	-3.1
Intermediate imports/manufacturing output, 1986 (%)	21.1	-1.3	-0.6	-1.1	-0.9
Shares in real GDP, 1986 (%)					
Petroleum	24.0	-0.8	-0.1	-1.1	-0.8
Agriculture	21.8	0.1	0.4	0.0	0.3
Manufacturing	10.3	0.0	-0.2	0.1	0.2
Domestic	43.9	0.7	-0.1	1.0	0.3
Domestic oil demand (mbd)	0.307	-0.051	-0.058	-0.045	-0.050

optimistic assumptions regarding export response elasticities). The alternative package also induces less inflation and real wage loss.

6 Conclusions

This paper aims at developing two points. The first is that a simple computable general equilibrium model can be put together to say something about major policy issues in a developing country. The relevance and realism of the model results are best left to the reader to judge, but at least the technical feasibility of the enterprise is established here.

The second point is that within the model a case can be made for sector-by-sector policy interventions to improve economic performance, as opposed to economy-wide changes such as devaluation. The reason is that the shifts in relative prices and in income distribution required for real exchange depreciation may prove to be infeasible. They can soon be eroded by inflation induced by organized groups (such as workers who strive to maintain their real income positions). If real depreciation proves impossible to achieve, then even if there are ample possibilities for substitution at the micro level, macro interventions aimed at changing resource allocation will be relatively ineffective. The reason lies with the model's Keynesian description of the macro economy of an oil exporter. This 'closure' of the macro system obviates much of the neoclassical apparatus that is built in.[8] With macro tools relatively ineffective, the case becomes stronger for more detailed interventions such as tariff and subsidy or dual exchange rate policies. Whether the practical difficulties of implementing such policies can be overcome is, unfortunately, a question that a macro model cannot easily address.

NOTES

* This macro model was prepared initially as an input into the work of a World Bank economic mission which visited Nigeria in May and June of 1982. It was developed subsequently for use by the Nigeria Division of the World Bank. The views and interpretations in this document are those of the authors and should not be attributed to the World Bank, to its affiliated organizations, or to any individual acting on their behalf. Comments by Paul Isenman, Alan Gelb, Sweder van Wijnbergen and William S. Humphrey are gratefully acknowledged.
1 The burgeoning literature on the macro difficulties of mineral exporters is reviewed by Corden (1984) and the other papers in this volume.

2 Please (1967) presents evidence that governments' marginal propensity to consume from additional tax (and by extension other) revenue is high.
3 For simplicity, only a verbal description of the model is given here. Equation sets and a description thereof are available from the authors.
4 Prices of imported goods within the country are set by the rule: Internal price = exchange rate × (one + tariff rate) × border price. This standard formula implies that there are no scarcity premia accruing to holders of import licences, monopoly trading positions etc. Such phenomena are discussed informally in Nigeria, but are difficult to capture in a model based on national accounts. In so far as both import demand and the home goods price rise with the level of economic activity, then higher import volume will be associated with increased income flows or 'rents' in the hands of producers of non-traded transport and commercial services. An oil boom stimulates rent-seeking in this sense.
5 Lancaster (1966) originated tree structures of consumer choice.
6 For descriptions of models based explicitly on social accounting matrices, see, for example, Pyatt and Roe (1977) or Taylor (1983).
7 Krugman and Taylor (1978) discuss contractionary vs. expansionary effects of devaluation in a model similar to the one here. Porter and Ranney (1982) argue that contraction is the typical case for developing countries.
8 Bell and Srinivasan (1984) summarize a large recent literature on closure, or how a model's specification of the macro mechanisms that equate savings and investment predetermines its results. As they put it, 'if the choice of closing rule is changed, the system dances to a different (and predictable) tune, however intricate and impenetrable the background music of its structure may appear at first glance!'

REFERENCES

Bell C. and T. N. Srinivasan (1984) 'On the Uses and Abuses of Economy-Wide Models in Development Policy Analysis', in M. Syrquin, L. Taylor and L. Westphal (eds), *Economic Structure and Performance: Essays in Honor of Hollis B. Chenery*, New York: Academic Press.
Corden W. M. (1984) 'Booming Sector and Dutch Disease Economics: Survey and Consolidation', *Oxford Economic Papers*, **36**, 359–80.
Krugman P. and L. Taylor (1978) 'Contractionary Effects of Devaluation', *Journal of International Economics*, **8**, 445–56.
Lancaster K. (1966) 'A New Approach to Consumer Theory', *Journal of Political Economy*, **74**, 132–57.
Please S. (1967) 'Savings through Taxation: Reality or Mirage?', *Finance and Development*, **4**, 24–32.
Porter R. C. and S. I. Ranney (1982) 'An Eclectic Model of Recent LDC Macroeconomic Policy Analyses', *World Development*, **10**, 751–65.
Pyatt F., G. Roe and A. Roe (1977) *Social Accounting for Development with Special Reference to Sri Lanka*, New York and London: Cambridge University Press.
Taylor L. (1983) *Structuralist Macroeconomics*, New York: Basic Books.

COMMENT   M. HASHEM PESARAN

In the case of most developing countries construction of a macro-econometric model suitable for short- to medium-term policy analysis is a formidable undertaking. The modeller often has to contend with small data bases of doubtful quality and 'imported' theories of questionable relevance to the specific historical and institutional realities of the economy concerned. As a result, the models constructed for developing countries generally have a rather weak basis in data and are best viewed as simulation tools by means of which the properties of a particular theoretical construction are investigated quantitatively. Such models, often referred to as computable general equilibrium (CGE) models, reflect largely the theoretical properties of the framework adopted by the modeller rather than the realities of the economy subject to the modelling exercise. Given that the data situation in Nigeria is worse than in many other developing countries, a point emphasized in the paper, the model constructed by Lance Taylor and his collaborators is more heavily theoretically based than is usual even in the case of CGE models. The 'unusually heroic assumptions' made by Taylor *et al.* to produce a consistent data set for the base year, and the particular procedure followed by them to 'assign' values to the unknown parameters of their model, make it very difficult to ascertain the degree to which the model they have constructed actually corresponds to the Nigerian economy.

Some of the assumptions made by the authors in order to set up the accounts for the base year are not described fully enough to enable the reader to make an independent judgement of his own. One is told that the intermediate flows were estimated from 'secondary sources', but no indication of how this was in fact done is provided. Nor is it made clear how the breakdown of a number of key aggregates into their components is carried out. The estimation of the model, or in the terminology preferred by the authors, the assignment of values to the parameters of the model, also leaves a great deal to be desired. In the majority of cases the authors offer little or no justification for their particular choice of the parameter values. They allude to '(scant) international evidence', 'expert opinion', or simply state that the parameter values were postulated to be 'consistent with recent Nigerian experience'. While the imposition of parameter values on the basis of qualitative information is, and ought to be, an important method in quantitative economic analysis (especially in the case of developing countries), from the description given by Taylor *et al*. it is not possible to ascertain how their experience of the Nigerian economy or the experience of the experts they are relying upon is converted into quantitative values for the parameters. The authors' method of obtaining 'estimates' of the key parameters of the supply and import demand functions is, however, more traditional and involves choosing values of these parameters such that the movement of output and prices are accurately replicated in a simulation of the model over the late 1970s and early 1980s. The paper does not, however, provide any information on the reliability of these parameter estimates. Thus, despite the authors' plea that 'The relevance and the realism of the model results are best left to the reader to judge ...', I for one have found it extremely difficult to judge the realism of the model from the description given by them.

Admittedly, given the data limitations, a detailed econometric investigation of the Nigerian economy seems to be out of the question. But there are other possibilities open to the authors. They could have carried out a 'sensitivity analysis' of their results to changes in key parameters or functional specifications. As it stands it is not possible to say how robust the policy conclusions of the paper are to the particular relations specified or the parameter values chosen. Another simple procedure for checking the model's realism would be to see how well it forecasts the main aggregates (outputs and prices) over the years 1983 and 1984. Considering that the current version of the model was completed in June 1983 it would have been quite feasible for the authors to evaluate the reliability of their model by checking its forecast performance.

As far as the theoretical underpinning of the model is concerned, Taylor *et al*. describe their model as a price-sensitive Keynesian model, but at the same time they also claim that 'It [the model] relies on the substantial body of theory that has grown up in the past few years on mineral or oil-exporting economies'. The literature they have in mind is the tradables/non-tradables framework advocated, for example, by Corden, which in the case of oil-exporting countries is modified by further disaggregating the tradables sector into booming-tradables and the other tradables sub-sectors. Two important assumptions underlie this analytical framework: the law of one price, and full employment, neither of which, however, is maintained by Taylor *et al*. It is therefore not clear in what sense their model is based on recent theoretical developments in the literature on oil-exporting countries. It is more appropriate to regard the model as representing an eclectic Keynesian framework where price responsiveness is built into the traditional

IS–LM income-determination model using familiar neoclassical tools such as the CES and Cobb–Douglas production functions, a complete system of demand equations and price-sensitive export and import functions. The main feature of the model which distinguishes it from other CGE models constructed in the literature lies in the specification of the agricultural supply function, and the detailed treatment of the oil sector. It is assumed that agricultural output is determined endogenously in response to changes in an 'input package variable' both directly, and indirectly through the process of capital accumulation. By contrast, productivity in the manufacturing sector is assumed to grow at an exogenously given rate of 3.5 per cent per annum. The rationale behind such an asymmetrical explanation of productivity changes in the agricultural and the manufacturing sectors is not clear. The assumption that productivity growth in the manufacturing sector is independent of the process of capital accumulation can be valid only in a very short-term model and is unlikely to hold in a medium-term model intended for policy analysis.

The model also has a number of rather odd features that are difficult to explain. The domestic demand for oil is assumed to depend on the absolute level of oil prices. The aggregate consumption function is specified in terms of nominal rather than real magnitudes. There are no wealth effects in the consumption function, which, in view of the fact that the interest rate is also assumed to be an exogenously determined policy variable, causes the model to have the important property that disequilibrium in the monetary sector has no repercussions on the real side of the economy. The degree of monetary disequilibrium in this model is used simply as an indicator of the extent to which a particular policy mix is financially viable with no consequence for the growth of output or the rate of inflation. The model can clearly benefit from a more careful integration of the financial and the real sectors. This is especially so, since in this model the availability of credit to the industrial and the agricultural sectors plays a crucial role in the determination of productive capacity.

The various simulation runs reported in the paper are of considerable interest and in a way represent the highlights of the modelling exercise. I am personally sympathetic to the main policy conclusion reached by the authors, namely, that 'With macro tools relatively ineffective, the case becomes stronger for more detailed interventions such as tariff and subsidy or dual exchange rate policies.' I have myself argued along similar lines elsewhere (Pesaran, 1985). But I am not at all convinced that the model constructed by Lance Taylor and his collaborators provides the empirical backing for such a policy recommendation. At this stage in the development of macroeconometric models for developing countries, I believe emphasis should be placed on compilation of more and better data, rather than on construction of more CGE models based on weak or non-existent data.

REFERENCE

Pesaran M. H. (1985) 'Structural Keynesianism as an Alternative to Monetarism', unpublished manuscript.

7

A commodity export boom and the real exchange rate: the money–inflation link*

SEBASTIAN EDWARDS

1 Introduction

A number of papers have recently analysed the way in which commodity export booms affect production in other sectors of the economy. Most of these studies have focused on the behaviour of the real exchange rate as the main transmission mechanism from the booming sector to the rest of the economy. This literature, which has come to be known as the Dutch Disease literature, has postulated that a commodity export boom will generally result in a real appreciation of the domestic currency, increased production of non-tradable goods and a decline in production and employment of the rest (i.e., non-boom) tradable sector.[1] However, commodity export booms can also have important short-run monetary effects, which will spill over to the real exchange rate. For example, a resource-based export boom will typically result in a balance of payments surplus and in the accumulation of international reserves. If this increase in reserves is not sterilized, the monetary base will increase and an excess supply of money may develop. If this is the case, the final effect will be inflation. This increase in the price level will, in general, be one of the mechanisms through which the real appreciation will actually take place.[2] It is possible, however, for the short-run increase in the rate of inflation to exceed what is required to bring about the equilibrium real appreciation generated by the export boom; in this case, the real exchange rate will appreciate in the short run by more than what real factors only would indicate. These short-run monetary effects of commodity export booms have recently been important in a number of developing countries, including Indonesia, Kenya and Colombia.

In this paper a model of a developing country that relies heavily on the exports of a particular good (the 'commodity export' for short) is fully worked out. The model emphasizes the effects of changes in commodity export prices on money creation and inflation. The model also allows for a fairly general exchange rate policy, ranging from a fixed nominal rate to a crawling peg based on a PPP rule. The model is empirically tested using data for Colombia. Experts have generally argued that fluctuations in Colombia's real exchange rate have been mainly determined by world coffee price movements, with most observers emphasizing the consequences of coffee price changes for money creation and inflation.

2   The model

In this paper a model that can be used to analyse the way in which commodity export prices, money creation, inflation and the real exchange rate interact is presented.[3] The model is developed for the case of a small developing country, with capital controls and no domestic financial market.

The model consists of three interrelated main building blocks – a money market block, an inflation block and an exchange rate block.

2.1   *The monetary block*

The first equation in the monetary block describes the process of money creation.

$$\hat{M}_t = \alpha \, \hat{R}_t + (1-\alpha) \, D\hat{C}R_t \tag{1}$$

As usual $\hat{X}$ denotes the percentage change in variable X. $\hat{M}_t$ is, then, the rate of growth of nominal money, $D\hat{C}R_t$ is the rate of growth of domestic credit and α and $(1-\alpha)$ are base year shares. Domestic credit creation, in turn, is assumed to depend on the fiscal deficit as a proportion of high powered money (DEF). This assumption captures the fact that in most less developed countries (LDCs) the creation of money is an important source of financing for government expenditure.[4]

$$D\hat{C}R_t = \beta DEF_t. \tag{2}$$

Regarding international reserves behaviour through time, it is assumed that reserves respond to two factors. First, an excess flow demand or supply for money will be reflected in accumulation or decumulation of reserves. Secondly, changes in the domestic price of the commodity export in period t will be translated, in the same period, into corresponding changes in reserves.[5] These assumptions regarding reserves behaviour are captured by equation (3).

$$\hat{R}_t = \gamma_0[\hat{M}_t^d - \hat{M}_{t-1}] + \gamma_1 \hat{P}_t^c \tag{3}$$

where R are international reserves expressed in domestic currency; M^d is the nominal quantity of money demanded, and P_t^c is the price of the commodity export expressed in domestic currency. The world and domestic prices of the commodity export are linked by the following equation:

$$P_t^c = E_t P_t^{c*}$$

where P_t^{c*} is the world price of this commodity and where E_t is the nominal exchange rate in period t, expressed as units of domestic currency per unit of foreign currency.

The novelty of equation (3) is that, contrary to most monetary models of open economies, it explicitly allows for international reserve shocks to be a source of money creation in the *short run*. In the long run, however, $\hat{P}_t^{c*} = 0$, $\hat{M}_t^d = \hat{M}_t = \hat{M}_{t-1}$, and reserves will not change (i.e., $\hat{R}_t = 0$).

The monetary side of the model is closed by an equation for the rate of change of the nominal demand for money. Assuming that the demand for money function depends only on real income, we have:

$$\hat{M}_t^d = \hat{P}_t + \sigma \hat{y}_t \tag{4}$$

Combining equations (1) through (4) we can obtain a first order semi-reduced form that describes the motion of money through time:

$$\hat{M}_t = -a_0 \hat{M}_{t-1} + a_1 \hat{P}_t + a_2 \hat{y}_t + a_3 \hat{P}_t^c + a_4 DEF_t \tag{5}$$

Since $0 < a_0 < 1$ the convergence of (5) will be oscillatory.[6]

2.2 Inflation block

The inflation side of the model is formed by four equations. The first one is the definition of the price level. Expressed in percentage changes we have:

$$\hat{P}_t = (1 - \Psi)\hat{P}_{Nt} + \Psi\hat{P}_{Tt} \tag{6}$$

Where $\hat{P}_{Nt}$ is the rate of change of non-tradable prices and $\hat{P}_{Tt}$ is the rate of change of the price of tradables other than the commodity export, or 'other tradables'.[7] The rate of change of the price of these other tradables, in turn, is assumed to be equal to the rate of change of the nominal exchange rate plus the rate of change of the world price of the other tradables:

$$\hat{P}_{Tt} = \hat{E}_t + \hat{P}_{Tt}^* \tag{7}$$

The rate of change of the price of non-tradables will depend on the change in the price of other tradables, real income and the excess flow supply of money in period t:[8]

$$\hat{P}_{Nt} = \phi \hat{y}_t + \Pi(\hat{M}_t - \hat{M}_t^d) + \hat{P}_{Tt} \tag{8}$$

Combining (6), (7) and (8) with equation (4) on the demand for money, we obtain the following semi-reduced form for the domestic rate of inflation:[9]

$$\hat{P}_t = b_0\hat{M}_t + b_1(\hat{E}_t + \hat{P}_{Tt}^*) - b_2^*\hat{y}_t \tag{9}$$

where $b_0 + b_1 = 1$.

3   The rate of crawl and the definition of the real exchange rate

The model is closed with three equations: the first one defines the rate of devaluation of the nominal exchange rate, or rate of crawl; the second equation relates real income to the price of the commodity export; and the third equation provides the definition of the real exchange rate.

The following expression summarizes the rule of the rate of crawl assumed to be followed by the monetary authorities at any moment in time:[10]

$$\hat{E}_t = \epsilon_0\hat{P}_t - \epsilon_1\hat{P}_{Tt}^* - \epsilon_2\hat{P}_t^{c*} \tag{10}$$

This is a fairly general equation that allows for a number of possible exchange rate policies. For example, if $\epsilon_0 = \epsilon_1 = \epsilon_2 = 0$, the country in question will have a fixed nominal exchange rate. If $\epsilon_0 = \epsilon_1 = 1$ and $\epsilon_2 = 0$, the country will have a strict PPP nominal exchange rate rule, where in each period the nominal exchange rate will be adjusted by the differential between domestic and world inflation. If, however, $\epsilon_2 > 0$, it means that the authorities in the country in question recognize that changes in the commodity export price will have an impact on the real exchange rate, and will try to accommodate this effect through a slowing down of the rate of devaluation. In the present paper it will be assumed that $\epsilon_0 \geq 0$.

Regarding real income, it is assumed that changes in the real price of the commodity export (i.e., changes in the terms of trade) generate deviations of real income from its long-run trend:

$$\hat{y}_t = g + \rho(\hat{P}_t^{c*} - \hat{P}_{Tt}^*) \tag{11}$$

Where g is the long-term trend rate of growth of output.

Finally, the real exchange rate (e) is defined as the domestic relative price of other (i.e., non-commodity export) tradables to non-tradable goods.[11] In terms of rates of change:

$$\hat{e} = \hat{E}_t + \hat{P}_{Tt}^* - \hat{P}_{Nt} \tag{12}$$

4 The solution to the model

4.1 *Permanent monetary equilibrium*

The model can be further divided into a real and a monetary block. The real side, which is composed of equations (8) and (11), can be solved under the assumption of full and permanent monetary equilibrium. In this case the model becomes similar to most models of the Dutch Disease which have traditionally concentrated on real aspects only. Assuming permanent monetary equilibrium, $\hat{E} = 0$, substituting (11) into (8) and using the definition given by equation (12), the change in the real exchange rate resulting from changes in the commodity export world price is:

$$\hat{e}_t = -\phi\rho\hat{P}_t^{c*} < 0 \tag{13}$$

This means that a (permanent) increase in the world price of the commodity export will generate a real appreciation of the domestic currency. In fact, equation (13) is the *spending effect* of a commodity export boom emphasized in the Dutch Disease literature (Corden, 1984). This real appreciation takes place because, as a result of the boom, there is an increase in expenditure on non-tradables. In order to maintain equilibrium in the non-tradable goods market, its relative price has to increase. Note from equation (13) that the extent of the real appreciation depends on the value of ϕ, the income elasticity of demand for non-tradables. If $\phi = 0$, that is, if none of the increased real income is spent on non-tradables, the commodity export boom will have no effect on the real exchange rate. This, of course, is a standard result in the Dutch Disease literature. However, the model derived in this paper goes beyond the real effects of a commodity export boom, emphasizing the monetary and inflationary repercussions of changes in commodity export prices.

4.2 *Short-run monetary disequilibrium*

Allowing for short-run monetary disequilibrium, the complete model works in the following way. As in the real side model, an increase in the real world price of the commodity export results in higher real income, through equation (11), and in an increased demand for non-tradables. This higher demand, in turn, affects, through equation (8), the relative price of non-tradables, generating the already discussed *spending effect*.

On the money side, the higher price of the commodity exports with its resulting higher real income and price of non-tradables affects both the demand and the supply for money. From equation (4), a higher demand for nominal (and real) money will result. The few Dutch Disease models that have incorporated monetary factors have emphasized this increase in the demand for money as a result of the export boom.[12] A particularly important effect of this higher demand for real money is that, if an excess demand for money results, some deflationary effect of the boom can take place. This is because if after the boom the supply of money does not change, monetary equilibrium can only be re-established if $\dot{P}_t$ decreases or if $\hat{y}_t$ goes down (equation (4)).

However, an excess demand for money is only one of the possible monetary consequences of the export boom. In fact, according to equations (3) and (1), after the boom international reserves will accumulate, and the rate of growth of money will also be higher. Whether the final result is an excess demand or an excess *supply* of money will depend on the relative values of some of the parameters in the model. In particular, if $\alpha\gamma_1 > (1 - \gamma_0)\sigma$, the commodity export boom will result in a short-run excess *supply* of money. In the rest of this section it will be assumed, unless otherwise indicated, that the export boom will generate an excess supply of money.

Under this assumption, the resulting excess supply of money will impact the nominal price of non-tradables, further appreciating the real exchange rate. What is the role of the nominal exchange rate policy in our story? Two things will happen according to equation (10). First, as a result of the higher commodity export price, the rate of the crawl will be slowed down in period t, helping to accommodate the real appreciation generated by the spending effect. Second, there will be a tendency partially to compensate the nominal exchange rate for the higher rate of inflation, through $\epsilon_0 \hat{P}_t$. The final effect will be a real appreciation resulting, partially, from the slowing down of the rate of the crawl and partially from higher inflation. If the liquidity or money creation effect generated by the higher price of coffee is large enough, the real appreciation can be larger in the short run than in the long run (see Edwards, 1984c).

The model can be formally solved for the rate of change of the real exchange rate as a function of exogenous variables only. Equations (6), (9) and (10) are first solved for $\hat{E}_t$, $\hat{M}_t$ and $\hat{P}_t$. Then, the definition of the real exchange rate is used to find $\hat{e}$:

$$\hat{e} = k - b_0 \delta_1 (\epsilon_0/(1+\Psi)-1)D^{-1}\hat{M}_{t-1} + b_0 \delta_4 (\epsilon_0/(1+\Psi)-1)D^{-1} DEF_t$$
$$-[A+B]\hat{P}_t^{c*} \tag{14}$$

where k is a constant which includes the trend rate of real income growth (g) and

$$D = 1-(b_0\delta_1 + \epsilon_0 (b_0\delta_3+b_1))$$

$$A = [b_2(\epsilon_0/(1+\Psi)-1)+b_0\epsilon_0(1-\epsilon_0/(1+\Psi))]\rho D^{-1}$$

$$B = [\epsilon_2(1-b_0\delta_1)/(1+\Psi)+b_0\delta_3(\epsilon_0/(1+\Psi)-1)-\epsilon_2(\delta_3 b_0+b_1)]D^{-1}$$

$$\delta_1 = \gamma_0\alpha$$

$$\delta_2 = \gamma_0\alpha\sigma$$

$$\delta_3 = \alpha\gamma_1$$

$$\delta_4 = (1-\alpha)\beta.$$

From this expression we can find how an increase in the world price of the commodity export affects the real exchange rate in the short run. Furthermore, from the comparison of equations (14) and (13), it is possible to find out the extent to which, after the boom, the short-run real exchange rate diverges from the new long-run equilibrium real exchange rate.

Let us now focus on the way in which changes in the commodity export price affect the short-run real exchange rate. Term A captures the spending effect of a change in the price of the commodity export on the real exchange rate. Since stability requires that $D > 0$, the spending effect will, as expected, generate a real appreciation. Let us now turn to the inflation and exchange rate effects. These are captured by term B. As can be seen from this expression, there are three different channels, in addition to the spending effect, through which changes in the commodity export price will affect e. Two of these channels indicate that a higher commodity price will generate a real appreciation. The third channel, however, suggests that $\hat{e}$ and $\hat{P}^{c*}$ are positively related.

Let us first look at the forces that suggest that there is a negative effect of $\hat{P}^{c*}$ on $\hat{e}$. First, a higher world price of the commodity results in an increase in international reserves and money growth in the same period. Assuming that, as a consequence, an excess flow supply of money results, this will generate inflation and, with other things given, a real appreciation. Secondly, according to equation (10), an increase in the world price of this commodity slows down the rate of the crawl. This also works towards generating a real appreciation, with other things given. The forces that tend to generate a real depreciation as a consequence of the export boom are of a second order of magnitude, and work through the following channel. The higher world commodity export price reduces the rate of the crawl and consequently, through equation (10), the domestic price of tradables and inflation. These lower rates of inflation and devaluation, in turn, will tend to result in a lower rate of domestic money creation, through equation (5), and even lower inflation. This lower inflation, of course, will generate with other things given, a real depreciation. However, given the second order nature of this effect, the strong presumption is that under normal circumstances (i.e., under plausible values of the parameters involved), the appreciation effects will dominate. This is, however, an empirical issue, which can be resolved by estimating the model.[13]

5   An application: coffee and the real exchange rate in Colombia

In this section the model developed above is applied to the case of Colombia. The performance of the Colombian economy has been traditionally linked to the behaviour of the world coffee market.[14] A number of authors have argued that changes in the world price of coffee have been transmitted into Colombia mainly through the effect that they have on the real exchange rate (Weisner, 1978; Urrutia, 1981;

World Bank, 1984; Edwards, 1984c, 1986). Increases (decreases) in the world price of coffee have generated real appreciations (depreciations) of the Colombian peso. These variations in the real exchange rate, in turn, have affected the degree of competitiveness of the non-coffee tradables sectors, with a real appreciation generating loss of competitiveness or exchange rate 'deprotection'. For example, the coffee bonanza of 1975–9 resulted in a sharp real appreciation, which negatively affected the ability of the domestic sector to compete in international markets. Earlier episodes of sharp increases in the price of coffee (1950, 1954 and 1956, for example) have also been related to steep appreciations of the peso (Weisner, 1978; World Bank, 1984). In table 7.1, data on real effective exchange rates, coffee prices, terms of trade, rate of growth of reserves and high-powered money, inflation and the nominal rate of devaluation for 1968–82 are presented.

In the Colombian case, the monetary and inflationary effects of coffee price increases have been important. For example, as the data in table 7.1 show, the 1975–9 coffee bonanza generated a steep increase in international reserve holdings and in money creation. The crucial role of the increase in the rate of money creation after the different coffee booms has been forcefully pointed out by a number of experts on the Colombian economy, including Urrutia (1981) and Weisner (1978).

Since World War II, the Colombian authorities have tried to use several schemes to reduce the impact of changes in coffee prices on the real exchange rate and on the rest of the economy. The main objective of the government during this period has been to reduce the undesirable short-run effects that temporary changes in coffee prices have on the degree of profitability, production and employment in the rest of the economy.[15] For many years returns from coffee exports were subject to a lower net rate of exchange. Also, in the past, the degree of import protection was altered depending on the behaviour of coffee prices; it was reduced as a consequence of increases in the price of coffee and raised when the world price of coffee declined. In addition, several monetary measures – including steep increases in the banking system's reserve requirements – have been implemented when the price of coffee has risen.[16]

A number of experts have indicated that the adoption of a crawling peg system in 1967 responded to the need to reduce the dependence of the real exchange rate on coffee price fluctuations (Weisner, 1978; Urrutia, 1981; Ocampo, 1983). However, since the inception of the crawling peg system, the decision on the rate at which the peso should be devalued has been highly influenced by coffee prices. For example, according to Weisner (1978), once the crawling peg was adopted, one of

Table 7.1 The price of coffee and the real exchange rate in Colombia

Year	Real price of coffee (1980 = 100)	Terms of trade (1980 = 100)	Rate of nominal devaluation (%)	Rate of growth of high-powered money (%)	Rate of growth of real reserves (%)	Real effective exchange rate (1980 = 100)
1968	64.3	62.0	12.3	23.9	—	104.9
69	66.9	61.6	6.3	25.7	37.3	105.3
70	83.4	75.0	6.5	19.1	-3.1	108.8
71	71.0	70.1	8.1	12.9	-0.5	111.3
72	75.7	73.7	9.7	16.5	64.0	112.5
73	83.5	78.5	8.1	24.3	67.0	113.9
74	69.6	81.9	10.3	22.8	-16.5	120.1
75	68.4	75.8	18.7	21.2	10.2	126.7
76	126.5	106.3	12.2	29.2	131.8	123.6
77	182.0	147.5	6.0	34.2	58.7	104.5
78	125.3	110.1	6.3	39.7	35.4	101.7
79	112.5	98.4	8.8	33.0	62.5	99.8
80	100.0	100.0	11.1	25.5	25.7	100.0
81	67.5	83.4	15.3	23.5	-0.6	95.2
82	72.3	81.9	17.6	18.4	-19.6	99.0

Note: The real price of coffee is defined as the US dollar coffee price deflated by the US dollar import price index. The effective exchange rate was computed using trade weights and taking into account Colombia's ten major trade partners. The partners (and weights) are: US (0.507); UK (0.047); France (0.037); Germany (0.163); Italy (0.033); The Netherlands (0.044); Japan (0.058); Sweden (0.032); Spain (0.035); and Venezuela (0.045). According to the definitions of real exchange rate used in this paper, an increase in the index reflects a real depreciation, whereas a decline in the index reflects a real appreciation. The raw data were taken from *International Financial Statistics* (IMF).

the main problems was to decide 'at what pace to devalue when coffee prices rise' (p. 203). This problem has been compounded by the existence of a trade-off between the rate of nominal devaluation and inflation. In practice there has been an inverse relationship between the rate of devaluation of the peg and coffee prices. The high coffee prices of 1976–9, for example, were accompanied by a significant slowdown of the rate of devaluation; when the price of coffee began to fall in 1980–2, the rate of the crawl was rapidly accelerated. This inverse relationship between world coffee prices and the nominal rate of devaluation constitutes another mechanism – in addition to the money creation inflationary effect – through which higher (lower) coffee prices have been translated into a lower (higher) real exchange rate.

In this section annual data for Colombia for 1960–82 are used to analyse econometrically the extent to which changes in coffee prices have, in fact, influenced the real exchange rate in that country. This empirical analysis is carried out in two ways. First, a reduced form equation for the rate of change of the real exchange rate is estimated. This equation, which is in some ways similar to equation (14) above, relates changes in the real exchange rate in Colombia to changes in the price of coffee and other real exogenous variables suggested by the theory. Second, the model developed in section 2, which incorporates the role of monetary factors in the short run, is explicitly tested by estimating simultaneously the money, inflation and rate of crawl equations from the model of sections 2 and 3.

6 Real exchange rate behaviour in Colombia: reduced form analysis

In this section some preliminary econometric evidence on the behaviour of the real exchange rate in Colombia is presented. The analysis is based on the estimation of reduced form equations and, as in Barro (1983), focuses on the role of real determinants of the real exchange rate.

In the empirical analysis of this section two definitions of the real exchange rate are used: *RER* is a bilateral measure of the real exchange rate computed as the nominal rate with respect to the US dollar (pesos per dollar), times the US WPI and divided by Colombia's CPI. *REER*, on the other hand, is an index of the effective real exchange rate, computed relative to a basket of ten currencies where a weighted average of the trade partner's WPIs is used in the numerator and Colombia's CPI is used as a deflator in the denominator. According to these definitions of the real exchange rate an increase in these indexes denotes a real depreciation, whereas a decline indicates that the domestic currency is appreciating in real terms.

In addition to investigating the nature of the relation between coffee price (and terms of trade) changes and the real exchange rate, two other hypotheses are tested. The first is that the rate of growth in income per capita and the rate of change of the real exchange rate are negatively related. This hypothesis is derived from the Ricardo–Balassa effect, which states that countries with a higher rate of productivity gain will experience a real appreciation in their currency. In the model derived above this effect of the rate of growth of real income on the real exchange rate was captured by the term k in equation (14). In this study the rate of growth of per capita income is used as a proxy to measure these productivity gains. The other hypothesis being tested refers to the relationship between the levels of import protection and the real exchange rate.[17] Even though in a general equilibrium setting with exportables, importables and non-tradable goods the effect of changes in import tariffs on the real exchange rate cannot be determined a priori, the presumption is that for most countries higher tariffs result in a real appreciation (Edwards, 1984a). In the regression analysis the following reduced forms for the real exchange rate were estimated:

$$\hat{e}_t = a_0 + a_1\hat{y}_t + a_2\,\hat{\tau}_t + a_3\Delta D_t + v_t \tag{15}$$

and

$$\hat{e}_t = b_0 + b_1\hat{y}_t + b_2\,\hat{p}_t^c + a_3\Delta D_t + u_t \tag{16}$$

where:

$\hat{e}$ = percentage change of either *RER* or *REER*

$\hat{y}$ = percentage change in real GDP per capita

$\hat{\tau}$ = percentage change in the terms of trade, measured as export prices over import prices

ΔD = change in a dummy variable that measures the level of protection in every period

$\hat{p}_t^c$ = percentage change in the real price of coffee, defined as an index of the dollar price of coffee deflated by an index of import prices for Colombia

u, v = error terms.

It is expected, then, that a_1, $b_1 < 0$, and that a_2, b_2, a_3, $b_3 < 0$. In equation (16), changes in the real price of coffee ($\hat{p}_t^c$) are used instead of the change in the terms of trade ($\hat{\tau}$), since changes in coffee prices are the main determinants of $\hat{\tau}$ and because our main interest is to investigate how changes in the price of the main commodity export affect the real exchange rate.

The results obtained from the estimation of equations (15) and (16), as well as some variants, using OLS, are presented in table 7.2. As can be seen, while all the coefficients have the expected signs, only a few are significant at conventional levels. On the other hand, the goodness of fit, as measured by the R^2, is rather poor. Nevertheless, these results provide some preliminary evidence that the hypothesized negative effect of terms of trade changes – and especially coffee's terms of trade changes – on the real exchange rate in Colombia is indeed present.

A problem with these estimates is that by concentrating on reduced forms they do not capture most of the action, missing in particular the mechanisms through which coffee price changes are transmitted into the real exchange rate. For this reason, in the next section the model developed in section 2 is explicitly tested.

7   Coffee, money, inflation and the real exchange rate in Colombia

In the preceding section, results obtained from the estimation of reduced form equations for changes in the real exchange rate in Colombia were presented. These regressions indicated that changes in the world (real) price of coffee have had a (marginally) significant negative effect on the real exchange rate in Colombia. However, a problem with these results is that, as in most analyses based on reduced form regressions, the mechanism through which a particular exogenous variable (the price of coffee) affects the endogenous variable (the real exchange rate) is not explicitly presented. In the Colombian case this is particularly troublesome, since by basing the analysis on reduced forms the possible monetary effect of higher prices of coffee is missed. In this section this problem is faced by directly estimating a version of the model presented in section 2.[18]

In this section the three main equations from the model (equations (5), (9) and (10)) are estimated simultaneously. The estimation was performed using annual data for 1952–80, with an explicit distinction made between the pre-1967 period and the post-1967 period. The

Table 7.2 The real exchange rate in Colombia: reduced form estimates

EQ.	Dep. var.	Period	Constant	$\hat{p}^c$	$\hat{\tau}$	$\hat{y}$	ΔD	R^2	DW
(15.1)	RER	57–83	0.022 (1.009)	−0.159 (−1.942)	—	—	—	0.082	1.394
(15.2)	RER	57–83	0.024 (1.106)	—	−0.257 (−1.787)	—	—	0.113	1.293
(15.3)	RER	57–83	0.108 (1.590)	−0.146 (−1.322)	—	−0.018 (−1.240)	−0.006 (−0.102)	0.162	1.303
(16.1)	REER	57–83	0.028 (1.178)	−0.122 (−1.027)	—	—	—	0.041	1.803
(16.2)	REER	57–83	0.030 (1.284)	—	−0.293 (−1.891)	—	—	0.125	1.737
(16.3)	REER	57–83	0.103 (1.233)	−0.120 (−0.957)	—	−0.017 (−0.019)	−0.030 (0.471)	0.085	1.615

Ordinary least squares. The numbers in parentheses are t-statistics. R^2 is the coefficient of determination and DW is the Durbin–Watson statistic.

following variant of the money creation equation (5) was estimated (where the v_is are error terms):

$$\hat{M}_t = \alpha_0 + \alpha_1 \hat{M}_{t-1} + \alpha_2 \hat{y}_t + \alpha_3 \hat{P}_{t-1} + \alpha_4 \hat{P}_t^{c*} + \alpha_5 DEH_t + v_{1t}$$
$$(17)$$

DEH is the fiscal deficit in nominal terms as a proportion of the lagged quantity of high powered money.

The following version of the inflation equation (9) was estimated, where *DUM* is a dummy variable that takes a value of zero up to 1967 and a value of one from there onwards.

$$\hat{P}_t = \delta_0 + \delta_1 \hat{M}_t + \delta_2 \hat{y}_t + \delta_3 (\hat{E}_t + \hat{P}^*_{Tt}) + \delta_4 DUM_t + v_{2t} \quad (18)$$

Finally, the exchange rate devaluation equation (10) was the following:

$$\hat{E}_t = \mu_0 + \mu_1 \hat{P}_t + \mu_2 (\hat{P}_t DUM_t) + \mu_3 \hat{P}^*_{Tt} + \mu_4 \hat{P}_t^{c*} + \mu_5 DUM_t + v_{3t}$$
$$(19)$$

The estimation of (16) using two stages least squares yielded the following result:

$$\hat{M}_t = -0.030 + 0.607 \, \hat{M}_{t-1} + 0.318 \, \hat{y}_t + 0.137 \, \hat{P}_{t-1} + 0.095 \, \hat{P}_t^{c*}$$
$$(0.883) \quad (4.067) \qquad (0.768) \quad (1.373) \qquad (2.776)$$

$$+ 0.125 \, DEH_t$$
$$(2.345)$$

$$DW = 2.03 \qquad SEE = 0.035$$

The most interesting result from the estimation of this equation is that it confirms the hypothesis that higher (domestic) prices of coffee have resulted in *short-run* increases in the rate of money creation. As discussed above, the mechanism through which this takes place is the accumulation of international reserves that are monetized by the Central Bank. Also, estimates of the coefficients of the lagged $\hat{M}$ suggest that the effect of changes in coffee prices on money growth have some persistence through time. The estimation of the money growth equation, then, provides statistical support to the claim made by numerous authors (i.e., Weisner, 1978; Urrutia, 1981) that in Colombia the ability to perform monetary policy has been hampered by the dependence of money creation on the behaviour of coffee prices. Also, these results support the hypothesis that the process of money creation in Colombia has been critically influenced by the behaviour of the fiscal side of the economy. An increase in the fiscal deficit – measured as a proportion of lagged base money – of 10 percentage points has resulted, on average, in an increase in the rate of growth of money of approximately 1.25 percentage points. This finding points out that the separation of the fiscal and monetary sides in traditional macroeconomic analysis might not be fully applicable to LDCs.[19]

The estimation of the inflation equation using two stage least squares yielded the following results:

$$\hat{P}_t = -0.006 + 0.705 \, \hat{M}_t - 0.040 \, \hat{y}_t + 0.311 \, (\hat{E}_t + \hat{P}^*_{Tt}) + 0.010 \, DUM_t$$
$$\quad (-0.729) \quad (2.669) \quad\quad (-0.363) \quad (2.182) \quad\quad\quad\quad (0.314)$$

$$DW = 2.23 \quad SEE = 0.060$$

With the exception of income growth and the dummy variable, the coefficients are significant and have the expected signs. The coefficient of $\hat{M}_t$ indicates that, with other things given, an increase in the rate of money creation by 10 percentage points has resulted in an increase of inflation of approximately 7 percentage points. On the other hand, according to the coefficient of $(\hat{E}_t + \hat{P}^*_{Tt})$, a higher rate of devaluation and/or higher world inflation, will be passed on almost one-third to price increases.[20] As the model indicates, the sum of the coefficients of $\hat{M}_t$ and $(\hat{E}_t + \hat{P}^*_{Tt})$ is not significantly different from one. However, the coefficient of real income growth was, in all runs, insignificant.

Finally, the estimation of the crawling peg equation yielded:

$$\hat{E}_t = -0.006 + 1.333 \, \hat{P}_t - 0.850 \, (\hat{P}_t \, DUM_t) - 0.060 \, \hat{P}^*_{Tt} - 0.198 \, P^{c*}_t$$
$$\quad (-0.119) \quad (2.569) \quad (-1.678) \quad\quad\quad\quad (-0.063) \quad (-1.604)$$

$$+ 0.043 \, DUM_t$$
$$(0.469)$$

$$DW = 1.728 \quad\quad SEE = 0.108$$

These results confirm the hypothesis that the Colombian authorities have taken into account the behaviour of world coffee prices when deciding by how much to devalue the nominal exchange rate. Lower (higher) world coffee prices result in higher (lower) rates of devaluation of the crawl. Also, according to this equation, in the post-1967 period – after the crawling peg was adopted, and with other things given, the exchange rate tended to be adjusted by less than the ongoing domestic rate of inflation. On the other hand, while the coefficient of the world rate of inflation is negative, as expected, the absolute value of its point estimate is very small and not significant.[21]

8   Concluding remarks

In this paper, the interaction between changes in commodity export prices and the real exchange rate has been investigated. In section 2 a model that relates coffee price changes to money creation, inflation and the rate of devaluation was developed. The model was then estimated for Colombia. A virtue of this model is that it highlights two of the channels that have been traditionally pointed out in casual discussions on the effect of commodity price changes on the real exchange rate: money creation and inflation and the rate of adjustment of the nominal exchange rate (i.e., the rate of devaluation of the crawling peg).

The model shows that commodity export booms will generally generate short-run increases in money creation, inflation and a real appreciation. In fact it is possible that the real appreciation generated through this channel exceeds the 'equilibrium' real appreciation resulting from the boom. If this boom is perceived as temporary, the real appreciation will be smaller, but could still be significant.

The model presented in this chapter was empirically tested for the case of coffee in Colombia. Two approaches were taken in the empirical sections. First, a reduced form equation that relates changes in the real exchange rate to changes in the price of coffee, and other exogenous variables, was estimated. The results obtained provided preliminary evidence indicating that increases (reductions) in the world price of coffee have indeed resulted in a real appreciation (depreciation). Secondly, the model developed in sections 2 and 3 was explicitly tested using a simultaneous equations approach. The results obtained indicate that coffee price changes have indeed been closely related to money creation and inflation. Also, coffee price changes have been negatively related to the rate of devaluation. These results indicate that in Colombia, the real appreciation resulting from coffee price increases has been accommodated, partially by money creation and inflation, and partially by an adjustment in the nominal exchange rate. The model used in this paper has been deliberately kept small and simple. As a result, it has been possible to pinpoint clearly the role of coffee in the inflationary and devaluation process. A cost of this approach, however, has been that some simplifying assumptions had to be made.

Appendix Data sources

All data refer to annual averages.

E = Pesos per US \$ nominal exchange rate, taken from *International Financial Statistics* (*IFS*).

M = M_2 definition of money, taken from *IFS*.

P = Consumer price index (CPI) taken from *IFS*.

y = Real GDP, taken from *IFS*.

P_T = Price of tradables in pesos. Constructed as the product of the US wholesale price index (WPI) and the Colombian exchange rate.

P^{c*} = Price of coffee in dollar terms. Constructed from data in the *IFS*.

DEH = Fiscal deficit, in nominal terms, scaled by the lagged quantity of high-powered money. From 1970 to 1980 data that correct for the *Cuenta Especial de Cambio* are used. (These data were supplied by Colombia's *Departamento Nacional de Planeacion.*)

NOTES

* A previous version of this paper was presented at the CEPR Conference on 'Natural Resources and the Macroeconomy,' London, 10–11 June 1985. Financial support from NSF grant SES 84 19932 is gratefully acknowledged.
1 On Dutch Disease see Corden (1984) and the papers in this volume.
2 On some of the monetary aspects of the Dutch Disease see, for example, Neary and van Wijnbergen (1984).
3 This section draws partially on Edwards (1986).
4 See Edwards (1983).
5 Notice that, for simplicity, the model ignores issues related to the demand for international reserves. For an integration of the demand for reserves literature with a balance of payments equilibrium analysis, see Edwards (1984b).
6 For exact expressions for the as in terms of the structural parameters, see Edwards (1986).
7 Notice that in defining the price level, we have assumed that the commodity export price does not enter into this index. This is a realistic assumption, since developing countries usually consume very little of their main export.
8 This equation is derived from assuming equilibrium in the non-tradables sector.
9 For expressions of the bs in terms of the structural parameters, see Edwards (1986).
10 In Edwards (1986) a more general rule of crawl is assumed.
11 It is also possible to define the real exchange rate as the PPP real rate. See Edwards (1986) for the derivation of a similar model, where the real exchange rate is defined in that way.

12 See, for example, Neary (1985).
13 Notice that the model presented here has ignored the distinction between permanent and transitory changes in the price of coffee. In Edwards (1986) a similar model is developed where this distinction is explicitly taken into account.
14 On the Colombian economy see, for example, Diaz-Alejandro (1976), Ocampo (1983), Weisner (1978), Kamas (1983), World Bank (1983). Coffee represents approximately 55 per cent of Colombia's foreign earnings from legal exports. It is important to notice that the presence of important illegal exports makes the empirical analysis of Colombia's external sector quite difficult. For obvious reasons there are no reliable data on the magnitude of these illegal transactions. On the importance of illegal exports in Colombia, see Junguito and Caballero (1978).
15 See Weisner (1978).
16 In that regard, the results from this reduced form can be viewed as preliminary, since they ignore the possible short-run effects of monetary variables.
17 The effects of commercial policy changes on the real exchange rate have traditionally been emphasized in the literature. In order to simplify the discussion, the model of sections 2 and 3 ignored commercial policy. However, the result reported in this section indicates that for the case of Colombia the effects of changes in trade taxes have not been very important in determining the behaviour of the real exchange rate.
18 Some of the results reported in this section draw on Edwards (1986).
19 The positive effect of changes in coffee prices on the rate of money creation is very robust to changes in the specification of the money growth equation. For alternative specifications, see Edwards (1986).
20 These results are consistent with those reported in Hanson (1982).
21 See Edwards (1986) for a detailed analysis of alternative specifications of a crawling rule equation for Colombia.

REFERENCES

Artus J. and M. Knight (1984) *Issues in the Assessment of the Exchange Rates in Industrial Countries*, Washington, DC: International Monetary Fund Occasional Paper 29.
Barro R. (1983) 'Real Determinants of the Real Exchange Rate', unpublished manuscript.
Cline W. C. (1983) *International Debt and Stability of the World Economy*, Washington, DC: Institute for International Economics.
Corden W. M. (1984) 'Booming Sector and Dutch Disease Economics: a Survey, and Consolidation', *Oxford Economic Papers*, **36**, 359–80.
Cumby R. and S. van Wijnbergen (1984) 'Fiscal Policy and Speculative Runs on the Central Bank under a Crawling Peg Exchange Rate Regime: Argentina 1979–1981', Washington, DC: The World Bank, unpublished paper.
Diaz-Alejandro C. (1976) *Colombia*. Cambridge, Mass.: Ballinger.
Edwards S. (1983) 'The Short-Run Relation between Growth and Inflation in Latin America: Comment', *American Economic Review*, **73**, 477–88.
Edwards S. (1984a) 'Exchange Rates in Developing Countries', Los Angeles, Ca: University of California Working Paper.

Edwards S. (1984b) 'The Demand for International Reserves and Monetary Equilibrium: Some Evidence from Developing Countries', *Review of Economics and Statistics*, **66**, 500–5.

Edwards S. (1984c) 'Coffee, Money, and Inflation in Colombia', *World Development*, **12**, 1107–17.

Edwards S. (1984d) *The Order of Liberalization of the External Sector in Developing Countries*, Princeton, NJ: Princeton Essays in International Finance No. 156, International Finance Section.

Edwards S. (1985) 'Money, the Rate of Devaluation and Nominal Interest Rates in a Semi-Open Economy: Colombia 1968–82', *Journal of Money, Credit and Banking*. **17**, 59–68.

Edwards S. (1986) 'Commodity Export Prices and the Real Exchange Rates in LDCs: Coffee in Colombia', in S. Edwards and L. Ahamed (eds) *Economic Adjustment and Exchange Rates in Developing Countries*, forthcoming.

Edwards S. and M. Aoki (1983) 'Oil Export Boom and Dutch Disease: Dynamic Analysis', *Resources and Energy* **5**, 219–42.

Hanson J. (1982) 'Short-Run Macroeconomic Development and Policy in Colombia 1967–82', Washington, DC: The World Bank.

Harberger A. C. (1983) 'Dutch Disease: How Much Sickness, How Much Boon?', *Resources and Energy*, **5**, 1–22.

Junguito R. and C. Caballero (1978) 'La Otra Economia', *Coyuntura Economica*, **8**, 101–41.

Kamas L. (1983) 'External Disturbances and the Independence of Monetary Policy under the Crawling Peg', Wellesley College, Department of Economics Working Paper No. 74.

Neary J. P. (1984) 'Real and Monetary Aspects of the Dutch Disease', in K. Jungenfeld and D. C. Hague (eds) *Structural Adjustment in Developed Open Economies*, London: Macmillan.

Neary J. P. and S. van Wijnbergen (1984) 'Can an Oil Discovery Lead to a Recession? A Comment on Eastwood and Venables', *Economic Journal*, **94**, 390–5.

Obstfeld M. (1984) 'Capital Flows, the Current Account and the Real Exchange Rate: Consequences of Liberalization and Stabilization', Washington, DC: Paper presented at the NBER/World Bank Conference on Structural Adjustment and Real Exchange Rates in Developing Countries, 30 November–1 December.

Ocampo J. A. (1983) 'En Defensa de la Continuidad del Regimen Cambiario', *Coyuntura Economica*, **13**, 198–214.

Urrutia M. (1981) 'Experience with the Crawling Peg in Colombia', in J. Williamson (ed.), *Exchange Rate Rules,* New York: St Martin's Press.

Weisner E. (1978) *Politica Monetaria y Cambiaria en Colombia*, Bogota: Asociacion Bancaria de Colombia.

Williamson J. (1983) *The Exchange Rate System*, Washington, DC: Institute for International Economics.

World Bank (1983) *Colombia: Economic Development and Policy Under Changing Conditions*, Washington, DC: The World Bank.

World Bank (1984) *Macroeconomic and Agricultural Policy Linkages for Adjustment and Growth: The Colombian Experience.* Washington, DC: The World Bank.

COMMENT PATRICK HONOHAN

Sebastian Edwards is to be congratulated on an interesting and worth-while integration of theory and empirical evidence in this paper. Colombia seems a good subject for analysis in view of the tripling of real coffee prices between 1975 and 1977 followed by a return within the following four years to the 1975 price – a price boom quite out of phase with that of petroleum.

Edwards stresses the role of monetary factors in the short-run response of the economy to this resource boom. Many writers have seen the role of money as having a potential deflationary or dampening effect in a resource boom, arising from a possible failure of the nominal money stock to expand to meet increased demand from those who have gained by the boom. Here, in contrast, coffee price inflation spills over into the money stock thereby generating domestic inflationary pressure. The difference between these two perspectives lies, of course, in the implicit model of monetary policy, and it seems that the authorities are not to be thought of as directly controlling the money supply path in this model.

I think the author is right in allowing for a semi-automatic increase in the money stock arising from the deposit of increased export receipts. It would be worth exploring this question a little further at the empirical level to see, first, what proportion of the extra export receipts went into the money stock and secondly, whether the money supply effect exceeds the demand effect from the extra income or wealth. To do this would mean looking, not so much at coffee prices as at the product of coffee prices and coffee output. Indeed, considering the sharp fluctuations there have been in the volume of coffee exports, inversely correlated with the price, I suspect that using coffee prices alone may be a mis-specification. After all, between 1977 and 1980 real coffee prices fell by almost 50 per cent but the volume of Colombian coffee exports more than doubled, so that the real value of coffee exports actually increased.

Looking more generally at the specification of the model, I would make two points. First, it is implied in the text that one is exploring a situation where the real exchange rate can appreciate by more than what real factors alone would indicate. But the empirical implementation of the model does not really endogenize the effect of 'real factors' on the real exchange rate. For instance, real income is not modelled as a function of the price of coffee and overall we do not see in the model the classic 'Dutch Disease' mechanism at work. As a result, it could be argued that the real exchange rate effect coming through the monetary channel in this model is an alternative monetary expression of the more familiar real effects, rather than being entirely additional.

The second general point on specification is to express a little concern over the exclusively short-run orientation which leaves long-run equilibrium values of the variables – prices, exchange rate, money – undefined. Inclusion of an error-correction factor, defining convergence towards long-run equilibrium, would help interpretability. I would guess that it might also improve the empirical estimates, whose dynamic structure is somewhat undeveloped and which seem to have a relatively poor degree of goodness of fit.

Turning to the empirical results, I notice a great number of insignificant coefficients. My own bias is towards parsimony, and for deleting insignificant variables. While accepting the statistical risks that that can entail, it would be interesting to know what one would be left with. Of course anything can happen because of correlation between explanatory variables, but looking at the significant coefficients, the data seem to be telling us that we do not need some of the theoretical elaboration of the model. In particular, the use of the excess supply of money idea is not justified either in the money equation (where the coefficient has the wrong sign) or for non-traded prices, where a simple quantity theory formulation – prices rising in line with the money supply – will do. Real income is also insignificant in the equations.

In sum Sebastian Edwards' paper tells me that a satisfactory and concise story can be told about the monetary and inflation consequences of coffee price movements in Colombia. A coffee price boom causes an expansion in the money supply and in non-traded goods prices. But by slowing the rate of nominal depreciation, the authorities can moderate the domestic price inflation needed to achieve the real exchange rate appreciation.

8

Booming sectors and structural change in Australia and Britain: a comparison*

PETER J. FORSYTH

1 Introduction

Within the past two decades both Britain and Australia have experienced resource booms; Britain with North Sea oil and Australia with its growth in the mining sector. As is well known now from the literature, such booms can increase a country's welfare, but they also bring adjustment problems. The central problem is that of the 'Dutch Disease', which refers to the adverse effects of a boom on the tradables sector, including manufacturing.

A number of important policy questions arise from resource booms. Overall, there is the question of how well a country adjusts to its new circumstances. There is the question of how large the gain in wealth is, and how large the sectoral adjustment problems are. An issue that has not been adequately resolved is that of what the appropriate macroeconomic policy response – in terms of fiscal, monetary and, perhaps, wages policy – should be. The actual, and efficient, distribution of the wealth gains between public and private sectors is an issue which has not been much analysed. It is worth exploring how countries such as Britain are managing temporary windfalls: can they create, and are they creating problems for the future? In the main, the burden of policy responses falls upon governments. They may or may not make efficient decisions. If they do not, there is the question of whether the private sector, through markets such as capital and foreign exchange markets, can make efficient choices and possibly counteract any inefficient decisions by governments.

In general, it will be concluded that the policy problems in Australia are significantly less difficult than those in Britain. The workings of the resource boom have been more straightforward, even though the value of the windfall is comparatively less. The evidence suggests that Britain has not made the most of its good fortune. It has not adjusted well to the structural change. It appears to be using up the temporary gains immediately, and, by doing so, making the adjustment costs now and in the future greater.

In the following section the nature of the booms is described. Then, in the next section, they are fitted into the context of the 'Dutch Disease' analysis. The macroeconomic effects merit some discussion, especially for the British case. It is not possible to be conclusive about these, however. The consequences for government revenues can be important, and they are discussed next, along with intertemporal issues. This is an appropriate stage to examine how well markets have worked.

The resource booms of Britain and Australia have often been likened, but they differ in important ways. These differences can be used to illustrate some distinctions noted in the literature. First, the 'spending' and 'resource-movement' effects, analysed by Corden and Neary (1982), have different roles in Britain and Australia. The spending effect is more important in Britain, while the resource-movement effect dominates in Australia. The problems raised differ accordingly. Secondly, the North Sea boom is short-lived, whereas the mining boom in Australia can expect to be long-lasting. A comparison of the two countries illustrates distinctions made in the literature.

2   Resource booms in Britain and Australia

2.1   *A brief history*

The booming sector in the British economy has been North Sea oil and gas. It has grown from virtually nothing to a major industry in ten years. Britain has other natural resources, such as coal, but this sector has not evidenced any sharp rises or falls over recent history. Britain as an economy has experienced various shocks, though they have not been resource-related (apart from the oil price rise).

The natural resource sector has, for most of Australia's history, been very significant (see Doran, 1984; Helliwell, 1984). The most spectacular resource boom was that of gold in the mid-nineteenth century analysed in Dutch Disease terms by Maddock and McLean (1984). Apart from this, production of silver, lead, copper and coal has meant that the mineral sector in Australia has been large. In fact, the proportion of GDP accounted for by the sector in the 1950s and 1960s, around 2 per cent, was atypically small. Recently, Australia experienced two resource 'booms' – a major boom in the period about 1968–74, and a minor boom about

1978–82. The first was associated with iron ore and bauxite/alumina mining and exports, along with off-shore oil. The second was energy-related and associated with coal and uranium production. Even after two 'booms', the proportion of GDP accounted for by the mineral sector is low compared to the pre-World War I period.

2.2 Characteristics

The mineral boom in Britain is simple to characterize. Oil and gas are produced on off-shore installations, at some distance from Scotland. Considerable investment was needed to make production possible. The labour requirements are very small relative to the British labour market. Gas is used domestically. By far the major output is oil, which is easily traded internationally. Britain can be considered a price-taker on world markets since even substantial changes in production are unlikely to result in much alteration of prices in the long run.

The Australian mineral sector is much more mixed. It produces several outputs, the main ones of which have been mentioned. For the most part, mines are located in remote regions. Several coal mines are situated in the Sydney region, and the off-shore oil operations are close to the Melbourne region. Only the coal industry is labour-intensive.

The source of the boom lies not only in the discovery of mineral deposits, though this was clearly important (especially for oil). Technological change, demand factors, price changes and regulatory controls have influenced the way the booms have developed. Falls in transport costs, with bulk ore carriers, have enabled Australia to supply distant markets, as well as move minerals to ports, at competitive prices. The development of Japanese industry has meant a relatively close market. The opening of many mines, especially for iron ore and coal, has been closely tailored to Japan's requirements. The viability of mines is directly affected by world prices, and much of the 1978–82 boom can be related to higher expected energy prices. Finally, government regulations, such as an embargo on the export of iron ore until 1960, restrictions on uranium exports and coal export levies, have altered the size and direction of the boom. A question that emerges from this is whether Australia possesses any market power in resources. It has been suggested that it may do so in uranium and bauxite/alumina, where it accounts for a significant proportion of world production, and coal, where it accounts for a high proportion of world trade, though not production. The imposition of a coal export levy may indicate that governments believe that such market power exists, though this has been disputed by economists.

254 **Peter J. Forsyth**

2.3 *Size and timing*

In Britain, North Sea oil and gas has grown from close to zero to about 6 per cent of GDP as of 1984 (table 8.1). Output is nearing its peak though there is doubt as to how rapidly it will fall off (see Devereux and Morris, 1983). Britain achieved self-sufficiency around 1980, and around double self-sufficiency in 1981 (table 8.2). Further finds of oil are possible, and some are likely, though there is doubt as to whether finds are likely to be as important as those which have already been made. It must be recognized that exploration depends on expected prices and existing reserves, and alterations in these could induce further exploration and discovery. Future reserves may be more expensive to exploit if, as is likely, the good prospects have been explored first.

While Britain is a net exporter at present, the long-run position in terms of present value may be one of approximate self-sufficiency. The depletion policy will be taken as given here, though it is recognized that it could be too rapid or too slow. Intertemporal problems emerge and are discussed in section 5. The optimal rate of extraction may have little to do with the efficient policy of spreading the benefits of the resource over time since prices are unaffected by output and revenues can be

Table 8.1 United Kingdom: contribution of oil to GDP and employment income, 1973–83

	GDP in mineral oil and natural gas (£m)	Income from employment in mineral oil and natural gas (£m)	Index no. of output (1980 = 100)	Total GDP (£m)	Proportion of GDP (%)
1973	58	7	2.2	66,013	—
74	24	19	0.1	75,101	—
75	9	29	0.3	95,007	—
76	602	51	16.2	110,844	0.5
77	2100	77	47.4	128,967	1.6
78	2777	98	68.9	148,059	1.0
79	5705	155	98.7	171,265	3.3
80	8809	217	100.0	198,830	4.4
81	11,994	288	110.3	216,965	5.5
82	13,898	337	126.6	235,997	5.9
83	16,193	362	137.6	259,831	6.2

Source: United Kingdom, Central Statistical Office, *United Kingdom National Accounts*, 1984 edition, London: HMSO.

Table 8.2 United Kingdom: balance of payments impact of oil and gas, 1973–83

	Value of sales			Interest profits dividends due abroad	Trade in oil			Current account balance
	Gas	Oil	Total		Exports	Imports	Balance	
1973	133	2	135	−9	344	1285	−941	−979
74	166	3	167	−10	710	4067	−3357	−3278
75	190	58	248	−23	734	3791	−3057	−1523
76	258	645	903	−24	1172	5119	−3947	−846
77	317	2226	2543	−550	1198	4750	−2771	53
78	432	2805	3237	−744	2235	4219	−1984	1162
79	538	5689	6227	−1368	4158	4889	−731	−525
80	648	8851	9499	−2215	6133	5818	315	3629
81	844	12,340	13,184	−2355	9107	5996	3111	7221
82	957	14,431	15,388	−2623	10,686	6130	4556	5206
83	1110	17,018	18,128	−3023	12,525	5650	6875	2916

All values are £m.

Source: Central Statistical Office, *United Kingdom Balance of Payments*, 1984 edition, London: HMSO.

invested. It will depend upon expected future prices, interest rates and the technical difficulties of extracting the oil over short and long periods.

The value of the resource deposit is naturally dependent on the price. In the short run, supply elasticities are low, since it takes a number of years to establish additional wells. In the long run, supply elasticities will be higher, though it is difficult to obtain reliable evidence on them. Supply is unlikely to be highly elastic even in the very long term, governed, as it is, by physical factors.

The Australian mining boom, by contrast, has been smaller and more gradual. This can be seen in tables 8.3 and 8.4. The period of greatest growth was between about 1968 and 1974, when the sector increased its share of GDP from around 2 per cent to around 4 per cent. Since then it has not shown a consistent pattern. While in value terms it has continued to grow, in quantity terms it tailed off in the late 1970s, as the constant price series (table 8.4) shows. The second boom, around 1980, was of much less importance than the first, and did not live up to expectations.

Mining sector growth in Australia is a much more sustained affair than in Britain. There is an exception to this – oil, which has a similar profile to oil in Britain, though it is tailing off more gradually than North Sea oil is expected to. With many resources such as iron ore, bauxite and coal, reserves are large relative to annual production. Thus production can be expected to last for a long period. More rapid depletion would be possible and probably not significantly more expensive (on supply elasticities, see Freebairn, 1985). Limits on the size of ready markets are a possible explanation of the depletion rate.

Table 8.3   Australia: percentage share in GDP of selected industries, 1963/4–1981/2

	Mining		Agriculture		Manufacturing	
	A	B	A	B	A	B
1963/4	1.8		10.0		27.1	
1968/9	2.2		9.2		27.4	
1973/4	4.2	6.6	7.1	6.3	27.2	22.7
1978/9		6.7		7.8		20.2
1981/2		5.9		6.6		20.2

Column A at 1968/9 prices.
Column B at 1979/80 prices.

Source: Reserve Bank of Australia, Occasional Paper 8A, *Australian Statistics 1948/50–1982/83*, vol. I, tables.

Table 8.4   Australia: percentage share of total GDP, 1960/1–1982/3

	Mining		Agriculture		Manufacturing		Electricity & water		Construction		Other	
	Curr.	Const.	Curr.	Const.	Curr.	Const.	Curr.	Const.	Curr.	Const.	Curr.	Const.
1960-61	1.7	3.6	11.4	8.7	29.3	23.6	2.9	1.7	7.0	8.1	47.7	54.2
61-62	1.7	3.5	10.8	8.9	29.0	23.3	3.0	1.8	7.1	7.8	48.4	54.7
62-63	1.6	3.1	11.6	9.0	28.4	23.7	3.2	1.9	7.1	7.8	48.0	54.6
63-64	1.8	3.0	12.8	8.8	27.7	23.0	3.1	1.9	7.1	8.3	47.6	55.0
64-65	1.9	2.8	11.6	8.5	28.1	23.7	3.2	2.1	7.4	8.3	47.8	54.5
65-66	2.0	3.1	9.7	7.3	28.4	23.5	3.4	2.1	7.7	8.6	48.7	55.3
66-67	1.9	3.4	10.8	8.5	27.5	23.1	3.2	2.2	7.6	8.2	49.0	54.7
67-68	2.0	3.4	7.9	7.0	28.0	23.5	3.3	2.2	7.6	8.7	51.2	55.3
68-69	2.1	3.7	9.0	8.1	27.2	23.3	3.2	2.2	7.5	8.6	50.9	54.1
69-70	3.0	4.7	7.3	7.3	26.7	23.5	3.2	2.2	7.6	8.4	52.2	54.0
70-71	3.1	5.8	6.1	7.0	26.5	22.8	3.1	2.3	7.7	8.3	53.5	53.9
71-72	3.5	6.2	6.3	7.3	25.6	22.4	3.1	2.3	7.7	8.2	53.8	53.6
72-73	3.4	6.5	7.6	6.3	24.6	22.7	3.1	2.4	7.5	8.0	53.8	54.2
73-74	3.5	6.6	8.5	6.2	24.3	22.7	3.0	2.4	7.3	7.6	53.4	54.4
74-75	3.8	6.7	6.3	6.7	21.9	20.0	2.9	2.5	7.6	7.0	57.5	57.1
75-76	4.2	6.2	5.5	7.1	21.2	19.4	2.9	2.6	7.5	7.0	58.6	57.7
76-77	4.3	6.6	5.4	7.0	20.7	19.1	3.0	2.7	7.2	6.6	59.4	57.9
77-78	4.5	6.6	4.7	6.8	20.3	18.8	3.1	2.8	7.1	6.5	60.3	58.4
78-79	5.2	6.5	6.6	7.7	19.4	18.7	3.0	2.8	6.6	6.2	59.3	58.0
79-80	6.1	6.1	6.7	6.7	19.2	19.2	3.0	3.0	6.2	6.2	58.8	58.8
80-81	6.4	6.0	5.8	5.9	19.3	19.0	3.1	3.0	6.3	6.5	59.2	59.6
81-82	5.8	5.7	5.2	6.5	19.2	18.6	3.2	3.1	5.9	6.3	60.7	59.8
82-83	6.3	6.3	3.8	5.5	18.0	17.6	3.5	3.3	5.6	6.1	62.8	61.3

Curr., Current price shares; Const., Shares at constant 1979/80 prices.

Source: Australian Bureau of Statistics, *Australian National Accounts, Gross Product by Industry*, various years.

Expectations are for continued, though slow, growth of the mineral sector (see Bureau of Industry Economics, 1981). Growth is expected to be concentrated in energy resources, and a new form of export, liquefied natural gas, is likely to be exported around the early 1990s. The effects of the changes in production which constitute the mineral boom can thus be considered more or less permanent.

Given that supply elasticities are distinctly not zero, resource price changes have, over time, quantity and revenue consequences. As can be seen from table 8.5, real resource prices rose in the late 1970s. This is the main explanation of the second mineral boom of 1978–82. Optimistic price forecasts for coal, uranium and aluminium (an energy-intensive metal) induced a boom in investment in these industries (and expectations of an even larger expansion of investment to follow). In the event the growth in actual output was modest, and resource prices declined

Table 8.5   Australia: GDP deflator and mining output price, current and deflated, 1960/1–1982/3

	GDP deflator	Mining output price	Real price of mining output
1960–61	29.1	13.9	47.7
61–62	29.3	13.9	47.2
62–63	29.4	15.4	52.5
63–64	30.7	17.9	58.2
64–65	31.6	21.0	66.4
65–66	32.4	21.0	64.8
66–67	33.9	19.5	57.6
67–68	34.5	20.1	58.4
68–69	35.6	20.5	57.6
69–70	37.2	24.0	64.4
70–71	39.2	21.2	54.1
71–72	42.1	23.4	55.7
72–73	46.5	24.2	52.0
73–74	52.3	27.3	52.1
74–75	60.7	34.5	56.9
75–76	70.2	47.4	67.5
76–77	77.4	50.7	65.5
77–78	82.9	56.3	67.9
78–79	90.1	71.8	79.7
79–80	100.0	100.0	100.0
80–81	110.8	117.0	105.0
81–82	120.4	122.0	101.3
82–83	136.2	136.6	100.3

Source: as for table 8.4.

before many planned investments were made. Some mines which were already in production incurred losses. In the longer term, mining sector output and revenues appear to be sensitive to prices.

2.4 The rental component of the mineral sector

Britain is undoubtedly better off having North Sea oil than if it did not. Since it is approximately self-sufficient, and the oil is relatively expensive to extract, Britain may be no better off than it was as an importer when oil prices were low. Rises in price are to Britain's advantage since it is, at the margin, an exporter. North Sea oil involves some labour and materials, and heavy capital investment. The rent component is large, however. Some of these rents accrue to the companies developing the fields (though much of their profit is a return on their investment). Most of the rent accrues to the government, which levies a de facto resource rent tax (Devereux and Morris, 1983). Government revenues are a high proportion of the value of output (see tables 8.6 and 8.7). A rise in oil prices is akin to the imposition of an indirect tax on fuel – it raises the cost of fuel to the private sector, and the government gains additional revenue.

In Australia, the oil sector is similar to the British oil sector. Rents are high, and the government obtains most of them (see table 8.8). However, oil accounts for only a modest proportion of mining output.

Table 8.6   United Kingdom: government North Sea oil and gas receipts (excluding Corporation Tax), 1977–84

	Oil tax and royalties	Oil tax and royalties plus gas levy	Consolidated revenue fund receipts
1977	153	153	42,395
1978	457	457	49,776
1979	1170	1170	57,924
1980	3076	3076	71,087
1981	5321	5576	82,352
1982	6535	6973	89,237
1983	8015	8549	96,257
1984	9119	9621	103,385

All values are £m.

Source: United Kingdom, Central Statistical Office, *Financial Statistics*, various issues, London: HMSO.

Table 8.7   United Kingdom: total oil and gas revenue estimates, 1981/2–1985/6

	Oil revenues	Gas levy	Total	Consolidated revenue fund receipts
1981/2	6.4	0.4	6.8	76.3
1982/3	6.1	0.5	6.6	82.9
1983/4	8.9	0.5	9.4	88.7
1984/5	12.0	0.5	12.5	98.4
1985/6	13.5	0.5	14.0	106.5

All values are £b.

Source: HM Treasury, *Financial Statement and Budget Report*, various years.

Table 8.8   Australia: petroleum and LPG revenue and total government revenue, 1978/9–1983/4

	Petroleum and LPG revenue ($A m)	Total government revenue ($A m)
1978/9	1227.0	33,390
1979/80	2270.2	38,619
1980/1	3107.9	45,395
1981/2	3163.3	57,972
1982/3	3486.0	58,712
1983/4	3664.5	65,021

Note: Rapid growth in petroleum revenue in the late 1970s is due primarily to changes in the structure of taxation.

Sources: Australian Bureau of Statistics, *Taxation Revenue Australia 1983–84* and *Government Financial Estimates, Australia 1984–85*.

In the main, the rental component of the mining sector is low (see table 8.9, from Porter (1984)). As has been indicated above, many mines are marginal and output price changes have a substantial effect on their viability. In short, the resource transfers needed to enable production are large relative to the value of that production.

Table 8.9   Australia: mineral sector expenditure proportions, 1981/2

	% of Total revenue
Labour costs	26.3
Purchase of goods and services	45.5
Depreciation, amortization and interest	18.5
Direct and indirect taxes	7.4
Net profit	2.3
Total revenue	100.0

Source: Australian Mining Industry Council Survey, reported in Porter (1984), p. 10.

2.5   *Balance of payments effects*

Both in Britain and Australia the resource booms involve tradable
outputs (gas, a small proportion of both countries' resource output, is
partly tradable). Prior to the North Sea boom, Britain was an importer
of oil: currently it is an exporter. The impact on the balance of payments
should be measured by import substitution as well as exports, and it is
large. This is shown in table 8.2.

Most mineral production in Australia is destined for export, except
for oil. This has been directed mainly towards import substitution.
Hence the growth in mineral exports corresponds to, though it under-
estimates, the impact on the trading position. As with Britain, the
importance to the trading position is greater than the contribution to
GDP. In table 8.10 the shares of various exports from Australia are
shown. While mining exports have been rapidly growing over the two
decades, they have been matched by the decline of wool.

3   Resource booms and structural change

3.1   *Applying Dutch Disease models*

The basic results of Dutch Disease models have been articulated by
Neary and van Wijnbergen in chapter 1 of this volume. Such models
have been applied to the Australian and British cases. The original
application to Australia was that of Gregory (1976), subsequently
elaborated by Snape (1977). Further analysis, including empirical
analysis, of the Australian mining boom has followed (see, for example,
Cook and Sieper, 1984). The approach was applied to the case of North

Table 8.10   Australia: exports by selected commodity groups, 1965/6–1982/3

	Wool	Coal	Iron ore	Alumina	Other ores	Metals	Total: ores, coal and metals
1965/6	28.8	2.4	—	—	3.6	10.3	>16.3
1970/1	12.6	4.7	8.5	2.2	5.8	9.8	31.0
1975/6	10.1	11.1	8.0	4.5	6.0	8.8	38.4
1980/1	9.8	10.3	5.8	5.2	6.3	8.8	36.4
1982/3	8.2	13.9	6.7	4.8	5.3	8.6	39.3

Values are percentages of total.

Source: Reserve Bank of Australia, as in table 8.3.

Sea oil in Britain by Forsyth and Kay (1980). Since then there have been many analyses of the impact of North Sea oil in Dutch Disease terms.

In dealing with the problem of applying the model to Australia and Britain several empirical problems are encountered. Both countries are far enough into their booms for real effects to have taken place. However, in neither case are the effects likely to prove sufficiently large to be unambiguously evident in the data. As noted, the actual rise in production of the minerals sector in Australia was not large at all. It is not easy to detect the effects of an expansion in one sector equivalent to 2 per cent of GDP. In Britain the changes were larger and quicker, but other large changes took place at the same time. There is some doubt, on theoretical grounds, as to how large any particular change should be, since expectations of changes, of themselves, have real effects. In both countries it is easier to identify some relative price changes than structural shifts. With Britain, the observations are consistent with Dutch Disease effects – the problem is that the changes are too large. There is the question of the extent to which the observed changes are due to these, or other, effects. This question has not been resolved.

3.2   *Basic structural effects*

There is no difficulty in perceiving changes consistent with Dutch Disease effects in Britain. As oil production grew, towards the end of the 1970s, the nominal exchange rate rose (see table 8.11). In 1979 real oil prices rose. Since 1980, they have fallen, and sterling has fallen. If day-to-day movements are any guide, 'news' about oil prices seems to

Table 8.11   United Kingdom: price indices and nominal exchange rate, 1965–83

	Relative export prices	Export unit value	GDP deflator (factor cost)	Weighted nominal exchange rate
1965	84.7	20.7	21.5	—
1970	80.9	25.8	26.4	133.2
1975	77.9	58.0	52.0	104.1
1980	100.0	100.0	100.0	100.0
1981	98.1	108.5	110.4	98.9
1982	92.7	116.7	117.7	94.2
1983	90.1	126.6	124.3	86.7

Source: Central Statistical Office, *Economic Trends Annual Supplement*, 1985 edition, London: HMSO; and IMF, *International Financial Statistics*.

be quickly translated into changes in sterling's value. To this extent, sterling is perceived as a petro-currency. Nominal exchange rate movements can be misleading; however, the various measures of real exchange rates and competitiveness confirm the view (see table 8.11).

The British boom has been characterized (section 2 above) as one with a large spending effect. Thus it could be expected that tradables production would fall, and non-tradables production would increase. Primary production, which is tradable, has been increasing, but it is a special case, because of the effects of the Common Agricultural Policy. Manufacturing might be identified as the tradable sector, and services (perhaps loosely, because of Britain's exports of financial and transport services) as the non-tradable sector. The decline in the manufacturing sector, especially since 1979, is dramatic (table 8.12). Its growth since 1982 can be explained in terms of the recovery from the recession and the fall in the exchange rate. At the same time, the service sector has expanded. This has happened in most industrial countries, but in Britain it has been more pronounced. Care must be used in interpreting shifts around 1980, since changes in relative shares might be explained in terms of manufacturing's greater sensitivity to the recession. Thus, in broad terms, British experience is consistent with the Dutch Disease approach. However, important questions remain, and they are examined later.

In contrast to the British case, the Australian one was characterized as one with a substantial resource-movement effect. To an extent, these resources came from overseas, through investment in the mining sector

Table 8.12   United Kingdom: GDP by sector, 1973–83

	1973	1979	1980	1981	1982	1983
			(current £m)			
Agriculture	2006	3910	4268	4775	5536	5535
Energy & Water Supply	3018	13,508	19,926	22,757	25,779	29,645
Manufacturing	20,919	48,298	54,490	53,883	58,282	62,258
Construction	4995	11,204	12,687	13,611	14,289	15,319
Services	37,731	100,518	115,874	131,741	144,817	158,928
Total	68,669	177,438	206,245	226,767	248,703	271,685
			% of total			
Agriculture	2.9	2.2	2.1	2.1	2.2	2.0
Energy & Water Supply	4.4	7.6	9.2	10.0	10.4	10.9
Manufacturing	30.5	27.2	26.4	23.8	23.4	22.9
Construction	7.3	6.3	6.2	6.0	5.7	5.6
Services	54.9	56.6	56.2	58.1	58.2	58.5
Total	100.0	100.0	100.0	100.0	100.0	100.0

Source: Central Statistical Office, *United Kingdom National Accounts*, 1984 edition, London: HMSO.

(see table 8.13), but there was still a substantial resource pull on the rest of the economy. In such a case, the effect on the non-tradables sector is ambiguous. It might expand or contract, depending on relative prices of non-tradables and labour. It is quite likely that the non-tradable sector would be relatively unaffected, and the main shifts would be between the booming and non-booming tradables sectors.

Evidence on real exchange rates (see table 8.14) seems consistent with the Dutch Disease approach, though for the earlier boom it is patchy. During this period, nominal exchange rates were fixed, though they altered slightly from time to time. Of course, real exchange rates can still change, through differential rates of inflation. The current account balance could also be allowed to vary, and for a period in the early 1970s Australia ran a current account surplus – unusual for a country which is normally a capital importer. At around this time, tariffs were cut across the board by 25 per cent (see Gruen, 1975). With the second, 1978–82 boom, the rise in real exchange rates is quite perceptible. Since then there

Table 8.13   Capital expenditure and overseas borrowing, Australia, 1959/60–1982/3

	Gross fixed capital expenditure		Increase in stocks	Net lending overseas	Statistical discrepancy	Total
	Private	Public				
1959–60	15.9	8.8	1.2	−2.5	−0.3	23.3
60–61	16.5	8.6	3.3	−4.4	−0.7	23.3
61–62	15.6	9.2	−1.5	0.3	−1.3	22.3
62–63	15.9	8.9	1.6	−2.3	−1.0	23.1
63–64	16.2	8.8	0.7	0.4	−0.8	25.3
64–65	17.2	9.4	2.8	−3.4	−0.1	25.8
65–66	17.6	9.9	0.5	−3.8	−0.4	23.9
66–67	16.7	9.6	1.6	−2.5	−0.8	24.6
67–68	17.1	9.7	0.5	−3.8	−1.3	22.1
68–69	17.2	9.2	2.5	−2.8	−0.3	25.7
69–70	16.9	9.0	1.4	−1.7	0.2	25.8
70–71	17.3	8.7	1.3	−1.7	0.1	25.7
71–72	16.8	8.7	—	−0.4	0.5	25.7
72–73	15.6	8.1	−0.7	2.2	1.2	26.5
73–74	15.1	7.7	2.3	−1.1	2.9	26.9
74–75	13.8	9.2	1.6	−1.6	1.9	24.9
75–76	14.2	9.2	0.2	−1.2	0.6	22.9
76–77	14.2	8.6	1.4	−2.3	0.4	22.3
77–78	14.0	8.8	−0.5	−2.7	0.8	20.4
78–79	14.7	8.0	1.2	−3.0	—	20.9
79–80	14.5	7.7	0.5	−1.1	−0.4	21.1
80–81	16.6	7.7	0.2	−3.7	0.4	21.2
81–82	18.2	7.4	0.8	−5.9	0.1	20.5
82–83	15.3	8.4	−1.3	−4.2	−0.3	17.8

Values are percentage of GDP.

Source: Reserve Bank of Australia, Occasional Paper 8A, *Australian Statistics 1948/50–1982/83*, vol. 1, table 6.1c.

has been a depreciation, consistent with the view that the earlier price forecasts have proved too optimistic.

The two booms were imposed on an economy undergoing gradual structural shifts. Services have been growing and agriculture and manufacturing declining (see table 8.4). The growth of mineral output in 1968–74 seems to have had little effect on services output, but to have taken place at the expense of the tradable sectors. The changes are, however, small.

Table 8.14   Australia: real exchange rates and competitiveness, 1970–83

	Trade weighted nominal exchange rate (Calendar year starting 1970)[a]	Real effective exchange rate		Rates of nominal assistance for manufacturing industry
		A[b] (March 1969 = 100)	B[c] (Calendar year starting 1970)	
1969–70	113.9	98.0	94.1	23
70–71	114.5	96.7	94.6	23
71–72	114.8	99.2	94.0	22
72–73	129.5	101.3	107.9	22
73–74	133.3	119.5	125.4	17
74–75	119.5	109.5	114.2	15
75–76	115.9	113.6	116.9	16
76–77	104.5	108.0	106.4	15
77–78	102.2	103.0	98.8	15
78–79	97.9	94.2	96.8	15
79–80	100.0	94.1	100.0	15
80–81	110.4	—	107.2	15
81–82	104.9	—	98.0	16
82–83	97.2	—	97.2	—

Column A, March 1969 = 100; Column B, calendar year starting 1970.
Our calculations: Australian CPI (Reserve Bank of Australia) divided by industrial countries' CPI (IMF *IFS*), multiplied by nominal trade weighted index.

Sources: [a] IMF *International Financial Statistics*.
         [b] Hollander and Marsden, 1980.
         [c] Reserve Bank of Australia, as in table 8.3.

In both countries relatively modest intersectoral shifts may mask sharper changes taking place within sectors. Sectors are aggregations of diverse industries, and these will be differentially affected by relative price changes. A contraction of, say, 4 per cent in a sector's output may not be especially significant, but if it is made up of contractions of 20 per cent in some industries, and expansions of others, it could pose serious adjustment problems.

It is worth examining this, especially for the British case. In table 8.15, changes in output for specific industries over the period of decline and recovery of manufacturing output are given. There is a wide spread of changes, not all of which are negative. This could be due solely to the recession, and were manufacturing to recover to 1979 levels, there might be little change in industry composition. Yet the data suggest that

Table 8.15   United Kingdom: index numbers of output by industry at constant factor cost[a]

	1973	1979	1980	1981	1982	1983
Metals	154.8	132.1	100.0	106.2	103.8	104.2
Other minerals and mineral products	128.0	111.8	100.0	89.7	94.9	94.3
Chemicals	96.4	110.5	100.0	100.2	100.8	107.0
Man-made fibres	175.6	137.0	100.0	84.9	68.1	78.1
Metal goods	141.8	121.6	100.0	92.6	94.3	97.0
Mechanical engineering	115.1	108.3	100.0	88.0	89.0	85.7
Electrical and industrial engineering	95.0	101.0	100.0	92.9	97.4	106.7
Motor vehicles and parts	137.8	115.7	100.0	83.0	79.8	84.0
Other transport equipment	101.5	92.4	100.0	103.5	100.5	97.1
Food	99.0	100.5	100.0	99.1	99.1	102.5
Drink and tobacco	89.8	101.9	100.0	95.2	91.7	94.5
Textiles	149.3	121.0	100.0	91.3	87.7	89.5
Clothing, footwear and leather	111.3	115.2	100.0	92.9	89.0	91.2
Paper, printing, publishing	109.6	108.0	100.0	94.9	91.4	91.7
All other manufacturing	120.3	116.0	100.0	91.2	88.1	91.9
Total manufacturing	114.1	109.3	100.0	93.7	93.7	95.9

[a] 1980 = 100.

Source: Central Statistical Office, *United Kingdom National Accounts*, 1984 edition, London: HMSO.

some industries may be contracting permanently. The changes taking place within manufacturing are greater than those taking place between manufacturing as a whole and services.

A final point to note is that terms of trade effects can add to the original Dutch Disease effect. Countries need not be small countries, taking prices as given. When exchange rates rise, they may be able to sell some of their exports at higher world prices, and purchase imports at lower prices. Thus, larger changes in exchange rates than otherwise will be called for, and the structural shifts will, in quantity terms, be larger. This possibility has been suggested by Forsyth and Kay (1980) in the context of Britain, and by Stoeckel (1979) and Cook and Sieper (1984) for Australia. It is very difficult to test how important this effect might have been. If elasticities are high in the long run, it will not be large.

3.3   *Some problems in interpretation*

The Australian case is straightforward, but the British case gives rise to problems. As mentioned, many of the shifts are greater than might be explained solely in terms of North Sea oil. There are other factors affecting the variables we are interested in. For example, monetary factors are likely to be a partial explanation of the rise in sterling around 1980 (Niehans, 1981). In addition, some markets may not work as quickly as others, and this may manifest itself as overshooting in the exchange rate (see chapter 1 of this volume). The rise, and subsequent fall, of sterling may indicate some overshooting.

Rather more problematical is the timing and absolute size of the boom. If Britain is approximately self-sufficient in oil, it would be, on balance, not much better or worse off as a result of the oil price rise combined with the discovery of oil (see Bank of England, 1982). One might not expect much change over the period, and especially around 1980, the large real appreciation would not be called for. Furthermore, sterling should not have declined so much in real terms after 1974.

Expectations are important determinants of real events. The 1978–82 boom in Australia was largely a boom in expectations, which has failed to be transformed into a boom in actual production. Yet it affected exchange rates and investment. By contrast the expectations of the importance of North Sea oil were probably too low in 1974–6, but were revised upwards between 1976 and 1980, a period during which many finds were announced and oil prices rose. The optimism surrounding the size of the deposits may have since faded. The recession which followed the 1974 oil shock may have halted any reverse Dutch Disease effects, but the subsequent recovery in industrial production until 1979 may have been a lagged response to the low exchange rate. None the less, it must be noted that industrial production in Britain, over the 1970s, grew less than in most other countries. The deindustrialization process, which has been affecting most industrial countries, has been more marked in Britain over this period.

Conceivably it is not changes in the long-term sustainable position which have determined actual structural shifts. Rather it has been what the country is actually doing with its resources. If Britain is only self-sufficient, in present value terms, in oil, a prudent policy would be to save a high proportion of oil revenues. If, on the other hand, it spends the revenues as they come in, in periods of oil surplus the shifts will be greater (later they will have to be reversed). There is some evidence that this is what Britain is doing (see section 5).

A related question is why the value of sterling is sensitive to the oil price. When Britain is approximately self-sufficient, a rise in the price of oil does not alter its long-term trading position (though, at the margin, Britain may be a net exporter). Several explanations may be suggested for why sterling and oil prices should nevertheless move together.

The first is that the discount rates of those involved may be high. In present value terms, Britain may then be a net exporter of oil. This is consistent with the possibility that oil revenues are being spent rapidly. This explanation requires the discount rate of private agents also to be high. Otherwise they would increase their saving to offset the government's expenditure to a degree, holding down exchange rates and inducing a balance of payments surplus. There would be no national spending effect, in spite of the government's increased spending.

A second explanation may be that anticipations take the form of expectations of greater oil deposits than have been announced. It is well known that explorers have no incentive to discover new resources which will not be needed for a considerable time – thus further discoveries, in addition to those announced, can be confidently expected. It is possible that information about some discoveries may be withheld for a time because of fears of differential tax treatment. This explanation would be consistent with apparently high rates of spending out of the oil revenues as they accrue (high current spending may be efficient). It should be recognized that if expectations are for large deposits, they can be either justifiable or false.

A final explanation moves away from the one-country model. When oil prices change, Britain's position relative to that of its competitors, such as Germany (an oil importer), will alter. A three-country model, with an oil exporter, an oil importer and a country which neither imports nor exports, may yield different results from a single-country model (see Forsyth and Kay, 1981; Krugman, 1983). Britain will revalue relative to its trading partners and competitors because, unlike them, it is not adversely affected by higher oil prices.

4   Macroeconomic effects of resource booms

4.1   *The effects of resource booms in economies with unemployment*

The simple comparative static analysis of the Dutch Disease effect presupposes an economy in macroeconomic equilibrium, with no unemployment problem. When the economy is not in such equilibrium, there are many more possibilities. For example, the presence of unemployment may indicate that labour markets are not working efficiently. If so, the factor reallocation called for in the model may not take place. Contraction of the tradables sector may not be needed to supply factors to the non-tradables sector because factors may already be available. On top of this, the way in which the resource boom affects spending and the balance of payments can have macroeconomic implications.

For a number of countries, the macro consequences of a resource boom are not of particular interest, since before and after the boom they were in macro equilibrium. This is true of Australia during the 1968–74 boom. Unemployment was low before, and during, the boom, though it rose soon after, due to other factors. This is not true of the second, minor boom of 1978–82. In Britain's case, North Sea oil was imposed on a poorly performing macroeconomy, and its timing coincided with a worsening of performance and policy changes. It is possible that some aspects of the boom made macro equilibrium more difficult to achieve.

The macroeconomic consequences of resource booms are less thoroughly analysed than the structural change aspects. Several possibilities have been identified by Corden (1981, 1982), Eastwood and Venables (1982), Buiter and Purvis (1983), Neary (1985) and Neary and van Wijnbergen (1984, and chapter 1 of this volume). These are unlikely to prove a complete listing. A range of effects can take place, and their relative importance, and the way they interact, are difficult to determine a priori. In principle, governments may be able to counteract certain effects, such as those in the monetary sector, but they need to know exactly which model fits the economy to do so effectively. Thus it is likely that their policy responses to the boom will be inappropriate, and fail to improve macro performance.

The possible macro effects of a boom are several. There will usually be an investment boom prior to actual production; this can stimulate the economy. The monetary effects, via changes in money demand associated with additional spending, and supply changes associated with balance of payments changes, have received some attention (Eastwood and Venables, 1982; Neary and van Wijnbergen, 1984). There will be fiscal effects associated with the likely inflow of revenues to the government. These effects will depend on how the government disposes of the revenues.

Much may depend on how labour markets work (see Corden, 1984, p. 370). The demand for labour will shift, and if real wages are rigid, employment will alter. Labour may not be very mobile between sectors. If so, declines in demand for labour in one sector may result in additions to unemployment, yet the additions to employment in the expanding sectors may be supply-constrained. This could happen if sectors are regionally based. An alternative model might be one where real wages set in one sector become accepted in others. Real wages in the expanding sector may be bid up, but if wages in the contracting sector are set with reference to these, relative wages will not alter sufficiently. All that will happen is that the real wage will be forced up, worsening unemployment.

4.2 Resource booms and macroeconomic performance in Britain and Australia

It is not possible to look back at the experience of Britain or Australia and come to firm conclusions about the macroeconomic effects of the booms. Apart from the inherent complexity of the issue, there is the additional complication that there were substantial policy shifts during the period. For example, in Britain, for part of the time, the growth of oil revenues coincided with severe monetary contraction (Niehans, 1981). There are few observations, and many variables which have changed.

Econometric models can provide some insights, though they are unlikely to resolve empirical issues, such as whether the impact of the boom has been to reduce or increase employment. Tracking the effects of North Sea oil in models such as the National Institute Model (Atkinson, Brooks and Hall, 1983) or the London Business School Model (Beenstock, Budd and Warburton, 1981) is a moderately difficult task. Since the models differ in structure, it is to be expected that their results differ. For example, whether the model allows for the possibility that anticipations of the boom affect real variables has a considerable bearing on its output. Unless it can be shown that a particular model is clearly superior to others there is little strong evidence on the importance of different effects. Macroeconomic models which specifically address the question of North Sea oil have been developed (see Bond and Knoble, 1982), though these are subject to the same qualifications.

A related approach is to use a computable general equilibrium model to simulate the effects of the boom. This is done by Dixon, Powell and Parmenter (1979) and Cook and Sieper (1984). Such models can indicate how large given effects might be, given the structure and parameters of the model. This can be useful, but it cannot provide an answer to the empirical question of whether these effects were present, and how significant they were.

With Britain, it seems unlikely that the North Sea oil boom has been associated with any straightforward and dominant macro effects. The growth in production has occurred at a time of sharp recession followed by moderate recovery. Anticipations of the size and value of the boom probably changed most during the 1976–80 period, when the exchange rate rose. Changes in the exchange rate are one proximate cause of the decline in manufacturing output from 1979 onwards. However, the boom would have had other effects which would have been expansionary.

The Australian boom of 1978–82 was more of an anticipated boom than an actual one, but none the less it had real consequences. Demand for labour in the investment goods industries rose, and wages were bid up. The optimistic environment facilitated matching of this wage increase in other industries. During this period, real wages throughout the economy rose (table 8.16). The rise in wages probably could not have been sustained even had the boom been a genuine one. The change in real wages can be regarded as a determinant of the sharp rise in unemployment in 1982–3. As a result of this mechanism operating through the labour market, the anticipated boom may have contributed to a worsening of unemployment.

5   Government revenue effects and the intertemporal problem

5.1   The problems defined

Two quite distinct issues are discussed here. One is the effect that a resource boom has on government revenue. The other is the problem that arises because the rents from the boom may accrue over a short period, raising the question of the extent to which the benefits should be spread over subsequent periods. The two issues are discussed together because often the rents mainly accrue to the government, and the intertemporal problem is the government's problem.

The point that rents may accrue to the government, which may have a different spending pattern than individuals, has been recognized (see, for example, Neary, 1985). As an empirical matter, the government may spend the rents in many different ways. There will, however, be an efficient pattern of spending, since the boom and its effects on taxation have altered the relative prices of public and private expenditure. The actual public expenditure need not be optimal, but the boom may have an impact on its size. If the government spends all the rents as they accrue, and on non-tradable goods, the Dutch Disease effects will be exacerbated. Many government services, such as education and welfare services, may be non-tradable. Even if the government restricts its spending increase to that amount which is optimal, there will be real resource allocation effects as a result of the boom. These effects will be present in all types of economies, but they are likely to prove most

Table 8.16   Australia: macroeconomic variables, 1960–82

	CPI	Average weekly earnings	Real wage index	Unemployed (%)	Balance of payments on current account ($A m)	% of GDP	GDP at 1975 prices ($A m)
1960	28.4*	46.0*	57.6*	1.4	−893	−5.8	35,974
61	28.5	47.7	59.5	2.8	−220	−1.3	36,403
62	28.6	49.0	60.9	2.6	−365	−2.2	38,897
63	28.9	51.6	63.5	2.5	−204	−1.1	41,664
64	29.9	55.5	66.0	1.6	−469	−2.3	44,606
65	31.0	58.0	66.5	1.3	−1139	−5.2	45,540
66	31.8	61.9	69.2	1.7	−718	−3.1	48,534
67	32.9	65.5	70.8	1.7	−994	−3.7	50,267
68	33.7	70.4	74.3	1.6	−1375	−5.0	55,074
69	34.8	76.3	77.9	1.5	−922	−3.0	58,182
70	36.5	84.8	82.6	1.4	−837	−2.5	61,283
71	39.0	93.4	85.1	1.6	−857	−2.3	64,416
72	41.3	101.8	87.6	2.5	438	1.0	66,998
73	46.7	118.3	90.1	1.8	425	0.8	69,959
74	54.5	148.3	96.7	2.3	−2828	−3.7	71,047
75	61.5	169.7	98.1	4.5	−1009	−1.2	72,826
76	70.1	190.7	96.7	4.7	−1949	−2.1	74,817
77	76.7	209.5	97.1	5.6	−3088	−3.4	75,492
78	83.0	225.6	96.6	6.2	−4533	−4.4	79,177
79	91.4	247.9	96.4	5.8	−2662	−2.3	80,148
80	100.0	201.3	100.0	5.8	−4141	−3.3	83,053
81	110.4	307.0	98.9	5.5	−8269	−5.4	85,130
82	123.1	341.9	98.7	6.7	−8607	−5.2	

* July to June, beginning in year shown.

Source: Reserve Bank of Australia, as in table 8.3.

significant in less developed economies. Such economies have fewer effective taxation options than developed economies, and resource rents may make a large difference to the government budget.

The intertemporal question has been discussed by several authors (Forsyth and Kay, 1980; Flemming, 1982; Buiter, 1983; Krueger and Porter, 1984; Corden, 1984; Neary and van Wijnbergen in this volume). On grounds of welfare maximization, the benefits of a temporary boom in real income, and perhaps government revenues, should be spread out over the future – the interest on the present value of the benefits can be consumed indefinitely. This has the advantage of restricting the structural change to that which is required in the long term, and there is no need to reverse the changes when the physical resource runs out. If the government is the primary recipient of the revenues, the savings decision initially falls upon it. It is possible for the private sector to make a different savings decision from the government, and to counteract the government's actions. If the economy as a whole spends the revenues as they accrue, the Dutch Disease effects will be larger as long as the boom lasts, but they will need to be reversed as the boom is exhausted. The policy question of how well the economy manages the temporary boom is thus an important question.

5.2   *A model of revenue effects*

Suppose a situation whereby a discovery is made of a valuable resource. It is possible that the government will own the resource and the right to the rents from it. Alternatively, the government may not own the resource but it may be able to impose a form of taxation which creates little or no distortion so it can share in the rents. It is often argued that resource rent taxation is such a form. If the government has access to other forms of costless taxation, such as lump sum taxes, its budgetary position need not be changed. The marginal cost of raising revenues stays constant at $1 per $1.

Most of the recent literature on public economics suggests that this is unlikely to be the case. (See the optimal tax literature, e.g. Diamond and Mirrlees, 1971). Governments rely on distortionary taxation, and the marginal cost of raising $1 will normally exceed $1 (see, for example, Browning, 1976; Findlay and Jones, 1982; Stuart, 1984). If a new, low-cost source of funds becomes available the government's budgetary options change, and the optimal level of spending will alter.

This can be seen in figure 8.1. The curve M_1 shows the marginal cost of raising funds in period 1. Curve B_1 shows the marginal benefits of government spending in this period. Before the resource boom the

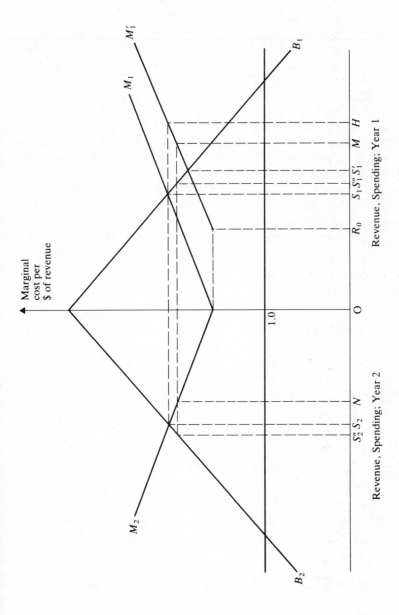

Figure 8.1   Effects of a resource boom on optimal levels of taxation and public spending.

efficient level of government taxation and spending is shown as OS_1. Suppose that, during the resource boom, the government gains an extra OR_0 in revenue which has a marginal cost of \$1 per \$1. The marginal cost of funds curve shifts laterally, by the amount OR_0, to M'_1. The new efficient level of spending is OS_1, and the level of taxation should fall by $OR_0 - S_1 S'_1 (=S'_1 H)$. The marginal cost of publicly provided goods has fallen relative to that of privately provided goods and spending shifts towards the publicly provided goods.

The analysis can be generalized to the case where there is more than one period, and the resource boom lasts for only one of the periods (not necessarily the first). A second period is shown in the left hand quadrant of figure 8.1. For convenience, it is shown as the mirror image of period 1. In the absence of the resource boom, the efficient level of spending, OS_2, is equal to OS_1. Suppose the resource boom yields revenues only in period 1. Efficient intertemporal allocation of revenues requires that the marginal cost of funds be equated in the two periods. This does not happen when spending rises to OS'_1 in period 1. Since the marginal cost of funds is lower in period 1 than in period 2, it is efficient to transfer funds from period 1 to period 2. Efficiency is achieved when the marginal cost of funds is equated. This involves saving an amount $S''_1 M$; this increases resources in period 2 by $S''_2 N$. Of this, an additional $S''_2 S_2$ is spent by the government and NS_2 represents the reduction in taxation. In period 1 spending increases only to S''_1 and the taxation reduction is confined to MH. For a boom which is anticipated but which does not provide immediate benefits, period 2 could be reinterpreted as the period before period 1.

In the boom period, the extra revenues can be split three ways. Some can be saved for the future, some can be returned to taxpayers and some can be spent. If the marginal cost of funds curve is steep (as it would be in less developed countries) the impact on spending could be large. If the government appropriates only part of the resource rents the demand for publicly provided goods will change (B_1 and B_2 will shift) due to the income effect. Most likely, they will shift outwards. It is possible that (some of) the increased government spending in period 1 will consist of direct investment by the government. This would be a substitute for saving by the government followed by provision of consumption goods in period 2. Finally, it should be recognized that the reduction in taxation will have some real effects. For example, in less developed countries a resource boom may result in lower taxes on exports and imports.

An alternative, and probably more realistic case, is where the price of a resource rises. Suppose that a country is self-sufficient in this resource over the longer term. The country neither gains nor loses, on balance, by the price change but there is a change in the domestic distribution of income. Suppose that the government owns the resource, or can tax it cheaply; there will be a shift of real income to the government. For a time the government will enjoy high revenues, but when the resource is exhausted the revenue flow ceases. In this case, there will still tend to be a real reduction in the marginal cost of funds to the government, though matters are not as clear cut as before.

The government, as before, has access to an efficient source of revenue and so the M curve shifts out as before. However, real incomes elsewhere in the economy have fallen, and this increases the cost of raising a given amount of non-oil revenue. Tax rates would increase and the marginal cost of revenue would increase. This is shown by curve M'_1 in figure 8.2. The resulting cost of revenue curve is shown as M''_1. Likewise, the marginal cost of revenue in the second period would rise. The likely, though not inevitable, result is that at the new equilibrium, E, the revenue boom is only temporary. There is an intertemporal allocation problem, which can be solved as before. On the part of the domestic users of the resource there is no intertemporal problem since they will be paying the increased price both now and in the future. As

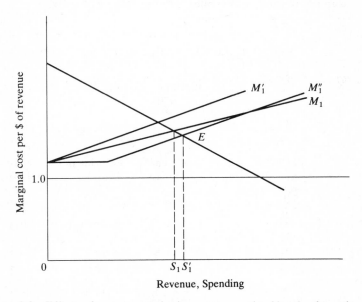

Figure 8.2   Effects of a resource price increase on optimal levels of taxation and public spending.

before, the tax mix will change and this will have an impact on real magnitudes.

The above analysis is a partial one, and subject to qualifications. First, the price of non-tradables will be bid up, partly because of the spending effects discussed here, and possibly because of resource-movement effects. This will affect the new equilibrium. Secondly, the demand for publicly provided goods may alter as a result of changes taking place in the economy. Thirdly, government investment in revenue-producing assets may be affected by demand shifts, but not by the changes in the cost of taxation. This is because, since they are self-financing, they are not affected by the overall budget constraint.

5.3   *Government revenues and saving in Britain*

The government revenue effects in Britain are relatively larger than in Australia, and attention will be focused on them here. But, as table 8.8 shows, the revenue effects in Australia from oil are quite significant. The rapid growth in revenues can be ascribed to a change in pricing and taxation policies (a movement to world parity pricing and taxation of rents). In addition there are some revenues from other minerals. The public/private balance and intertemporal questions for Australia, which arise from temporary oil revenues, are the same as for Britain.

The growth in UK oil revenues, and their significance as a component of the budget, are shown in tables 8.6 and 8.7. Given the relative magnitudes, it is difficult to track exactly the response to oil revenues,

Table 8.17   United Kingdom: nominal and real PSBR and domestic saving, 1970–83

	PSBR			Real saving	
	Nominal (£b)	Real (£b)	% of real national increase	Government (£b)	Total domestic (£b)
1970–2	−1.1	1.9	3.5	5.0	6.7
1973–5	−7.0	1.4	1.7	−7.5	7.3
1976–8	−7.8	—	—	−4.5	11.3
1979					
1980 }	−11.8	1.6	0.8	−5.7	14.1
1981				4.8	15.1
1982	−5.4	1.8	0.8	1.6	15.2
1983	−11.7	5.8	−2.1	−1.5	16.7

Source: Bank of England (1984).

but some rough tests are possible. A simple way for the government to save revenues for the future would be to reduce the budget deficit and retire debt. As table 8.17 indicates, there is no clear-cut evidence that this has been happening. Alternatively, the government may be investing more directly, though this does not seem to be the case. The government could be maintaining the deficit, and handing back the revenues to the private sector. This is rather more difficult to test, since we need to know what government spending would have been in the absence of the boom. An adequate test would involve correcting expenditure to allow for the level of unemployment and phase of the cycle. Much of the current unemployment may not be cyclical, hence it would be difficult to know what the appropriate corrections would be. As table 8.18 indicates, government spending has continued to rise. If anything, it seems that the government has been spending the revenues as they come in.

This need not hold back the private sector from making the appropriate responses. If the government is using the revenues too quickly, private agents might perceive that in the future, taxes will be higher, or government service levels be lower. In either case, it is open to the private sector to invest more now, in order to have higher real incomes when the oil revenues run out. The simplest method of investment would be to invest overseas. Except for differential sectoral effects, the oil boom has made investment in Britain neither more nor less attractive. If so, additional saving will be channelled into investment overseas, and a balance of payments surplus will be recorded. Alternatively, higher direct investment in Britain might occur.

Britain has had a balance of payment surplus over the past few years, though it has been falling as North Sea oil revenues have been rising (table 8.2). If, to use some hypothetical figures, current net benefits from the oil were £10 b, and the sustainable consumption were £5 b, then £5 b would be invested. If all of this were to be invested overseas, a sustained balance of payments surplus of around £5 b could be expected. This does not seem to be occurring. There does not seem to be any clear evidence of a shift in domestic investment (see table 8.18).

It is very difficult to discern the effects of a revenue boom of the size of North Sea oil on an economy which has been changing as rapidly as Britain's. In 1980 and 1981 it entered a deep recession, and it has been recovering quite rapidly since then. During this period, government spending policies can change, and to a degree, were forced to change (e.g. by the rise in unemployment). The recession and subsequent recovery also have implications for the balance of payments. A completely satisfactory disentanglement of the effects of revenue changes

Table 8.18   United Kingdom: macroeconomic variables, 1970–83

	Basic weekly wages, all industries (1975 = 100)	General index of retail prices (1975 = 100)	GDP 1980 prices (£m)	Gross fixed domestic capital formation (£m 1980 prices)	Total government consumption (£m)	Total unemployment (10³)
1970	44.1	54.2	190,158	39,925	38,406	555
71	49.8	59.3	195,272	40,700	39,557	724
72	56.7	63.6	199,836	40,594	41,188	696
73	64.5	69.4	215,599	43,535	43,148	557
74	77.2	80.6	213,332	41,734	43,858	528
75	100.0	100.0	211,827	41,808	46,268	838
76	119.3	116.5	220,050	42,434	46,889	1265
77	127.2	135.0	222,215	41,323	46,109	1359
78	145.1	146.2	230,290	42,938	47,125	1343
79	166.8	165.8	235,221	43,925	48,089	1235
80	196.9	195.6	230,197	41,628	48,810	1513
81	217.0	218.9	227,555	38,075	48,811	2395
82	231.9	237.7	231,895	40,645	49,224	2770
83	245.0	249.6	239,626	42,348	50,523	2984

Source: Central Statistical Office, *Economic Trends Annual Supplement*, 1985 edition, London: HMSO.

from macroeconomic effects that have in turn been influenced by the resource boom is not possible.

Notwithstanding this, there seems to be little evidence that the government, or economy as a whole, have made efficient decisions as to the disposition of the temporary revenues. If anything, it looks as though the government is devoting much of the revenues to increasing current public consumption itself, and the private sector is not making any adjustment to this. If this is the case, Britain is using up its benefits with little thought for the future, but, more importantly, exacerbating the effects on its tradable industries, and creating further structural adjustment problems for the future.

6 Conclusions

The most significant of the differences between the Australian and British cases is that the rental component of British North Sea oil is proportionally very high, so that the spending effect dominates, whereas the rental component of the Australian mining output is relatively small. This has several implications.

The nature of the structural changes required depends on the size of the spending effects. In the case of Britain, there is a need to increase output in those industries whose output is subject to greater demand; in the main, these will probably be non-tradables. In Australia, the structural shifts arise largely from the increased demand for factors of production from the mineral sector. In both cases, the shifts which take place will be of differing magnitude and direction for different industries, and a simple classification into tradable and non-tradable sectors hides much of what happens.

The structural changes take place with different time patterns in the two countries. In Britain, there is a rapid increase in real spending power. The structural shifts required come once the value of the discovery is perceived. In Australia, the structural shifts are related to production, not consumption changes, and these take longer to develop. Once the discovery of the resources is made, the direction of the changes becomes clear, but it may take some time before the factor flows need to be made. In addition, the distinction between the investment and production phases is important as these put different demands upon factor supplies. To a degree, factor imbalances are resolved by capital flows. The gradual build-up of mining investment and production flows in Australia gives factor markets time to adjust.

282 Peter J. Forsyth

Only in Britain will the effect on government revenue be large. This effect has an impact on the efficient pattern of government spending. The government is inevitably placed in the position of needing to decide how to use the large, but temporary, source of revenue. If the government uses the revenue in a myopic way, there is still scope for individuals to compensate for this in their own savings plans – this requires them to be well-informed and long-sighted. While it is difficult to test, the evidence suggests that the government has not been using the revenue efficiently.

In both countries, there is evidence of Dutch Disease effects, but it is impossible to measure the precise impact of the booms on structural change. In the Australian case, for the major boom of 1968–74, the macroeconomy was in balance, but the mineral boom was small compared to the size of the sectors it was affecting. There are many more problems of interpretation in the British case. The broad pattern of changes is consistent with the Dutch Disease model, but other factors have had a significant influence. In particular, it must be recognized that North Sea oil was imposed on a macroeconomy that was performing poorly, and the boom itself probably affected this performance. There are, in addition, questions of timing and of the long-term value of the boom which remain unresolved. To a degree, Britain appears to be reinforcing the structural effects by using up its benefits over a short period.

NOTE

* This chapter has benefited very much from comments from and discussion with several people. In particular I would like to thank John Black, Max Corden, Fred Gruen, Bob Rowthorn, Peter Warr and the discussant, John Flemming, as well as the editors, Ted Saxerud for excellent research assistance and Marti Pascall for expeditiously typing the manuscript.

REFERENCES

Atkinson F. J., S. J. Brooks and S. G. F. Hall (1983) 'The Economic Effects of North Sea Oil', *National Institute Economic Review*, No. 104, March, pp. 38–44.
Bank of England (1982) 'North Sea Oil and Gas: Costs and Benefits', *Bank of England Quarterly Bulletin*, March, pp. 56–73.
Bank of England (1984) 'Inflation Adjusted Saving and Sectoral Balances', *Bank of England Quarterly Bulletin*, June, pp. 231–4.
Beenstock M., A. Budd and P. Warburton (1981) 'Monetary Policy, Expectations and Real Exchange Rate Dynamics', in W. A. Eltis and P. J. N. Sinclair, *The Money Supply and the Exchange Rate*, Oxford: Clarendon Press.

Bond M. E. and A. Knoble (1982) 'Some Implications of North Sea Oil for the UK Economy', *International Monetary Fund Staff Papers* **29**, 363–97.

Browning E. K. (1976) 'The Marginal Cost of Public Funds', *Journal of Political Economy*, **84**, 283–98.

Buiter W. H. (1983) 'Measurement of the Public Sector Deficit and its Implications for Policy Evaluation and Design', *International Monetary Fund Staff Papers*, **30**, 306–49.

Buiter W. H. and D. D. Purvis (1983) 'Oil, Disinflation and Export Competitiveness: a Model of the Dutch Disease', in J. S. Bhandari and B. H. Putnam (eds), *Economic Interdependence and Flexible Exchange Rates*, Cambridge: MIT Press.

Bureau of Industry Economics, Australia (BIE) (1981) 'Mining Developments and Australian Industry: Input Demands During the 1980s', Research Report No. 9, Canberra, AGPS.

Cook L. H. and E. Sieper (1984) 'Minerals Sector Growth and Structural Change', in L. H. Cook and M. G. Porter (eds), *The Minerals Sector and the Australian Economy*, Sydney: Allen and Unwin.

Corden W. M. (1981) 'The Exchange Rate, Monetary Policy and North Sea Oil; the Economic Theory of the Squeeze on Tradables', *Oxford Economic Papers*, **33**, 23–46.

Corden W. M. (1982) 'Exchange Rate Policy and the Resources Boom', *Economic Record*, **58**, 18–31.

Corden W. M. (1984) 'Booming Sector and Dutch Disease Economics: Survey and Consolidation', *Oxford Economic Papers*, **36**, 359–80.

Corden W. M. and J. P. Neary (1982) 'Booming Sector and De-industrialization in a Small Open Economy', *Economic Journal*, **92**, 825–48.

Devereux M. P. and C. W. Morris (1983) 'North Sea Oil Taxation: The Development of the North Sea Tax System', London: Institute for Fiscal Studies, Report Series No. 6.

Diamond P. A. and J. A. Mirrlees (1971) 'Optimal Taxation and Public Production', *American Economic Review*, **61**, 8–27 and 261–78.

Dixon P. B., A. A. Powell and B. Parmenter (1979) *Structural Adaptation in an Ailing Macroeconomy*, Melbourne: Melbourne University Press.

Doran C. R. (1984) 'An Historical Perspective on Mining and Economic Change', in L. H. Cook and M. G. Porter (eds), *The Minerals Sector and the Australian Economy*, Sydney: Allen and Unwin.

Eastwood R. K. and A. J. Venables (1982) 'The Macroeconomic Implications of a Resource Discovery in an Open Economy', *Economic Journal*, **92**, 285–99.

Findlay C. C. and R. Jones (1982) 'The Marginal Cost of Australian Income Taxation', *Economic Record*, **58**, 253–62.

Flemming J. S. (1982) 'UK Macro-Policy Response to Oil Price Shocks of 1974–75 and 1979–80', *European Economic Review*, **18**, 223–34.

Forsyth P. J. (1980) 'North Sea Oil and Revaluation: the Impact on Individual Industries', Institute for Fiscal Studies, Working Paper No. 13, July.

Forsyth P. J. and J. A. Kay (1980) 'The Economic Implications of North Sea Oil Revenues', *Fiscal Studies*, **1**, 1–28.

Forsyth P. J. and J. A. Kay (1981) 'Oil Revenues and Manufacturing Output', *Fiscal Studies*, **2**, 9–17.

Freebairn J. (1985) 'Natural Resource Industries', in R. Maddock and I. McLean (eds), *The Australian Economy Since 1980: Performance and Policies*, Cambridge: Cambridge University Press.

Gregory R. G. (1976) 'Some Implications of the Growth of the Mineral Sector', *Australian Journal of Agricultural Economics*, **20**, 71–91.

Gruen F. H. (1975) 'The 25% Tariff Cut: Was It A Mistake?', *Australian Quarterly*, 7–20.

Helliwell J. F. (1984) 'Natural Resources and the Australian Economy', in R. E. Caves and L. B. Krause (eds), *The Australian Economy: A View from the North*, Sydney: Allen and Unwin.

Hollander G. and J. S. Marsden (1980) 'The Effect of Internal Cost and Exchange Rate Changes on the Competitiveness of Australian Industry', Centre for Economic Policy Research, Australian National University, Discussion Paper No. 3.

Krueger A. D. and M. G. Porter (1984) 'The Asset Theory of Exchange Rate Determination and the Resources Boom', in L. H. Cook and M. G. Porter (eds), *The Minerals Sector and the Australian Economy*, Sydney: Allen and Unwin.

Krugman P. (1983) 'Oil and the Dollar' in J. S. Bhandari and B. H. Putnam (eds), *Economic Interdependence and Flexible Exchange Rates*, Cambridge, Mass.: MIT Press.

Maddock R. and I. W. McLean (1984) 'Supply Side Shocks: the Case of Australian Gold', *Journal of Economic History*, **44**, 1047–69.

Neary J. P. (1985) 'Real and Monetary Aspects of the "Dutch Disease"', in K. Jungenfeld and D. Hague (eds), *Structural Adjustment in Developed Open Economies*, London: Macmillan.

Neary J. P. and S. van Wijnbergen (1984) 'Can an Oil Discovery Lead to a Recession? A Comment on Eastwood and Venables', *Economic Journal*, **94**, 390–5.

Niehans J. (1981) 'The Appreciation of Sterling – Causes, Effects, Policies', SSRC Money Study Group Discussion Paper, February.

Porter M. G. (1984) 'Mining and the Economy – Some Key Issues', in L. H. Cook and M. G. Porter (eds), *The Minerals Sector and the Australian Economy*, Sydney: Allen and Unwin.

Snape R. H. (1977) 'Effects of Mineral Development on the Economy', *Australian Journal of Agricultural Economics*, **21**, 147–56.

Stoeckel A. (1979) 'Some General Equilibrium Effects of Mining Growth on the Economy', *Australian Journal of Agricultural Economics*, **23**, 1–22.

Stuart C. (1984) 'Welfare Cost per Dollar of Additional Tax Revenue in the United States', *American Economic Review*, **74**, 352–62.

COMMENT   JOHN FLEMMING

This paper sets out many of the relevant facts relating to the booming resource sectors of the Australian and British economies since 1970. It also deploys much useful analytical material, primarily relating to equilibrium resource allocation issues. References to the Public Sector

Borrowing Requirement are in the context of intertemporal resource allocation rather than the management of demand. The equilibrium bias comes out when a valid point about heterogeneity of 'expected' changes in individual sub-sectors is illustrated by *actual* changes in UK manufacturing sectors (section 3.2) whose experience has been dominated by macro developments.

As the co-author, with John Kay, of the most influential single paper on the impact of North Sea oil on the UK economy, Peter Forsyth was applying and developing a set of ideas already circulating in Australia. This adds interest to his comparative review of both economies; in particular it is interesting to note that many of the Forsyth and Kay (FK) arguments apply more starkly to the UK than the Australian case. In other respects I found this example of the comparative method disappointingly short on synergy. It is not clear how interpretation of either picture is enhanced by an examination of the other.

As all that I know about the Australian economy was learnt from this paper, I shall concentrate in my more detailed comments on the UK and analytical material.

(1) A key issue, on which I have never accepted the FK line, relates to the order in which North Sea oil reserves were discovered, revalued by OPEC and tapped (see Flemming, 1982, especially p. 225). This is relevant to effects on asset prices which might be expected to react to 'news'. In the version of his paper presented at the conference, Peter Forsyth stated 'North Sea oil came after the first of the oil price shocks, and to an extent its development was conditional on high oil prices'. The second part of this sentence is unobjectionable and the first is true of production but not of discovery; official estimates of reserves barely changed between 1973 and 1983. The implication of the *ceteris paribus* approach adopted here is that any references to 'required deindustrialization' should be read historically as 'avoiding required industrialization'.

(2) There is another way in which oil could affect sterling which involves things sufficiently difficult to observe with any precision that it offers ample scope for *ex post* rationalization. Consider the demand for sterling as an asset. It should, according to portfolio theory, depend not only on expected relative returns but also on the variance–covariance matrix. Suppose that there is a small direct effect of the oil price on sterling. This makes the covariance of sterling with oil prices significantly different from that of other currencies. This in turn means that a rise in the *variance* of oil prices should increase oil consumer's hedging demand for sterling, pushing it up.

Agents face a difficult signal extraction problem in identifying from historical data the magnitude of the direct oil–sterling link which is crucial to the determination of their covariance. Suppose that a jump in the oil price is associated – as seems likely – with a jump in its *ex ante* variance. Both these factors will boost sterling and this could easily lead to an exaggerated estimate of the covariance strengthening the indirect effect and thus leading to further exaggeration.

(3) Peter Forsyth includes much valuable material on the public finance implications of resource rents. At one point (section 5.2) he considers the possibility of the government expropriating only part of them. This possibility clearly exists when the private ownership of the resource rents is well defined – as I imagine is the case with Australian minerals. It does not, however, in the case of North Sea oil. In the absence of taxation it is hard to imagine the government giving away exploration and production rights. In particular, in an equilibrium framework the rents necessarily accrue to the government which owns them. It is, however, true that if these rights were sold for a lump sum the relevant uncertainties and capital market imperfections might reduce the present value of government receipts (though bringing them forward in time) while increasing *ex post* the wealth of the oil companies, with the effects described.

(4) Uncertainty and capital market imperfections would be less helpful to Peter Forsyth's argument (section 6) that British consumption patterns respond quickly to changes in expected real income, as soon as the value of the discovery is perceived, in fact. As far as private agents are concerned this may involve anticipating future tax cuts unless the government is willing to borrow, if necessary, to implement the steady-state tax cuts immediately – as is also indicated by Barro-type arguments for tax rate smoothing.

(5) There is a hint (section 5.2) that as resource rents are a low-cost revenue source the opportunity cost of a given revenue has fallen and public expenditure in the UK should have risen. More explicitly British governments are criticized for saving too little (section 5.3): presumably tax rates are unsustainably low? I would agree that on an optimal path the (suitably adjusted) fiscal deficit should, *ceteris paribus*, have fallen as North Sea revenue rose. The question of its level is more difficult. It could be argued along these lines that more should have been borrowed while oil production was below its peak. Going back to my first point, the UK did not get richer, it merely avoided getting poorer. Thus, there was no income effect generating additional demand for public goods. Moreover the slow response of public expenditure to the slowdown of

productivity growth about the time of OPEC I meant that public expenditure ratios had become inflated. Correction for this will have masked any effect of a lower opportunity cost of resource revenues – not to mention the heightened perception of the deadweight burden of other taxes.

REFERENCE

Flemming J. S. (1982) 'UK Macro-Policy Response to the Oil Price Shocks of 1974–5 and 1979–80', *European Economic Review*, **18**, 223–34.

9

Indonesia's other Dutch Disease: economic effects of the petroleum boom*

PETER G. WARR

1 Introduction

Indonesians have sometimes joked that their country suffers from a 'Double-Dutch Disease'. One 'Dutch Disease' is the legacy of Dutch colonial control, which ended when Indonesia achieved independence in 1949. The other, the 'Dutch Disease' now familiar to students of international economics, is the effect on the Indonesian economy of the international oil price shocks of 1973–4 and 1978–9. This second Dutch Disease is the subject of this paper. We shall focus on the effects that increased revenue from petroleum exports has had on relative prices within Indonesia, on the sectoral structure of production and on the distribution of income, and finally we shall discuss the policy response of the Indonesian government.

Indonesia is a significant but not a major exporter of oil, accounting for around 7.5 per cent of OPEC output and 2.4 per cent of world output.[1] These exports are of great importance for Indonesia. In 1983, revenues associated with petroleum accounted for 76 per cent of Indonesia's total export earnings and taxes on oil companies contributed no less than 64 per cent of total government revenue.[2] Nevertheless, Indonesia remains primarily an agrarian economy with 56 per cent of its population of 147 million employed in agriculture. Manufacturing accounts for another 9 per cent of total employment and services for 30 per cent. Employment in the petroleum and mining industries accounts for only about 0.7 per cent of the total work-force.[3] In these respects Indonesia resembles Egypt and Nigeria, and to a lesser extent, Mexico.

The comparison between Indonesia, Egypt, Nigeria and Mexico can be developed briefly with the data provided in table 9.1. Indonesia and Egypt achieved high rates of growth of GDP per capita and moderate inflation through the 1970s and early 1980s. External debt rose as a

Table 9.1   Comparative economic indicators for Indonesia, Egypt, Nigeria and Mexico

		Indonesia	Egypt	Nigeria	Mexico
Petroleum exports /total exports (%)	1982	75	69	95	77
Real GDP growth rate per capita	1960–1970	1.8	1.8	0.6	4.3
(% per capita, p.a.)	1970–1982	5.4	5.9	1.2	4.6
Inflation (% p.a.)	1975–1982	14.2	13.3	17.7	25.6
External public debt/GNP (%)	1973	33.5	23.0	7.0	10.2
	1982	21.1	52.4	8.5	32.7
Debt service /total exports (%)	1973	6.3	40.2	4.0	22.2
	1982	8.3	70.9	9.5	29.5
Gross international reserves (months of imports)	1982	3.0	1.9	1.1	0.6
Current account balance/total merchandise exports (%)	1982	−3.3	−7.7	−37.6	−13.2
Central government expenditure/GNP (%)	1972	16.2	n.a.	9.9	12.1
	1981	27.3	n.a.	(22.3)[a]	20.8

[a] Relates to 1978; later data unavailable.

Sources: World Bank, *World Development Report*, 1983 and 1984; World Bank, *World Debt Tables*, 1983–4; and International Monetary Fund, *International Financial Statistics*, various issues.

proportion of GDP between 1973 and 1982 in all countries shown except Indonesia, which began the period with substantial but highly concessionary bilateral debt. By 1982 Indonesia's debt servicing represented the smallest proportion of total exports of the countries shown, its reserves were relatively substantial and its current account deficit was small. The final point to notice from the table is the rapid growth of the central government in the three countries for which data are available (all but Egypt). Since petroleum export revenues accrue largely to the governments of these countries, this is unsurprising; but it is of great economic importance for the countries concerned.

Indonesia's macroeconomic performance over the period of the oil boom is described further in table 9.2. It is notable that the monetary growth rate exceeded the sum of the rate of growth of real GDP and inflation through almost all of the period. The average rate of monetary growth over the period was around 33 per cent compared with a 17 per cent average rate of inflation and 8 per cent average growth rate of (real) GDP. The residual, 8 per cent, is partly accounted for by increased monetization of subsistence economic activity.[4] Over the period neither total debt outstanding nor total debt servicing increased markedly as a proportion of GNP and reserves increased relative to the volume of imports by about 50 per cent. The gross value of Indonesia's oil exports over this period was around US$130 billion. The increase in reserves accounted for only 3 per cent of this total and was only one-fourth as large as the increase in total debt. In brief, Indonesia absorbed all of its petroleum revenues during this period, but essentially no more than that. Indebtedness did not increase very significantly and reserves were not depleted.

Indonesia's petroleum sector is described in detail in the tables presented in the Appendix. The contribution of the petroleum sector to gross domestic product increased from 10 per cent in 1972 to 19 per cent in 1982. The real value of total petroleum output rose by 490 per cent over this period, but this was due overwhelmingly to international price increases. The unit value of Indonesia's petroleum exports rose by 350 per cent in real terms and thirteen-fold in nominal terms (see table 9.7); but physical output rose by only 23 per cent (see table 9.6).[5] Domestic consumption as a proportion of domestic output increased from 13 to 34 per cent over this decade (see table 9.8).[6]

A substantial theoretical literature on the economic effects of booming sectors has now developed, but empirical testing of the predictions of these analyses has necessarily lagged behind.[7] The purpose of the present paper is first to ask whether the empirical evidence available for Indonesia confirms the qualitative predictions of this literature. Second, we look at the way the Indonesian government has responded to the domestic effects of the petroleum boom. In particular, we discuss the most important of these policy responses, the large devaluation of the Indonesian currency in November 1978.

Specifically, we ask four questions:

1 Have the average *prices* of traded goods declined relative to those of non-traded goods (section 2.2)?

Table 9.2 Macroeconomic indicators for Indonesia, 1972–82

	1972	73	74	75	76	77	78	79	80	81	82
Gross national product ($ b)	11.02	15.68	23.19	29.12	36.90	44.23	49.49	49.02	69.28	82.47	87.20
Growth rate of real GDP (%)	9.4	11.3	7.6	5.0	6.9	8.8	7.8	6.3	9.9	7.6	2.3
Inflation (%)	6.6	31.0	40.6	19.1	19.8	11.0	8.1	20.4	15.4	8.5	9.5
Growth rate of money supply (%)	47.7	41.1	40.1	33.4	28.2	25.1	24.0	36.1	47.6	29.6	10.0
Debt outstanding ($ b)	4.08	5.25	6.86	7.99	9.31	11.66	13.11	13.23	14.88	15.74	18.42
Debt outstanding/ GNP (%)	37	34	32	27	25	26	27	27	22	19	21
Debt service/GNP (%)	1.4	1.3	1.6	1.8	2.1	2.9	4.2	4.3	2.6	2.4	2.6
Reserves ($ b)	0.8	0.8	0.7	0.6	1.3	2.5	2.7	4.2	6.8	6.2	4.6
Reserves as months of imports	2.2	2.5	1.8	0.9	1.7	2.8	2.5	3.5	4.2	3.0	3.1

Source: as in table 9.1.

2 Has the *structure* of domestic production outside the oil sector shifted away from traded goods and towards non-traded goods (section 3)?

3 What have been the *income distributional effects* of Indonesia's petroleum boom (section 4)?

4 How has the *policy response* of the Indonesian government to the effects of the oil boom modified the effects discussed above (sections 2.3 and 3.2)?

Readers familiar with the 'Dutch Disease' literature will require no explanation for the first two questions and little for the third. The literature establishes the presumption that a booming sector will lead *ceteris paribus* to a decline in the ratio of tradables prices to those of non-tradables and to a contraction in the output of tradables sectors other than the booming sector, relative to those of non-tradables. According to the literature, the implications of this for factor incomes will depend on factor intensities in these sectors. Factors used intensively in tradables sectors will lose absolutely while those used intensively in non-tradables will gain.

The fourth question requires more explanation. By 1978 the relative price effects of the oil boom were the subject of policy interest in Indonesia at the highest levels of government. The perceived decline in the profitability of the non-oil traded goods' sectors led in November 1978 to a 33 per cent devaluation of the currency. Judging from official announcements made at the time and subsequently, this devaluation was motivated primarily by the desire to protect the domestic traded goods sectors from the effects of the oil boom (i.e. to counteract its effects on relative prices) and not (to the same extent at least) by balance of payments considerations. The effectiveness of this policy response continues to be the subject of economic debate and we shall review the empirical evidence on its effects.

In view of the importance of exchange rate policy for our discussion, and especially the November 1978 devaluation, it is convenient to divide the period from 1971 onwards into three intervals.[8] From 1971 to 1978 Indonesia's exchange rate was fixed relative to the US dollar. This period divides into two intervals: the years from 1971 to 1973 represent the pre-oil shock period; the years from 1974 to November 1978 cover the period when the domestic effects of the first oil shock were first felt. Thirdly, from then until 1982 these effects were mixed with the impact of the devaluation and that of the second oil shock. A second large devaluation occurred in March 1983, but since this devaluation was apparently motivated by balance of payments considerations and not by protectionist objectives, our discussion will not extend beyond the end of 1982.

2 Relative price effects

2.1 *Some caveats*

The theoretical expectation of a decline in the prices of tradable goods and services relative to non-tradables as a consequence of a resource boom is, of course, based on a comparative static analysis with all other determinants of relative prices held constant. When comparing this expectation with the historical record, we obviously confront the difficulty that these other determinants of relative prices are not necessarily stationary. These factors include domestic monetary and fiscal policy, domestic price interventions of various kinds, exogenous domestic supply shocks and international commodity price movements. We must therefore attempt the counter-factual exercise of comparing the observed historical experience in which the petroleum boom is present, with the hypothetical situation that would have arisen in its absence but in which all 'other' factors were the same as those observed.

A second difficulty is that while the conceptual dichotomy between 'tradable' and 'non-tradable' goods and services is convenient for theoretical purposes, it does not mesh closely with the available data. Most of the goods produced in Indonesia's import-competing sector, for example, are imperfect substitutes for imported commodities. To this extent they are only partially tradable. Moreover, the protection of Indonesia's import-competing industries is accomplished by a Byzantine combination of tariffs, import quotas and direct subsidies to both outputs and inputs. The existence of binding quantitative import restrictions moves goods from the 'tradable' to the 'non-tradable' category so far as the standard theory is concerned because given the size of the quota their domestic prices are determined by domestic supply and demand conditions rather than by international prices and the exchange rate. But the commodities subject to quantitative restrictions are scattered widely within the available data and it is virtually impossible to separate them from the rest of the import-competing sector given the information available.

A further problem is that the prices of some important commodities are administratively controlled in Indonesia. As in the case of many other LDCs this is especially significant in the case of major food crops, particularly the most important of these, rice. Rice is imported into Indonesia but these imports are exclusively controlled by the government's rice marketing agency. Domestic prices are also controlled by the government and while there is some evidence that the long-term movement of the domestic price roughly follows movements in international rice prices, there are often wide discrepancies between the two in the short run.[9] In brief, rice does not fit either of the conceptional categories of 'tradable' or 'non-tradable' especially well, although within this spectrum it is probably closer to the 'tradable' extreme.

2.2   *Impact of the petroleum boom, 1974–8*

Despite these problems, it remains possible to extract a relatively clear picture of the impact that Indonesia's petroleum boom has had on relative domestic prices. Indices of some of the most important aggregate price series are presented in table 9.3. The first five series shown are (roughly) indices of traded goods prices. The second last series (Jakarta consumer prices) combines traded and non-traded goods prices and the last, the housing component of the consumer price index, is a frequently used proxy for non-tradables prices.

As an index of tradables prices, the series representing the wholesale prices of imported goods is the most useful. Fluctuations in international prices are more significant in the case of the non-oil export price series and these international price movements are extraneous to our discussion. As an index of non-tradables prices the housing series is more useful than the consumer price series but it also has major deficiencies. The 'housing' index incorporates data on housing rents, prices of electricity and water, costs of home maintenance and domestic servants, all of which are non-traded, but it also includes fuel and household equipment prices, which clearly involve traded commodities.

In table 9.4 these data are converted to relative price form with a base of 1974 equal to 100. The impact of the petroleum boom may be thought of as occurring from 1974 onwards. We shall discuss first the period up to 1978 inclusive. The indices of wholesale prices of imports and (non-oil) exports declined significantly relative to the consumer price index between 1974 and 1978. This is even more true when we look at the ratio of these import and export price series to the 'housing' price series. Both these price ratios rose until 1974, after which they declined rapidly until 1978. This is also true of the ratios of the wholesale prices of manufactures to the housing series. The decline after 1974 is much smaller in the case of the agriculture/housing price ratio but it must be recalled that price controls for food crops, especially rice, have a dominant effect on the behaviour of agricultural wholesale prices.

It is helpful to construct an index of tradables and non-tradables prices which improves upon the indices shown in tables 9.3 and 9.4.

Table 9.3   Aggregate price indices, Indonesia, 1971–82[a]

	1971	72	73	74	75	76	77	78[b]	79	80	81	82
Imports (wholesale prices)	54	60	76	100	109	117	122	130	188	217	243	255
Exports (wholesale prices)	27	32	47	100	98	104	119	121	258	391	416	432
Exports, non-petroleum (wholesale prices)	46	48	76	100	83	103	132	140	238	289	340	350
Agriculture (wholesale prices)	46	54	73	100	117	147	180	194	261	327	378	422
Manufacturing (wholesale prices)	53	58	81	100	107	126	140	153	205	250	279	307
Jakarta consumer prices (general)	51	54	71	100	119	143	159	166	216	256	285	310
Jakarta consumer prices (housing)	72	73	83	100	125	157	184	199	255	308	338	386

[a] 1974 = 100.
[b] Data for 1978 cover only the pre-devaluation period of January to October.

Source: Central Bureau of Statistics, Jakarta, Indikator Ekonomi, various issues.

Table 9.4 Selected aggregate relative price indices and 'competitiveness', Indonesia, 1971–82[a]

	1971	72	73	74	75	76	77	78	79	80	81	82
Imports/CPI	106	111	107	100	92	82	77	78	87	87	85	83
Exports (non-oil)/CPI	88	89	107	100	70	72	83	84	111	113	119	113
Manufacturing/CPI	103	108	114	100	89	88	88	92	95	97	97	99
Agriculture/CPI	90	100	103	100	98	103	113	117	121	128	133	136
Imports/housing	75	82	93	100	87	75	66	67	74	71	72	67
Exports (non-oil)/housing	63	65	92	100	66	66	72	75	93	93	101	90
Manufacturing/housing	73	79	98	100	85	80	76	77	80	82	82	80
Agriculture/housing	64	74	88	100	94	94	98	97	102	106	112	109
'Competitiveness'	130	130	122	100	100	82	87	95	132	110	98	95

[a] 1974 = 100.

Sources: as in table 9.1 and International Monetary Fund, International Financial Statistics, various issues.

Such an index is shown by the solid line in figure 9.1.[10] The dashed line labelled 'competitiveness' should be disregarded for now. The index of relative prices is constructed as follows. The index of tradables prices is the Indonesia-wide wholesale price index for imported commodities. Export prices are excluded for the reasons indicated above. The index of non-tradables prices is drawn from components of the consumer price index.

From April 1979 onwards the Bureau of Statistics has published monthly data giving 26 components of the Indonesia-wide consumer price index. From this series an index of non-traded goods prices has been constructed from eight CPI components seemingly belonging to the non-traded category.[11] Prior to April 1979 data were published for a 'cost of living' index for various cities, disaggregated to only four categories: housing, food, clothing and miscellaneous. Unpublished price data using the post-April 1979 CPI classification have been obtained from the Bureau of Statistics for the period January 1971 to April 1979, but relating to Jakarta only, and these data are used in the calculations underlying figure 9.1.

The series declines steadily from an index of roughly 120 at the beginning of 1974 to an index of roughly 70 in late 1978. The rapid decline from mid-1973 to mid-1974 should not be attributed directly to the petroleum boom. It appears to have been due primarily to the effects of a very large rise in rice prices following a poor rice harvest in

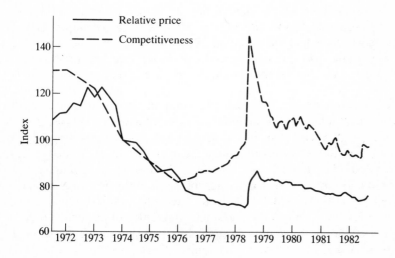

Figure 9.1   Aggregate tradable/non-tradable price ratio and 'competitiveness',
1971–83 (1974 = 100).

late 1972, followed by a major monetary expansion in 1972 and 1973. The inflationary effect of this expansion, concentrated in the prices of non-tradables, seems to be the explanation for the decline in the tradables/non-tradables series up to mid-1974. But the subsequent steady decline of at least 30 per cent up to the end of 1978 can be attributed more directly to the petroleum boom.

2.3   *The devaluation of November 1978*

By late 1978 the apparent decline in the profitability of the non-oil traded goods producing sectors was the subject of widespread public discussion within Indonesia. The outcome was the 33 per cent devaluation of the Indonesian rupiah in November of that year. Short-run balance of payments considerations apparently played some role in determining the timing of this devaluation, since there was a small but noticeable deterioration in Indonesia's current account in the months preceding the devaluation. But this cannot explain the magnitude of the devaluation which ensued.

The 1978 devaluation provides a relatively clear example of a devaluation motivated primarily by protectionist considerations. This is clear from various official statements made at the time and shortly afterwards. An example is a subsequent article by the Director of Bank Indonesia, who states that the devaluation

> was carried out with a view to improve Indonesia's international competitive position and thus to stimulate the development of export and import substitution industries which had been under increasing cost pressure due to a faster rate of inflation in Indonesia in the recent years than the rate abroad.[12]

In most countries a dramatic decline in the profitability of the import-competing sector might be expected to lead to increased protection for that sector. But in Indonesia there are complicating factors. Indonesia's import-competing manufacturing sectors are already highly protected (Pitt, 1981; Boediono, 1983). Moreover, smuggling is widespread and this implies that further increases in tariffs, or tightening of quota restrictions, will be likely to have only muted effects on the domestic prices of these commodities. Tightening of protective barriers increases the attractiveness of smuggling and this smuggling response dilutes the degree to which protectionist policies have the desired effects of raising the domestic prices of the target commodities. In such circumstances, the use of exchange rate adjustments in an effort to raise the domestic profitability of these industries has obvious political attraction.

Indonesia's freely convertible currency means that everyone, smugglers included, must convert domestic currency into foreign exchange at the official exchange rate. To the extent that devaluation has the effect of raising the domestic prices of traded goods relative to non-traded goods, then, this device may be capable of achieving, albeit temporarily, protection of the non-oil traded goods producing sectors of the economy that would not be possible through other means.

Support for the policy objective of shielding Indonesia's non-oil traded goods producing sectors from the general equilibrium effects of the oil boom derived from more than simply the sectional interests of producers in those industries. It also reflected the generally held presumption that Indonesia's oil exports would inevitably decline in volume terms within the foreseeable future, possibly vanishing entirely within 20 years. This presumption was based on extrapolations of recent trends in Indonesia's production and domestic consumption of petroleum and petroleum products. Production showed negligible growth while consumption was expanding at 10–12 per cent per annum.

It was contended that, if oil exports were to run out so quickly, it was both economically wasteful and politically dangerous to allow the non-oil traded goods sectors to contract in the short run only to be required to expand again a decade or two later. In addition, it was widely agreed that the rate at which Indonesia's oil revenues could productively be absorbed was limited and that short-run accumulation of foreign exchange reserves was desirable. According to this argument, these resources would be absorbed more efficiently if the rate of absorption was slowed, and this time phasing could be facilitated by temporary exchange rate protection.[13]

It is important to realize that the effects of using the exchange rate for protective purposes differ from the effects of the conventional instruments of commercial policy – including tariffs and import quotas – in several important respects. First, they differ in their relationship to smuggling, as described above. Secondly, unlike tariffs and import quotas, which affect the domestic prices of traded commodities relative to one another, exchange rate protection aims to influence the domestic prices of traded commodities as a group relative to non-traded commodities. Its impact is consequently much less specific. If the aim is to protect *particular* traded good industries, exchange rate manipulation is a very crude instrument.

A third difference is that while the relative price effects of tariffs and import quotas are permanent, those of exchange rate changes are likely to be temporary.[14] Finally, we should note that in a country like Indonesia, where a high proportion of export revenue accrues directly to the government in the form of petroleum taxes, exchange rate adjustments have major (but temporary) implications for government revenue.[15] Devaluations raise revenue, but this effect persists only as long as the relative price effects persist.

The relative price effects of the devaluation are clearly indicated in figure 9.1. The tradables/non-tradables price ratio reached a peak 4–5 months following the devaluation, by which time it had risen by 23 percentage points above its value immediately before the devaluation. At this point a little over half of the decline in the tradables/non-tradables price ratio since mid-1974, and around one-third of the decline since mid-1973, had been reversed. After this, the relative price effect fell away gradually and this process of decay had a half-life of approximately a further 25 months. By the time of the March 1983 devaluation roughly one-fifth of the initial relative price effect of the devaluation remained.

Indices of tradables/non-tradables price ratios relating to narrower groups of traded commodities show a common pattern of a rise in the price ratio following the devaluation, reaching a maximum after 3–5 months, followed by the gradual decay of this impact.[16] By the time of the March 1983 devaluation most of these indices had reached, or almost reached, their values just prior to the 1978 devaluation.

Turning to the impact of the devaluation on specific broad sectors, two points are especially striking.[17] First, it was a considerable time before the prices received by these sectors adjusted fully to the devaluation (i.e. rose by 50 per cent in rupiah terms). For the agricultural, mining and quarrying and manufacturing sectors this required 15, 16 and 17 months, respectively. Consumer prices (as measured by the CPI) had risen by a comparable amount after 23 months. The second point is that even by the time of the March 1983 devaluation, the ratios of the average wholesale prices of the products of these sectors to the CPI had still not returned to their pre-devaluation values. Of course, these sector-wide price movements were influenced by many factors other than the devaluation and it would be a gross oversimplification to say that any one of these sectors produced only 'traded' commodities. Nevertheless, these observations do suggest that the validity of the 'law of one price' assumption requires closer examination.

Not only did the domestic prices of imported goods take several months to respond to the devaluation, but the prices of their domestically produced substitutes took longer still.[18] This can be shown by examining the prices of pairs of imported goods and their apparent substitutes produced domestically. The time required for full response of the prices of domestically produced import substitutes to the devaluation averaged around 14 months whereas the time required for their imported substitutes averaged around 10 months. But these observations in turn cast doubt on the usefulness of 'indices of competitiveness' (table 9.4 and figure 9.1), since they rest so heavily on the assumption of the 'law of one price'.

2.4 Changes in 'competitiveness'

The account presented above is: (a) that the impact of the devaluation on relative prices was considerably smaller than the relative price effect of the petroleum boom which it was intended partly to offset; and (b) that this impact was subsequently dissipated, but only slowly. This contrasts sharply with the picture presented in earlier commentaries. These discussions have suggested that the impact of the devaluation on relative prices was very large in relation to the effects of the oil boom, but that this effect was eroded extremely quickly, having largely vanished within 7–12 months after the devaluation.[19]

The differences between these accounts resides in the fact that in earlier discussions the analysis of the relative price effects of both Indonesia's petroleum boom and the 1978 devaluation was conducted almost exclusively with the use of indices of 'competitiveness'.[20] These indices are widely used in applied work on international economics. They are calculated by taking the nominal exchange rate between the home country (Indonesia) and each of its major trading partners and multiplying it by the ratio of consumer prices in the foreign country to consumer prices at home. The resulting numbers are then aggregated using the various countries' shares of the home country's trade as weights. Such an index is presented in the final row of table 9.4 and by the dashed line in figure 9.1.[21]

The importance of this type of index for our discussion goes well beyond its use in studying the impact of the 1978 devaluation. Calculations based on this type of index, showing a substantial decline between 1971 and 1978, similar to that indicated in table 9.4, played an important part in the policy discussions that preceded the devaluation.[22] According to one source, the International Monetary Fund and the Dutch government argued at the Inter-Governmental Group for Indonesia meetings in mid-1978 essentially in favour of a devaluation to restore 'competitiveness', drawing on these sorts of calculations, while the World Bank argued against it.[23]

We shall argue that these indices provide a misleading indication of relative price movements, and before comparing the two series shown in figure 9.1, it is helpful to review the economic properties of the 'competitiveness' index.

Competitiveness is usually defined as in equation (1),

$$C = ep^*/p, \tag{1}$$

where C denotes competitiveness, e denotes the official exchange rate (units of the domestic currency for unit of foreign currency), and p^* and p denote the foreign and domestic price levels, respectively. For simplicity, we are ignoring the multiplicity of foreign countries. Changes in 'competitiveness' are given by

$$\hat{C} = \hat{e} + \hat{p}^* - \hat{p}, \tag{2}$$

where '^' denotes proportional changes (e.g. $\hat{C} \equiv dC/C$). Denoting domestic prices of traded and non-traded goods by p_T and p_N, respectively, change in the real exchange rate $R \equiv p_T/p_N$ are given by

$$\hat{R} = \hat{p}_T - \hat{p}_N. \tag{3}$$

For simplicity, we are also ignoring the multiplicity of traded and non-traded goods. Changes in the domestic price level (the consumer price index, let us say) are given by

$$\hat{p} = \alpha\hat{p}_T + (1 - \alpha)\,\hat{p}_N, \tag{4}$$

where α is the share of traded goods in consumer expenditure.

Now, if the 'law of one price' held at all times, the domestic prices of traded goods would be given by

$$p_T = e\,p_T^*. \tag{5}$$

Changes in the deviation from the law of one price can thus be measured by $\hat{D}$, where

$$\hat{D} = \hat{e} + \hat{p}_T^* - \hat{p}_T \tag{6}$$

Rearrangement of the above expressions with the assumption that the foreign real exchange rate is constant (i.e. $\hat{p}_T^* = \hat{p}^*$) now gives

$$\hat{C} = (1 - \alpha) \hat{R} + \hat{D} \tag{7}$$

It is obvious from inspection of equation (1) that if 'purchasing power parity' held at all times the index of competitiveness would be constant. Movements in it can consequently be thought of as capturing deviations from purchasing power parity. A decline in this type of index is usually interpreted as reflecting a rise in costs in the home country in comparison with those abroad and so a decline in the 'competitiveness' of producers of traded goods in the home country.

The basis of this reasoning is apparent if we consider a situation where the nominal exchange rate and foreign prices remain constant and the domestic price level rises due, say, to the spending effects of an oil boom (i.e. $\hat{e} = \hat{p}^* = 0$ and $\hat{p} > 0$). The index of 'competitiveness' falls, but whether the true competitiveness of any group of producers has risen or fallen depends entirely on the composition of the price rise – whether the prices they receive have risen or fallen relative to the prices they pay. Now if traded goods prices are determined by international prices and the exchange rate (i.e. the 'law of one price' holds and $\hat{D} = 0$) they will have remained constant and so the rise in the domestic price level will have been dominated by rises in the prices of non-traded goods. The competitiveness of firms producing non-traded goods and services will have improved (on average) while that of traded goods producers will have declined. Of course, the decline in the index of competitiveness will understate the decline in the tradables/non-tradables price ratio ($\hat{R} < \hat{C} < 0$) because the domestic price level depends on both tradables prices (which are constant) and non-tradables prices (which have risen).

Now suppose we have a devaluation, but that the 'law of one price' does not hold in the short run for the domestic prices of tradables. For the discussion of this case it is convenient to rearrange equation (7) further, holding foreign prices constant ($\hat{p}_T^* = 0$) to give

$$\hat{C} = \hat{e} - \alpha\hat{p}_T - (1 - \alpha) \hat{p}_N. \tag{8}$$

In the immediate aftermath of the devaluation tradables prices will have responded only marginally ($\hat{p}_T \simeq 0$ and $\hat{p}_N = 0$). But by feeding the new (higher) exchange rate into the calculation of 'competitiveness', the index will imply that they have already adjusted in full. Since neither tradables nor non-tradables prices have in fact risen very much at this stage, domestic consumer prices have not risen much either. The result will be a dramatic increase in the measure of competitiveness ($\hat{C} \simeq \hat{e}$), even though the true competitiveness of tradables producers, as measured by the relative prices they actually face, will have improved only marginally.

Following this, as tradables prices do in fact rise significantly in terms of non-tradables, improving the true competitiveness of tradables producers, this fact will be reflected in the index only through its effects on the domestic price level, causing the 'competitiveness' index to *fall*. That is, the index will misinterpret the *actual* increase in tradables prices as an increase in *costs*, through its effect on the price level. This will appear as an erosion of the dramatic (but fictitious) gain in competitiveness achieved with the devaluation (i.e. $\hat{p}_T > 0$ and $\hat{p}_N = 0$ implies $\hat{C} = \hat{e} - \hat{p}_T < \hat{e}$). In its subsequent movements the index will make no distinction between rises in tradables and non-tradables prices – both cause the index to fall to the extent that they affect the domestic price level – and so it will fail to capture both the true gain in competitiveness as tradables prices respond to the devaluation and the later erosion of this gain as non-tradables prices begin to catch up.

Now comparing the two series shown in figure 9.1, we see exactly the difference in the pattern of price adjustments predicted by the reasoning presented above. Over the period 1974 to 1978 the competitiveness index understates the decline in the tradables/non-tradables price ratio induced by the oil boom. Following the devaluation, from 1979 onwards, the 'competitiveness' index suggests a much larger initial effect which then eroded much more quickly. To a considerable extent, the impression that earlier discussions of the Indonesian economy have given – of large initial relative price effects of devaluation relative to the impact of the oil boom, followed by their rapid erosion – must be seen as a statistical aberration, an artefact of the 'competitiveness' index itself. As an instrument for counteracting the relative price effects of the petroleum boom the devaluation was less effective immediately, but also much longer-lasting, than previous discussions indicated.

3   Structural effects

3.1   *Composition of gross domestic product*

Indonesia's petroleum boom has had clearly identifiable effects on domestic relative prices, but it is much more difficult to identify clear effects on economic structure. The time period over which we are attempting to observe these shifts is relatively short and the movement of resources in response to the price signals discussed above is presumably slow. Moreover, the data on the composition of Indonesia's gross domestic product (GDP) which we will be studying do not permit a satisfactory separation to be made between 'tradables' and 'non-tradables' sectors. Most of the sectors appearing in the data include some industries belonging to both categories as well as state enterprises and industries subject to direct price controls. Of course, structural change would have occurred in Indonesia without the petroleum boom. As in our examination of relative price effects, we are interested in comparing the observed data on the one hand with the hypothetical situation which might have arisen in the absence of the boom on the other.

Figure 9.2 shows the components of Indonesia's GDP from 1960 to 1982 measured at constant 1973 prices. In figure 9.3 these data are expressed in proportional form, showing each sector's percentage contribution to total non-petroleum GDP (total GDP minus the petroleum sector's contribution), all at constant 1973 prices.

Now, focusing on figure 9.3, suppose we had only the data shown for 1960 up to 1972 and that we were to predict the changing composition of GDP up to 1982 on the basis of this. In particular, consider the extrapolation of the trend in agriculture's contribution to GDP over the period from 1960 to 1972 up to 1982. It seems clear that the observed decline in agriculture's contribution to GDP from 1973 to 1982 was more rapid than this crude extrapolation would predict; but a more systematic test of this proposition is easily provided.

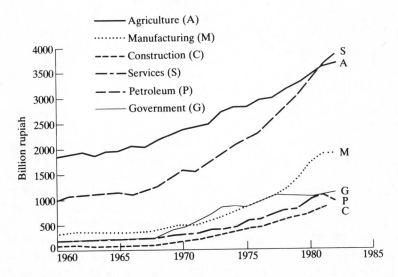

Figure 9.2   Components of Indonesian GDP, 1960–82 (constant 1973 prices).

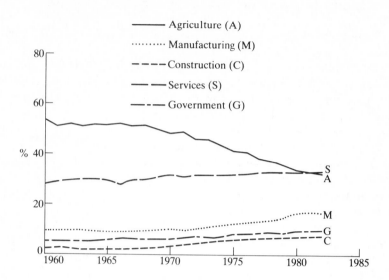

Figure 9.3   Components of Indonesian GDP as percentage of total non-petroleum GDP, 1960–82 (constant 1973 prices).

The existence of sustained structural change due to the petroleum boom has been tested statistically by fitting a time trend to agriculture's share of non-petroleum GDP separately for the periods before and after the first oil shock and then testing whether the two trends were significantly different. We estimated the equation

$$x_t = a_i + b_i t + u_t, \tag{9}$$

where x_t denotes agriculture's contribution to GDP expressed as a proportion of total non-petroleum GDP in year t, a_i and b_i are constants and u_t is an error term. This equation was estimated by ordinary least squares regression separately for each of the two periods: 1960–72 ($i = 1$); and 1973–82 ($i = 2$). We then tested the null hypothesis that $b_1 = b_2$. This hypothesis was rejected at a 5 per cent level of significance.[24]

The same exercise was then repeated for four components of agricultural GDP. Equation (9) was re-estimated for the above two periods as before, but with agriculture's contribution to GDP replaced by the contribution of: (a) farm food products; (b) farm non-food products; (c) estate crops; and (d) forestry products. The null hypothesis was again rejected in cases (*a*) and (*d*), narrowly accepted in case (*c*) and accepted in case (*b*).[25]

The rate of decline in agriculture's contribution to GDP was quite high by international standards. The same decline which took a decade in Indonesia (from 44 per cent to 31 per cent of GDP from 1971 to 1981) took 25 years in Japan (1902 to 1927), for example.[26] It occurred despite rapid growth of agricultural output (4 per cent from 1971 to 1981, about double the rate of growth of agricultural output in India during the period), heavy public investment in the agricultural sector (see section 3.2), and direct agricultural price supports, especially for food crops.

When the data for the agricultural sector are disaggregated we find that the rate of decline in the non-food crop agricultural industries' proportional contribution to non-petroleum GDP exceeds that of the agricultural sector as a whole. Comparing 1974 and 1982, the contribution of agriculture as a whole to non-petroleum GDP declined from 43.9 to 32.2 per cent. Food crops' contribution declined from 26.2 to 20.2 per cent, a decline of less than one-quarter. The contribution of the rest of agriculture declined from 17.7 to 12.0 per cent, a decline of almost one-third.[27] Loosely speaking, the decline in agriculture's contribution to non-petroleum GDP at constant prices was concentrated in those agricultural industries where prices are not controlled by the government, and where the economic effects of the petroleum boom could be expected to occur more freely.

The proportional contribution of services to GDP increased gradually and roughly linearly throughout the period, but the contribution of government, construction and especially manufacturing increased more rapidly from the mid-1970s onwards. All this is broadly consistent with theoretical expectations except the growth of manufacturing. The growth in the contribution of manufacturing partly reflects the growing importance of the petroleum refining sector. This sector is a large component of total manufacturing activity but its growth reflected government policy rather than market forces.

Comparing Indonesia with its South-East Asian neighbours, perhaps the most striking feature of figure 9.3 is the *absence* of a really dramatic expansion of the contribution of manufacturing from the mid-1970s onwards. This occurred in each of the other ASEAN countries, and in this light, extrapolation from the earlier years is presumably an especially bad predictor of what would have happened to Indonesia's manufacturing sector in the absence of a petroleum boom. It seems likely that Indonesia's petroleum boom held back the rapid growth in manufacturing that would otherwise have occurred.

3.2   *Government revenue and expenditure*

The data presented in figures 9.2 and 9.3 above present a misleading indication of the behaviour of Indonesia's public sector in that the data include only government consumption (classified as 'routine' expenditures in the Indonesian accounts) and do not reflect the increasingly important role of public sector investment. Figure 9.4 provides a more meaningful picture of government revenues and expenditures, and of their composition. It should be noted that Indonesian government accounts are presented in such a way as to give the impression that the budget is balanced and that the budget deficit is financed almost entirely by foreign aid and commercial borrowings. In the financial year 1981/2 total revenue and expenditures accounted for 22.5 and 25.8 per cent of total GDP, respectively, and the deficit accounted for 3.2 per cent.

The composition of expenditures is detailed further in table 9.5. The substantial public expenditure on agriculture, especially on irrigation,[28]

Table 9.5   Budgeted expenditures as a proportion of GDP, 1975/6–1982/3

Sector	% of GDP							
	1975/6	76/7	77/8	78/9	79/80	80/1	81/2	82/3
Agriculture and irrigation	2.5	2.4	2.0	1.9	1.3	1.7	1.8	2.0
Industry and mining	1.7	2.5	2.0	2.2	2.5	1.7	1.9	2.1
Education and health	2.4	2.3	2.8	3.0	2.8	3.1	3.7	4.4
Defence and security	3.6	3.4	3.3	3.1	2.9	2.9	3.2	2.9
Regional development	3.6	3.3	3.7	3.5	3.1	3.2	3.5	3.3
Government apparatus	4.7	4.2	4.3	4.4	5.8	7.0	8.2	6.0
Other[a]	3.1	4.7	4.2	3.2	3.3	3.6	3.6	4.1
Total	21.6	22.8	22.3	21.3	21.7	23.2	25.9	24.8

[a] Transport and tourism comprise approximately one-third of this category.

Source: Department of Finance, Jakarta, *Nota Keuangan*, various issues.

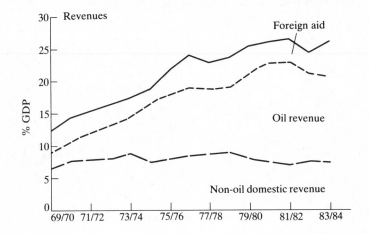

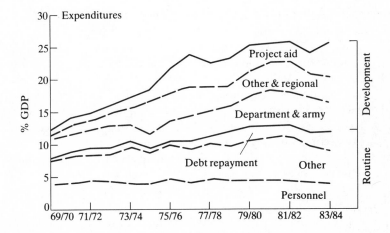

Figure 9.4   Budget revenues and expenditures as percentages of GDP,
1969/70–1983/4.
Source: *Nota Keuangan*, various issues.

is especially notable, as is the sizeable expenditure on industry. The
latter consists mainly of investments in large public enterprises engaged
in steel, fertilizer and cement production and in petroleum refining. As
a component of total expenditure, and more especially as a component
of GDP, expenditure categories of an investment character (loosely

called 'development' expenditures in the data) have become very much more important over the period of the petroleum boom. Expenditures on education and health have also grown significantly. Investments in rural health and family planning programmes have been a significant component of this. By contrast, the proportion of GDP spent on defence and internal security has been squeezed.

In short, while examples of corruption and wasteful public expenditure can easily be found, both the Indonesian data and the judgements of informed observers indicate that Indonesia's petroleum revenues have largely been invested in relatively sensible public investments, especially in the 'tradables' sectors, partly offsetting the contraction in those sectors that the petroleum boom would have produced. Whether one approves of such an expansion in the role of the public sector or not, it certainly cannot be said that Indonesia's petroleum revenues have been wasted.

4   Income distributional effects

The theoretical literature dealing with the impact of a resource boom on the functional distribution of income has focused largely upon Heckscher–Ohlin models with two factors of production which are fully mobile domestically but immobile internationally.[29] For our present discussion a more readily applicable model would be a Jones-type model with only one domestically mobile factor of production, 'labour', and all other factors sector-specific. In such a model a decline in the prices of traded goods relative to non-tradables, induced by a resource boom, would be accompanied by a shift of labour from the former to the latter industries. Wages would rise relative to the prices of tradables and fall relative to the prices of non-tradables. But the theory is ambiguous as to whether real wages – wages relative to an index of consumer prices – would rise or fall.

We shall review briefly the limited available evidence on movements in real wages in Indonesia. Figure 9.5 summarizes the most reliable data available on the behaviour of real wages in Indonesia's manufacturing sector over the period 1975 to 1982.[30] Two points are especially clear. First, there is an overall trend of rising real wages over the period. Secondly, this trend was interrupted by the devaluation in late 1978. The devaluation caused consumer prices to rise faster than wages and it was roughly 2 years before real wages returned to their pre-devaluation levels. Over this 7-year interval average real wages in manufacturing rose by 68 per cent according to these data. Real GDP per capita rose by

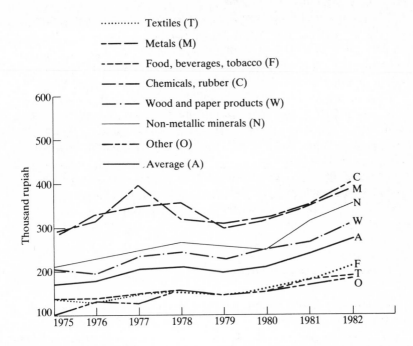

Figure 9.5   Annual real wages, manufacturing, 1975–82 (constant 1975 prices).

37 per cent over this same period, so according to this crude calculation, both real manufacturing sector wages and the share of national income going to industrial sector labour rose over this period.

Other sources of urban sector wage data are less satisfactory but point in roughly the same direction. Data on wages for construction workers in Jakarta are available from 1975 onwards.[31] These data distinguish between labourers, foremen and head carpenters. Deflating these data by the Jakarta consumer price index we find total increases in real wages over the period 1975–82 of 95 per cent for labourers, 21 per cent for foremen and 31 per cent for head carpenters. These data also reveal a dip in real wages following the 1978 devaluation, lasting for 2–3 years.

The best data available for rural sector wages are a series of daily wage rates for three activities (hoeing, transplanting and weeding) collected since 1976 by the Bureau of Statistics. When these data are deflated by the price of rice (in the absence of a suitable consumer price index for rural workers), we find increases in real wages for three regions of Java and a small decline in a fourth.[32] Wage data for estate

312 **Peter G. Warr**

workers also point to rising real wages. Deflating published wage data by the price of rice as before the data indicate increases in real wages from 1976 to 1980 of between 3 and 39 per cent.[33]

Independent survey data point to a significant decline in both rural and urban poverty in Indonesia. In these data poverty is defined in terms of ability to purchase a specified bundle of staple commodities. The percentage of the surveyed population with household incomes per member falling below the cost of this bundle fell from 40 per cent to 27 per cent for the country as a whole between 1976 and 1981. For rural areas the drop was from 40 to 26 per cent and for urban areas it was from 39 to 28 per cent.[34]

These trends cannot possibly be attributed solely to the oil boom, but it seems clear that over the period of the boom real wages have risen, and the frequency of absolute poverty has apparently declined. The oil boom has not led to the immiserization of Indonesian wage earners.

5   Summary and conclusions

Indonesia's petroleum boom was accompanied by a rapid expansion of public spending and by growth of the domestic money supply at a rate far in excess of the rate of growth of real GDP. Since this occurred during a period (1974–8) in which Indonesia's exchange rate was fixed relative to the US dollar, the resulting inflation led to a decline in the ratio of traded goods prices to those of non-traded goods and services. Because of the fixed exchange rate the inflation induced by the monetary expansion was concentrated in the prices of non-tradables.

In the absence of a petroleum boom this combination of macroeconomic policies would have led to a massive balance of payments deficit, to the depletion of Indonesia's foreign exchange reserves, and probably to increased indebtedness. A large devaluation would have been inevitable by around 1975. The petroleum boom enabled the authorities to defer such a devaluation and this provided the mechanism by which the petroleum revenues were absorbed.

By late 1978 the authorities judged the resulting rate of absorption to be excessive and devalued the Indonesian rupiah. Commentators have debated whether the deteriorating profitability of non-oil traded goods industries or an anticipated balance of payments problem provided the main motivation for this devaluation, but the two are obviously closely related. The result of the devaluation was a partial amelioration of the decline in the tradables/non-tradables price ratio which had occurred over the previous 5 years. This effect reached a peak after 5 months and then eroded slowly with a half-life of roughly a further 2 years.

Unlike several other oil-exporting countries, Indonesia did not borrow heavily on international capital markets in the late 1970s. This enabled Indonesia to avoid the worst problems of the LDC debt crisis of the early 1980s. The reason for this appears to have been a debt-wariness on the part of the government induced by Indonesia's own 'mini-debt crisis' in 1975. This took the form of a financial burden for the central government created by the imprudent borrowing and investment behaviour of the Indonesian government-owned oil company, Pertamina (McCawley, 1978). It is ironic that this event, though scandalous in terms of the waste of public funds which it involved, apparently led to an unexpected benefit. It fortuitously induced the Indonesian government to restrain its subsequent borrowing abroad and thus to avoid even greater financial hardships in the next decade.

Appendix   Indonesia's petroleum sector

Tables 9.6–9.8 on the following pages provide information on the structure of the petroleum sector and its importance in the Indonesian economy.

Table 9.6 Oil production, Indonesia, 1972–83

| | Total production (crude oil) | | | | | By company[b] | | | Disposal[d] | | Exploration expenditure[e] ($ m) |
	Thousand bpd[a]	Million barrels	% increase	As % of World	As % of OPEC	A (%)	B (%)	C (%)	Export[c] (%)	Domestic (%)	
	(1)	(2)	(3)	(4)	(5)	(6)	(7)	(8)	(9)	(10)	(11)
1972	1081	396	22	2.1	4.0	84	7	10	87	13	286
73	1338	489	23	2.3	4.3	77	15	8	87	12	393
74	1375	502	3	2.4	4.5	69	23	8	85	14	807
75	1306	477	−5	2.4	4.8	66	27	7	84	16	1047
76	1508	550	15	2.5	4.9	58	36	5	88	16	830
77	1685	615	12	2.7	5.4	50	45	5	87	17	870
78	1636	597	13	2.6	5.5	48	46	5	84	19	860
79	1594	580	−3	2.5	5.1	48	47	5	77	22	1080
80	1577	577	−1	2.5	5.8	47	48	5	73	24	2080
81	1602	585	1	2.7	7.1	46	49	5	72	27	3060
82	1338	488	−17	2.4	7.2	39	55	6	71	34	3924
83	1343	490	0	2.4	7.5	46	49	6	74	32	3953

[a] Barrels per day.
[b] A, Contract of work (of which 93–95% is Caltex). B, Production-sharing (new) companies. C, Pertamina.
[c] 8–15% of total exports in the form of refined products.
[d] Columns (9) and (10) do not add to 100% because of stock changes and imports of refined products.
[e] Petroleum company expenditures (does not include Pertamina).

Sources: Columns (1) to (10), Central Statistical Bureau.
Column (11), Annual Petroleum Sector reports, US Embassy, Jakarta.

Table 9.7 Oil sector exports, Indonesia, 1972–83

	Volume (million barrels)		Value ($ b)							Unit value ($)	
			Gross								
	Crude	Products	Crude	Products	Total oil	LNG	Total oil sector[a]	Total exports (incl. oil gross)	Oil (as % of total exports)	Nominal	Real[b]
	(1)	(2)	(3)	(4)	(5) = (3)+(4)	(6)	(7) = (5)+(6)	(8)	(9) = (7)/(8)	(10)	(11)
1972	299	46	0.8	0.1	0.9	—	0.9	1.8	50	2.79	1.85
73	370	56	1.4	0.2	1.6	—	1.4	3.0	47	3.74	2.67
74	379	45	4.7	0.5	5.2	—	4.6	6.8	68	12.35	6.71
75	363	37	4.9	0.4	5.3	—	5.1	6.9	74	13.59	6.98
76	449	36	5.7	0.4	6.0	—	6.1	8.6	71	13.59	5.86
77	484	51	6.8	0.5	7.3	0.1	7.3	10.8	68	14.10	6.27
78	462	40	7.0	0.4	7.4	0.5	7.4	11.0	67	15.18	6.22
79	394.3	54	8.1	0.7	8.9	1.3	10.3	15.6	66	20.62	5.96
80	361.7	60	14.4	1.2	15.6	2.2	16.5	21.9	75	39.86	9.91
81	362.2	56	17.0	1.2	18.2	2.5	18.9	22.3	85	46.81	12.13
82	301.7	44	14.9	0.6	15.5	2.9	15.9	22.3	71	49.24	12.13
83	314.8	47	12.6	1.0	13.6	2.6	13.7	21.2	65	40.03	8.15

Totals may not add owing to rounding.

[a] Bank Indonesia data (foreign exchange) differ from CSB (customs) data in columns (3)–(6).

[b] Deflated by general import price index (1971 = 100).

Sources: Columns (1), (2), (7)–(10), Bank Indonesia, Indonesia Financial Statistics, various issues.
Columns (3)–(6), (11) Central Statistical Bureau, Jakarta, Indikator Ekonomi, various issues.

Table 9.8 Oil tax revenue and domestic consumption of oil products, Indonesia, 1972–83

	Government revenue			Domestic consumption of oil products[b]				
	Total domestic revenue (Rp b)	Oil company (Rp b)	Tax (%)	Autur and Avgas	Gasoline	Kerosene	Diesel and fuel	Total[c]
	(1)	(2)	(3)	(4)	(5)	(6)	(7)	(8)
1972	591	199	34	1.3	11.0	21.8	13.6	47.7
73	968	345	36	1.8	12.1	23.1	23.2	60.2
74	1754	973	56	2.3	12.8	26.8	27.3	69.2
75	2242	1249	56	2.7	14.3	30.6	30.4	78.0
76	2906	1620	56	2.1	16.3	33.2	35.2	86.8
77	3536	1949	55	2.4	18.0	36.7	40.7	97.8
78	4266	2309	54	2.6	20.3	41.7	47.6	112.2
79	6697	4260	64	2.9	21.9	45.5	53.8	124.0
80[a]	10,277	7020	69	3.4	23.8	49.0	62.5	138.7
81	12,213	8628	71	3.9	26.2	52.6	77.1	159.8
82	12,418	8170	66	4.0	26.1	51.9	82.9	164.9
83	14,433	9520	66	3.8	24.6	48.1	80.0	156.5

[a] For columns (1)–(3), fiscal year beginning 1 April.
[b] Million barrels.
[c] Excluding small quantities of 'other' products.

Sources: Columns (1)–(3), Department of Finance, *Nota Keuangan*, various issues.
Columns (4)–(8), American Embassy, Jakarta, *Indonesia's Petroleum Sector*, July 1984, p. 41.

NOTES

* This paper has benefited from the research assistance of Lorraine Dearden and from the comments of J. Peter Neary and seminar participants at the Australian National University, May 1985. Discussions with H. W. Arndt, A. E. Booth and P. T. McCawley have been especially helpful.

1 *Source: Petroleum Economist*, August 1984, p. 316.

2 *Source*: American Embassy, *Indonesia's Petroleum Sector*, American Embassy, Jakarta, July 1984.

3 *Source: 1980 Indonesian Population Census*, Central Bureau of Statistics, Jakarta, Series S(2), table 45.9.

4 See Arndt and Sundrum (1984) for further discussion.

5 If 1973 is used as the base then there was essentially no increase in physical output between then and 1982 or 1983, although output was somewhat higher in most intervening years.

6 For further detail on Indonesia's petroleum sector, see Arndt (1983).

7 See McKinnon (1976) for an early discussion and Corden (1984) for a survey of the recent literature.

8 On 15 November 1978 the exchange rate was devalued from Rp. 415/US$, at which value it had been pegged since August 1971, to Rp. 625/US$. This rate of devaluation was 50 per cent when measured in terms of the home currency and 33 per cent when measured in terms of the dollar value of the rupiah. The rate was subsequently allowed to float downwards gradually, until 30 March 1983 when it was devalued from Rp. 700/US$ to Rp. 970/US$.

9 See Rosendale (1984).

10 The vertical marks appearing on the horizontal axis of figure 9.1 represent the *mid-points* of the years indicated beneath them.

11 These commodities and their respective weights, based on the weights used in the construction of the CPI, are: rent 41.2 per cent, household operations 14.9 per cent, meat 7.8 per cent, vegetables 7.9 per cent, fruits 4.5 per cent, soft drinks 7.9 per cent, medical care 7.5 per cent and education 8.3 per cent.

12 Ismael (1980), p. 103. See also the 1978/9 Annual Report of Bank Indonesia (especially p. xi) and the public statements referred to in the coverage of the *Far Eastern Economic Review*, 1 December 1978.

13 For further discussion of this debate see Paauw (1978a,b), McCawley (1980a,b) and Corden and Warr (1981). The theory of 'exchange rate protection' is developed in Corden (1977) and especially Corden (1981).

14 For discussion of the relative price effects of devaluations in a large number of LDCs see Cooper (1971a,b, 1973) and Connolly and Taylor (1976a,b).

15 See Gray (1982) for a useful discussion of this issue.

16 These indices are discussed in Warr (1984), pp. 72–3.

17 See tables 9.2 and 9.3, for example, and Warr (1984), pp. 74–5.

18 Warr (1984), pp. 78–9. Evidence for other countries is discussed in Isard (1977) and Gregory (1978).

19 See, for example, Garnaut (1979), pp. 20–1, and Healey (1981), pp. 12–21.

20 These indices have often been called 'real exchange rates' but this term leads to confusion with indices of tradables/non-tradables price ratios, which have also been referred to in this way. See the analytic discussion which follows.

21 The index shown is calculated from exchange rates and consumer price indices published in International Monetary Fund, *International Financial Statistics*, various issues. Indonesia's seven major trading partners were included, using Indonesia's import shares as weights. The countries included and their respective weights are: Japan 0.45, USA 0.21, Germany 0.11, Singapore 0.09, Britain 0.05, The Netherlands 0.05 and Australia 0.04.

22 The decline in the index from 130 in 1971 to 95 in 1978 occurred in spite of the depreciation of the US dollar, to which the rupiah was pegged, relative to the currencies of Indonesia's other trading partners, principally the Japanese yen. On this account, the trade-weighted rupiah cost of foreign exchange rose from an index of 100 in 1971 to 135 in 1978. But the rate of inflation in Indonesia over this period was almost double that of its trading partners. Prices in Indonesia's trading partners rose from 100 to 181 over the 8-year period, while in Indonesia they rose from 100 to 334.

23 *Far Eastern Economic Review*, 6 June 1978. Note also the wording of the explanation for the devaluation given by the Director of Bank Indonesia, cited above.

24 The estimated values were $b_1 = -0.414$ and $b_2 = -1.539$, with t-statistics of -4.6 and -22.9, respectively, and the null hypothesis was rejected by means of a Chow test for the equality of two regressions. The critical F-statistic for this test corresponding to the relevant degrees of freedom and a 5 per cent level of significance is 4.38 and the estimated F-statistic was 71.82. The R^2 statistics for the two regressions were 0.66 and 0.98, respectively.

25 The estimated F-statistics were: farm food crops 21.07; farm non-food crops 0.09; estate crops 3.83; and forestry 7.01. The result for forestry should be treated with caution because the overall quality of fit of the regression for the first period was quite low.

26 *Source*: Ohkawa (1957).

27 The percentage contributions of broad non-food crop agricultural sectors to non-petroleum GDP were, in 1974 and 1982 respectively: farm non-food crops 4.8 and 4.0, estate crops 2.7 and 2.5; livestock 2.9 and 2.0; forestry 5.1 and 1.7; and fishing 2.2 and 1.8. (*Source*: Bureau of Statistics, Jakarta, *National Income of Indonesia*, July 1979 and August 1983).

28 See Warr (1980) and especially Mears and Moeljono (1981).

29 Effects analogous to the Stolper–Samuelson 'magnification' theorem then dominate the results. See Corden and Neary (1982) and Cassing and Warr (1985).

30 These data provide one of the few consistent time series on wages in Indonesia. They are derived by taking the total wage bill payment and dividing by total employment. The data are from manufacturing industry surveys. (*Source*: Bureau of Statistics, Jakarta, *Statistik Industri*, various issues.) I am grateful to Dr P. T. McCawley for assistance with these data.

31 These data are based on surveys conducted by the Department of Public Works as a guide to building costs. They probably do not represent a statistically representative sample but should be reasonably reliable over time. (*Source*: Department of Public Works, Jakarta, *Daftar Harga Satuan Bahan Bangunan*, various issues. Rice prices are from Bureau of Statistics, *Indikator Ekonomi*, various issues.)

32 The increases over the 1976–82 period were 11 per cent in Yogyakarta, 30 per cent in Central Java and 37 per cent in East Java. A decline of around 2 per cent occurred in West Java. (*Source*: Bureau of Statistics, Jakarta, *Statistik Harga*

Produsen dan Eceran Pedesaandi Jawa Madura dan Beberapa Propinsi Luar Jawa, July 1982.)
33 For casual sugar estate workers in Java the increases were: males, 28 per cent; females, 39 per cent; and for tobacco estate workers in Sumatra they were: males, 3 per cent; females, 35 per cent. (*Source*: Bureau of Statistics, Jakarta, *Average Wages of Estate Workers*, 1976–9 and 1978–80. Rice price data are from *Statistical Year Book of Indonesia*, 1982.) I am grateful to Dr A. E. Booth for assistance with these data.
34 *Source*: Bureau of Statistics, Jakarta, *Indicators of Income Levels: Number and Percentage of Poor People in Indonesia, 1976–1981*, table 8, p. 48.

REFERENCES

Arndt H. W. (1983) 'Oil and the Indonesian Economy', in *Southeast Asian Affairs 1983*, London: Heinemann (for the Institute of Southeast Asian Studies, Singapore), pp. 136–50.
Arndt H. W. and R. M. Sundrum (1984) 'Devaluation and Inflation: the 1978 Experience', *Bulletin of Indonesian Economic Studies*, **20**, 83–97.
Boediono (1983) 'Manufacturing Protection in Indonesia', paper presented in 1983 to ASEAN–Australian Trade Workshop, Canberra, August (to be published in a forthcoming volume edited by C. Findlay and R. Garnaut).
Cassing J. H. and P. G. Warr (1985) 'The Distributional Impact of a Resource Boom', *Journal of International Economics*, **18**, 301–19.
Connolly M. and D. Taylor (1976a) 'Testing the Monetary Approach to Devaluation in Developing Countries', *Journal of Political Economy*, **84**, 849–59.
Connolly M. and D. Taylor (1976b) 'Exchange Rate Changes and Neutralization: a Test of the Monetary Approach Applied to Developed and Developing Countries', *Economica*, **46**, 281–94.
Cooper R. N. (1971a) *Currency Devaluation in Developing Countries*, Essays in International Finance No. 86, June, Princeton University, New Jersey.
Cooper R. N. (1971b) 'An Assessment of Currency Devaluation in Developing Countries', in G. Ranis (ed.), *Government and Economic Development*, New Haven, Conn.: Yale University Press, pp. 472–513.
Cooper R. N. (1973) 'An Analysis of Currency Devaluation in Developing Countries', in M. B. Connolly and A. K. Swoboda (eds), *International Trade and Money*, Toronto: University of Toronto Press, pp. 67–196.
Corden W. M. (1977) *Inflation, Exchange Rates and the World Economy*, Oxford: Clarendon Press.
Corden W. M. (1981) 'Exchange Rate Protection', in R. N. Cooper et al. (eds), *The International Monetary System under Flexible Exchange Rates: Global, Regional and National*, Cambridge, Mass.: Ballinger, pp. 17–34.
Corden W. M. (1984) 'Booming Sector and Dutch Disease Economics: a Survey', *Oxford Economic Papers*, **36**, 359–80.
Corden W. M. and J. P. Neary (1982) 'Booming Sector and De-industrialization in a Small Open Economy', *Economic Journal*, **92**, 825–48.
Corden W. M. and P. G. Warr (1981) 'The Petroleum Boom and Exchange Rate Policy in Indonesia', *Ekonomi dan Keuangan Indonesia/Economics and Finance in Indonesia*, **29**, 335–59.

Garnaut R. (1979) 'Survey of Recent Developments', *Bulletin of Indonesian Economic Studies*, **25**, 1–42.

Gray C. S. (1982) 'Survey of Recent Developments', *Bulletin of Indonesian Economic Studies*, **18**, 1–51.

Gregory R. G. (1978) 'Determination of Relative Prices in the Manufacturing Sector of a Small Open Economy: the Australian Experience', in W. Kasper and T. G. Parry (eds), *Growth, Trade and Structural Change in an Open Economy*, Sydney: University of New South Wales Press, pp. 219–38.

Healey D. T. (1981) 'Survey of Recent Developments', *Bulletin of Indonesian Economic Studies*, **27**, 1–35.

Isard P. (1977) 'How Far Can We Push the "Law of One Price"?', *American Economic Review*, **67**, 942–8.

Ismael J. E. (1980) 'Money and Credit in Indonesia, 1966 to 1979', *Ekonomi dan Keuangan Indonesia/Economics and Finance in Indonesia*, **28**, 97–101.

McCawley P. T. (1978) 'Some Consequences of the Pertamina Crisis in Indonesia', *Journal of Southeast Asian Studies*, **9**, 1–27.

McCawley P. T. (1980a) 'Indonesia's New Balance of Payments Problem: a Surplus to Get Rid of', *Ekonomi dan Keuangan Indonesia/Economics and Finance in Indonesia*, **28**, 39–58.

McCawley P. T. (1980b) 'The Devaluation and Structural Change in Indonesia', *Southeast Asian Affairs 1980*, London: Heinemann (for the Institute of Southeast Asian Studies, Singapore), pp. 145–57.

McKinnon R. I. (1976) 'International Transfers and Non-traded Commodities: the Adjustment Problem', in D. Liepziger (ed.), *The International Monetary System and the Developing Nations*, Washington, DC: USAID.

Mears L. and S. Moeljono (1981) 'Food Policy', in A. Booth and P. McCawley (eds), *The Indonesian Economy During the Soeharto Era*, Oxford: Oxford University Press, pp. 23–61.

Ohkawa K. (1957) *The Growth Rate of The Japanese Economy Since 1878*, Tokyo: Kinokuniya Shoten.

Paauw D. S. (1978a) 'Exchange Rate Policy and Non-Extractive Exports', *Ekonomi dan Keuangan Indonesia/Economics and Finance in Indonesia*, **26**, 205–18.

Paauw D. S. (1978b) 'The Labor-Intensity of Indonesia's Exports', *Ekonomi dan Keuangan Indonesia/Economics and Finance in Indonesia*, **26**, 447–56.

Pitt M. M. (1981) 'Alternative Trade Strategies and Employment in Indonesia', in A. O. Krueger et al. (eds), *Trade and Employment in Developing Countries, vol. I: Individual Studies*, Chicago: University of Chicago Press.

Rosendale P. (1984) 'Survey of Recent Developments', *Bulletin of Indonesian Economic Studies*, **20**, 1–29.

Warr P. G. (1980) 'Survey of Recent Developments', *Bulletin of Indonesian Economic Studies*, **26**, 1–31.

Warr P. G. (1984) 'Exchange rate Protection in Indonesia', *Bulletin of Indonesian Economic Studies*, **20**, 53–89.

COMMENT DOUGLAS D. PURVIS

Peter Warr's paper chronicles the effects of the two world oil price shocks on the Indonesian economy. That economy – which one might describe as 'second generation Dutch' – is a prototype candidate for the 'Dutch Disease'. The oil sector is a large sector within the economy, accounting for roughly three-quarters of export earnings and two-thirds of government revenue in 1983. But the economy is a small player in world oil markets – Indonesian oil production accounted for 2.4 per cent of world output and 7.5 per cent of OPEC production in 1983. Further, the output of oil as a share of GDP doubled over the 10-year period 1972–82.

The first sign of the second Dutch Disease is the rapid growth in the government sector – as a share of GNP, government expenditures in Indonesia rose from 16.2 to 27.3 per cent between 1972 and 1981. Otherwise, macroeconomic variables mask any Dutch disease symptoms: growth and inflation were good by contemporary standards, and debt and reserves remained stable relative to GNP and imports.

Clearly, any Dutch Disease that did occur was not of the 'macroeconomic' type but rather of the 'sectoral shift' type. (For a discussion, see the introductory essay in this volume and the references cited there – Buiter and Purvis, for example, focus on the former type while Corden and Neary focus on the latter.) Accordingly, the paper focuses on changes in relative prices, output shares and income distribution. However, in developing the basic questions to be examined, it would have been helpful had the paper distinguished more carefully between booms resulting from resource discoveries and those resulting from (essentially exogenous) increases in resource prices.

For purposes of discussion, the post-1971 period is divided into three sub-periods:

1 1971–3   fixed exchange rate and no oil shock.
2 1974 to November 1978   fixed exchange rate and oil shock I.
3 December 1978 to 1982   devaluation and oil shock II.

Warr then presents an extremely useful discussion of the problems involved in using conventional price indices to examine the central questions addressed in the paper. One of the real contributions of this paper – both to the debate of the Indonesian case and in terms of the standards he sets for other researchers – is the careful construction and interpretation of some new time series to cast light on the problem.

Focusing on OPEC I, Warr shows that according to the 'conventional' approach – using conventional price indices – the oil price hike reversed the rising trend of the ratio of tradable to non-tradable prices. Warr's own measure of relative prices behaves in a roughly similar fashion, although he emphasizes that the initial rapid decline starting in mid-1973 is not the result of OPEC I. Warr then turns to the 1978 devaluation. This devaluation appears to have been of a classical protectionist-inspired kind, with the added twist that temporary protection was required in anticipation of the exhaustion of domestic oil reserves and hence the ultimate need to maintain non-oil exports. The relative price impact of the devaluation is undeniable however one slices the data. Nevertheless, Warr's own numbers suggest a considerably smaller relative price effect from the devaluation than does the accepted wisdom based on the conventional numbers. In this I found his arguments quite convincing, although I am not familiar enough with the specifics of the Indonesian situation to form a firm judgement. In any event, I have no doubt that his contribution will raise the level of the debate in Indonesia.

However, I found Warr's discussion here a bit confusing. He uses the persistence of the relative price effect to infer that the 'law of one price', which he comes close to treating as synonymous with purchasing power parity, does not hold. I think of the two concepts as being logically distinct, and it is not clear that my usage of either conforms to his (common) usage of both.

The law-of-one-price, or LOOP, is an arbitrage relationship – it holds if one cannot make super-normal profits by buying a commodity in one currency and then selling it in another. As such, there is considerable empirical basis for economists to use LOOP when formulating models. Note that there is nothing in LOOP which holds that relative prices should remain unchanged – the only implication of LOOP for relative prices is that they should be invariant to the currency in which they are measured.

Purchasing power parity, or PPP, I take to be quite different. Although the term PPP is used in a wide variety of ways in the literature, I think the only meaningful interpretation is the following (which I accept may be somewhat revisionist): PPP is a comparative statics statement about the neutrality of money; in particular, about the invariance of relative prices in response to monetary changes. If domestic prices (traded or non-traded) change in response to a monetary disturbance, PPP requires that the exchange rate adjust so as to offset any relative price effect vis-à-vis foreign goods. PPP does not imply that relative prices should remain unchanged; the possibility of real shocks is admitted. Further, there is ample evidence to suggest that PPP does not hold in the short run (i.e., there are short-run non-neutralities), but that it is a useful working hypothesis for long-run analysis.

I believe that a more carefully articulated theoretical framework, incorporating these issues and outlining the determinants of the equilibrium real exchange rate, would have improved the discussion immensely. In particular, while I am sympathetic to Warr's warnings about inference based on the standard measure of competitiveness, I was not enlightened by it. It would have been helpful, for example, for the discussion of real wages to take place here, rather than later in a different context.

As a final comment on this section of the paper, I note that while Warr's calculations undoubtedly reduce the relative price movements, such movements as do remain are still quite significant.

Turning to the Dutch Disease proper, Warr discusses the data problems involved in describing the structural changes in the economy and the inference problems in explaining them. (However, apart from some estimated trend equations, we are nowhere treated to any formal attempts at statistical inference.) He finds little evidence of any Dutch Disease; such as there is was apparently rather benign. Manufacturing output continued to grow during the period, although Warr suggests its growth was probably slowed by the oil price shocks. Government consumption was constant, so no Netherlands-type Dutch Disease of a rapid absorption of resources into government services was witnessed. Most of the expansion of government was apparently in the form of public sector investment.

Perhaps the major symptom of any disease is Warr's argument that increased government revenues from OPEC I allowed a devaluation 'necessary' in 1975 to be postponed until 1978. Fortunately, this is a mild, likely non-fatal strand of the Dutch Disease. But Warr's analysis is a reminder that induced reactions of government policy are an important, if not *the* important aspect of any economy's response to major disturbances. Using newly found revenues to 'finance rather than adjust' is just one of many possibilities, although a common one.

10
Round-table discussion
J. PETER NEARY – *Chairman*

This has been a conference about oil booms that are not really booms
and Dutch Diseases that are neither Dutch nor diseased, so it is perhaps
appropriate that we conclude with a round-table discussion around a
rectangular table! I will start by calling on the members of the panel,
Max Corden, John Kay, Doug Purvis and David Newbery, after which I
will open the discussion to the floor.

W. Max Corden

Three main issues have surfaced at various times during this conference.
First of all there are the effects of the spending or overspending
following a natural resource boom, which depend on whether the boom
is temporary or permanent and so on: these are essentially issues of
stabilization policy and have nothing to do with the Dutch Disease as
such. Secondly, there is the Dutch Disease aspect, that is to say that
there are some adversely affected sectors and some relative price
changes which accompany the boom. The third issue concerns the
optimal rate of resource extraction. I shall not discuss this further
because it has not been central to this conference. Thus we have two
main themes running through this conference and in each case positive
and normative analyses are required. Most of the discussion has been
positive and this positive analysis can be sub-divided further.

Firstly, there are the consequences of what might be called neutral
policy; i.e., what happens if the government in some sense stands by and
does nothing? 'Doing nothing' is itself an ambiguous concept: do we
mean constant nominal money supply, constant rate of interest, etc.?
Secondly, there is the question of what the actual policy reactions have
been. I will say something on that in a minute. Finally, there is the

normative question that really has not been discussed much at all: what are the optimal policies in each case?

Coming back to the two main topics, in each case they are really old topics in new guise but with many additional twists. The first of the two topics that I mentioned is the stabilization issue: if a country suddenly gets a rise in income does it spend it all now? How temporary can the rise in income be assumed to be? Are there tendencies to overspending? Are there downward rigidities in spending so that a rise cannot easily be reversed? I feel this has been one of the main subjects of the conference. Alan Gelb's paper was the key paper in that area, since it took a wide-ranging view of the experience of this particular kind of boom and slump, looking at how different countries and governments have behaved and speculating as to how they should have behaved. Clearly some policy reactions have been much wiser than others. We have just come across Indonesia which has been much better than Nigeria, for example.

The second topic is the one that has fascinated us all, namely the Dutch Disease aspect. It is also an old subject both in the historical and the analytical sense. For example, the idea that labour-saving technical progress can have an adverse effect on labour even though it is potentially Pareto-improving is an old one, and the preoccupation of the Luddites with the harmful effects of technical progress is really a version of the Dutch Disease problem. This issue also arose in the 1950s when the United States gave food aid to many countries, including India, under programme PL480. At the time there were long discussions about the adverse effect that this might have on food production in India. At the analytical level, those of you who are familiar with the growth and trade literature associated with Harry Johnson, concerned with the effects of biased technical progress – how technical progress in one industry leads to resource movements out of other industries and so on – will recognize that all Dutch Disease models are really a branch of that literature.

Hence we have been concerned here with an old subject and an old body of theory. But the special feature is the focus on industries and on factor incomes via effects on industries. We first look at the effect on an industry and then we ask what are the factors specific to or intensive in that industry, hence showing that there are indirect income distribution effects. By contrast, in a one-sector model with two factors, capital and labour, it is well known that labour-saving technical progress could have an adverse effect on labour. To some extent therefore we have generalized this one-sector approach a little bit, but it's all the same sort of thing.

All these issues lend themselves very readily to empirical work, and I think it is a very important subject we are working on. And if some of the work here has not been adequate and has not been sorted out sufficiently, that is simply a challenge to straighten it out. There are so many examples both in history and currently of the two separate issues to which I have referred, that I think it is well worth getting it all straightened out. I do not think we have any simple answers, as borne out by various cases we have discussed, for example that of Indonesia. In any case, the study of booming sector and Dutch Disease economics ought itself to be a booming sector for many years because of its relevance for historians; indeed the whole of economic history could be looked at in terms of some of these issues and concepts.

Finally, I have been asked to say what, in the main, did I get out of the conference? I felt that the government policy reaction issue and, in particular, the way governments spend their extra revenues resulting from the booms, has been somewhat underplayed, or at least not sufficiently highlighted, in the literature and yet this has been the major concern in many of the developing countries. Some of the papers at the conference, especially Alan Gelb's, have usefully drawn attention to this aspect.

John Kay

I thought I would say something about natural resources and the microeconomy – if the word microeconomy exists, that is. (I rather hope it doesn't, just as I hope the word macroeconomy doesn't exist except in the title of this conference!). At any rate, I thought I would concentrate on some microeconomic issues and try to spell out what I thought I had learned from some of the papers at this conference and which subjects seem to me to need further consideration and analysis.

The first thing I learned is that I got a lot of reinforcement of a distinction I was already aware of but not perhaps sufficiently aware of, namely, the distinction between enclave and resource-transfer effects. That distinction was made very clearly in the theoretical survey paper and it was reinforced again in, indeed it was one of the strongest points to emerge from, Peter Forsyth's British/Australian comparison. And indeed that comparison had a rather piquant aspect, as John Flemming picked up. Peter and I in a sense imported these Australian ideas into the UK, but actually, on reflection, they are ideas that are very different in their application to the two countries. Probably the reality is that the thesis as presented does not apply at all well to Australia but does apply very much better to the UK. And one tends to forget that these enclave and resource transfer phenomena have been going on for a very long time. We've had booming sectors, as Max has pointed out, for many centuries. We've had booming enclave sectors since gold discoveries and perhaps before that, and we've had booming resource-transfer sectors of a variety of kinds. If we go back to the kind of economics people wrote in the nineteenth century, they wrote a great deal about railway booms and the like in precisely this kind of booming sector analysis. And one of the points to emerge from that of course is that the tradable/non-tradable distinction does not have the same relevance and importance in relation to booming resource transfer sectors as it does in relation to the enclave issues.

The second thing I picked up from the introductory survey paper was that fix-price disequilibrium models are beginning to yield answers to some of the questions people have kept raising in analysing booming sectors over the past few years. In particular, people have asked whether unemployment is an inevitable outcome of a boom, and the answer seems to be in principle, no; but somehow it looks very likely in practice. I think the analysis we were given in the survey paper may help us to give some theoretical explanations of why that is so.

I'd like to go off on a slight tangent from that because one of the things that emerged there was the distinction between the experience of Latin American countries and Persian Gulf countries, which was expressed in terms of a condition on relative supply elasticities or, more precisely, on supply elasticities relative to the importance of goods in consumption. Now I suspect that's a condition which we're going to come up against again. In particular, I suspect it provides a partial answer to one of the questions that emerged from this morning's discussion; namely, since in present value terms Britain is no more than, and perhaps slightly less than, self-sufficient in oil, why is it that the sterling exchange rate goes up and down with the oil price (which is a very clear empirical observation)? Now I believe that the reason for that and the reason why some of the Bank of England's critique of the relevance of booming sector analysis to the UK was misplaced was that it supposed that Britain, as a country broadly self-sufficient in oil, was somewhere in the middle of a spectrum which was a symmetric spectrum. But it seems to me that the position of, let us say, Germany and Japan at one end of that spectrum of countries, which are very much less than self-sufficient in oil, and the main oil exporters at the other end, which are very much more than self-sufficient in oil, is not actually at all a symmetric spectrum. More precisely, while one could imagine contraction and expansion of the manufacturing sector in Germany and

Japan, one could not envisage contraction and expansion of the tradable sectors of Saudi Arabia in quite the same way. Now I'm clear that there is a point here, but I have found it difficult to put my finger on exactly how one defines what the issue is and I think Peter and Sweder's condition on supply elasticities relative to the importance of consumption is probably the expression of that condition. What this may lead to is the application of that condition not so much in their fix-price model as in a simple international general equilibrium model of how exchange rates get determined. I think that's one of the exercises which needs to be done if we are to understand these very marked empirical observations which are not at the moment very clearly explained by the analysis which we have.

There were three particular microeconomic points I wanted to pick up. One was the fact that, in the enclave model, what booming sectors do is to redistribute resources between the public and private sector, because most of these rents accrue to the government. That point was emphasized in relation particularly to Holland and Nigeria and in the context of Nigeria I learned about Please's law which was a *phenomenon* I'd certainly been conscious of before but not a *name* I'd been conscious of before for the fairly obvious empirical observation that if you give governments a lot of money they tend to spend it. I think there are two aspects to that, if one is trying to look at it more precisely. One is a justified point that if governments derive a lot of additional revenue from the taxation of rents, the shadow price of public sector revenue falls and therefore the optimal proportion of publicly provided commodities in overall national income actually does increase. To that extent the Dutch reacted correctly by increasing publicly provided commodities when government revenues were boosted in this particular way. That point may actually get more emphasis than it deserves because what happens is not only that the economic shadow price of government revenue falls but also the political price of government revenue falls, if you believe in governments which broadly seek to maximize their activities subject to some sort of electoral constraint or whatever. The way in which these electoral constraints operate is probably that raising nominal tax rates loses votes whereas a big increase in rent taxation gives you an opportunity to derive more revenue without having to increase nominal tax rates. That is a phenomenon that one has seen in all these enclave sector countries, and it is a phenomenon that has been followed by that money being spent in some way or another. In the British case revenues have been spent on funding a high level of unemployment without having to make more than modest increases in nominal tax rates. So the government's propensity to consume that revenue is very high, whereas the value of that consumption in some of these cases appears to be quite low.

My second point related to some microeconomic policy issues which arise out of these kind of developments and I picked up three particular issues there. One was that the transitional costs of the kind of structural adjustments which were being implied could be very large and there were strong arguments for microeconomic interventions to reduce these; that was cited in the cases of Norway and Nigeria where it was suggested that the relative price changes and particularly the real wage changes required to bring about structural adjustments might well be impossibly large for a whole variety of reasons and that provided a case for direct intervention. A second interesting issue relates to a belief I have always held that the argument that we should use our North Sea oil to provide cheap energy for manufacturers was self-evidently absurd. Looking at some of the arguments raised in the Dutch case I wondered whether it was quite so self-evidently absurd, because that may be a way of, in effect, using your resources to achieve import savings at some efficiency cost but at an efficiency cost which is less than the transitional costs of making other kinds of adjustments in the microeconomy. At any rate it seems to me that there were questions there which are worth exploring. And the third microeconomic policy issue was that one of the things that a nation with oil or other reserves wants to do is diversify. Part of that is obviously portfolio diversification in which you get the oil out of the ground and buy other assets. But another kind of diversification may be an industrial structure that gives you a permanent base of industries producing tradable goods.

The final issue which I wanted to note very briefly was that of uncertainty. It arose in a number of papers, particularly in relation to Norway, although Alan Gelb raised it in a rather interesting way when he noted the ratchet effects which arose from oil price and other fluctuations. And there were other transitional costs of varying prices noted, most of which are very high. I think that raises a final policy question: if these costs of uncertainty and adjustment are so high, why is so little being done in the way of institutional arrangements to reduce them? After all, most of the costs of fluctuating oil prices are not net costs for the world economy taken as a whole. That is, there ought to be contracts which people could make to eliminate or reduce the impact of these fluctuations, yet we've seen virtually no such arrangements. There are futures markets in these commodities, but they only exist for rather short periods and they are not very active. We have certainly seen very few actions such as long-term supply contracts between western governments, for example, which might reduce the various costs which were identified in a number of papers.

Douglas D. Purvis

As noted in the opening survey paper, the motivation for this conference came essentially from two observations: first, that we are all getting a bit repetitive in our theoretical analysis and, secondly, that rather little empirical evidence has been brought to bear on the fairly extensive theoretical developments. I agree completely with these two observations and I think it is fair to ask now, what have we learned from the conference?

First, I think we have learned that it would be premature for the theoretical study of the Dutch Disease to come to a halt. There clearly remain theoretical issues that have not been properly explored and I think this conference has succeeded in bringing some of them out. Secondly, I am impressed at Peter and Sweder's ability to marshal so many empirical case studies of the Dutch Disease, and I think we have learned a lot from the empirical analyses presented at this conference. I am also struck by how different the empirical papers are in approach: we have had planning models, models of intertemporal optimization, a couple of econometric papers and a number of 'data organization and description' papers. This variety is all the more striking when it is recognized that there is, much more than at most conferences, a coherent theme to the questions being studied.

I thought that two theoretical issues which got short shrift in the survey paper but which arose more in the conference were the intertemporal issue and the related one of uncertainty. I was pleased that we had an extensive paper dealing with each of those and that the discussants were so thorough on each that I don't feel the need to try to remind you of the lessons that we learned. In particular, I feel that there is a lot to be learned from the Aslaksen–Bjerkholt paper combined with David Newbery's excellent discussion of it.

One distinction that I think needs more attention in the Dutch Disease literature is the distinction between permanent and transitory effects. This distinction, common in many other branches of the literature trying to deal with uncertainty, is crucial to many of the issues raised at this conference, but by and large the Dutch Disease literature has not been as careful with that distinction as it might have been.

Another important distinction that surfaces occasionally but that I would like to see brought to the fore is that between a boom that occurs because a country has a resource that the world suddenly decides is more valuable and a boom caused by a discovery of additional supplies of a resource; in other words, the distinction between a price shock and a quantity shock. I think they are very different in a number of ways. The key way in which they are different is that a price shock that is world wide affects your trading partners as well as yourself. Single-country models sometimes leave something to be desired in dealing with those price shocks. The relative price implications of a price shock, once you recognize that it is generalized to your trading partners, are not nearly as straightforward as the relative price implications of a quantity shock. So I think that, when we go out and do the empirical case studies, it is very important to bear in mind which type of shock we are talking about.

There is another distinction that has been raised but that I want to emphasize again. I have always thought of there being two different types of Dutch Diseases. One is the type motivated by real trade theory analysis where we examine sectoral effects in the real economy. The other is what I think of as the macroeconomic aspect of the Dutch Disease which essentially comes from short-run exchange rate responses combined with some sort of macroeconomic story of sticky prices. The macroeconomic aspect receives less attention in the survey than I think it deserves: I think it needs to be brought up front in some of the other papers as well. I am rather surprised at this because my first exposure to the Dutch Disease debate came while I was spending a year in England in 1979 and 1980. At that time the controversial issue was whether the overvaluation of sterling was caused by Mrs Thatcher or by North Sea oil. That debate at first tended to dismiss the North Sea oil story from a macroeconomic perspective since, given a wealth boom which raises the demand for tradables directly and an indirect effect coming through the exchange rate, the Dutch Disease outcome requires that the exchange rate effect not only mitigate the wealth effect on the demand for tradables but also reverse it. The surprising result that came out of the macroeconomic analysis was that, within the confines of fairly general model specification and without violating the usual norms of stability, such a reversal is, in fact, a possible outcome.

So, if Mrs Thatcher was not ill-conceived, she was probably ill-timed; it was very unfortunate that monetary contraction coincided with North Sea oil. As Max Corden says, he doesn't like to call this monetary aspect part of the Dutch Disease at all but prefers to call it simply a stabilization problem. In fact, stabilization policy was running in the wrong direction at the time given the effects of North Sea oil.

I think that the macro story has to be brought up front because it is a competing hypothesis and should be kept in mind if we are going to do our hypothesis tests correctly. It also has to be up front for other reasons, some of which I indicated in my discussion of Peter Warr's paper. In trying to decide how much responsibility for macroeconomic performance to attribute to the oil price booms we have to control for those phenomena, and a number of papers did not give sufficient attention to this.

There is another reason for bringing up the macro effects and this is also particularly relevant to the distinction between price and quantity shocks. Once you adopt a macroeconomic perspective on the policy response that has been a big part of many of the papers, we can no longer think of the oil price shocks as being purely exogenous events. Instead, we have to think of them as being either mitigated or reinforced by the aggregate demand stance of a broad class of oil-importing industrialized countries, in particular the United States. I think one of the big differences between the 1974 oil shock and the 1979 oil shock was the stance of aggregate demand that was taken in a number of major oil-importing countries following the oil price shock.

Let me mention a couple of other minor issues. First, repeating a point that John Kay made, the key aspect in many of these questions is adjustment policy and it strikes me how little we know about that. Economics has made great progress in generating theorems about the role of markets in achieving an efficient equilibrium allocation of resources. But it has paid very little attention to the process by which those resources actually get allocated and therefore very little attention to the role of policies in influencing the actual adjustment process by which we move from one equilibrium to the other. It seems to me that we have now run into a central policy issue which requires us to know more about that and I would like to see adjustment assistance policies and those sorts of factor mobility issues brought to the fore.

Finally, the other comment I have was stimulated by a remark that David Newbery made at an early stage in the conference. He suggested that an important aspect of an oil discovery is that it might relax a borrowing constraint, in the sense that a lot of less developed countries are essentially quantity-constrained in world capital markets for a wide variety of reasons, and one of the major impacts of a resource boom is to relax that borrowing constraint so that they suddenly become much more credit-worthy. David suggested that in a number of countries this increased ability to borrow might be used to finance an industrialization process so that we could have a proindustrialization rather than a deindustrialization response. It seems to me that a lot of the evidence we have seen in this conference indicates that, although this relaxation of the borrowing constraint did occur in many of these countries, it was the government that managed to borrow the money. In many cases this proved to be unfortunate since the government failed to invest the proceeds well. So the relaxation of the borrowing constraint has in fact worked against many of those countries: given how they chose to invest the proceeds of their borrowing, they would have been better off had they remained constrained in world credit markets.

David M. G. Newbery

After three discussants there are not many issues left unexposed. I will start by saying what I have learned from the conference and what I have found most interesting. They are, first, the fact that some of these booms are temporary and of uncertain duration (now that we have seen that the price of oil not only goes up but sometimes comes down, oil is beginning to look more like a commodity and obviously one then starts thinking of the commodity price fluctuations aspect); and, secondly, the closely related problem of modelling the response of governments to fluctuations in price and revenue.

When Stiglitz and I were thinking about rather more straightforward commodities and their price fluctuations, we were aware that the macroeconomic responses were important but most of our story was about the microeconomic behaviour of agents. Roughly speaking, that story was that, for the kinds or risks that seemed to be prevalent in commodity markets, the costs of adjustment at the microeconomic level did not appear to be very large and so the benefits of reducing those fluctuations also appeared to be modest. Of course there was the tantalizing prospect that the macroeconomic disturbances of a commodity boom and the consequent adjustment costs might be very large and might justify some kind of international stabilization policy. So we attempted to build a model, which now that I look back on it, was very much like a Dutch Disease model. It had two sectors, a traded goods sector which produced an exported commodity whose price fluctuated in a random way but with known mean and variance, and a non-traded goods sector. Labour was allocated between the two sectors and the change in income in the traded goods sector generated changes in demands for non-traded goods and obviously changed the income of that sector. We then asked some rather microeconomic questions: what kinds of contracts would agents who knew the structure of the economy sign in the non-traded and traded goods sectors? Could we explain unemployment? Would contracts be too rigid in money terms to deal with the fluctuations in demand? As it turned out, it was really quite difficult to think of good reasons, profit-maximizing rational reasons, why agents would sign sufficiently inflexible contracts. We came up with some and they could account for some unemployment in response to fluctuations in the export price, but the costs looked very small. They were not enough to change our view that the macroeconomic consequences of price fluctuations were not very large.

The missing element in our story is provided I think by Alan Gelb's paper. We were assuming a world with no government, really very much like the framework paper for this conference in which agents optimize rationally and operate in a competitive environment. Whereas the truth is of course that governments do exist and if they optimize they don't optimize the sorts of things that we think are important and it is probably a mis-specification to suppose that they do systematically optimize. Their behaviour is really the key element in explaining what actually happens and in particular in accounting for the costs, and that is rather embarrassing because we have very poor theories of government. It comes back to the issue that Doug just raised: what is adjustment? How do we think about adjustment policy? Well, you have got to have some theory about what gets chosen and we are a bit short on those. It is also I suppose encouraging for economists because it must surely be very easy to go round and advise countries that experience booms to do various things which would clearly make things better. They make such large and obvious mistakes.

One theme I want to pick up which I was very pleased to see that both Kay and Forsyth raised is that the availability of these relatively low fiscal cost rents to the public sector lowers the marginal cost of raising public revenue and is in itself a case for expanding the public sector. It also raises the question of reducing the distortions of the existing tax system and one looks around to see which are the most important ones and the macroeconomic costs are again terribly important. If the argument is that real wages are slow to adjust and if it is the case, as is frequently true, that the tax on wages is quite large in various forms, then one very obvious way of reducing the distortion costs (which in this case are largely macroeconomic distortion costs) is to use some of the oil revenue to reduce the wage cost of employment without reducing the wage to the employed person. Had that been done, presumably all sorts of good things might have happened. That seemed to come out quite clearly in the Dutch case as well.

I think those are the two things that I find most exciting and potentially fruitful for further consideration. There are a number of other points that I also find intriguing. One is that there is a big difference between oil and gas. It is fairly obvious that in many cases gas is non-traded and even where it is tradable, as in the case of The Netherlands, it is not quite so straightforwardly tradable as oil. As a result, the issue of what exactly is its right price is not so straightforward and saying that the Dutch subsidized energy is not in itself a very straightforward statement. We were told that the domestic price of gas was by and large above the export price of gas and that the export price of gas was set at what one deduces was an aggressive long-run dynamic profit-maximizing level. So you could argue that the Dutch were not being subsidized as far as energy was concerned. They were paying above the border price, certainly well above the marginal border price. The other interesting thing about gas is that, because it is non-traded, it suggests a large number of associated, typically mega-project, investments like fertilizers, LNG and petrochemical complexes. All of those investments produce industrial tradable goods, so in the first place that alters the Dutch Disease story. The other thing is they are big complex projects which usually go wrong, which is also bad news.

I was struck by a quick calculation I did when I was in the World Bank. You can turn gas into nitrogenous fertilizer and the question I asked was, what fraction of currently flared gas which is being wasted would you use if you made all the world's nitrogenous fertilizer out of gas? The answer is 15 per cent; in other words you could flood the fertilizer market remarkably quickly if you went in for a number of these mega-projects, especially if different people went in for them in different places at the same time, all on the optimistic assumption that the world price of fertilizer was insensitive to their own project. So I think there are a whole range of very interesting issues that are peculiar to gas.

Coming back to the risk aspect, I didn't mention it when I was commenting on the paper on risk before but if I were thinking about what is the really tricky and important issue to model, particularly with Norwegian gas (which comes back to the question of what is the peculiar characteristic of gas, particularly gas in deep, chilly waters a long way from where you might want to use it), it is this: that the costs of getting it out are lumpy and large. The key question therefore is not how do you adjust the depletion rate in response to changes in the world price of energy, because by and large once you've put the infrastructure in you get it out as fast as you possibly can. It would take an enormous change in expectations, which in some sense would not be rational at the global level, for you to want to change that. The issue is rather *when* do you incur these large lumpy fixed costs? That is a really hair-raisingly difficult problem because of its lumpiness and riskiness and because it is

essentially intertemporal. Each one of those separately is quite difficult
to handle but this is the issue that presumably has to be faced by the
Norwegians and, to some extent, the British.

The other thing I learned, which I find fascinating as an intellectual
puzzle that seems to me to warrant a great deal more thought, is what
exactly is the nature of the absorptive capacity of a country and what is it
that limits the rate at which it can expand and use resources intelli-
gently? Is it just government behaviour which is the problem or is there
more than that? Indeed Sweder in his model explicitly models absorptive capacity, though in a rather *ad hoc* way because we know so little
about it. It is quite clear from Alan Gelb's paper that absorptive
capacity is a terribly important factor in different countries' responses to
these commodity booms but I feel analytically rather unclothed when it
comes to thinking about what exactly absorptive capacity is. Learning-
by-doing is a similarly difficult problem but at least we have ways of
thinking about that and I feel much more confident about what
learning-by-doing is. As regards absorptive capacity and the associated
problem of structural adjustment, I just don't feel confident that the
analytical tools, even the micro analytical tools we have, are really
adequate. These are crucially important issues and it therefore seems to
be sensible to try to think about them in the future.

J. Peter Neary

Thank you very much. In opening the discussion to the floor, I would
like to return to the concluding section of Sweder's and my paper where
we listed a number of questions which have been asked about the
consequences of natural resource booms. They fell into two groups:
positive questions, such as, does deindustrialization take place and does
the real exchange rate appreciate?; and normative questions, as to what
governments should do when they benefit from a resource boom.
Without wishing to structure the discussion too much, it might be
interesting to focus initially at least on those positive questions. In our
paper and in Sweder's opening remarks it was to some extent suggested
that the issues here are clear cut. They certainly are as far as the
theoretical models are concerned. However, looking at the papers from
the conference that focused on those positive questions, it is not obvious
to me that we have any as yet clear cut examples of the Dutch Disease
that conform exactly to the pattern of the theoretical models. One
example that seemed to come close was that of Indonesia, and since the
earlier discussion of that case had to be foreshortened, I wonder if Alan

Gelb or Peter Warr would be willing to give a direct answer to the question, does Indonesia provide an example of the Dutch Disease or not?

Alan H. Gelb

This is a very interesting question. When I started looking at the countries that I am currently examining I expected the predictions of the theoretical models to hold. What really threw me as I went from country to country was that I started to find deviations from the predicted pattern of changes in both sectoral structure and the real exchange rate. (The nature of the deviation depends on how you measure these of course.) There are certain countries for which you can see very clear real exchange rate trends as predicted but there are others where you don't see them; and there are certain countries where you see sectoral shifts as you expect but there are a few countries where you don't see them clearly. Moreover the correlation between sectoral and relative price shifts is not always very good.

In fact it is interesting that Indonesia – although its government adjusted the nominal exchange rate far more rapidly than any other country – did not avoid a decrease in the competitiveness of its so-called traded goods sectors. So their expansion was in spite of relative price changes rather than because of them. The story here seems to come closer to the question of the relationship between technical change and resource rents. I believe that Indonesia is distinctive in that it had a conservative government under which it was recovering from previous internal political and economic shocks and it put a high priority on rural reconstruction which is very unusual for developing oil exporters. Moreover, by 1973, it had developed some effective institutional mechanisms for affecting what happened in the rural sector. The Green Revolution – new rice strains which raised yields – coincided with the first oil boom but needed effective rural management to work. So it was a combination of luck and the fact that Indonesia had these mechanisms – for example, to deliver cheap fertilizer to rural areas. Most other developing countries wouldn't have had such administrative capability even if they had attempted to use oil income to subsidize fertilizer. It would appear that there you had a case where the expansion of non-traded sectors such as communications, roads and so on, really was complementary to the expansion of the traded sectors. One of the remarkable things about Indonesia is that the degree of dependence on imported food did not rise during this period, which is very unusual since most of these countries shifted over to become food importers.

Looking across the countries that I have seen I would say probably the clearest case of a country that seems to conform to both the price and the quantity predictions of the Dutch Disease is Trinidad and Tobago. Nigeria comes very close but only if you break agriculture into export agriculture and food agriculture and if you can say that food agriculture was almost non-traded because it was shielded by inadequate port facilities. If you do that for Nigeria, you come pretty close to the theoretical model both in prices and quantities but otherwise you don't.

Sweder van Wijnbergen

You said that part of agriculture in Nigeria was effectively non-traded because of port facilities. A similar point may be relevant to Indonesian food policy. Even if agricultural goods can be traded in principle, if the government puts on a quota they become effectively non-traded. So the extent to which you should look on food in Indonesia as part of the non-traded sector depends on their trade policy.

Alan H. Gelb

Yes, I agree. This brings up some very interesting trade-offs for these countries. Clearly, if you limit food imports so that food is effectively non-traded, you will have a much greater rise in the overall level of domestic prices relative to foreign prices because you are forcing adjustment on to a smaller section of the economy. On the other hand, this might have some distributional implications that are quite favourable since it allows the rural sector to get some of the benefits of the oil income.

M. Hashem Pesaran

First, as a matter of historical record, I think it should be noted that the Dutch Disease problem was first discussed, in my view quite comprehensively, in a paper by Rollins as early as 1956 in which the direct and indirect effects of a resource discovery are distinguished. Other early work in this field, not covered by the main speakers, includes papers by Seers (1964) and Mahdavy (1970). These papers are published in rather obscure places, at least to economists, but they are cited in my paper in *Economica* (1984).

On the point made by John Kay and emphasized by David Newbery, the possibility that with higher oil revenues governments could reduce taxation, it is probably right in the case of the United Kingdom and maybe The Netherlands. But it is certainly not right for countries like Iran, Nigeria or even Mexico where non-oil taxes are only a very small proportion of total government revenues. I believe that in the case of countries like Iran we should in fact do the reverse. We need a more rationalized taxation system with more rather than less revenues from non-oil incomes. I think therefore it is important to make a distinction between whether one is dealing with developing countries or developed countries where a comprehensive system of taxation already exists.

Finally, on the Indonesian case, it has often been pointed out and it was pointed out by the main speakers today that the 1978 devaluation would have had to come earlier and would have been more severe if the oil had not come on stream when it did. But, if the Indonesian government had not had the oil, they probably would not have expanded the economy the way they did and therefore it is not possible to say whether they should have had a larger or a smaller devaluation. The approach underlying the standard view seems to be to take government policy as given and then to ask what would have happened if the increases in oil revenues had not materialized. But this is not quite right: one really needs to have a model of how the government would have behaved in the absence of increases in oil revenues, and this has not been offered.

Peter G. Warr

Yes, that's certainly correct, the government could not have behaved as it did in the absence of their oil reserves. Following on Alan Gelb's excellent comment on the Indonesian case, I feel it is only accurate to point out that the Indonesians were lucky. One respect in which they were quite lucky was that the high-yielding rice varieties came along at just a very nice time for them when they had the foreign exchange revenues to import fertilizers on which the new high-yielding rice varieties are very dependent. That was purely fortuitous and we cannot congratulate the Indonesians for that. However, we can in a sense congratulate them for being what Gunnar Myrdal calls a 'hard state'. They were able to resist political pressures to spend indiscriminately, which many other countries were not able to resist, largely because of their highly centralized government apparatus without much semblance of democracy.

Jeroen J. M. Kremers

I don't really see how you can build a general case for expanding the government sector on the basis of a decline in the shadow price of government revenues, if non-neutral macroeconomic effects are taken into account.

John Kay

It's simply a fairly obvious point that the optimal level of provision of public goods is calculated using efficiency conditions that take account of the shadow price of public revenue. If that shadow price of public revenue falls, it follows that consumption of public goods relative to private goods at any given overall income level should increase.

Jeroen J. M. Kremers

Are you not really using static equilibrium efficiency considerations? If you take all the feedback and macroeconomic effects into account, do you get the same results? I doubt it.

John Kay

I don't quite see what are the factors omitted from my model that you would want to introduce. Certainly if there are some other inefficiencies in the economy it might well be that this argument doesn't hold and if you want to identify particular inefficiencies that mean it doesn't hold please do so. But it is simply a general proposition that, if you decrease the price of one good relative to another, you will want to increase the supply of the first good.

Jeroen J. M. Kremers

My point is analogous to a critique of Barro's work on tax smoothing. There, if you impose standard microeconomic optimality conditions, you get his tax smoothing result, but if you have any non-neutralities you don't. In the case of a resource boom, why increase government spending? Why not decrease other taxes for example?

John Flemming

But you certainly would do both, surely, because you have to equate the marginal cost of revenues from different sources, so if they go down as the rents increase, then some of the adjustment must come in the form of reducing the tax wedges elsewhere.

Peter G. Warr

The efficient solution will not be that all of the increase in revenues will be reflected in additional spending. [*John Kay:* Agreed.] There will be a combination of reduced taxation and increased spending, the combination reflecting the slopes of the relevant schedules.

John Kay

The proposition is essentially that, as between two countries with the same overall real income level, the one which has more real income in the form of rents accruing to the government will have a higher level of government expenditure than the one that doesn't; that's the claim and I would have thought that that was a fairly robust proposition.

J. Peter Neary

But could I add, picking up on an earlier point: we have a clear divergence here between a normative model of public sector behaviour – public sector shadow pricing rules which imply that it is better to have a bigger public sector – contrasted with the actual experience Alan Gelb documents showing that in fact government sectors did get bigger but the revenues were blown on crazy projects. Political economy and cost–benefit analysis don't coincide.

Christopher Bliss

A view seems to be emerging from our discussion that I should like to expose. I will no doubt be accused of parodying people's views but I accept that risk. Put simply, the view seems to be that it makes a big difference whether the booming sector is in the public sector – of its nature controlled by government and I suppose off-shore energy is a prime example of that – or whether on the other hand it is in the private sector. In the first case the revenue will accrue as it were naturally and automatically to the government which will spend it on bad and wasteful forms of expenditure. While if the booming sector is in the private sector the rents will accrue to private individuals and they spend it much better.

Now it seems to me that that cannot be right; it's too simple. If there is an increase in income in a country which accrues in the first place to the private sector it provides a government with an opportunity to tax. You can no doubt think of special cases where Colombian coffee growers will run the coffee across the border if the government tries to tax them and so on. There are also cases where it is not that easy in fact either to identify or to get hold of the rents even when those rents are seemingly directly in the government's control. One sees this very clearly in the pricing of energy in the North Sea and somewhat similar things happen in the case of the United States. There are rents there, they accrue from the increase in the price of energy, but the people who are going to pull the oil out of the ground are in the case of the North Sea international oil companies and in the case of the United States private oil producers, and there is then quite a political struggle over the division of those rents: how much of them are going to go to the government and how much not. There are private individuals who think that they have a right to a certain share of those rents and try to get hold of them and we are into a political process. Now that political process is not wholly different from the political processes where there's a coffee boom and the government says: 'Why should coffee growers benefit from the increase in the world price? We are going to come in and tax it away and use it to build universities or whatever'. I think too strong a contrast has been drawn between the two cases.

John Kay

Can I come back and press the point that the central distinction is between taxes on rents and taxes on other things; and the greater the element of rent in what it is that is taxed, the lower the cost of raising tax revenue. Now it may well be that some of your coffee revenues do in fact represent rent but the particular characteristic of oil revenues is that a very high proportion of them represent rents.

Patrick Honohan

Could I just add a caveat. Obviously when the boom has happened you've got your resource rents, but in a situation where you're trying to encourage people to explore in the hope that they may find oil, then of course there are very strong disincentive effects of an announced taxation policy.

John Kay

Right: the marginal cost of raising tax revenue from these sources is much higher than the average cost and, of course, it ought to be if you are designing your tax structure efficiently.

Alan H. Gelb

I want to take up the question why it makes a difference whether the government gets the revenue or not. I think there is a difference between oil and coffee booms and one reason is just the magnitude of the effects: oil booms are far bigger. But apart from that, I think the real problem is not so much the taxation of rent versus other sources, but how you *spend* rent income relative to other sources. If you look across countries there is a very peculiar feature which is common to almost all governments, and that is that all governments are really quite puritanical: even though rent derives from no particular 'activity', there is a great reluctance actually to give it away. Rather than give it away what you do is you invest it, you increase construction activity, you hire people and so on. The way in which oil incomes in these countries have been channelled into private spending has to a large extent been through an increase in construction activity. If you think of this from the viewpoint of the private sector, the way to get access to these rents is through the demand-side effects of the public investment programme. You can see this very clearly if you look at what has happened in Alaska. In the north of Alaska, where the trust funds of certain Eskimo groups have increased very rapidly, there is quite a reluctance actually to give the money away. Oil income filters through to the local communities but it is pumped in through quite intensive work programmes. For example, in order to get access to this money you may have to build a road. It seems that it doesn't really matter whether or not the road is used much or whether the road will be there next year when the permafrost changes shape or whatever. I think this is one of the reasons why these construction programmes have gone as fast as they have: they have been the main way in which the oil income has been distributed to the private sector. From many perspectives it might have been better just to give a larger share of it away.

Sweder van Wijnbergen

One other issue which ties in a little bit with Alan's point is that the government may worry that the private sector is not an infinitely-lived Barro-type family. So it may not want to give all the revenue away because it is concerned about the intertemporal distribution of income and it is worried that private individuals do not put a very high value on their children or subsequent generations. This means that, apart from reasons of efficiency or a preference for services, the government may want to keep some of the revenue and somehow share it intergenerationally, perhaps by undertaking very long-term investment projects.

Michael Beenstock

I was interested in some of the remarks of David Newbery and John Kay with regard to the normative aspects of handling the uncertainties in the oil sector. Following up some of the ideas, and thinking particularly of the UK, one question is, does the government have any better view about the future course of oil prices or the future course of reserves than agents in the private sector? I don't know what the answer is but I suppose it is no: there is equal ignorance all around. A second question is, does the private sector in some sense not care about the future in the way that the government does? I'm just raising these questions in this context without necessarily postulating answers.

A separate issue relates to the point made in the initial survey paper that as long as we have fluid factor and product markets then there need be no unemployment: everybody effortlessly moves from one sector to the other, the coal miners become ladies' hairdressers overnight and there are no mismatch problems. We obviously know that that is an extreme situation but it seems to me that a lot of the normative issues that have been raised in the discussion don't particularly relate to oil. I mean we would want to make factor markets more competitive in any case; it's not as if oil is the only source of structural change in the economy. So I ask myself then, what is it, as far as policy response is concerned, that is peculiar to oil, rather than being generally good in any case, like improving the competitive environment? What are the quintessential oil-related or raw materials-related policy response issues apart from this question about irrational expectations on the part of the private sector as to how much oil there is? I can't really think of any specifically oil-related policy response issues. I wonder whether the panel has any suggestions in that regard.

M. Hashem Pesaran

It seems to me what is important is not that a change in oil prices brings about a corresponding change in rents; after all, both the Soviet Union and the United States are major oil producers and are therefore subject to the same rent effect. What makes countries like Iran, Nigeria and now Britain different, and why we need a different framework for their analysis, is because in such small open economies a change in oil prices simultaneously affects not only the government budget (since oil and non-oil income are taxed at substantially different rates), but also and more importantly the balance of payments current account position. The change in oil prices shifts both constraints at the same time, and so what the government does with the proceeds of oil exports and what effect it has on import propensities is crucial and must be studied in a different manner from how you would study the effects of changes in oil prices in a closed economy. So, although there may be a lot of similarities, an investigator who wants to look at oil-exporting rather than just oil-producing nations should explicitly recognize both the government budget and the external account constraints in order to answer some of the pressing policy questions.

J. Peter Neary

I think before this conference I would have given a different answer to Michael Beenstock's question, namely, that typically the rents accruing from natural resources tend to be very large and tend to come suddenly; therefore, although the adjustment problems that they produce may not differ qualitatively from those that arise from other sources, they may in practice pose much greater costs simply because of their scale. Now, of course, what we have found in many cases, even perhaps the best known, such as Britain, The Netherlands and so on, is that the scale of these oil discoveries does not seem to have been so enormous in relative terms. We come back therefore to Trinidad and Tobago as the archetypal and perhaps sole case where oil has posed a distinct problem simply because its effect was so large.

Michael Beenstock

But the issue there is simply one of discontinuity, nothing peculiar to oil.

Sweder van Wijnbergen

The fact remains that oil has greatly raised the cost of imperfections in the economy.

Patrick Honohan

I have a different kind of answer to Michael Beenstock's question. What is special about these resource booms is the typical policy response which they evoke. As we saw in some of the papers, governments tend to react to a price boom by saying 'This sector is important: we must make use of this newly valuable resource'. If lots of countries are thinking the same way there will tend to be a hog-cycle effect where everybody invests in the same sector. Even if there are no cost overruns, such simultaneous investments will cause problems.

There seems to be a natural temptation for governments to wish to integrate the enclave formed by the newly valuable resource into the economy by developing processes which use the resource as an input. I would have thought that most economists would come out with guns firing against this presumption. The correct response, I would have thought, is to say that the boom represents wealth which should be secured and allocated without reference to the sector it comes from. That is why I have been a bit uneasy about suggestions here that a government should subsidize the use of valuable resources that happen to be available in its country.

John Black

I want to cast some doubt on whether the distinction between price shocks and quantity shocks is as important as Doug Purvis suggests. I take the point that a price shock affects all countries and not just one, whereas quantity shocks are often specific to a single country: an oil strike in an area that has never been surveyed before, or political disturbances such as war or a breakdown in public order. However, many quantity shocks are not specific to any one country: geologists discover that certain forms of strata are likely to contain oil, or technical advances allow oil to be extracted from greater depths or in greater proportions. These types of shocks typically affect many countries simultaneously.

Douglas D. Purvis

If the North Sea was attached to the United States I think I would be willing to accept that point. But the fact that OPEC influenced the United States whereas the North Sea discoveries did not, seems to me a fundamental difference.

Ronald W. Jones

I want to go back to the question of what happens to the price of public sector activities. I tend to think of them as being rather labour-intensive and rather non-traded and so one consequence of either a quantity or a price boom is that the cost of government services goes up fairly substantially. Admittedly you have more revenue, but the cost effect may outweigh that.

Jean M.G. Frijns

I have two points about the price boom. If rent income for the government depends on a price boom, you could see it as an additional tax on the private sector so in that case there is ample reason to reduce other taxes in order to try to maintain the original ratio of taxes to GNP. Further, if the fraction of non-traded goods in government spending is high, then the additional crowding-out of the traded goods sector will, in combination with the learning-by-doing effect of van Wijnbergen and given the *transitory* character of additional gas or oil revenues, imply negative long-run aspects. We had discussions in The Netherlands in the late 1970s about the loss of market position of many of our important multi-national firms. Labour market crowding-out as a result of increased government spending on non-traded goods proved to be an important factor in this deindustrialization process.

Patrick Honohan

I would like to throw in something which I am surprised has not come up more, and that is migration. It may be empirically more important than people give it credit for and it is an easy (and technically not very interesting) theoretical addendum. I would have thought that in several countries which have experienced resource discoveries there have been important migration effects, and of course that dampens the wage effect. It is fairly obvious what sort of things happen but if we want to make our analysis empirically relevant then migration within countries as well as between countries seems to me something that has been unduly neglected.

Sebastian Edwards

One conclusion which has been fairly general is that if you want to avoid a real appreciation, the government should not spend too much on non-traded goods. A danger with giving that advice to governments of developing countries is that they may be encouraged to spend most of the revenue on arms and weapons, and that has occurred in many countries.

J. Peter Neary

Well, it is clear, perhaps to our surprise, that we have not exhausted the issue of the Dutch Disease. Hopefully the many gaps in our knowledge which this discussion has revealed will inspire future research into the consequences of, and the appropriate policy response to, natural resource booms.

Index

Page numbers in italic refer to figures and tables.